"I laughed so hard at times that my jaws ached!"
– Dennis N. Griffin, award-winning true-crime author of *The Rise and Fall of a "Casino" Mobster: The Tony Spilotro Story*

UNDERWORLD

How To Survive and Thrive in the American Mafia

A Self-Help Book By
Roman Martín

WildBluePress.com

UNDERWORLD published by:
WILDBLUE PRESS
P.O. Box 102440
Denver, Colorado 80250

Publisher Disclaimer: Any opinions, statements of fact or fiction, descriptions, dialogue, and citations found in this book were provided by the author, and are solely those of the author. The publisher makes no claim as to their veracity or accuracy, and assumes no liability for the content.

Copyright 2019 by Roman Martin
All rights reserved. No part of this book may be reproduced in any form or by any means without the prior written consent of the Publisher, excepting brief quotes used in reviews.

WILDBLUE PRESS is registered at the U.S. Patent and Trademark Offices.

ISBN 978-1-948239-88-2   Trade Paperback
ISBN 978-1-948239-89-9   eBook

Interior Formatting/Book Cover Design by Elijah Toten
www.totencreative.com

"Better to live one day as a lion than a thousand like a lamb."
– Nicodemo "Little Nicky" Scarfo

"In his book UNDERWORLD, *Roman Martín has hit a home run. It is amazingly well-researched and jam-packed with stories by sources whose names will be very familiar to Mob enthusiasts. While the stories and other matters addressed are accurate descriptions of serious things, such as murder and mayhem, they are told with humor and may often have you laughing hysterically. Congrats, Mr. Martín, on a job well done."*
– Dennis N. Griffin, author of *Surviving the Mob* and *Rogue Town*

"I couldn't let go of it! I read and laughed out loud the whole LA-to-Amsterdam flight. I feckin' love Martín's 'voice.' Kudos!"
– Alex Rotaru, award-winning documentary filmmaker and playwright

"As a decades-long associate of the Chicago Outfit, I thoroughly enjoyed Roman Martín's book UNDERWORLD. *He accurately describes 'the Life,' and the pros and cons of becoming a mobster. But he does it in a very unique manner that will no doubt have you in stitches at times. I highly recommend it."*
– Frank Cullotta, co-author of *CULLOTTA: The Life of a Chicago Criminal, Las Vegas Mobster, and Government Witness*, and former crime partner of Tony "the Ant" Spilotro (Joe Pesci in *Casino*)

"If you only read one book about the Mafia in your entire life, you should read this book. Actually, you should probably read The Godfather *by Mario Puzo instead. But*

if you only read two books about the mob, uh, well, never mind – you should then maybe read Wiseguy *by Nicholas Pileggi. Okay, fuck it, if you read only three books about Cosa Nostra, then you should read* UNDERWORLD!"
– Marco "Babar" Falcón (self-proclaimed
ex-half-assed wiseguy)

"As a former associate of the Colombo organized crime family, I thoroughly enjoyed reading UNDERWORLD *by Roman Martín. If you are into true accounts of organized crime told with a sense of humor, this book is a must read."*
– Orlando "Ori" Spado, the "Godfather of Hollywood"
and co-author of *The Accidental Gangster*

"At the end of a global thermonuclear war, there will be two things left on this planet: cockroaches and Roman Martín."
– J.R., former federal public defender
(Northern District of California)

*"Hemingway, Faulkner, Steinbeck, Fitzgerald, Twain, Salinger, and Martín.
No doubt history will find Don Roman taking his rightful place among the pantheon of America's greatest auteurs."*
– Roman Martín (no relation to the author)

UNDERWORLD

TABLE OF CONTENTS

DISCLAIMER	9
WHY I WROTE THIS BOOK	11
WHO THE HELL AM I TO WRITE THIS BOOK?	13
DEDICATIONS	17
CHAPTER ONE – THE BENEFITS OF A CAREER IN THE MAFIA	19
CHAPTER TWO – THE DOWNSIDE OF BEING MOBBED UP	38
CHAPTER THREE – HOW TO BREAK INTO THE MOB	56
CHAPTER FOUR – HOW TO PREPARE FOR LIFE IN THE MAFIA	71
CHAPTER FIVE – HOW TO DRESS, BLING, AND PREEN LIKE A MOBSTER	86
CHAPTER SIX – HOW TO BEHAVE YOURSELF AS A WISEGUY (PART ONE – THE DOS)	98
CHAPTER SEVEN – HOW NOT TO BEHAVE AS A WISEGUY (PART DEUX – THE DON'TS)	113
CHAPTER EIGHT – HOW TO DISTINGUISH YOURSELF AS AN UP & COMING MAFIOSO	132
CHAPTER NINE – HOW TO GIVE AND TAKE TUNE UPS	156
CHAPTER TEN – MAKING YOUR BONES	163
CHAPTER ELEVEN – HOW TO PROPERLY DISPOSE OF DEAD PEOPLE	186
CHAPTER TWELVE – HOW NOT TO GET BUSTED	204
CHAPTER THIRTEEN – HOW TO DEAL WITH RATS, UNDERCOVERS, AND WITNESSES	223

CHAPTER FOURTEEN – HOW NOT TO GET WHACKED	247
CHAPTER FIFTEEN – EXTORTION, LOANSHARKING, AND DEBT COLLECTION	270
CHAPTER SIXTEEN – SHAKEDOWNS	283
CHAPTER SEVENTEEN – HEISTS AND SCORES	303
CHAPTER EIGHTEEN – HIJACKING	320
CHAPTER NINETEEN – ROBBERIES	329
CHAPTER TWENTY – BOOKMAKING AND GAMBLING	341
CHAPTER TWENTY-ONE – BURGLARIES AND HOME INVASIONS	358
CHAPTER TWENTY-TWO – BANK JOBS	375
CHAPTER TWENTY-THREE – ARSON	390
CHAPTER TWENTY-FOUR – WHAT TO DO WITH YOUR ILL-GOTTEN GAINS	402
CHAPTER TWENTY-FIVE – FLIPPIN' AIN'T EASY	429
CHAPTER TWENTY-SIX – LAMMIN' IT (GETTIN' THE FUCK OUTTA DODGE)	455
EPITAPH	478
PRINCIPAL SOURCES, QUOTES, AND REFERENCES	480
BIBLIOGRAPHY	487
ROGUES' GALLERY	492

Disclaimer

Are you tired of taking shit from some loser with a plastic nametag and chronic halitosis? Sick of that bespectacled fuckface hovering over your cubicle, constantly harping on you to file those inane TPS reports? Are you secretly praying for the slow, sweet embrace of Death to take you away?

Well, if you're considering suicide as a possible career option, then the Mafia could be just the ticket!

I would, however, like to make something perfectly clear right off the bat: I strongly discourage organized crime as a potential career path – it typically ends badly. However, if you absolutely, *positively* have to be a gangster, then you need to read this book.

In other words, if you're gonna be a bear, be a grizzly.

WHY I WROTE THIS BOOK

I don't much like cops. The feds I like even less. That includes in order of ascending power: the FBI, the US attorney's office, and the Department of Justice. Plus, the feds don't play fair (and never have) so none of these people are on my Christmas-card mailing list. So this book is my way of recalibrating the scales of justice ever so slightly towards the bad guys.

Also, there's never been another book like this, and there should be. Why should lawyers, doctors, and hedgefund douchebags have entire libraries devoted to their professions, and not a single book dedicated to improving one's criminal skills? Mobsters need love too, you know.

The idea for this book came to me in an epiphanous moment after reading about three particular mobsters. The first was Boston mob boss James "Whitey" Bulger. In 1969, he emerged from prison after a nine-year bank-robbery stretch with an insatiable appetite for criminal knowledge and advancement. Whitey was a voracious reader who never passed a bookstore without checking out its true-crime section. He paid particularly close attention to those memoirs that discussed law enforcement operations and investigative techniques, as well as the tools professional criminals used. Jimmy (as he was known on the streets) was always looking for info that would give him an edge over both competitors and coppers.

The second was LA *Mafioso* Anthony "the Animal" Fiato, the baddest mofo who ever cock-swaggered down Sunset Boulevard during the late '70s and '80s, and with whom I once had the pleasure of speaking to by phone. He bemoaned the fact that "it's not like there's some manual you can go out and buy to learn to be a gangster. Hollywood only teaches you so much, and the real tough guys don't talk about what they do. They just do it."

The third was fabled Mafia hitman Richard "the Iceman" Kuklinski, who plausibly boasted of committing more than a hundred contract killings. In the '50s and '60s, when he was just coming up, he scoured pulpy crime rags, not only for information about murder methods and investigations, but on human psychology. He always strived to understand what made his victims and enemies on both sides of the law tick.

Oh, and let's not forget those poignant lyrics from Coolio's 1995 hit song "Gangsta's Paradise:" *They say I gotta learn, but there's no one here to teach me.*

Well, now there is, friends! So fret no longer, for now there is indeed a single written source for all your criminal needs!

Yes, I realize I'm going to stir up a freakin' hornet's nest with this manifesto. First Amendment free speech rights notwithstanding, the feds will not appreciate my revealing their most closely guarded Mafia secrets.

What the hell, let's have some fun and see where the chips fall.

WHO THE HELL AM I TO WRITE THIS BOOK?

I've been obsessed with organized crime since I was a wee lad. I've read virtually every major non-fiction book ever published about *La Cosa Nostra* ("our thing" in Italian). I've also watched almost every documentary, feature film, and TV series ever made about the mob. As a Mafia fanboy, I feel compelled to share my infinite wisdom with you fine folks. In short, this book more or less gives you a roadmap on how to become a successful mobster.

In researching it, I read more than fifty true-crime tomes about the American Mafia. Most of these I'd read at least several times before, and all I've devoured at least twice over the past two-plus years. I also perused many hundreds of newspaper, magazine, and Internet articles, and traveled extensively throughout New York City, Italy, and even Greece as part of my research (I'll explain that last one later). Next, I spent many months deep thinking, sometimes standing in place for hours at a time, lost in thought, not unlike Socrates or Aristotle.

Finally, I interviewed a number of high-profile ex-mobsters, most of whom had spent at least several years in WITSEC, a.k.a. the Federal Witness Protection Program. It wasn't hard to do – these gentlemen often have websites and even blogs. I found all of them to be extremely helpful, cooperative, and eager to share their rich experiences with the world. Those who don't do social media were more or less readily accessible through their publishers, and to them I am eternally grateful.

Some I had to track down through a private investigator. This is their story – warts and all. With the passage of time, I think they came to realize they had played an important role in the history of the mob, which itself has played an important part of American history and popular culture.

I am particularly indebted to two former career criminals. The first is Kenny "Kenji Snaps" Gallo, a former associate of both the Milano and Colombo crime families in Los Angeles and New York, respectively. (For those of you who recently awakened from a coma, since 1931, organized crime in New York City has been controlled by five *Cosa Nostra* "Families" – the Gambinos, the Genoveses, the Colombos, the Luccheses, and the Bonannos.)

The second is Marco "Babar" Falcón, a former associate of … well, Kenny Gallo. Out of all the interviewees, these two were the most generous with their time and attention, so *grazie mille, signores.*

I'd also like to give a shoutout to all the other ex-gangsters who provided me with so many wonderful anecdotes about their lives. These men – some who will remain anonymous, including the former street boss of the LA Family – were so kind to me, and so intelligent, insightful, and humorous it was often difficult for me to reconcile the persons they are now with their violent pasts. At the very top of that list ranks former Gambino soldier (made man *or* associate, but typically the former) Andrew "Good News" DiDonato, for whom I sincerely hope will someday be reunited with his long-lost son, Andrew Junior. Special thanks also to ex-Chicago wiseguy (made man or Mafia associate) Frank Calabrese Jr., Anthony Fiato, Sal Avila, Detective Jerry H., "Mr. 187" (sergeant-at-arms/enforcer for the Hells Angels in NorCal), Jerry Zimmerman, Jack Rausch, attorney Roger H., undercover FBI agent Big Mike, Kevin Beachum, Barry (R.I.P.), Peter North, Buck Adams (R.I.P.), Tabitha Stevens, and the late Johnny Fratto. Rest in peace, Johnny.

Also, respect to the *carnale* (brother) from the Mexican Mafia prison gang (a.k.a. *La Eme,* for the letter *M* in Spanish) for his insight into the California prison system and his own clique.

And may the Buddha bless you as well, Dr. E., Joe D., Jimbo X, and Tony Serra.

As for the other good guys who helped me with this book, I'd like to thank the two high-profile criminal defense attorneys who advised me on the various legal issues addressed herein, as well as several former federal Organized Crime Strike Force prosecutors, including one from the Southern District of New York (Manhattan). They too shall remain unsung heroes as I sincerely doubt they would want to be publicly associated with this book in any way (or with myself, for that matter).

As Jimmy "the Weasel" Fratianno would say, "It is what it is."

Oh, and don't forget to peruse the Rogues' Gallery at the end of this book in case you forget who any of the characters are herein.

Dedications

To that very special someone in my life – you know who you are – I say this:

Thank you for always telling me what a total loser I am, that I would never amount to anything, and that writing this book was an absolute waste of the last two and a half years of my life. But in the immortal words of my favorite nineteenth-century German philosopher, Friedrich Nietzsche, "What doesn't kill you makes you stronger."

Just kidding, Moo-Moo!

Big ups are also due to my manager for instantly recognizing the sheer breathtaking genius of this masterpiece. Unfortunately, I'm probably going to fire him the instant I latch onto someone higher up than him on the Hollywood food chain. He's such a sweet guy though that I think he'll understand. If not, I'll simply recite the old scorpion and the frog parable.

Also, I *sincerely* want to dedicate this book to all the authors who've spent so much of their lives writing about organized crime in general, and about the Italian-American Mafia in particular. Thank you all for the years and even decades of sheer bliss you have provided me. This book is a platonic love letter to all of you. And, of course, I greatly appreciate them, their estates (for those who are sadly no longer with us), their publishers, and all the other copyright holders for generously allowing me to quote at length from their selected works.

Next, I want to make a particularly special and heartfelt dedication to Sabur Moini – you would have loved this book.

In the immortal words of the Bard himself, "Goodnight, sweet prince."

Penultimately, I'd like to give a shout out to my next-door neighbors for the two weeks I was in Hell's Kitchen researching this book — FDNY Rescue 1 at 530 W 43rd Street. They just celebrated their 104th birthday. More importantly, these were the first guys on scene after the September 11 attacks, and they lost nearly half their company. Love and respect. I hope you guys enjoyed the bottle of 15-year-old Macallans!

Last but certainly not least, I am eternally grateful to Denny Griffin for his unwavering support, enthusiasm, and encouragement.

As the late, great true-crime writer and former G-man William "Bill" Roemer Jr. used to say, "Keep punchin'!"

Chapter One – The Benefits Of A Career In The Mafia

"I'd rather laugh with the sinners than cry with the saints." – Billy Joel

In deciding whether a career in organized crime is right for you, you should first consider all of the ins 'n' outs, the ups 'n' downs, and the what-have-youse of *La Cosa Nostra*. In other words, the good, the bad, and the fugly. Let us begin on a happy note with the *benefits* of being a mobster.

"Good times, baby!"

Whenever Marco "Babar" Falcón found himself in jail (or rehab) and someone asked him what he was in for, that was always his response. It also sums up the best that "the Life" has to offer. The hedonistic opportunities and orgiastic excesses of being a *Mafioso* (made man or higher rank) are truly limitless, as exemplified by Anthony "the Animal" Fiato.

During his ten-year reign (late '70s to late '80s) in Tinsel Town, Fiato always ate at the finest restaurants, hobnobbed with the glitterati, and schtupped the most aesthetically-pleasing women. They included Alana Stewart (Rod the Mod's then wife) and later, Denise Brown (O.J.'s sister-in-law). A-list actors begged to hang out with him, including James Caan, who reportedly swam in his cocaine slipstream like an insatiable remora fish for days on end.

Where was I? Oh yeah, models and starlets would claw over each other to velcro themselves to Anthony's Herculean physique and inhale his man-scent. Fiato is a testament to the undeniable truth that power, even more than money or fame, is the ultimate aphrodisiac.

And that really is what being a made man – a formally inducted member of the LCN (*La Cosa Nostra*) – is all about. The power, the money, the lifestyle, and the ladies. What's *not* to like about it?

(Um, quite a lot as it turns out, but we'll get to that in the next chapter.)

Doing Whatever the Fuck You Want, When You Want, to *Whom* You Want

This is arguably the ultimate perk of being a gangster. In the immortal words of Bonanno soldier Benjamin "Lefty Guns" Ruggiero (Al Pacino in 1997's *Donnie Brasco*), as told to Donnie Brasco (undercover FBI agent Joe Pistone) in Pistone's eponymous book:

"As a wiseguy, you can lie, you can cheat, you can steal, you can kill people – *legitimately*. You can do anything you goddamn want, and nobody can say anything about it. Who wouldn't want to be a wiseguy?"

Who, indeed?

Personally, I think that being a gangster means never having to say you're sorry, and most certainly never having to take shit from anything that walks, crawls, or breathes. *Amen.*

In 1964, Jon Roberts was a connected guy (an associate, *not* a made man) with the Gambino crime family in New York. This was over a decade before he moved to Miami and became one of the biggest cocaine traffickers in the history of the United States. He smuggled in *tons* of cocaine from the late '70s to the late '80s, and was considered by the DEA to be the Medellín Cartel's top distributor in North America.

One particular evening, Roberts was besieged by a marauding band of Hells Angels. The bloodthirsty bikers were seeking retribution for some perceived slight and decided to storm his bar. Terrified and alone, he locked the door and called his mentor, fellow Gambino soldier Andy Benfante.

Roberts braced the door with whatever was at hand, but the wood buckled and strained from the weight of the invading Hessians. "You fucking guinea!" the barbarian horde screamed through the thick oak. "We're gonna stuff you like a Christmas goose!"

Roberts held out as long as he could, then BOOM! The door exploded inward, and twenty leather-clad Neanderthals burst through the entryway. Roberts saw his twenty-one years of life flash before his eyes. He knew he was a dead man, so he braced for impact and prayed for a miracle...

The miracle barged in hot on the heels of the Angels – it was Andy Benfante and two refrigerator trucks' worth of 300-pound monsters. These were massive Italians from a nearby meat-packing plant, armed with baseball bats and metal hooks. They crushed the invading Huns and turned the Harleys parked outside into scrap metal.

It was in that instant that Jon Roberts truly understood that by being formally associated with a Mafia family, he had virtually unlimited power in the underworld. He knew that after stomping the Angels, there was nobody he couldn't fuck with.

Fiato summarizes this mob mindset. "Being a gangster isn't about being Italian or Sicilian. It's simple, really. When you're a criminal, when you have people behind you, you're a mobster. If you have a mob behind you, you're a mobster. That's what makes you dangerous. It's not one gun, it's many guns. It sends a message that's powerful: if you fuck with me, you're fucking with them."

Now if these illuminating vignettes don't give you at least half a chub, perhaps you should seek another line of work. I hear Foot Locker is hiring. For the rest of you, I'd suggest that power is, again, the number-one perquisite enjoyed by knockaround guys.

But don't get me wrong – there are *plenty* more benefits...

The *Goomaras* (The Women)

Personally, my favorite bennie of livin' *la vida loca* – even more than the cash, flash, pizazz, and champagne – would most definitely be the *chicas*. And plenty o' goodfellas out there will wholeheartedly agree with me. There's nothing quite as intoxicating as a sublime one-night stand. "How *you* doin'?"

Vegas-by-way-of-Chicago mobster Frank Cullotta was astounded at the raw animal magnetism that even a squat, unappealing toad like Anthony Spilotro (Joe Pesci in 1995's *Casino*) exuded. According to a bewildered Cullotta, "broads" in Rolls Royces, including movie stars, would shamelessly throw themselves at Spilotro because of his unmistakable power.

Of all the gangsters I've interviewed or even read about, nobody got as much action as Kenny Gallo, even as a youngster. (Ever heard of another high schooler taking *two* dates to prom?) After producing and directing pornos became too much like a real job in the '90s, he started collecting debts for infamous Hollywood madam Heidi Fleiss. Once, he even had to slap around her most famous client (you know who I'm talking about) for shorting her three K.

(This same client testified at her criminal trial. "I'm a famous actor – I didn't pay Heidi's girls for sex. I paid them to *leave* when I was done with them." *Ouch.*)

Gallo then segued into working for Michelle Braun, the proprietor of Nici's Girls, a phenomenally successful online escort business that allegedly provided $10,000-a-night sex workers to Tiger Woods. All the top porn stars, and even several future big-name Hollywood actresses, turned tricks for Michelle. After partnering up with her, Gallo single-handedly created a new *niche* in gangsterdom – the "ho wrangler" (not *my* term). It worked like this:

Throughout the '90s, Arab sheiks from Kuwait or Dubai would order a Gulfstream packed with Nici's Girls, for which Michelle would receive $50,000 per girl *per* weekend. Gallo would come along to ensure nobody shorted them.

His primary function, however, was to make sure that the girls didn't take too many sleeping pills at night, woke up on time, and timely made their fellatio appointments. And, of course, when the ladies got bored and nothing good was on TV, they'd shag the hell out of eager-to-please, too-polite-to-say-no Kenji.

Earning with Both Fists and Spending Like a Drunken Sailor

These are two more obvious upsides to the Life that spring to mind. Take the high-rolling lifestyle of John Alite for starters. He was an Albanian-American associate of John A. Gotti Jr., son of the late not-so-great Dapper Don. For over a decade, beginning in the '80s, Alite earned as much as $75 million for the Gambinos. Of that, approximately $10 million went into his own pocket and $6 million into Junior's. (He shorted Junior $4 million.)

Alite bought dozens of luxury cars, $3,000 Brioni suits, $500 Bruno Magli shoes, and watches, including an $80,000 diamond-studded gold Rolex. He also invested in expensive real estate, including a weekend home in the Poconos and a huge home in Massapequa, Long Island. He owned a trucking company and valet parking concessions, as well as stocks, gold bars, and diamonds.

One of the biggest earners in Mafia history was also Anthony "Big Tony" Peraino, a badged (made) member of the Colombo crime family. In 1972, he and his brother Joseph invested $25,000 in the production of *Deep Throat*, the most successful film in porn history.

By the mid '70s, it had grossed $25 million and would ultimately gross more than $600 million. This enabled the Perainos to build an empire that included garment companies in New York and Miami, a string of triple-X-rated movie theaters, record and music publishing companies, and a 65-foot yacht in the Bahamas. Sweet *fortunatu*!

So what do these guys do with their filthy lucre? Spend!

When Anthony Fiato wasn't busting up loanshark victims, he shopped like Paul Manafort in Beverly Hills. He bought $1,500 sport coats, $1,000 cashmere sweaters, and handmade Italian loafers. At night, he'd blow more money on a dinner tab than his father earned in three months tending bar. He'd spend three grand just on Dom Pérignon and Kristal champagne. Wherever he dined, the waiters would hover around him like Tinkerbell in heat. Like Jimmy "the Gent" Burke (Robert DeNiro) in 1990's *Goodfellas*, he'd tip the bartender a hundred bucks for a single round of drinks. He'd even toss a sawbuck to the bathroom attendant just for spritzing him with Giorgio cologne.

Similarly, during Gallo's eight-year run in New York, whenever he wanted to buy anything that caught his fancy – clothes, guns, computers, or cars – he simply peeled off Benjamins from his four-inch-thick gangster roll. The cost of any particular item never once crossed his mind.

Indeed, throughout the '90s, Gallo was raking in $700,000 a year in cash. And when I say all cash, I mean he paid zero income taxes. Even if he wanted to, he couldn't because he'd been a gangster so long that he literally had no idea what his social security number was.

Crime Doesn't Pay

Another major perk for wiseguys is they rarely, if ever, have to reach into their own pockets to pay a tab.

In the summer of 1976, John Gotti was just a freshly-minted *Mafioso* with the Gambinos. He also became a secret owner in a Queens discotheque from which one night Son of Sam serial killer David Berkowitz followed home one of his female victims. Gotti's crew then organized nightly, heavily-armed lynch mobs which trolled the local streets searching for Berkowitz. I can only imagine what they would have done with him had they caught his insane ass.

Anyways, the original owner defaulted on a loansharking debt to Gotti. Big John wasted no time in sending over his Bergin crew, named after their then social club, the Bergin Hunt and Fish Club in Ozone Park, Queens. (Not a lot of marlin catching went on there.) The visiting gangsters included John's brother Gene Gotti, Tony "Roach" Rampino, and Matthew Traynor, who were armed to the teeth. In no time at all, Gotti had a new income stream, and his loyal *goombata* (criminal associates) had a new place to drink for free. Needless to say, they never paid a cover charge.

Similarly, before he hooked up with Lefty Guns Ruggiero in the mid '70s, Joe Pistone was with Anthony Mirra. Tough Tony – everyone's least favorite psychopath – was a made man with the Bonannos. On the plus side of this relationship, Pistone never once paid for a drink while he bounced around Manhattan's hippest night spots with Mirra, including the red-hot Hippopotamus club. There they would post up at the bar all night while wiseguys lined up to kiss Mirra's ass (even though they all hated his guts) and pay for his and Pistone's libations.

The downside was the fact that if you got into an argument with Terrible Tony, you'd best stay out of his reach, as he was likely to stab you. Thank God somebody finally whacked this psychotic prick! Actually, you can thank Pistone, who was the reason Mirra got clipped, for bringing an undercover fed into the fold.

Full disclosure, pals – free drinks could come back and bite you in the ass if you're not careful. Case in point: in June 2008, centenarian Colombo underboss John "Sonny" Franzese was indicted for shaking down the Hustler and Penthouse strip clubs in Manhattan. He eventually served eight years in the can for too many lap dances on the arm, as well as other racketeering, loansharking, and extortion charges involving a Long Island pizzeria.

Free Stuff

Besides free drinks and copious blowjobs, wiseguys also get lots of swag (stolen property) *gratis*. During his early days in the LA mob during the '60s, a teenage Anthony Fiato was introduced to a Sicilian gangster named Blackie Gallo. Speaking in broken English, Blackie brought him back to his apartment, which was bulging with designer clothes pilfered from the finest boutiques in Beverly Hills. Everyone from movie producers to cops to gangsters bought stolen merchandise from Blackie. Even famous local hoods like Mickey Cohen and Jimmy "the Weasel" Fratianno shopped at Blackie's. Thus, after selecting from hundreds of suits, shoes, shirts, ties, and cufflinks – for which he paid pennies on the dollar – Fiato was bedecked like a movie star.

Particularly pleasurable is glomming off rich folks. In the days when Anthony "Gaspipe" Casso was comin' up the ranks of the Luccheses in the early '80s, a true Mafia bromance sprung up between him and Russian mobster Marat Balagula. They loved frolicking on each other's yachts and dining with their wives together at Manhattan's finest restaurants.

Gaspipe loved being treated like a visiting dignitary at Balagula's chic, expensive nightclub in Brighton Beach (called – what else? – Odessa). There, attractive, disturbingly young Ukrainian "models" latched onto him like an *Alien* baby. Hopefully those glorious, on-the-cuff nights provided Gaspipe with enough masturbatory fodder to last him the rest of his life in federal prison.

Rub one out for me, little buddy!

Nobody freeloaded off the jetset crowd better than Gallo, who explains in his autobiography *Breakshot,* that as a "ho wrangler," he would spend weeks at a time living like Scott Disick sucking on the teet of Kimye (or whatever they call those blithering idiots). This means Gallo would travel around the world in first-class seats or PJs (private jets), and stay at only five-or-more-star hotels. (That's right, ignoramuses – the Burj Al Arab in Dubai is the only seven-star hotel in the world, and offers an indoor ski run.) He would also eat at only Michelin-starred restaurants. All of this, of course, was on somebody else's dime – specifically, the johns who had hired one or more of Nici's girls. See, Gallo's nut was included as an ancillary expense.

Gallo's dining exploits as a world-class mooch would have turned even Ivan Boesky green with envy. One of Gallo's duties as a ho wrangler was to accompany the woman and her date to fancy restaurants like Morton's or Peter Luger (the famous, over-the-top-expensive steakhouse in Williamsburg, Brooklyn). There, he would keep an eye on her and the john. During these outings, Gallo would order the five most expensive entrées, take a few bites of each, then doggy-bag the rest back to his hotel. The next morning, he would wake up to lobster, steak, and a hummer – all comped.

Oh happy day!

The Fistfights

Okay, 'nuff said about the obvious perks – let's examine a few of the not-so-apparent bennies. Few things in life produce a pure adrenaline rush like a bench-clearing bar brawl. Gallo described one particular evening when he was chaperoning for porn superstar Jenna Jameson at a strip club in NYC, Howard Stern's then favorite hangout, the infamous and now-defunct Scores. That night, a drunken buffoon tried to grab a handful of Jenna's twenties off the stage.

Gallo immediately charged out from backstage like Ferdinand the Bull, plowed into the buffoon, and smashed him back into the slathering crowd. Gallo then pie-faced him with one hand and retrieved the pilfered cash with the other. Unfortunately, this landed Gallo on the disgustingly sticky floor, giving the buffoon and his fellow assholes the chance to stomp and kick him.

But Gallo managed to grab the buffoon's leg and bite it to the bone. The buffoon screamed so loudly that his friends temporarily stopped their shit-kicking. Gallo popped up and bashed a few of their faces. At that sweet moment, several gigantic bouncers joined the fray, knocking over the buffoon and attached bungholes like ten pins. *Strike!*

Moments later, the troublemakers were unceremoniously dragged out and tossed into the warm embrace of the waiting coppers. Kenji, Jenna, and company trailed after them, enjoying a hearty laugh at the sight of the buffoon sobbing hysterically as he was being handcuffed. *Boo hoo hoo!*

I like the old-school brawl that Jimmy "the Gent" Burke, Tommy DeSimone, and Joe "Buddha" Manri got into with some white-trash racists at Robert's Lounge in 1978. That night, their friend, African-American credit card scamster

Parnell "Stacks" Edwards (Samuel L. Jackson in *Goodfellas*) was playing guitar and singing.

Cody, a blond, goateed, and tatted-up out-of-towner, who had been hassling Stacks, warned him to stop playing his "nigger music" or he was going to catch a beating. Overhearing this, Burke stood up from his bar stool and nudged Manri, who nodded in agreement: *let's fuck him up.*

Burke grabbed Cody by his lapel and reared back to smash his jaw. But before he could launch his punch, one of Cody's confederates smashed a chair across The Gent's spine. Jimmy kissed the floor, blinded by pain and temporarily rendered breathless.

Manri grabbed the confederate (another *Deliverance* extra), hoisted him up with both arms, and launched him across the room. The confederate landed on a table, and it was game over for him. Two more peckerwoods jumped on Manri like tigers on an elephant. As Manri fought to shake them off, Tommy DeSimone entered the bar and joined the fray. He grabbed one of the 'woods by the hair, yanked him backwards, and repeatedly smashed his fist into his face.

Finally, Jimmy the Gent regained his breath, stood up, and smashed into Cody like an NFL linebacker. With his huge left hand encircling Cody's throat to hold him steady, the right shot forward like a bazooka, shattering his nose. Cody slumped to the ground, unconscious, spewing blood.

Meanwhile, Manri grabbed the third confederate in a bear hug, squeezing him until he heard ribs crack. Someone in the bar yelled something about cops, so Jimmy, Manri, and Tommy fled into the night, laughing.

Cue Queen's "We Are The Champions."

The Gunfights

Even more exhilarating than fistfights are *gun*fights. Nothing cures erectile dysfunction like the sound of a 9mm, full metal jacket round grazing your skull as it shatters the sound barrier.

On October 1, 1979, a firefight involved Anthony "Nino" Gaggi, a powerful Gambino *caporegime* (captain, for you dunskies), and off-duty NYPD police sergeant Paul Roder, who was moonlighting as a car service driver at the time. The incident occurred only minutes after Nino and Mafia serial killer Roy DeMeo (the Gambinos' most prolific hitman ever) murdered two men. The victims were father-son gangsters, Gambino capo James "Jimmy the Clam" Eppolito Sr. and made man James "Jim Jim" Eppolito Jr. They were accompanied by an unsuspecting associate, Peter Piacente. Roder saw the bright flashes from the gunshots in the car and the three surviving occupants get out and flee. Gaggi and Piacente power walked in tandem down the street; DeMeo wisely went the other way. Roder trailed the former in his ride.

Roder screeched his sedan to a halt in front of Gaggi and Piacente, hopped out, and crouched behind the driver's door. "NYPD, freeze! Put your hands up!" he screamed, drawing a bead on them with his police-issued .38 revolver.

Rolling the dice with his life, Nino circled around Piacente, using him as a human shield against Roder. "Let me see your hands!" Roder bellowed, crouching into a shooting stance, left hand cupping the right with the revolver.

Nino suddenly appeared from behind Piacente, semi-auto in hand, pointed at Roder. BAM! BAM! BAM! Every shot went wide. Roder returned fire. BANG! BANG! BANG! One round pierced Nino's neck, barely missing his artery, and spun him around. The next bullet splattered Piacente's leg, and the third missed.

Nino face-planted onto the sidewalk, his arms outstretched like Christ on the cross. His right hand inched towards his gun. Roder yelled at him to stay still. "Don't touch it or I'll shoot again!"

Nino's trembling fingers closed around the firearm, but he was too weak to lift it. He finally let go, rolled onto his back, and stared at the sky. His dream was always to die in the street with a gun in his hand, and he came damn close. He was eventually convicted of assault with a deadly weapon and sentenced to five to fifteen years. But don't worry, folks – Nino had the last laugh in the end. After fixing the jury on his first trial, he was able to get his conviction overturned on appeal in 1981.

In *The Animal In Hollywood*, Tony the Animal describes the first time he shot someone. It happened during a robbery of a high-stakes card game in LA during the '60s, before he returned to his native Boston for a long spell. The game was attended by pimps, thieves, and dopers.

Fiato whipped out his trusty .32 semi-automatic and screamed for the players to put all their cash on the table. In the midst of everyone complying, a shotgun-wielding thug suddenly emerged from a back room. Without thinking, Fiato – BLAM! BLAM! – shot him twice, then fled.

But following close behind was a second, previously-hidden thug, who chased him down the block. Fiato spun around and – BLAM! BLAM! – pumped several bullets into the man.

Fiato laughed with exhilaration as he raced away from the scene, thrilled by the terrified looks of his victims. He nabbed almost 12 Gs from this score – a small fortune back then. He never found out whether the men he shot survived.

The Weddings

For all you weak sisters out there (and you know who you are, you candy-ass, salad-tossing, bubblegum-chewing yatches), have no fear – the Mafia offers plenty of non-violent fun too.

No other organized crime group on Earth has better matrimonial ceremonies than the LCN. Weddings like the one in the famous opening sequence of *The Godfather* are not uncommon. For example, every top mobster in the Big Apple turned up for the 1990 wedding of the Teflon Don's son, John Gotti Jr. It was held in a grand ballroom of one of Manhattan's swankiest hotels, the Helmsley Palace.

The groom's father insisted the hotel fly the Italian flag over its main entrance, an honor typically reserved only for visiting foreign dignitaries. Since the Dapper Don shelled out a cool $100K for the nuptials, the manager was only too happy to accommodate him. It was a good investment though, 'cause Big Daddy forced all the attendees to gift at least $5,000 in cash to the bride and groom. As a result, Junior made almost 400 large that day.

Jon Roberts once attended an equally sumptuous Mafia wedding reception in Manhattan that occurred during the early 1970s. Roberts' pal Vincent Pacelli sought to expand his heroin-trafficking business to the Midwest by marrying the daughter of one of Chicago boss Sam "Momo" Giancana's top lieutenants. The wedding reception was held at the famous Pierre Hotel, and was considered to be the social event of the season for LCN. Guests were entertained by no less than two orchestras, a rock band, and a bevy of bellydancers. Oldtimers breathing from oxygen tanks cavorted with young Turks powdering their noses with disco dust while undercover feds posed as waiters.

I highly recommend attending as many Mafia weddings as possible – they present invaluable networking opportunities. Just watch out for all the feds who'll be filming everyone coming in and out.

The Food

The next best thing to weddings for peaceful mob festivities is eating. Food is sacred to racketeers – it's like communion for lapsed Catholics. Even Gallo was amazed at how much the Bay Ridge, Brooklyn, boys revered food. They would lovingly film pasta-laden tables and show off the photos to their friends like proud parents bragging about their brood. And the meals would stretch on hour after hour, until lunch became dinner, dinner became supper, and supper became breakfast. The only thing missing was a vomitorium like in ancient Rome. If you don't believe me, ask former FBI agent Joaquín "Jack" Garcia, who gained eighty pounds(!) during his nearly three year stint working undercover against the Gambinos in the early oughts (the 2000s).

Without question, no OC (organized crime) syndicate has ever eaten like the Mafia. In his book *A Man of Honor*, Giuseppe "Joe" Bonanno describes feasting with Mustache Petes (pre-LCN Old World gangsters) back in the 1920s. On those glorious occasions, Don Bonanno, fellow boss Joe

Profaci, and Profaci's righthand man Joseph Magliocco would feast with Don Vincent Mangano at his country estate just outside the city.

Oh, what a delightful time they would have! They not only shared happy tales of murder, money, and bootlegging, but Mangano and Magliocco cooked up food that was superior to the best Italian restaurants in the tri-state area. These home-cooked meals were both elaborate and endless. Better yet, all the fresh food fell off the back of a truck or fishing boat, and therefore was F-R-double-E. For example, *il primi piatti* (the first course) was always halibut, red snapper, shrimp, clams, and lobster – all donated earlier that day by Sheepshead Bay fishermen.

Secondi would be huge platters of filet mignon and veal. By the time the pasta was served in the wee hours of the morning, these Mustache Petes would have been blissfully shitfaced on bottles of homemade *vino*. (Since Magliocco was the low man on the Mafia totem pole, it would be his fleshy feet stamping the grapes.) The foursome gorged, quaffed, sang Sicilian and Italian folk songs, recited poems, cracked jokes, and made toasts to their hearts' content. No surprise, then, that Bonanno considered these fraternal fiestas to be some of the most pleasurable experiences of his life.

Cue Dean Martin's *"Volaré."*

For you fatfucks with see-through socks out there, I *know* this has got your little soldier standing at attention. But even the New York wiseguys can't hold a candle to their Chicago *amico nostra*, whose single Family is known simply as The Outfit. Hitman Frank Sheeran illustrates in *I Heard You Paint Houses*:

> The Chicago Outfit guys liked to eat. They would bring in the food and the wine and the booze and put it all on big tables. It was a banquet with main dishes of veal, chicken, *baccala*, sausage, meatballs, different pasta dishes, vegetables, salad, different kinds of soup, fresh fruit, and cheeses, and all kinds of Italian pastry. They'd

eat and drink and smoke big cigars. Then they'd eat again. All the while they're joking and telling different funny stories. They'd drop off and go into a steam bath and sweat out all the food and alcohol. They'd come back after a shower and start eating again.

I'm going to pause here to give you a few related tips on how to conduct yourself at restaurants. Wiseguys *never* order off the menu, and always make special requests that are all but certain to infuriate the chef. They also never wait in line to be seated at restaurants. Instead, they simply shove all the other waiting diners out of the way, palm the *maître d'* a hunskie, and barrel towards the center table to hold court – regardless of whether it's already taken.

And when the bill finally comes, in the rare event the mobsters choose not to ignore it, they simply pull out a cauliflower-sized roll of bennies (wrapped in those giant blue rubber bands that bind broccoli bunches), and slap a handful down. Goodfellas always pay in cash because they don't have credit cards – at least not in their own name. Nor do they carry wallets or any form of ID, which only a square would do.

Oh, and connected guys never verbally express their enjoyment of the food since speaking to a lowly waiter is beneath them. Follow their lead and, instead, simply put your thumb and index finger together, and kiss them with a dramatic flourish.

Minghia!

If you're having a big dinner out with all your *goombata*, especially somewhere you'll be seen by other mobsters or feds, then bypass all that Italian cuisine and go straight for the beef. Order the biggest cut of meat on the menu – a straight-up brontosaurus steak that would make Fred Flinstone cry. (When I was in Florence, Italy, the bone-in *Fiorentina bisteca* I ordered at one of the city's oldest restaurants weighed over three and a half pounds!) And the rarer the better. Make sure that shit is swimming in blood. Let everyone around you see that you are a meat eater in every sense of the word. Do you really want your enemies talking about you the next day: "Yo, d'you see Roman last night eatin' that tiramisu?! He's goin' soft!"

The Lifestyle

I'd like to end this first chapter with a reminder about how incredibly glamorous and exciting a career in the Mafia can be. (A slight pause here to tell all my player-hating detractors to go eff themselves – just read the next chapter if you think I'm not being fair and balanced, you chode-gargling fuck toilets.)

Perhaps no mobster has ever lived it up as intensely as Anthony Casso. By the early 1970s, he was spending like the Kartrashians, frequently vacationing with his wife Lillian in the US Virgin Islands, Bermuda, the Caribbean, Florida, and Vegas. They also enjoyed the best the city had to offer, dining at Michelin-starred restaurants and taking in all the top Broadway shows. Then, once he dropped his wife off at home after their obligatory weekly date night, Casso would head off to hotspots like 21 and Regine's. There, he would impress the waiters by buying $5,000 bottles of wine, then horrify them by mixing the bottles with Dr. Pepper. *You can take the boy out of Bensonhurst...*

Age certainly didn't temper Gaspipe Casso's profligacy. By 1990, he was blowing thirty grand a week on wine, women, and song, dining at only the finest establishments in NYC and shopping at the most exclusive haberdasheries.

The only other *Mafioso* I can think of who lived it up almost as much as Gaspipe, but certainly over a longer period of time, was Aladena "Jimmy the Weasel" Fratianno. Jimmy was a made guy with The Combination (the Cleveland Family) before transferring to the so-called Mickey Mouse Mafia, as the LA Family has been derisively known since the '60s (after its legendary and very first boss Ignacio "Jack" Dragna died in 1956).

During the late 1940s in LA, Jimmy was living *la dolce vita*, with not one but two mistresses stashed away in deluxe *pieds*-à-*terre*. Nights were reserved for professional prize fights followed by Sunset Strip club-hopping at Ciro's, Mocambo, Slapsy Maxie's, and the Band Box.

During the '60s, when he wasn't breaking big rocks into little ones, Jimmy cavorted in Sin City, where he was fawned over by executives at all the major casinos, downtown and on the Strip. Everywhere he went, Jimmy reveled in his popularity, in the love and respect shown to him by all his old friends. None of them had bothered to visit him in the joint, of course, but now that he was free, everything was on the house – dames, chips, ringside seats, you name it.

During the early to mid 1970s, whenever he blew into Vegas, he was treated like a visiting king. Even Tony Spilotro rolled out the red carpet for him. The Weasel particularly enjoyed holding court in a huge, comped suite at Caesar's Palace as fair-weather friends lined up to pay homage.

Finally, I'd like to leave you with a quote from Marco "Babar" Falcón. In 2010, the Discovery Channel produced a one-hour documentary about Gallo entitled *Flipped: A Mobster Tells All*, which you should be able to catch on YouTube. Being a self-diagnosed toxic narcissist, Marco was only too happy to talk about their glory days in Newport Beach from the mid '80s to the early '90s:

> The best times were bouncing around the nightclubs. We were the kings then. They loved us because we were palming quarter-gram bindles of pure cocaine to everyone we shook hands with. It was a beautiful life. It was like a movie to us. We had all the guns and the cash, the girls, the glitz, the glamour. It didn't seem real.

The boys were millionaires before they could legally drink. *Namaste*, bitches!

Okay, if the foregoing doesn't convince you to make a Faustian bargain and join the Mafia *today*, then I'm sure I don't know what will. However, for all those of you who are ready to earn your wings and enter the most exclusive men's club in the world, a.k.a. the Honored Society, I say this: slow your roll, *pendejos*! Pump the friggin' brakes! Have you never heard of the flight of Icarus? Are you unaware of a phenomenon known as *gravity*? The primary law of physics is quite simple: what goes up must come down. Or as Dr. Eldon Tyrell once famously explained, "The light that burns twice as bright burns half as long." In other words, read the next chapter before you sign on the dotted line.

Lessons to Be Learned

Burke and DeSimone clearly displayed their genuine love for Stacks by coming to his aid and endangering themselves in this manner. Obviously, if you want to be a man's man in the mob, then you too should always back up your friends, regardless of the odds. (Or as the Hells Angels like to say, "One on all and all on one.")

However, in the event you are forced to permamently dispatch one of your friends down the road, please don't let these fuzzy feelings cloud your judgment. Indeed, this is precisely what Burke and DeSimone did to their beloved Stacks several years later. Stacks dropped the ball big time when, following the infamous 1978 Lufthansa Heist, instead of torching the work van as instructed, he instead left it parked on a street while he got high and shacked up with a girlfriend.

After several days, the cops found the van, which had been papered with parking tickets, and realized it had been used to transport the heisters and loot. More importantly, they found Stacks' fingerprints everywhere. The dumb shit had forgotten to wear gloves. Thus, it was with a heavy heart that Burke gave the nod to DeSimone, who sniffled with emotion as he blew Stacks' brains out on December 18, 1978, one week after the heist.

My award for best mob brawl of all time has to go to Kevin Weeks, Whitey Bulger's righthand man for twenty-five years. One night, Weeks accidentally walked into the wrong bar with seven drunk buddies – it was a lesbian bar packed to the brim with badass, lady-loving homegirls. Unfortunately, and *suicidally*, one of Kevin's seven dwarfs loudly cracked a homophobic joke.

As Weeks explains in his autobiography *Brutal*, before the doofus even spat out the punchline, the women attacked. In a riot reminiscent of the famous 1969 Stonewall uprising in Greenwich Village (which sparked the modern gay civil rights movement), every woman in the bar pounced with pool cues, beer bottles, and chairs. Weeks and comrades fought back with everything they had, but they were getting the shee-it beaten out of 'em. With every wave the now-shriveled menfolk beat back, another would crash over them like a tsunami. The emasculated eight somehow managed to fight their way outside, bloodied but laughing maniacally at their near-death experience.

Shameless Namedrop

FYI, the last time I was slummin' it in Beverly Hills, I had the distinct pleasure of meeting James "Jimmy" Caan himself at the Montage Hotel's rooftop restaurant. He was hanging out with two gorgeous blondes, who were either his granddaughters or his dates for the afternoon. During our brief repartee, he reminded me, "Ant'ny prefers to be called Craig."

When Mr. Caan asked me where Fiato was currently living, I chortled, "You know I can't tell you that, Sonny!"

Jimmy, who was dressed in a designer tracksuit and pristine white sneakers, gave me a knowing smile. See, Santino Corleone still knows lots of people who would be very interested in finding The Animal.

Chapter Two – The Downside of Being Mobbed Up

"There are no happy endings in the Life."
– Joseph "Joe Campy" Campanella

The mob ain't *all* fun and games, people. Plenty of bad shit happens – as with the upsides, some of the disadvantages are more obvious than others.

Getting Whacked

This is the first obvious downer that springs to mind. Indeed, the body count in LCN is so high that it's pointless for me to spend too much time on this subject. For example, during the Roaring Twenties, there were over a thousand mob-related murders in Chicago alone, most of which remain unsolved.

Or how 'bout this one: in researching this book, I stayed in an apartment in NYC's Hell's Kitchen on West 43rd Street between 10th & 11th Avenues. This neighborhood was the birthplace of the Irish mob in America, beginning in the mid nineteenth century after millions of immigrants poured into America to escape Ireland's catastrophic potato famine.

My original plan was to do a walking video tour of the neighborhood, pointing out the locations of the most notorious Irish mob killings in modern times. But I soon realized that this would be an overwhelming task. Between 1965 and 1985 alone, the NYPD attributes as many as one hundred murders to the so-called Westies. That's five murders a year, each and every year for twenty years, in one single neighborhood in the Big Apple alone.

For a more specific illustration of just how pervasive murder is in the Mafia, I'll defer to Beantown mobster Johnny "the Executioner" Martorano. After he flipped in 1995, the Boston Organized Crime Strike Force investigators gave him a list of eighty gangsters he had known since the early 1960s. They wanted him to identify which criminal clique each gangster had belonged to – In Town (the Boston LCN Family), The Hill (Bulger's Winter Hill Gang), and so forth. Martorano was dumbfounded when he realized that out of that entire list, seventy-five of the men had been murdered. That's almost a ninety-four percent attrition rate!

Thus, my precious time is better spent on discussing the likelihood of insult being added to injury when you get clipped. What I mean by that is, your murderer will probably be someone you *love* – maybe even your father, son, or brother. That sucks big time. In the Mafia, one day a guy is your closest friend, and the next day he is your undertaker.

Fratricide tops even friend-icide as the more offensive way to meet your maker. Here's a chilling example by way of Colombo Family *capo* Gregory "the Grim Reaper" Scarpa.

Just before midnight on January 14, 1987, The Grim Reaper's older brother, Salvatore "Sal" Scarpa, was drinking and playing cards in a Brooklyn social club. Sal was not having a good night, having recently been convicted of cocaine possession and now awaiting sentencing. It was about to get worse: five masked, armed gunmen suddenly burst into the club. "This is a robbery!" one of them screamed. "Everyone on the fucking floor now!"

Everyone in the club, including Sal, immediately kissed the ground. Several of the robbers began rifling through the patrons' pockets, snatching their cash and jewelry, while the other robbers stood guard. But when they moved onto Sal, they didn't bother taking his gold watch, gold necklace, or $313 in cash. Instead – Boom*!* – they blew the back of his head off.

Sal's murder was never solved, though it was common knowledge in the underworld that his own brother Greg had ordered the hit. See, for the last several decades, rumors had persisted that Greg was a rat. Sal had always defended him. However, as the years passed and Greg miraculously dodged every single federal case thrown at him, he began to suspect the same. Then he made a fatal mistake: he told one of their mutual associates of his suspicion.

Reporter Peter Lance reached out to Gaspipe Casso, who was (and still is) doing life in a federal hellhole, and asked him whether he believed Greg could have sanctioned his brother's murder. Casso responded in the affirmative, confirming that it was indeed Greg who had ordered the double-tap because Sal was telling everyone the Reaper was a rat. According to Mr. Lance, Greg Scarpa's daughter, "Little Linda" Schiro, was also convinced that her father had ordered her uncle Sal's murder.

An eerily similar incident occurred on April 14, 1973, in Chicago. The Outfit's boss, Joseph "Joey Doves" Aiuppa, issued a murder contract to Tony Spilotro. At the time, Spilotro was facing homicide charges with Mario DeStefano and his brother, Spilotro's mentor, Mad Sam DeStefano.

Mad Sam was a raging psychopath and out-and-out loony bird who could not be trusted to keep his mouth shut in court. He had recently stretched a simple traffic-violation hearing into a one-week trial and media circus where he represented himself, making a mockery of the proceedings. Mad Sam showed up daily in a wheelchair, wore pajamas, and addressed the court through a megaphone. The Outfit shotcallers were none too pleased with his antics.

Thus, on the day in question, Mario and Tony arrived at Mad Sam's house, ostensibly to discuss eliminating the key prosecution witness against them, co-killer Charles "Chuckie" Crimaldi. When they pulled up, Mad Sam was puttering in his garage. Mario approached him first, right arm extended to shake his big brother's hand. Tony was just behind him, concealing behind his back a sawed-off, double-barreled 12-gauge shotgun.

Mario suddenly stepped aside. Tony raised the shotgun and – BOOM! – blew Sam's right arm clean off. BOOM! The second blast caught Sam flush in the chest, killing him. Ironically, twenty years earlier, Sam had murdered his other brother Mike for disgracing The Outfit with his heroin addiction.

Good riddance, I say – couldn't have happened to a nicer guy. Mad Sam was the worst torturer-murderer in the history of the LCN. He soundproofed his basement so he could torture victims while his oblivious wife and three kids lived their lives upstairs. He was also crazy as a shithouse rat, always opening his front door to FBI agents while wearing only a robe and boxer shorts – with his monstrous, disfigured salami dangling out in all its hideously deformed glory.

Cue Juice Newton's "Angel Of The Morning."

The Paranoia

The constant fear of getting two in the back of your head from even your own flesh and blood results in another major Mafia bummer – paranoia. Constant, inescapable, endemic fear that permeates every fiber of your being.

Gallo recalls the constant dread experienced by John "JB" Baudanza, a.k.a. Johnny Goggles, a Lucchese made man. JB *should* have felt safe and protected in light of the fact that his father-in-law was the all-powerful Lucchese *capo* Domenico "Danny" Cutaia. Alas, twas not to be.

Baudanza's life was consumed by dread. Whenever they bounced around together, he would always have Gallo go into a place first to ensure assassins were not lying in wait. JB was perpetually concerned that the reckless and bloodthirsty Persicos (who ruled his previous Family, the Colombos) would eventually kill him for past indiscretions. For Baudanza, it was only a matter of time before they exacted their revenge against him for siding with the losing faction in the 1991-93 Colombo War.

Gallo personally experienced this foreboding on numerous occasions. Whenever Colombo made man Eddie Garofalo Jr. called for him, he never knew if he was going to be sent for in order to kill or be killed. Every call from Eddie would immediately cause Gallo to hyperventilate and break into a cold sweat. He was convinced that Garofalo was the only gangster in Brooklyn who could rub him out without any forewarning.

This paranoia occasionally takes a comical turn. Philadelphia underboss Philip "Crazy Phil" Leonetti describes in his autobiography *Mafia Prince* what happened at his son's tenth birthday party in 1984.

As the party was raging in the backyard with all of his kid's friends present, Leonetti and fellow *Mafioso* Lawrence "Crazy Larry" Merlino were inside the kitchen plugging candles into the birthday cake. Suddenly, a large masked figure appeared in the alley leading to the backyard. Phil and Larry looked at each other and shrieked, "It's a hit!"

Without thinking, they opened the side kitchen door, grabbed the guy, and pummeled and booted the poor bastard. It was a teenager in a dinosaur costume whom Leonetti's wife had hired to entertain the kids!

Crazy Phil and Crazy Larry pulled the kid's masked off – he was sobbing hysterically, begging them to stop, as all the attendees in the backyard stared in horror. This is how fucked up their lives had become.

Killing the Wrong Person

Only a pure psychopath like Gaspipe or Gambino button man Roy DeMeo actually enjoys whacking people out; Roy used to brag that it made him feel like God. Instead, old-school good guys like Johnny Roselli and Jimmy Fratianno simply did what they had to do ("It's just one o' dem t'ings"), and took no pleasure from it. Murdering *innocent* people, however, is downright unpleasant and can make you feel terrible about yourself. This presents our next organized crime buzzkill. Unfortunately, whether out of sheer stupidity or mere happenstance, this occurs far more often than you'd imagine.

The most obvious situation arises when you go out on a hit and accidentally kill the wrong person. In 1971, during the Irish mob war in Boston between the Killeen and the Mullens gangs, Whitey and his friend Billy O'Sullivan served as the two main shooters for the Killeens.

One night, Whitey went out hunting for members of the Mullens gang. He couldn't believe his luck when he came across their leader, Paulie McGonagle, sitting alone in his car. Paulie, who was parked directly in front of his own house, never saw Whitey coming from the opposite direction.

"Hey, Paulie!" Whitey called out as he pulled up right next to him. He shot Paulie almost point blank in the face, instantly killing him.

Oops. Whitey suddenly realized he had shot the wrong McGonagle. Instead of Paulie, he'd murdered his brother Donnie, who bore a startling resemblance to him. Donnie had never been involved in crime, much less in the Irish mob war. That'll put a damper on your evening. *Or not.*

Horrified, Whitey drove straight to O'Sullivan's apartment. Deeply shaken, Bulger staggered into the kitchen and put his head on the table. "I shot the wrong one," he said. "I shot Donald."

Billy O, as he was known on the street, told him to shrug it off, explaining that Donnie was a heavy chain-smoker who was probably going to die someday soon from cancer anyways. "Now, how do you want your pork chops?"

An equally unfortunate but certainly more gruesome example of smoking someone who found himself in the wrong place at the wrong time comes courtesy of John Gotti Sr. His "oops, my bad" moment occurred on April 29, 1987, when Jeffrey Ciccone, a mentally disabled citizen dressed in a black suit, was walking down the street across from the Bergin Social Club in Ozone Park.

Suddenly, a truck backfired just as the don himself, Gotti, was walking out the front door. Gotti regularly visited the Bergin before heading over to his new headquarters at the Ravenite Social Club in Manhattan's Little Italy. Located at 247 Mulberry Street, the Ravenite served as the Gambino Family's primary HQ for sixty-six years, from 1926 until 1992, when the feds seized it.

UNDERWORLD | 43

Gotti, fearing gunfire, ducked back into the Bergin. Several bodyguards, including his burly 6'3" chauffeur, Bartholomew "Bobby" Boriello, charged across the street at Ciccone, believing he was the shooter. Seeing their guns, Ciccone hightailed it. Boriello shot him once in the ass, bringing him down.

In broad daylight, in full view of numerous bystanders, who later told the police they saw nothing, Gotti's goons grabbed Ciccone, threw him into the trunk of 400-pound Dominick Borghese's tinted Benz, and roared off. They drove him to a store on Staten Island owned by a Gotti capo for a basement interrogation.

As Borghese would testify a decade later, the goons, including hitman Joe "the German" Watts, savagely beat and tortured thirty-seven-year-old Ciccone, demanding he tell them who had ordered the hit on Gotti. He pleaded for mercy, claiming he had no idea what they were talking about, and began frantically quoting Bible passages. The goons finally began to suspect that Ciccone was some type of insane vigilante who had acted entirely on his own.

The German was getting tired and hungry from all the exertion and so sent a message to Gotti asking what they should do with him. "Kill him" was the response, and so that's what they did. Watts and Borghese tied up Ciccone's hands and feet, and stuffed him into an orange body bag. He was sobbing and begging for his life when they zippered it shut. Five bullets to the dome from Watts' .380 automatic put an end to the cacophony.

The killers were starving so they decided to get supper, during which they would arrange a place to dump the corpse. They were only gone a few hours when, incredibly, burglars broke into the store. Although they didn't go down into the basement, they did leave the store's metal gates open when they left. A passerby noticed the open gates and called New York's Finest, who investigated and discovered Ciccone's body at 4:30 A.M. There were no arrests.

Man, I sure hope Johnny Boy – named *Time* magazine's "Man of the Year" in its September 19, 1986, issue, with his own Andy Warhol cover to boot – didn't lose too much sleep over this blunder.

Aw, fuck it, Dude – let's go bowling.

Inadvertently Killing Your Own Kin

If killing innocent people isn't bad enough, how about accidentally causing the deaths of your own (biological) family members? For example, if the mob wants you dead – presumably because of something you did – but can't find ya, it will occasionally eradicate an immediate member of your gene pool. The Mafia's fabled policy against killing innocent relatives is not exactly chiseled in stone.

During the '70s, George Jay Vandermark's title at the Stardust Resort and Casino in Las Vegas was Slot Machines Supervisor. His real job, however, was to manage the slot skim for The Outfit, which back then had a controlling interest in the casino. Prior to that gig, George worked as a slot machine thief in Chicago.

On May 18, 1976, the Nevada Gaming Control Board (NGCB) raided the casino and discovered that the coin scale in the Stardust count room had been set to undercount coins by one third. This resulted in the skimming of as much as $20 million from the slots in a single eighteen-month period alone.

Anyhoo, wily George skedaddled out the back door during the raid and got the heck outta Dodge. And for good reason too – turns out greedy Georgie was skimming from the skim, having helped himself to a cool three million. That's over thirteen big ones today. *Mama mia!* Realizing the raid would uncover his embezzlement from the mob, he fled to Mazatlán, Mexico, where he lived in a trailer park.

Since the boys from Chi-town couldn't find him, they did the next best thing. They tracked down his son Jeff, which wasn't particularly difficult since he was also a Stardust employee, and bashed in his skull with a mallet.

Cue The Beatles' "Maxwell's Silver Hammer."

So what happened to Georgie, the glomming grifter? Bet your sweet tukas he never returned to Vegas, though he apparently settled in Phoenix in early 1977. That summer, Georgie Boy disappeared forever. The FBI believes he was murdered and buried in the desert, although no one has ever been charged. However, according to Bill Roemer, The Outfit's Godfather Joey Aiuppa authorized Vandermark's murder, which took place in South America after Georgie fled there. The film *Casino* has a brief but memorable scene where hitters track down and shoot the elder Vandermark in Costa Rica.

No Money, Mo' Problems

Another big downer in mobland that may surprise you is the ever-present threat of financial insolvency. Contrary to popular belief, most goodfellows out there are not rollin' in dough and lighting Cohibas with hundred-dollar bills while high-class sex workers spray them with Evian Mist. In fact, you may be shocked to learn that just like the rest of the unwashed masses out there, most *Mafiosi* are broke dicks. "Say it ain't so!" you gasp. I'm afraid it is.

According to Kenny Gallo, aside from blood relatives of ruling Mafia clans like the Colombo Family's Garofalos or Persicos, most mobsters today are barely scraping by. Those on the bottom rung are relegated to dealing small amounts of poor-quality marijuana and blow, or are otherwise grinding out a living through low-level bookmaking, loansharking, or extortion rackets. In fact, made guys are often evicted or jailed for failing to pay rent or child support.

Long before he moved to Brooklyn, Gallo was exposed to the mundane reality of everyday mob life by top LA gangster Vincent "Jimmy" Caci. Caci showed him a lifestyle that hardly resembled the glamorous, carefree existence portrayed in films and TV shows. Caci's regular forays to the race track revealed the depressing lifestyle of deadbeat wiseguys and degenerate gamblers more suited to *Shameless* than *The Sopranos*. In the end, Gallo came to the sobering realization that outside of glitzy nightclubs, being a mobster was tantamount to holding down a dreary working-class job.

"Christ, Roman," you squeal, "next thing I know you're gonna be telling us mob guys are going on welfare – WTF???!"

Um, this is *precisely* what happened to the Gottis. In 1961, Mr. and Mrs. Gotti were so ass-broke when their first child Angela was born that Johnny had to sneak his wife and newborn out of the hospital to avoid paying the bill.

Things didn't improve much for the latex-averse Gottis as Victoria kept pushing out babies – Irish triplets, no less (three kids in three years). So between his wife, four brats, and a burgeoning gambling addiction, Gotti was perennially in the red. This resulted in ugly domestic tiffs and several separations for the besieged parents.

And just when it seemed things couldn't get any worse, in 1966, Big John was convicted of attempted theft and thrown into the clink. Although it was a short stay, the bust caused him to lose his day job loading trucks. As a result, Victoria was forced to go on welfare and sue her husband for unpaid child support in Brooklyn's domestic relations court.

Can you imagine wiseguys clipping coupons to survive? Shopping at Ralph's instead of Whole Foods? Lord, what is this world comin' to?!!!

No one would know this more than Vincent "Vinny" Asaro, once a legitimate, if not well respected or particularly liked, capo with the Bonannos. Asaro was the only mobster prosecuted for the 1978 Lufthansa Heist, but was acquitted in November 2015. He was universally considered to be a brokester who regularly mooched off friends and family, and was certainly not above sucking on the teet of the Social Security Administration. This constantly-bitching wiseguy was such a miserable fuck that he made Lefty Guns Ruggiero look like Deepak Chopra.

Finally, Gambino killer and Bergin crewmember Wilfred "Willie Boy" Johnson's wife was also forced to go on welfare when he was busted in 1966 and imprisoned for armed robbery.

His capo Carmine "Charley Wagons" Fatico broke his promise to care for his family while he was upstate, so he flipped.

The Heebie Jeebies

As everyone knows, good health is even more important than money, and this is particularly true for *mental* health. So if you'd like to avoid suffering from severe PTSD, you may want to consider another line of work. Who would've thought that blowing someone's brains out would give you the willies?

So too will the constant pressure of trying to stay alive in the treacherous world of LCN. Think I'm exaggerating? Just ask former Lucchese acting boss Alphonse "Little Al" D'Arco, who in late 1991 flipped against his superiors, boss Vittorio "Little Vic" Amuso and underboss Gaspipe Casso, who was the true power behind the throne. D'Arco also ratted out Genovese Godfather Vincent "the Chin" Gigante. Little Al suffered from post-traumatic stress disorder after doing so, and was plagued by constant nightmares wherein all three Mafia shotcallers chased him into the bowels of Hell.

Philip Carlo's *The Butcher* is the second-goriest Mafia book I've ever read (after Gene Mustain and Jerry Capeci's masterpiece *Murder Machine*). It tells the story of Bonanno soldier Thomas "Tommy Karate" Pitera, who easily murdered more than seventy-five humans. This puts him neck and neck with the Gambinos' Roy DeMeo and the Colombos' Greg "the Grim Reaper" Scarpa Sr. for being the most prolific hitman in modern mob history. Like DeMeo, Pitera's specialty was dismembering his victims' bodies to make them do the Houdini or to disappear 'em.

Tommy Karate Pitera's most gruesome post-murder disposal was that of Phyllis Burdi, an attractive young woman whom he shot to death while she slept in 1987. Pitera, who blamed Burdi for his wife Celeste's recent heroin-overdose death, ensnared his associate Frank Gangi into setting her up for the hit. Gangi watched in horror as Pitera used a dismemberment kit to slowly and methodically cut her body into six pieces.

Using a finely-honed Bowie knife, Pitera expertly severed Burdi's head and placed it on the edge of the tub, then separated her arms and legs. Gangi was nauseated at the macabre spectacle, particularly because he had been making love to her only an hour earlier. The grisly sight of her head and body parts, plus the stench of her blood and gore, would never leave Gangi. He would wake up from a nightmare in a cold sweat, the ghastly image of Burdi's decapitated head staring at him, her mouth open in a frozen scream. These nightmares would grow increasingly worse over the years.

The Rat Race

For Marco Falcón, a totally unexpected downside of the Life was the unbelievably exhausting work schedule. Running with Gallo while he made his rounds in LA after Gallo joined the Milano crime family in LA (named after boss Pete Milano) was the opposite of the lethargic lifestyle they had enjoyed when they were dopers in Newport. (In 1992, at age twenty-four, Marco fled Orange County for Miami when the feds closed in.) This was the typical schedule for them back in those halcyon days:

First, they'd wake up at the crack of noon and ride their $3,000 Japanese mountain bikes around the beach. They'd carry their guns in Gucci fanny packs, while conspicuously hoisting Motorola cell phones the size of small car batteries. They'd end up biking to Fashion Island for a delectable hundred-dollar sushi lunch. *Domo arigato gozaimasu!* Then they'd hit the payphones, feeding in quarter after quarter to line up the day's dope deals.

Afterwards, they'd lounge around their pool until late afternoon, perfecting their savage tans. Then it was time to hit the gym and pump up for the night's festivities. After a sauna and shower, they'd gear up in their finest Cavaricci acid-washed jeans, Guess? jackets, silver-tipped Zodiac cowboy boots, and silver bolo ties. Then they'd paint the town red in their gleaming Carnauba-hand-waxed sports cars, with disco music pumping from Bose speakers.

Several hours and many kilos later, they'd meet the rest of their crew to distribute more *schniffy-schniffy* by the fuckload. Finally, after dinner and business were completed, and the grocery bags bulging with street cash were safely tucked away in their beds, they'd hit the strip clubs, nightclubs, and after-parties. And, if they were still physically capable, the boys would crush Alotta Fagina before the sun came up and turned their bones to dust.

Hoo ah! Now that's what I call a civilized lifestyle.

Not so for the f'ing mob, however, which is a never-ending, eighteen-hours-a-day, seven-days-a-week, 365-days-a-year rat-fuck-race with no vacations, sick days or overtime. To give you an example of how hard Gallo worked, he literally put 50,000 miles a year on his custom ZR-1 Corvette tooling around SoCal. Marco tried to keep up with him when he was in town, and even though Gallo was doing all the driving and hustling, Marco was so exhausted at the end of the day that he immediately passed out when he got back to his hotel. *Fuck dat!* The next morning, Marco caught the next flight back home to Miami to convalesce.

Gallo, on the other hand, was the type of gangster who would leap out of bed early each morning like he was in a Lexapro commercial, clap his hands excitedly, and gleefully shout, "This is going to be a great day – to rob, cheat, and steal!" In other words, this maniacal, frenetic, grueling, workaholic hamster wheel actually appealed to go-get-'em Gallo. Go figure.

Okay, so let's look at some concrete examples of this hellish schedule. From age eighteen, Philip Leonetti was his psychotic uncle Little Nicky Scarfo's constant companion. Everywhere Scarfo went, he went. Everything Nicky did, he did. For nine straight years, Leonetti worked sixteen-hour days, every single day of the year. He attended every meeting and sit down, and participated in most of Scarfo's hits. And while it is certainly true that he earned millions of dollars for himself in the process, Philip was prosecuted twice for murder. In the end, he was bone tired.

Henry Hill (Ray Liotta in *Goodfellas*) endured an identical schedule with *his* boss, the all-powerful Lucchese capo Big Paulie Vario (Paul Sorvino). Henry also shadowed his boss's every move, chauffeuring him all over the five boroughs to conduct business. He would pick up Paulie at ten A.M. and drop him off *seventeen hours later* at three A.M.! This crime-perpetuating Batman-and-Robin duo never stopped moving as each day required them to pursue a hundred schemes, out of which maybe ten panned out. Every waking hour was spent hustling.

Prison

Let's start to wrap up this sobering chapter by talking about prison – you know, the slammer, the can, the big house, the paint, the hoosegow, *el cárcel, la pinta*. For the vast majority of career criminals, spending lots of time in the grey bar hotel is an inescapable occupational hazard. I don't know about you, but personally, I wouldn't particularly enjoy dropping timber in front of fifty guys who speak only Spanish (if you're in Cali). And if you think finding a cute date on a Saturday night is tough on the outside, imagine what it's like in the pen. And the worst part? Trust me, you nine-to-five, tax-paying squares out there don't want to hear about the worst part.

Aw heck, I'll tell ya anyway…

In prison, especially in California, unless you're willing to shank a motherscratcher in the throat, chances are you're going to be passed around like a collection box at Christmas mass. That means you're going to get "stretched out" by a group of overly-neighborly inmates. Some weak sisters get so stretched out that they literally have to shit into a colostomy bag for the rest of their lives.

It gets worse. Unfortunately, your prison paramours won't be wearing condoms during this amorous free-for-all. One ex-con, a former professional confidence man, confirmed to me what I had already discovered about him while researching on the Internet – he had contracted HIV after being beaten and sexually assaulted by two men in Lompoc federal prison.

Freaked out yet? How about this: in Pelican Bay, the only supermax state prison in California, the brothers will run a train on a new, unprotected white boy until he literally passes out from the pain. Then, to keep the party going, they'll put out lit cigarettes on his ass, which causes him to twitch and shake.

Screw that, you say? I will *cut* a bitch, you're thinking? Well, that's not as simple as it sounds. One of the many inconveniences of prison is the lack of pockets in which to conceal your sharpened spoon or finely-honed toothbrush. So how do you carry your weapon? Think about this for a few moments…

Cue *Jeopardy* theme…

Bingo! Congratulations, you figured it out. That's right, in the penitentiary, all those who wish to wear white at their wedding are forced to insert large hunks of metal into their rectum. This is done by wrapping your shank in Saran Wrap, which you then slather with Crisco so it slides nicely into your lower intestine — I'm pretty sure there's an instructional YouTube video on this. When he was doing time in Brazilian prisons, John Alite would tie a string around the handle of his homemade scimitar so it dangled out of his O-ring like a tampon for quick retrieval.

By the way, it should go without saying that the more attractive you are, the larger shiv you'll need to protect yourself. According to Marco, with his pretty-boy face and baby-soft skin, he was forced to walk the yard with freakin' Excalibur shoved up his ass.

Hello, vicar!

Still having fun? Still think I'm not being fair and balanced? I think it's safe to say that we've now covered the fugly. However, if after reading this chapter you're still dead set on getting your wings, then perhaps the Life *is* right for you. Now learn how to join the privileged ranks of the Men of Honor.

Lessons to Be Learned

While it is essential that you hitch your wagon to a rising mob star, try to find one who enjoys a healthy work-life balance.

After all, what's the point of breaking your back to be a wiseguy if you don't have the downtime to enjoy it? In other words, try to avoid workaholics like Scarfo and Vario.

So why *do* Mafia hoodlums work so damn hard? First, there is enormous pressure on wiseguys to keep earning for their bosses because in *La Cosa Nostra*, money *always* flows upward and *never* downward. This means that associates kick up a portion of their earnings to their soldiers; the soldiers kick up to the capos; and the capos, in turn, kick up to *their* bosses. In addition, gangsters spend like drunken sailors on shore leave in Manila so there is the constant need to bring home the bacon. A third reason is that most gangsters absolutely love being gangsters, and therefore hustling, scheming, and scamming is more fun than, well, having fun.

Having said that, however, I think there is a simpler explanation. Wiseguys by their very nature are financial carnivores (or blood-sucking parasites, to use a less flattering term) who can't help but screw suckers out of their money. But strangely, I've noticed that more often than not, this fast-buck mentality ultimately proves self-defeating and counterproductive.

For example, your typical braindead loanshark will bust out a recalcitrant debtor's successful business by draining all of its assets and even burning it to the ground for insurance money. This is just plain stupid and myopic. Instead, the *goombah* should become a secret silent partner and let the degenerate gambler continue running the business. That way you'd have a constant, long-term income flow. Makes sense, right?

I asked Dr. E., a renowned psychotherapist in Brentwood who's treated a number of ex-mobsters, about this bizarre phenomenon. Dr. E. explained that true sociopaths don't feel that they are alive unless they are screwing someone *American Me*-style, even if by doing so they make less money. Scorpion and the frog, gents!

Travel Tidbits

By the way, this frenetic work ethic is purely an American phenomenon. From what I can tell, no other criminal network in the world works as hard as our own LCN. This includes the three Mafias in Italy – the Sicilian Mafia, the Naples-based Camorra, and the Calabria-based 'Ndrangheta (pronounced "en-DRA-getta"). These gangsters across the pond take their vacations seriously, like most Europeans.

When I was doing research on the Amalfi Coast, just outside of Naples, I had the pleasure of conversing with my hotel's concierge, GianMarco, who, like most locals, has lived his entire life in the region. Can't really blame him – it's one of the most beautiful places on Earth.

GianMarco had once been engaged to the daughter of a Camorra boss, and had become quite close to his future father-in-law. The relationship didn't work out, but fortunately for GianMarco, he and his betrothed parted amicably, and he maintained his congenial relationship with her pops. So every summer, *il padrino* would seek out whatever fancy hotel Marco was working at and stay there for several months.

That's right, you heard me correctly – several *months*. And all the other top members of his crime family would also vacation in the region, whether it be in Sorrento, Positano, Capri, or Amalfi town. In fact, according to GianMarco, the entire region was a crime-free zone, as dictated by Camorra custom and tradition. This way, the *camorristas* were *forced* to relax and recharge their batteries for the coming stressful fiscal year.

More importantly, the Camorra has an arrangement with the federal Italian and regional Neapolitan governments similar to the one that the Mexican cartels are *supposed* to have with *their* federal government: no crimes, especially of violence, are to be committed in tourist resorts like the Amalfi Coast. In other words, the Camorra does not shit where it eats.

However, apparently the Sicilian Mafia needs a reminder of this unspoken agreement, judging by a huge banner my water taxi passed near the famous Rialto Bridge in Venice. It read:

No Mafia – Venezia è Sacra! ("Mafia Stay Out – Venice is Sacred!") I did a little digging and found out that this banner has been hanging in place since at least May 2016. Thus, it would seem that even my beloved *Venezia* is not necessarily off limits to the mob in Italy.

Fun Fact!

Would *you* accept coffee from this guy? Well, William F. Roemer Jr., my all-time favorite FBI agent, did *for years*. Sam would always tell him that he regularly imported "special" coffee beans from Sicily, and that's why the coffee tasted slightly bitter. It wasn't until Mad Sam bought a one-way ticket to the old harp farm that Roemer finally learned that during all that time, Sam had been *pissing into the coffee pot*! Needless to say, Roemer never drank coffee again.

Chapter Three – How to Break Into the Mob

"You don't choose to join the mob. The mob has to choose you."
– Nicholas "Nicky Crow" Caramandi

There's only four ways to break into the Mafia, which I've itemized in the following descending order of importance and effectiveness: (1) family connections (2) street gangs (3) living in a mob-dominated neighborhood and (4) befriending connected people through networking. Simple, right?

"Family Comes First"

You've obviously heard this expression before. Well, nowhere is this more *très a propos* than in *La Cosa Nostra,* whose shameless nepotism would cause even Herr Trump to give a tiny thumbs up. Thus, it should be patently obvious that the best time to join the mob is the moment you're shat out into this cold, cruel world.

With any luck, at that moment, the hospital's maternity ward waiting room will be stuffed with husky, overfed male relatives speaking in a distinctive *dees*-*dems*-and-*dos* accent. These loving, sensitive gentlemen will be eagerly rubbing their meaty hands and nervously chewing on satin-glossed nails as they discuss your future. Specifically, your future with the *uomini d'onore* (men of honor).

If indeed these are your *paisans*, then you are in luck, my friend, because most mob guys believe that their sons should follow in their own Ferragamo-clad footsteps. Now presumably, these men have your best interests at heart. In other words, they're thinking, "*Ming*, if *Cosa Nostra* is good enough for me, then *bada bing*! It's good enough for my precious Junior."

This myopia, coupled with your gangster father or uncle or older brother's instinctive sense of self-preservation, will ensure that your acorn will fall close to the Family tree. See, in the treacherous world of organized crime, trust is a rare commodity. However, without loyal and trustworthy *goombata* to watch your back, you're as good as dead. This obviously presents a conundrum. Family solves that problem – after all, who better to trust than your own flesh and blood? So mobsters naturally seek to envelop themselves in the protective cloak of blood relatives.

Take Philip Leonetti, who was literally born into the Mafia. His grandfather Christopher Leonetti was a *Cosa Nostra*-connected hood who was part of a crew in Manhattan's Little Italy. (Which, based on my recent foray to New York, now sadly consists of two tourist-infested blocks with virtually zero Italian-Americans in sight.) Crazy Phil's father Pasquale Leonetti oversaw Philadelphia don Angelo Bruno's dice and card games from the late '50s to the early '60s. And last but certainly not least, Leonetti's uncle was, of course, future Philly and Atlantic City boss Nicodemo "Little Nicky" Scarfo.

Being the sensitive, considerate uncle he was, the diminutive 5'5", 135-pound Scarfo took it upon himself to teach young Philip everything he knew about the mob. I've always been a big proponent of getting started in a life of crime as early as possible. But nobody got started as young as Philip.

In 1961, when Philip was only eight, Scarfo brought him along on a truck ride to New Jersey. In the back was a dead body. Scarfo prudently thought it would look less suspicious if he brought Leonetti along with him. During the drive, Scarfo patiently explained he had been forced to stab the man (twenty-three times) because he had been robbing bookies associated with their *borgata* (Family). The way Scarfo explained it, he had actually done a *good* thing by killing the man. Saint Nick swore little Philip to secrecy, and from that moment on, they developed a special bond. By the time he was eighteen, Philip had become Scarfo's closest confidante. He would later become his top killer and underboss.

Thus, for you kids out there who are considering a career in organized crime, I cannot impress upon you enough the importance of fostering these Mafia blood ties. Make sure you constantly kiss your *goombah* uncle's ass, and always appear eager to please. Jump at every opportunity to make yourself useful. And as James Burke tells Henry Hill in *Goodfellas*, "Always keep your mouth shut."

Listen, don't worry if your uncle is a caustic, sniveling little prick like Nicky Scarfo – once you get bigger, you can simply disappear him and take his place. For now, however, just be his little good little *soldato* and do everything he says without hesitation or question. Let him take you to the movies to watch inappropriate R-rated films so you can cheer on the bad guys together. Make sure you constantly spout out the funniest lines from all his favorite movies. Since he's a moron, there'll be only four – the first two *Godfather* films ('cause the third one sucks big wet donkey balls), *Goodfellas*, and *Scarface*. It doesn't matter that at your tender, young impressionable age, you'll likely suffer severe trauma from repeated viewings of these violent flicks. All that matters is that doing so will ingratiate you with your creepy uncle. And then you'll be on your way!

Not everyone is fortunate enough to have family members who are either formally inducted members of the Mafia, or who are otherwise connected. But if you want *in*, the next best thing is to have a clueless father who not only knows mob guys, but for some reason, brings you around them before you even reach puberty. With a little luck, these men won't molest you, and, instead, will stuff twenties in your pockets and slowly indoctrinate you into the ways of the Secret Society.

Such was the case with Anthony "Gaspipe" Casso, who would one day go on to great things like admittedly murdering thirty-seven people and becoming the underboss of the Lucchese crime family. Unlike many future *Mafiosi*, Gaspipe's daddy Michael Casso actually loved him. In fact, they were extremely close and did everything together. Michael was even thoughtful enough to bring Gaspipe around his best friend, Salvatore "Little Sally" Callinbrano, a powerful Genovese *capo* who controlled the Brooklyn waterfront in the late '50s and '60s. (Callinbrano was the Mafia inspiration for the 1954 Marlon Brando film *On the Waterfront*.)

Gaspipe saw firsthand how glamorous mobsters lived with their huge homes, shiny Cadillacs, camelhair overcoats, sharp fedoras, pointy shoes, and dazzling pinkie rings. Then Gaspipe took a good long look at his own father, a failed professional boxer living in a rundown tenement apartment, and wondered, *Hmmm, I wonder what path in life I should take?*

Amazingly, after Gaspipe joined the mob as an associate at age seventeen, the elder Casso expressed bewildered dismay, scratching his unusually dense skull and thinking, "*Marone!* How the fuck did this happen?" Gee, Papa, how indeed?

Anthony "the Animal" Fiato also had a loving but equally obtuse father, Johnny Fiato, who worked as a bartender at the Villa Capri in Hollywood during the swinging '60s. Back then, it was the hottest place in town for movie stars to rub shoulders with mob stars. Frank Sinatra himself co-owned the famous restaurant, where actor Robert Mitchum regularly drank himself blind at the bar. It was there that the teenage Fiato began meeting and doing favors for various wiseguys, who saw themselves in the brawny, violent delinquent.

Eventually, this resulted in Fiato becoming a full-time criminal with the LA Family. Poor beleaguered Johnny could only throw his hands up helplessly and wonder why his boy had strayed off the path of righteousness.

Street Gangs

If you aren't related to someone in the mob or who at least knows *Mafiosi*, have no fear, little buddy, because you can always join a street gang. I cannot overemphasize how helpful gangs can be in launching your career in organized crime. That is, assuming, of course, that you've got the bollocks *and* the brains to rise above the typical lowlife, dead-end losers with whom you'll be forced to associate therein.

It's in a street gang where you'll learn the fine arts of petty crime and inflicting senseless violence on your enemies and unsuspecting citizens. Your willingness and ability to put the hurt on people, especially by committing savage acts of mayhem, is certain to catch the eye of your local Mafia street boss.

Also, the great thing about being a teenage thug/wannabe wiseguy is you'll get used to being arrested and getting the crapola beaten out of you by the coppers. This way you'll become exposed to the criminal justice system and incarceration at an early age, which will help alleviate the uncertainty and mystery of prison when you get older.

Make sure you mouth off to your arresting officer to such a degree that you're guaranteed to catch a beating. Making racist jokes is a surefire way to get tuned up. Marco Falcón claims he's anything but a racist as his experiences as an amateur penologist have taught him to despise *every* ethnicity – including his own. However, he claims he's certainly learned the value of pushing someone's buttons when necessary.

If racist jokes don't work, cracking wise about an officer's mother will certainly do the trick. If you can't think of anything particularly clever to say, you can simply repeat Joe Pesci's famous line from *Goodfellas*: "Ming, what're you doin' here? I thought I told you to go fuck your mother!"

Why on God's green Earth would you intentionally provoke a police officer in this manner? Three simple reasons. First, it will prove to the local don that you can keep your mouth shut when getting arrested. The Mafia is always on the lookout for stand-up guys. Second, it'll prove that you can take a trimming like a man when getting pinched. Third, with a little luck, the cop will tune you up so egregiously that the DA will be forced to drop the charges against you in exchange for your agreement not to sue the police department.

In any event, committing heinous crimes as a juvenile will usually result in a relatively mild slap on the wrist, with probation, home detention, or, at worst, a short stint in juvenile hall. That is, if you're white, or even Asian. If you're black or Latino, however, you'll likely end up going to a gladiator academy for violent and incorrigible youthful offenders. For example, in California, if you're a person of color and do something particularly reprehensible, you'll end up in CYA (California Youth Authority). This is basically the same thing as an adult prison, except you'll be getting gang raped by gentlemen under the age of twenty-five. On the plus side, you'll learn how to duel with medieval weapons.

The best part about being a juvenile gangbanger, however, is that your criminal record will be permanently sealed when you turn eighteen. This means you can later become a doctor, lawyer, or even a commodities broker – like Gallo did after he entered WITSEC. He worked for the largest commodities firm in the world, MF Global in Chicago, before it went belly up in 2011. (The fact that Gallo had participated in a $20 million Wall Street pump & dump scheme with the Colombos didn't dissuade the feds from helping him obtain his Series 3 license.)

This, of course, will only happen if and when you finally get your shit together and realize there's easier – albeit less exciting – ways to get rich. In any event, the only way your record can be unsealed is by a court order, and even then, only under extraordinary circumstances. Otherwise, even an FBI background check typically won't pull up your youthful indiscretions.

****

The Colombos' Carmine "the Snake" Persico (who recently croaked in the can after doing thirty-four years) is a perfect example of this early teenage-gangster trajectory.

In 1950, Carmine dropped out of high school at the tender age of sixteen and became a shotcaller for a notorious Brooklyn street gang called The Garfield Boys. Back then, guns were scarce, so the Boys tooled up with bicycle chains, tire irons, crowbars, baseball bats, axe handles, and zip guns – in other words, your basic *Escape from New York* arsenal. The Boys, led by Carmine, gained notoriety by engaging in bloody street rumbles with rival gangs. Carmine, in turn, capitalized on his violent reputation by extorting money from weaker teenagers. He made up for his unintimidating stature (5'6", 150 pounds) through sheer ferocity.

In March 1951, Carmine, now seventeen, took his first major pinch after he beat a rival gangbanger to death in Brooklyn's Prospect Park during another rumble. He caught a break, however, and the murder charge was dropped. His reputation as a comer soared and caught the attention of Colombo *capo* Frank "Frankie Shots" Abbatamarco. Next thing he knew, Persico was apprenticing under Abbatamarco, first working in bookmaking and shylocking, and subsequently moving up to burglary and hijacking.

****

The Mafia cherishes brains far more than brawn, as anyone can be a knuckle-dragging leg-breaker. So if you can show that you possess intelligence and leadership qualities while banging heads in a street gang, your chances for future induction in the mob will increase exponentially.

Take John Gotti Sr., for example. Even though Gotti eventually became the most reckless and self-destructive mob boss since Al Capone, as a young thug he displayed unusual intellectual talents. Back in the 1950s, which was both the Golden Age of the mob *and* New York City street gangs, Gotti was a member of the Rockaway Boys, whose turf covered the Brownsville-East New York sections of Brooklyn.

In 1956, Johnny Boy (as he was affectionately called by his friends) dropped out of high school and became a full-time member of the gang, as well as an aspiring racketeer. He was only sixteen, which is an excellent time to start fucking up your life. The Rockaway Boys then merged with the nearby Fulton-Pitkin gang to become the powerful Fulton-Rockaway Boys. As a result, the huge, mostly Italian-American gang was able to successfully square off against local African-American gangs, such as the Brownsville Stompers, the Mau Mau Chaplins, and the Ozone Park Sinners.

On May 15, 1957, not unlike Persico, Gotti took his first felony arrest following a major brawl with the Ridgewood Saints. Cops swarmed the rumble after one of the Fulton-Rockaway Boys was killed after being stabbed and thrown through a plate-glass window.

Also like The Snake, young Gotti enhanced his street rep not only by his penchant for violence, but by his ability to keep a cool head under extreme duress. Even more importantly, Johnny Boy earned mad props from the local underworld players by displaying an uncommon proficiency in diplomacy. In other words, Gotti had heart, brawn, *and* brains. It wasn't long before the Mafia came calling in the guise of the infamous Fatico brothers, Carmine and Daniel. They dominated the hijacking trade for the future Gambino Family (then known as Albert Anastasia's *borgata*) in East New York and Brownsville.

Boyz in the 'Hood

If you are unable or unwilling to join a street gang for whatever reason, then you should convince your parents to move to a mob-controlled neighborhood. This shouldn't be as challenging as it sounds since these locales are typically free of street crime. (Mobsters do not tolerate junkies, muggers, pickpockets, drug dealers, prostitutes, or other ne'er-do-wells shitting where mobsters eat.) You'd better move fast though because gentrification is slowly but steadily extricating these areas from Mafia dominance. Just look at what's been happening for years in Brooklyn, which was once Ground Zero for *La Cosa Nostra*. Or in Chicago and Philly.

The reason living in a mob community is so important is that the local street guys will automatically feel comfortable with you if they've seen you around year after year. This is especially true if they know your parents, even if they're squares. Just being seen, of course, isn't enough to make yourself known and accepted – you must also excel at...

Networking

That's right, I said it – networking, just like in any other profession. This means that you'd better be someone that others – particularly hardcore criminals – enjoy spending time with. This means that you'd better develop above-average social skills. If you can't, then I strongly advise you to start shopping for Instacart.

Once you've mastered the gift of gab and grow the *gagoots* to back it up, then it's time to start hanging around places where mob guys chillax. In other words, do what Thomas "Tommy Karate" Pitera did when he wanted to join the Bonannos in Brooklyn: become a world-class martial artist and undefeated street fighter; hang out in local mob bars, restaurants, and social clubs; and treat everyone you meet with utmost deference and respect. Of course, it didn't hurt that Pitera had been born and raised in Gravesend and so was readily recognized and accepted by the local *Mafiosi*.

This seems like a good time to explain how to conduct yourself when you start hanging out at mob bars and want to be accepted. My first rule of thumb is to never go around flashing wads of cash, as that either gets you marked as a sucker, showoff, or, worse, an undercover cop. No authentic wiseguy will ever legitimately seek this type of negative attention.

Miami hipster-hoodlum Jimbo X once told me, "The worst advice you can give someone is to be themselves." Translation: if you are a self-loathing braggart prone to vulgar public displays, then by all means, shut the fuck up.

The first order of business for an up-and-comer is to show that you know how to keep secrets, mind your own business, and stay low key. So don't start pestering the barkeep at your favorite mobspot to identify all the wiseguys who enter or to run down their criminal rap sheets; asking questions gets you known for all the wrong reasons. Never seem eager to engage others. Always act like you've got *subrosa* shit going on, and that you're not particularly game to make new friends. Real players will eventually sniff you out as a man who knows how to carry himself, as a man who is both confident and streetwise.

Never volunteer more information about yourself than is absolutely necessary. Always talk about your extracurricular activities in vague terms like, "Uh, I do a little of dis, and a little of dat." Or, "I'm into a few different things, you know. Whatever looks good and carries low risk." Never be loud or obnoxious. In your own subtle and understated way, let the underworld know that you are disciplined, independent, and successful.

For you self-starters out there, I recommend laughing at other wiseguys' jokes but keep your opinions to yourself. It's okay to act a little cocky as long as you don't step on anyone else's toes. Or as the Hells Angels like to say, show some class.

Finally, I advise you to be proactive and walk away from conversations that don't concern you. Always do so before you are *asked* to step away. This is certain to impress your new friends, who will appreciate your judgment and discretion. Aside from breaking heads, this is the fastest way to establish your street cred.

In short, wiseguys do what they're told and never ask questions. You don't speak unless spoken to. When you're eating with your betters, make certain you're the first one finished. Open doors for them and pull up their cars when they're ready to go. Your job is to anticipate what they want before they even think about it. Don't joke or make unnecessary comments. Act seriously and you will be taken seriously. Act like a clown, and, well, you get it, right?

Get Noticed

Even if you join a gang, grow up in the right 'hood, and hang out in the local mob spots, you still need to rise above the human detritus that makes up the typical criminal echelon. Tommy Karate did this by beating up all the local tough guys with such ferocity that the Mafia hoods in Gravesend were practically forced to bring him into the fold. In other words, Pitera had all the makings of an excellent contract killer, which in fact he later became.

Similarly, when Gallo was just coming up in the Orange County drug world in the mid '80s, he got noticed by the Avila family as a result of his unparalleled ability to hustle and make money. The Avilas – a Mexican clan led by Joey Avila, his identical twin brother Sal, and their older brother Sergio – were allegedly the biggest cocaine trafficking group in Orange County, importing their *yeyo* by the planeload directly from the Medellín Cartel.

And when associates of the LA Family tried to rip Gallo off when he made his first foray into the porno-production world, he showed up with two truckloads full of Crips. This sudden influx of hard, pipe-hittin' homies convinced the *Mafiosi* to make Gallo a junior partner.

Now if you can't be the absolute best at something that inspires confidence, then try a new approach. Do what Gambino associate Andrew "Good News" DiDonato did as a teenager to get noticed – display tyrannosaurus rex-sized testicles. He accomplished this feat after shaking down two teenage dimwits who were with *capo* Nicky Corozzo's crew. The blowback from the shakedown had unexpected and, at least for Andrew, fortuitous consequences.

First, Nicky's favorite shooter, Michael "Mikey Y" Yannotti, approached Andrew and his partner Tommy. Mikey Y's murderous rep was well known throughout all five boroughs, and he was by far the most dangerous man Andrew met during his fourteen years as a gangster. So when he spoke, Andrew and Tommy listened.

In no uncertain terms, Mikey Y told them to back the fuck off. He explained that the two dimwits who worked at a bagel shop were into Little Nicky for big money from gambling debts – a pastime they had been financing by embezzling from the shop. In other words, it was Nicky first and Nicky last.

Several weeks later, one of the dimwits got caught red-handed by the bagel shop owners with his hand in the cookie jar. The punk immediately threw Andrew and Tommy under the bus, claiming the two budding Bowery Boys were forcing them to tap the till and hand over the dough. The owners – two brothers who were significantly older and girthier than Andrew and Tommy – dimed the bulls, then beelined across the street to a park to fight the boys.

As soon as the brothers pounced, out came Andrew and Tommy's brass knuckles (a must for every *bambino* bad boy). It was an ugly brawl, with one of the brothers later requiring one hundred stitches in his head. The cops arrived and arrested Andrew and Tommy for assault. But *they* immediately pressed assault charges against the two owners, claiming self-defense. Witnesses confirmed that the two older men had attacked the teenage thugs first. As a result, the four combatants agreed to drop all charges against each other.

Once the dust settled, Little Nicky sent for Andrew and formally put him on record as an associate. This means Nicky notified all Five Families that Andrew was now officially with him. So from that point on, anyone who fucked with DiDonato was fucking with Corozzo. As one of the strongest skippers (capos) in the Gambinos, this meant Andrew had serious weight behind him.

See, the Nickster was impressed by DiDonato's penchant for pugilism, as well as his aplomb in the face of police heat. But that was merely icing on the cake. Word of Andrew's entrepreneurial spirit in shaking down all of the neighborhood's young crooks had been reaching Corozzo's ears for the last six months. It was time to bring him into the Gambino fold. In doing so, Nicky also made Andrew a squire to Mikey Y.

Andrew was only sixteen years old – again, a perfect age to pop your Mafia cherry.

Now I know what you're thinking – what if Mikey Y (and, by extension, Nicky Corozzo) had clipped Andrew instead of bringing him on board? Certainly that was a possibility, but not a likely one. The reason is this: good talent like Andrew is hard to find. See, even though Andrew wasn't the biggest or toughest guy on his block, he was always willing to go the extra mile.

For example, if a tougher guy beat DiDonato in a fight, Andrew would wait for him the next day with crowbar in hand. When the guy came around the corner, Andrew would bushwhack him and beat him mercilessly. You bet your sweet ass that guy never dissed Andrew again. Nor did anyone who heard about Andrew's payback. In no time at all, he controlled all the teenage crooks in his 'hood. Just like Gallo would do several years later in Newport and Irvine.

Aside from sheer toughness, Andrew also displayed an uncanny knack for making money even as a young whippersnapper. For example, he shook down all the local weed dealers and started his own car-theft crew. One time he even stole a new Mercedes that contained hundreds of thousands of dollars in the trunk, which he quickly learned were gambling proceeds belonging to the Gambinos. He did the right thing and immediately returned the car and cash. By doing so, he earned the gratitude of none other than the boss himself, Big Paul Castellano. (He actually sent Andrew a bouquet of flowers and a thank-you card!) DiDonato also earned the respect of Little Nicky Corozzo.

Now *that's* how it's done, *lieblings*.

Lesson to Be Learned

Think of enterprising street gangs as farm teams for the Major Leagues of organized crime. Pearls of wisdom, honey babies. Pearls of wisdom.

By contrast, Gallo and Marco were *not* members of street gangs, as there is a paucity of such anti-social organizations along Orange County's Gold Coast. Instead, there was something far safer but equally instructive – a local phenomenon known as wrecking crews. These were loosely-knit groups of privileged, predominantly white teenagers who loved nothing better than to get wasted and brawl with wrecking crews from other affluent high schools.

Theirs was particularly vicious and in three years they never lost a single rumble. They even once beat the tar out of the entire UCI basketball team! The nice thing about these mêlées was that if you fucked up another crew, they wouldn't try to stab or shoot you afterwards in revenge. After all, these kids were just looking for good times, not to ruin their pampered lives.

Admittedly, the boys got a little carried away when going after a rival crew (the Punkers) from a high school in neighboring Irvine when they embarked on a car-bombing campaign in the late '80s. This brought down the full weight of the ATF (Federal Bureau of Alcohol, Tobacco, Firearms, and Explosives) on their incendiary asses. Fortunately, there were no arrests. However, the police brass did allegedly make a secret deal with Gallo – if he stopped blowing up people's cars, the local fuzz would stop pulling him over and searching him whenever he drove through town. Gallo agreed, and the bombings and police harassment stopped. Go figure.

Richard "the Iceman" Kuklinski grew up in Hoboken, New Jersey, during the '50s when there were no local street gangs, but he didn't let this deter his criminal ambitions. Kuklinski – who was 6'8" tall and weighed almost 300 pounds – quickly became known throughout Jersey City and Hoboken as an extremely violent man who was both fearless and reckless. As a result, like-minded young toughs naturally gravitated to him. The Iceman capitalized on this fealty and formed his own crew who swore an oath of loyalty to one another.

The Coming Up Roses Gang, as they self-deprecatingly called themselves, were soon pulling off robberies and stick-ups, including burglarizing warehouses and fancy homes. Thanks to Kuklinski's meticulous planning and shrewd judgment, the gang members' pockets were soon bulging with cash.

The Iceman handpicked only the most dangerous thugs to join his crew. They regularly engaged in ferocious bar brawls that typically resulted in E.R. visits for enemy combatants, with injuries ranging from cracked skulls to gaping knife wounds. In short order, the Coming Up Roses became known as the toughest gang in South Jersey. It didn't take long for the local DeCavalcante *Cosa Nostra* family (who inspired *The Sopranos*) to take notice.

If you can't join a gang, have a gang join *you*!

Chapter Four – How to Prepare for Life in the Mafia

"You can't learn about it at school and you can't have a late start."
– Carlito Brigante, a.k.a. Motherfucker to the Max

The margin for error in the Mafia is razor-thin – so slim that even one tiny misstep can result in your head being blown off, or even worse, a RICO conviction followed by lifetime imprisonment. (RICO is the acronym for the 1970 **R**acketeering **I**nfluenced **C**orrupt **O**rganizations Act, which is the federal government's primary OC statute.)

So if you're gonna go down this road, you can't do it half-assed. You have to be on point all the time. You can never ever get caught slippin'. You always have to be one step ahead of the law, and two steps ahead of your enemies. You have to be able to see two, three, and even four moves ahead of your opponents. You must be able to predict another person's behavior before they even *think* about doing something. Or as LAPD Detective Alonzo Harris says, "The shit's chess, it ain't checkers!" In short, you must be better and *badder*, meaner and smarter, more ruthless and cunning, than everyone around you.

"Jesus H. Christ, Don Martín!" you exclaim. "That is a *muchisimo* tall order, *señor*."

Baby steps, babies – one foot in front of the other. That's why I'm here.

The Ideal Childhood

If you're going to be a bad motherfucker, it's important that you have a really shitty childhood, which means growing up dirt poor. This should instill in you an overwhelming obsession with making money. Now for those of you who decide law school or business school is the best path for that, then more power to you. But for those of you who'd rather take a shortcut to riches and are willing to go to prison instead of grad school, then the mob is the way to go.

I know what you're thinking – plenty of people grow up impoverished and have no desire whatsoever to mob up. *Correctamundo!*

That's why, ideally, you'll have a really, *really* shitty childhood. By that I mean that with a little serendipity, you'll be physically abused by a world-class asshole of a father. This will instill in you a deep-seated hatred for authority, an ability to withstand severe punishment, and utter contempt for weakness – especially in yourself. Most importantly, it will provide you a hair-trigger temper that will result in instant, overwhelming violence against anyone whom you perceive to be a threat.

That pretty much sums up Babar's adolescence. He grew up poor with a very large, very scary stepfather who had a drinking problem and a penchant for bitch slapping him around whenever he was displeased. Marco is deeply indebted to his stepdad because it triggered in him an interesting psychological effect when he fought other kids: if someone attacked him, he'd actually try to *kill* them. Marco's shrink explained to him that he wasn't fighting his opponent, but his stepfather, who never laid a hand on him again once he turned fourteen and was big enough to fight back.

Similarly, the seeds were planted for Jimmy the Weasel to morph into the Mafia's top killer on the West Coast thanks to the brutal punishment he received at the hands of *his* father. Jimmy's pop used to beat the stuffing out of him while openly favoring his siblings. This painful injustice only made Jimmy more stubborn, resentful, and defiant. No surprise that Jimmy left home at an early age, ready to take on the world – and God help anyone who dared get in his way.

Kenny Gallo went through a comparable experience when he attended the Army and Navy Academy in Carlsbad, California (near San Diego). As a puny pre-teen cadet, the older boys brutalized him. The top six senior cadets who ruled the school even carved a *6* into his left forearm with a knife – a scar he'll carry to his grave. It didn't take him and his fellow plebes long to fight back and learn the number-one truism of the jungle: it's better to be stirring the pot than to be in it. It's this experience that later earned Gallo the colorful sobriquet "Kenji Snaps" because he'd be laughing with an unsuspecting enemy one second and "snap" into violence the next.

This latter attribute will make all your friends walk on eggshells around you because they never know when you're going to give them a brotherly hug or shove an ice pick into their ear. Niccolò Machiavelli said, "It's better to be feared than loved." *Word.* When swimming in a shark tank, it is critical that you at least *appear* to be a Great White.

The Ideal Mental Attitude

I realize it's a quantum leap to go from tuning someone up to strangling them with a length of piano wire. How do you develop this homicidal mindset? How do you get to that point where you can murder another human being in cold blood? Getting sexually molested as a child certainly helps. This will provide you with the necessary gusto and fortitude to do heavy work.

Take James "Jimmy the Gent" Burke, for example. From all accounts, Jimmy murdered well over forty men (and at least three women by my count). He personally clipped thirteen people just so he could keep the lion's share of the nearly six million dollar haul from the notorious 1978 Lufthansa Heist, minus Paulie Vario's $1 million end, as well as smaller token payments to several other Mafia bosses to keep the peace. He was such a scary guy that even other stone-cold Mafia killers were deathly afraid of him.

How did Jimmy get to be one of the most feared killers in mob history? By having the shittiest *childhood* in mob history. Jimmy never met his father and had no idea who he was. His mother dumped him in some hellish orphanage and never looked back. Little Jimmy, who was only two years old at the time, never laid eyes on her again.

From there, Jimmy was shuttled between so many foster homes that he couldn't remember the faces of the adults who took him in, much less their names. Not that he would want to, since many of them emotionally, physically, and sexually abused him. Time and time again he ran away, only to be captured and sent back. At age thirteen, he left the foster care system for good. He took to living on the streets, where he was mostly homeless, sleeping in cars and whatnot. And then, of course, both jail and the Mafia beckoned.

See, people aren't born monsters – they must be *made* into monsters. So good luck with that.

Oh, and in case you're wondering how to ensure you get molested, simply volunteer to be an altar boy at your local Catholic church. Get yourself assigned to whatever priest was transferred by the archdiocese to that particular church within the last two years – chances are he was moved there because of prior acts of molestation. Seriously, do you think it's just a coincidence that a disproportionately large number of mobsters *and* serial killers were altar boys?

If you don't believe me, ask John Alite, Billy Beattie (The Westies), Jimmy Coonan (choir boy but same thing – Westies boss), Larry Mazza, Francis "the Irishman" Sheeran, Joe "Mad Dog" Sullivan (molested by a nun), Danny Greene (Catholic orphanage), Ramon "Mundo" Mendoza (Mexican Mafia prison gang hitman who admitted to twenty murders), Johnny Martorano, his brother Jimmy, Eddie McGrath (Westies), Charles "Deanie" O'Banion (Al Capone's nemesis), Vincent "Vinny Ocean" Palermo (*de facto* boss of New Jersey's DeCavalcante Family and the inspiration for Tony Soprano).

Also altar boys were Andrew Cunanan (spree killer and Gianni Versace's assassin), Dennis Rader (the BTK Killer),

Richard Ramirez (the Night Stalker), and Charles Whitman (Texas sniper mass murderer). These are just a sampling.

And heck, when all else fails, join the fucking Boy Scouts!

Martial Arts

Now that you've fostered a volcanic rage, you still need the means with which to express it. What I mean is, you better know how to walk the walk instead of just talk the talk, pilgrim. Without the technical know-how, your pent up bloodlust will not be able to properly manifest itself. What's the use of being a homicidal maniac if you're just a little girlie-man in a street fight?

There is nothing more emasculating in this world, nothing more humiliating, and nothing more detrimental to your street rep than getting the shit kicked out of you. The downfallen looks on your friends' faces when you pick your ass off the ground after crying uncle will sear your soul 'til your dying day. Even worse, your embarrassing ass kicking could've easily been avoided if only you'd made the effort to take streetfighting seriously. I'm talking about training, baby. I'm talking about the motherflippin' martial arts!

Cue Carl Douglas' "Kung Fu Fighting."

"But Romie," you sob, "what's the point of being a gangster if you have to be *disciplined*? Oh, woe is to me! I'm a lazy piece of poopoo who just wants to party and count my money."

Or maybe you're thinking, "Why should I suffer to become an undefeated bare-knuckle warrior when I can simply pop a cap in the motherfucker's ass?" After all, as super-predator Jimmy Bulger (who hated the nickname Whitey) liked to say, "You know what beats a black belt? A gun belt."

Well, I'll tell ya, Mister Smartypants. Even if you're a worker with a gun, you will never earn true respect from the street unless you're good with your hands. Take a look at Thomas "Tommy Two Guns" DeSimone. Tommy D, as he was also known, murdered over two dozen people with his pistols. However, according to his good friend, Colombo associate Salvatore "Crazy Sal" Polisi, he couldn't fight his way out of a paper bag. Without his two guns, he was just a weak sister. And everyone knew it.

But still you bitch, "So fucking what – I am *always* strapped!"

Not in prison, baby. Not where it counts. Unfortunately, firearms are not allowed in the big house. When Tommy D was locked up, he shook like a windblown leaf because he knew he had made many enemies from all his senseless killings. He'd hide in his cell all day long when everyone else was in gen pop, quaking with terror. He was such a giant *mons veneris* that when he got into a fistfight with Gambino associate Ronald "Foxy" Jerothe, a trained boxer and Gotti Senior's "adopted" son, instead of fighting back, he simply shot Foxy in the face. Twice.

Ironically, killing Foxy on October 12, 1974, was one of the main reasons Tommy got his own head blown off over four years later on January 14, 1979. This was one month after Tommy participated in the December 11, 1978, Lufthansa Heist.

Anyways, you don't have to win a fight to get respect on the street or to avoid getting toilet-plunged by your nextdoor tiermate. You only need to take enough chunks out of him so that the next predator who comes along will think twice before trying to stuff you like a portobello mushroom.

Bottom Line: You must become a fearless, *skilled* streetfighter. It's do or die out there!

Don't worry if you're not physically imposing. You can always bulk up on anabolic steroids like 5'5" Sammy "the Bull" Gravano and 5'7" Gaspipe Casso. Juicing was very popular in Marco's social circle – all of the boys in their crew, including Gallo, would lovingly inject each other's cross-striated glutes with 'roids. They both shot past 200 pounds of shredded muscle. What a rush, baby!

Cue The Village People's "Macho Man."

Okay, I want to be a good role model for all the baby kingpins-in-training out there so I want you to just say no to 'roids. Aside from making you go bald, giving you acne, and causing you to develop gynecomastia (male breast tissue), the juice will destroy your liver. This means you can't drink or do drugs when you're cycling, which will only expedite the organ deterioration process. Gallo would get furious with Marco if he saw him hoover up a line of Peruvian booger sugar, and would immediately confiscate his 'roid stash. Not fair!

Besides, you don't need to be muscular to be a feared, respected thug. Look at Ralph "Sonny" Barger, Maximum Leader of the Hells Angels. Sonny is a short, skinny guy but he was a serious boxer and unstoppable scrapper who would easily knock out guys twice his size. Hail to The Chief!

Training, Exercise, and Nutrition

Bet you didn't think discipline was a key component of preparing for the mob, did ya? That's probably because you're a clueless idiot with a BORN TO LOSE tattoo on your hairless, concave chest. *You have to be highly disciplined to succeed in organized crime.* This starts with serious, daily training to develop into a top streetfighter. This means cross-training in multiple fighting disciplines. This is easy if you live near a UFC gym filled with lots of pros and top amateur fighters. For all you pimple-faced geeks out there, stop playing with yourself like the town freak and beeline to the nearest MMA school *pronto*. (As an ancillary benefit, once you become the toughest kid on your block, you can actually start having coitus with other humans.)

If you don't have access to an MMA gym, you should take Brazilian Jiu-Jitsu (BJJ), preferably the form taught by the world-famous Gracie family. Marco trained for several years with Carley Gracie, who is Royce (pronounced *H*oyce) Gracie's uncle. Carley holds both a ninth-degree black belt and the famed red belt in Gracie Jiu-Jitsu, and was undefeated as Brazil's national jiu-jitsu champion for eight years running before moving to the US.

Or sign up with Gallo, who now lives happily on a large farm near Chicago with a bunch of ducks, chickens, and other wildlife. Gallo has a black belt in BJJ, which was given to him by Lars Wallin, a Swedish *wunderkind* who trains movie stars at Fortune's Gym on Sunset Boulevard. Lars got *his* black belt from none other than Hélio Gracie (Royce's father), arguably the greatest jiu-jitsu practitioner in the history of the world. Lars trained for seventeen years on and off with Hélio in Sao Paolo, Brazil. Gallo got *his* black belt after training six days a week for ten years.

This is the kind of discipline you need, and these are the types of people you should seek out to train with and learn from.

George Rowe was an informant who went undercover for more than two years in the early oughts to rid his hometown (Hemet, California) of outlaw bikers. (One of Gallo's former Orange County crewmates, Chuck "Browntooth" V., was a sergeant-at-arms with the Vagos who went down as a result of Rowe's Operation 22 Green.) Aside from Joe Pistone, Jack Garcia, and Bill Roemer (who was undefeated for four years as Notre Dame University's heavyweight boxing champ), Rowe is the only *non*-gangster I can think of in that milieu who could have gone toe-to-toe with the toughest criminals they knew.

But George – who vanquished over *one hundred* adversaries in street brawls and illegal, underground bareknuckle matches – didn't suddenly wake up one morning with superhuman fighting abilities. He learned martial arts techniques from a man his father had befriended during the Korean War.

For more than four years, from age four to nine, George trained every day for two hours with the mysterious Master Lee, whom his father had imported for this purpose. Georgie Boy was forced to complete hundreds of pushups and perform endless drills. Without such relentless and brutal training, he would never have enjoyed his unblemished winning streak.

"But wait," you squeal, "that doesn't sound like fun at all!"

You know what's *really* not fun, sweeties? Getting the doodoo beaten out of you in front of lots of people. Marco never saw Gallo lose a single fight because the Snapster took his training seriously. Marco, on the other hand, did not and got his nancy ass kicked plenty of times. (But as he says in his own defense, "I won *half* my fights. If I was a baseball player batting .500, I'd be in the fucking Hall of Fame.") So sad! The agony of defeat is just that – it's *agonizing*.

When Marco was seventeen, Gallo told him to punch this tough rich kid Alex K. in the face for hitting on Gallo's girlfriend. So Marco did without question or hesitation. He simply walked up to Alex while he was sitting in his customized mini-truck, said hello, and cracked him in the kisser. Marco barely knew the guy.

Three years later, Marco ran into Alex at a gym in Irvine near John Wayne Airport. Alex challenged him to fight outside. Marco reluctantly accepted and so the entire gym poured out to watch. Marco didn't want to throw down as he was on probation at the time and had just gotten a luxe mani-pedi (paraffin wax, deep sea scrub, the works). But Alex charged him so it was *on*...

CRACK*!*

Marco shattered the dude's nose with one punch, and Alex squirted blood all over him. It was disgusting. Alex later went around town talking shit about him, so Marco caught up with him at a gas station and asked him if he still had a problem with him. Alex said he did not and so Marco let it go.

Seventeen years later, at their twentieth high school reunion, Alex showed up looking for Marco so they could have a rematch. This is how utterly humiliated Alex felt from his defeat. If Alex had kicked *Marco's* ass when they were young, Alex never would've given him a second thought. To this day, Alex still lopes around Newport, proudly displaying his misshapen nose like a badge of honor. Pa-thetic! Do you want to end up like this doofus? Get a life, Alex! Move out of your parents' house! And get some rhinoplasty, for Christ's sake!

Let's see, what else, what else... Oh yeah, eat right and exercise daily. This subject is so boring I don't even want to get into it. Just do it, *pendejos*! (I will, however, refer you to Bill Phillips' seminal diet-and-bodybuilding tome, *Body for Life*. Learn it. Know it. *Live it*.)

Streetfights

Alrighty then! Now that you've got the skills, the physique, *and* the stamina, it's time to go out and actually *become* a fearless streetfighting man. In short, you should get into as many fights as possible before you turn eighteen. That way you won't get into any serious trouble (unless you accidentally kill someone, in which case you'll do time for voluntary manslaughter).

Once you become an adult, fights are still lots of fun but the legal consequences are a bit more dire. For example, in California, you can get what's called a strike, which is a violent-felony conviction, on your record. Strikes add a helluva lot more time to your sentence, and when you get your third, you automatically get twenty-five-to-life. Even with good behavior, you'll still have to do eighty-five percent of your sentence with a single strike, instead of, say, two-thirds for non-strikes.

You can even get sued by the guy you pummeled. For example, if you plead "no contest" to an assault charge in criminal court, or are convicted of even a misdemeanor, your accuser can use that plea or conviction against you in *civil* court. That's because the assault has already been proven in a court of law with a higher standard of proof – a "proof beyond a reasonable doubt" standard in criminal court versus a significantly lower "preponderance of evidence" threshold in civil court. That means the only issue to determine in the civil case is how much you should pay in damages. So uncool!

Fortunately, most gangsters (and losers in general) are judgment-proof, meaning they have no assets in their own name or income to be garnished. So that should discourage the vast majority of civil lawyers (who get paid on contingency) from going after you.

If that doesn't work, you can always do what Gallo did when the divorce attorney of Tabitha Stevens, his pornstar, soon-to-be-ex-wife, aggressively threatened to take Gallo to the cleaners. Gallo simply hid out in the *scheister's* parking garage. When the pudgy blowhard got into his BMW, Gallo stuck a pistol in his mouth and promised to blow his head off if he ever heard from him again. Needless to say, blowhard dropped the case the next day.

****

Look, fighting is like humping – the more you do it, the better you get at it (at least in theory). So jump at every opportunity to show the world you can open a can o' whupass. *Let's get ready to rumble!*

Fights also present excellent opportunities for you to publicly display your savagery. When you're a budding mobster, honor should get tossed right out the window. Only a *pazzo* is honorable in a street fight. So if, for example, you've got your opponent down on the ground, *kick him in the fucking face*. Stomp the living shit out of him. If he turns his head, sucker punch him! Use headbutts, groin strikes, fish hooks, eye gouges – whatever it takes to put him down and keep him down.

One time in high school, Marco foolishly got into a scrap with a guy, Brandon J., who was not only twice his size but a damn good brawler. It wasn't long before Brandon was on top of Marco, beating his ass like a red-headed stepchild. Now, an honorable guy would've conceded defeat. But Marco had a rep to uphold so, instead, he took a three-inch chunk of flesh out of Brandon's ribcage with his teeth. Man, was he howling in pain! The dude finished kicking Marco's ass and went straight to the E.R. Even though Marco lost the fight in spectacular fashion, the word got out that he was a dirty fighter who would hurt you even if you won. And Marco even earned Brandon's respect. They became good friends, and Gallo absorbed Brandon into The Crew (the name of their high school and post-H.S. semi-organized crime group).

So, kids, try to emulate Kevin Weeks. Growing up in Southie as he did, a boy had to prove his mettle each and every day in street fights. According to Weeks, the most important thing was not to win, but just to fight back with everything you had. You had to show all the other tough kids that you were more than willing to stand your ground.

Trust me, Weeks should know – he easily had over *500* fights in his day, largely as a result of working four nights a week as a bouncer at Triple O's, the bloodiest bar in Boston. He got the job after slaving away as a barback one particularly memorable evening. That night, two huge thugs started brawling with each other, pausing only to summarily dispatch the two regular bouncers who attempted to intercede.

Weeks sailed across the bar and – P-POW! P-POW! – knocked out each combatant with one-two combos gleaned from his Golden Gloves boxing days. As fate would have it, Whitey Bulger was standing in the shadows watching this all go down. And so a star-crossed, symbiotic relationship was born.

Drop Out of School

If you want to join the Mafia, it's important you do super shitty in school, so be sure to drop out of high school no later than the eleventh grade (your junior year). I can only think of a handful of *Mafiosi* who actually graduated from high school, much less college. Hopefully you'll be expelled for being a baby kingpin and so this decision will be made for you.

If not, simply finish the tenth grade so you can get your driver's permit and *leave*. Release yourself on your own recognizance. If your parents don't approve, just tell them to fuck off and become an emancipated minor. Besides, there'll be plenty of time to get your GED and even a college degree when you're in prison.

Dropping out of school will leave you with enough free time to devote yourself to your criminal career, which will often require you to stay up way past your normal bedtime. Marco basically moved into Gallo's condo in Newport right after their junior year so they could scheme, scam, and deal full time.

Now pay attention, 'cause this is important: just because you drop out of school does not mean you should stop learning. *Au contraire, mon frère*. This is when your education *begins*, young Grasshopper. If you're going to be a master criminal, you must be extremely intelligent with a broad range of in-depth knowledge in many subjects. You should read up to fifty books a year, focusing on useful topics. For example, if you want to get a nice overview of how to dismember a corpse, study *Murder Machine* and *The Butcher*.

Similarly, if you want to find out how to dissolve a human being in a vat of acid (preferably *after* they're dead), then you should read Anthony M. DeStefano's *Mob Killer*. In fact, absorb every non-fiction book about organized crime you can find. (Prison provides a splendid opportunity for you and your cuddle-buddy to curl up together with a good book and catch up on your reading.)

You should even learn *culture* by, say, traveling extensively abroad, reading classical literature, and going to the opera.

Whatchoo talkin' 'bout, Willis?!

Listen, if you wanna bring your A-game, you're going to need to become a sophisticated international man of mystery. This way you can become friends with classy, sophisticated, and *wealthy* people – people that you need to get close to in order to rob, cheat, and fleece them. If you only prey on broke dicks, you too will be a broke dick. Figure it out, you friggin' dunskies!

Learn to Shoot

Become an expert marksman with every type of firearm. Guns are the primary tools of a gangster's trade so please become extremely familiar and comfortable with them. It could very well become a matter of life and death. If Nino Gaggi hadn't been such a crappy shot, he wouldn't have gotten one in the neck and been sentenced to prison. (Fortunately for him, he died of a heart attack at age sixty-two just before he was scheduled to begin his stretch. He was one of only a handful of Mafia bosses, including legendary godfathers Carlo Gambino and The Outfit's Tony Accardo, who died of natural causes without ever having spent a single night in jail.)

Gallo and his other BFF, fellow crewmate Lee Mathew Clyde (known simply as Clyde to his friends) both became crack sharpshooters in military school. By the time they were eighteen, they would regularly drive out to the desert near Palm Springs and target shoot for hours on end with assault rifles, hunting rifles, sniper rifles, submachine guns, shotguns, pistols, and revolvers.

Gallo became such a gun fanatic that he devoted an entire bedroom in his Irvine house exclusively to storing weapons. His collection included 37 assault rifles, but his prize jewel was a fully-automatic 1975 MAC-10 (a Miami chopper). This was a real one with .45 bullets, not the inferior semi-automatic MAC-11 version with 9mm rounds that was manufactured thereafter. And it even came with a suppressor (silencer).

Second place went to an authentic World War II-era .45 Tommy gun (Thompson submachine gun) with a round ammo drum. Do you have any idea how heavy that sucker is? Gallo would go nuts if he saw a movie where a Prohibition-era gangster was firing a "Chicago typewriter" with one hand – it's physically impossible.

Be All You Can Be (Join the Military)

I know what you're going to say – this is the most fucked up suggestion I've made thus far. But just hear me out. You would be bamboozled if you knew how many mobsters became superstars after emerging from combat tours. Calm down, baby boy, and take a moment to really think about this…

The military teaches you discipline, how to carry out orders competently and without question, and how to respect the chain of command – precisely what the Mafia requires. The armed forces you to get into peak physical shape and to keep your greasy piehole shut – which the Mafia appreciates. The military will break you down psychologically and build you back up into a remorseless killing machine – which the Mafia admires. The military will turn you into an expert in hand-to-hand combat and light weapons – which the Mafia rewards. With me so far, Forrest?

Participating in combat, where you'll see your closest friends getting shot or blown to pieces, will help you to emotionally detach yourself from other friends in later mob life. This is particularly useful when you are ordered to murder them. An even more subtle skill you'll pick up when you're blowing the heads off enemy combatants is learning how to shut off your fear and control your emotions. Now *this* is an absolutely invaluable trait for up-and-coming mob stars.

By the way, military school turned Clyde into such a badass that when he was only fourteen, still a freshman cadet, he stabbed an older man – a marine from nearby Camp Pendleton – after the marine and another jarhead beat the crap out of him in a McDonald's. Clyde kept pleading with them to stop beating him but they wouldn't, so he plunged a Bowie knife into the dude's heart. The judge ruled it a justifiable homicide committed in self-defense. However, Clyde was placed on six years' probation for carrying a concealed weapon.

Chapter Five – How to Dress, Bling, and Preen Like a Mobster

> *"My entire closet is filled with clothes that end in vowels – good vowels like Ferragamo, not bad ones like Aldo."* – Marco Falcón

Now that you can talk the talk *and* walk the walk, it's now imperative that you *look* like a gangster. This means that when you walk into a bar or restaurant or club, every heartbeat in the room should know you're a wiseguy. Now this will obviously attract undercover agents like flies to feces, but what's the point of being a mobster if nobody knows it?

The Threads

One of the reasons John Gotti Sr. was the most famous gangster in America since Al Capone was his sartorial splendor. After he and his ten pals (including Salvatore "Sammy Bull" Gravano) whacked Paul Castellano and his bodyguard Tommy Bilotti on December 16, 1985, Gotti became known as the Dapper Don.

Gotti singlehandedly made Brioni a household name. In fact, Gotti, who (foolishly) specialized in giving the press pithy sound bites, once emerged from a court appearance and bumped into his favorite fawning reporter. "John, what're you wearing today?" the reporter asked. "Brioni," he replied. "Three thousand dollars – *solve that one!*" Oh, how the press ate that shit up! What a freakin' *stunad*.

Aside from his dazzling collection of double-breasted, custom-tailored silk suits, Johnny Boy was also famous for wearing hand-painted silk ties, handmade alligator-skin Bally shoes, monogrammed silk socks, and cashmere overcoats. Gotti would boast that his public demanded that he look the part of a Mafia don, and that's why he dressed the way he did.

But Gotti didn't always dress like this. In fact, before Big Paul's farewell party, Gotti dressed like a total schlub. It was only after ascending the throne that his wardrobe underwent a radical transformation. As a *caporegime*, he had been partial to gaudy turtlenecks, polyester disco shirts open to the navel, and gold medallions gleaming through dense tufts of chest hair. He even occasionally rocked a poofy, nylon Oakland Raiders jacket with tasseled leather loafers. (*A Raiders jacket with loafers – what, are you fucking kidding me?!!!*)

In fact, when he was just a bottom-feeding soldier scraping by on low-level meat-and-potatoes crimes like hijacking and loansharking, the Daffy Don dressed like Bowzer from *Sha Na Na*. He wore black leather motorcycle jackets and white t-shirts with the shirt sleeves rolled up. This Fonzi-approved ensemble perfectly complemented his linebacker frame and greasy, duck-tailed pompadour. Gotti was also exceedingly fond of clashing plaids and stripes.

Even after he became don, however, John still had absolutely no sense of style. According to Gotti's pal Salvatore Polisi, every morning another mobster by the name of "Fat Bob" picked out John's clothes, which had all fallen off the back of a truck, of course. Bob had a fine eye and exquisite taste, and was a master of color coordination. But for Fat Bob, Gotti would have dressed like Steve Martin's "Wild and Crazy Guy" character from *Saturday Night Live*.

****

Frenchy Brouillette was the most notorious gangster-pimp in American history, eclipsing even Iceberg Slim. He was also a close friend of Louisiana godfather Carlos Marcello, who supposedly had a direct hand in JFK's assassination. Frenchy had slightly different tastes in threads than most styling mobsters, but clearly understood the importance of dressing a certain way.

At his prime, he was a rock star in the underworld – a glorious, preening peacock, bulging with anabolically-enhanced muscles. He would traipse down Bourbon Street, resplendent in Italian silk suits and handmade alligator-skin loafers that shined like mirrors. His pumped pectorals would strain through unbuttoned designer shirts. Diamond rings sparkled on all ten fingers!

Frenchy explains how to attract flies with honey in his autobiography *Mr. New Orleans*. See, Brouillette was his own best advertisement. By dressing and swaggering like Tom Jones at AARP Ladies Night, he convinced all manner of lowlifes that he was a "gin-soaked Moses" who would lead his degenerate entourage to nirvana. No wonder, then, that Frenchy spent his entire adult life leading a cavalcade of sex workers, johns, strippers, swingers, crackheads, junkies, gamblers, gangsters, dopers, and, of course, federal agents.

Ahhh, a man after my own black heart…

Whatever you wear, always look classy and successful but never boorish. And never, *ever* wear Versace – according to Marco, that's strictly for "wannabe Eurotrash." You want everyone around you to respect and admire you, so dressing elegantly and tastefully goes a long way towards achieving that goal. Always look like you take excellent care of yourself and people will treat you accordingly.

In addition, if and when you are officially made at a formal Mafia induction ceremony, you should wear either a black, dark grey or navy blue suit and sensible, rubber-soled footwear. Why sensible? Well, on the off chance you're going to get a shiny 9mm slug in your dome instead of a secret Mafia decoder ring, you may need to run for your life. *Arrivederci!*

By the way, for you nincompoops reading this, when you're told to "come dressed" to a score, it means you're supposed to bring a gun. Just before his first robbery in the '60s, Bonanno bozo and future rat Gaspare Valenti was given this precise instruction. Thus, for his first armed robbery, he arrived decked out entirely in burgundy: seersucker jacket, slacks, shirt, and patent-leather shoes. His fellow robbers burst out laughing.

Da Bling

We can't have an intelligent discussion about Mafia fashion without discussing jewelry. Now *this* is what separates the putzes from the players. All Marco had to do is glance at someone's watch to know if they're a loser or if they *possibly* have money. "With women, it's easier if they're married or engaged because I can size up their wallet with one look at their diamond ring."

The same obviously goes for guys with diamond pinkie rings. To further his criminal career, Marco studied under a top jeweler in downtown Miami's Diamond District who dealt exclusively in wholesale rocks. He is therefore intimately familiar with the four *C*s: cut, color, carats, and clarity. Legendary Gambino capo Gregory "the Old Man" DePalma used to carry a jeweler's loupe with him in case he needed to inspect someone's sparkle on a moment's notice.

Oh, where would the glorious history of *La Cosa Nostra* be without bling? Let us heave a nostalgic, world-weary sigh as we trip down memory lane…

First and foremost, there was the infamous pinkie ring – the bigger and gaudier, the better. This trend was started in the early 1930s by Mafia founding father Giuseppe "Joe" Bonanno. He had them made from every conceivable type of jewel – diamonds, rubies, sapphires, onyx, etc. With his superbly-cut suits and jaunty hats, Joe Bananas' pinkie rings made him the envy of the entire Mafia.

Nobody had a more expensive pinkie ring than Gaspipe Casso, whose walnut-sized diamond would have been worth well over $175,000 today. I bet he still thinks about that ring in his concrete box as he waits for the Boatman to ferry him across the river Styx.

Second prize for the glitziest pinkie ring goes to Kevin Weeks, whose five-carat solitaire diamond was worth $100,000. Whitey Bulger bought it for him after Kevin punched out the teeth of some guy who threatened Whitey – Weeks had dislodged his own original, smaller diamond in the process.

The most expensive watch award goes to my favorite Albanian-American knockaround kid, John Alite, whose diamond-studded gold Rolex was worth $80,000.

Finally, Johnny "the Executioner" Martorano, who admitted to murdering twenty people while rolling in Bulger's Winter Hill Gang, gets the prize for best watch-ring combo. For two decades, he sported a pinkie ring with a five-carat, internally-flawless diamond, and a Rolex President dazzling with emerald-cut diamonds. The authentic mahogany inlaid in the Rolex's face was identical to that in the dashboard of his black Mercedes 560 SEL. His customized thirty-three-foot Holiday Rambler RV gleamed with the same wood. Poor Johnny eventually was forced to sell all of these possessions to pay his defense attorney.

Cue Bobby McFerrin's "Don't Worry, Be Happy."

Gallo and Marco were certainly not immune to the gold bug – how could they be when they came of age in the roaring '80s in Newport? Oh, it was a glorious time for dopers! Back then, Orange County's Gold Coast was a-boomin' with yacht and Ferrari dealerships, which *all* had electronic money counters in the manager's office for special VIPs. The three oldest sons of Griselda Blanco, a.k.a. the Cocaine Godmother, bought a dozen Ferraris and Lambos from one Newport dealership alone. In fact, the manager let them use his office as an unofficial headquarters for their SoCal drug-distribution empire.

Dude, back then, the Pacific Coast Highway was gridlocked with exotic cars, like the white Lamborghini Countach with the vanity plate SNOWMAN. The real estate, stock market, and cocaine industries were on freakin' fire. Why did it have to end, Lord? They was havin' so much fun!

Anyhoo, during that time, Gallo, Marco, and the dozen-plus other hardcore members of their crew all got their dazzle on in a big way. They all rocked gold Rolies, gold Turkish rope chains like the one Al Pacino sports in *Scarface*, 24-karat gold bracelets, and only a single diamond earring in their *left* earlobe.

They even jokingly changed the name of The Crew to the Rolex Social Club. They'd be, say, playing blackjack in Vegas or snorting a line off someone's ass in Palm Springs when suddenly one of the boys would cry out, "Rolex-forearm-bash-Louis-Vuitton-wallet-slap!"

The fellas would instantly drop whatever (or whomever) they were doing and bash their Rolex-manacled forearms together, withdraw their LV wallets, and high-five-slap them in the air. This never failed to elicit awed looks from their legions of sycophants. Oh, how the mighty have fallen!

Marco considerably toned down his bling collection after he moved to South Beach. He did so after his first visit to a Sunday tea dance (afternoon DJ club), when the local hipsters expressed horror at his fresh-off-the-Newport-Beach-boat attire, heavily-gelled hair, and bulging package. He thereafter downsized to a stainless-steel Rolex (sans diamonds) and sold off the rest of his gold Mr. T starter set.

He also traded in his Ray-Bans, Oakleys, Vuarnets, and Persols for an extensive collection of high-end Japanese and French designer eyewear (Matsuda, Okio, Yoji Yamamoto, Jean Paul Gaultier). Other individuals wearing the same über-hip specs instantly recognized and accepted him as someone who was successful, stylish, and super-cool. This provided him an entrerez into the upper-crust feeding grounds.

Follow Marco's lead and limit your trinkets to only a steel or, at worst, a platinum Rolex – even white or rose gold is too gaudy – and (God forbid) a wedding ring. No necklaces, bracelets, earrings, pinkie rings, or piercings. If you're a made guy, you've already gotten the word: toss everything flashy and stop hugging 'n' kissing each other on the cheek. Only the New York *goombata* did this – the Chicago mobsters, for example, have always preferred to simply shake hands.

If you're painting the town red, then by all means wear shirts with French cuffs and pearl or silver cuff links. But if I see diamonds on any part of your face, body, or clothing, I'm gonna walk over and slap the shit out of you. Oh, and stop going to social clubs. If not, you might as well roll out in force like outlaw motorcycle gangs and wear a big sign on your back that screams organized crime member.

Hygiene and Grooming

Cleanliness is next to godliness. Ideally, you should shower three times a day. Once, after you chew your arm off to escape the clutches of whatever Dothraki wet-nurse you managed to drag home from the strip club the night before. Second, after your intensive, two-hour martial arts-crossfit-Zumba-dance workout. Third, just before you hit the town in search of – what else? – more easily-impressed women of ill repute, loose morals, and low standards.

As with clothing, John Gotti also immortalized Mafia grooming standards. Mob guys had always been known to pamper themselves – just look at Albert "the Mad Hatter" Anastasia, who was famously whacked on October 25, 1957, while getting a trim and hot shave at the Park Sheraton Hotel in Manhattan. Gotti, however, elevated primping and preening to an art form. Here was his daily schedule after he became boss in late 1985.

His right-hand man, Angelo "Quack Quack" Ruggiero, would call him at home at noon to wake him. Gotti, who'd been out all night getting his ass kissed at Regine's and 21 in the city, would answer gruffly then hang up. Fat Angie, a 300-pound killing machine with 24-karat balls and a cubic zirconia brain, would keep calling back until Gotti finally spoke to him. "Yeah, yeah, Ange – I'm up, I'm up." "Have ya had yer espresso yet, John?" (If Ruggiero could have deep-throated Gotti through the phone line, he would have happily done so.)

After showering, eating breakfast, and donning a velour tracksuit and pristine sneaks, Gotti would be picked up by

Ruggiero in a big, shiny, black Mercedes. Big John had bought it to celebrate his assassination of Paul Castellano in front of Sparks Steakhouse – the most audacious and spectacular hit on a mobster in NYC since Anastasia's demise almost three decades earlier.

They'd then drive over to the Bergin Hunt and Fish Club in Queens, where Gotti would spend hours getting his daily shave, trim, and manicure from a professional barber and a stylist. Then Fat Bob would dress him in his impeccably suave suits. By this time, it would be four o'clock – time to go to work at the Ravenite Social Club in Manhattan's Little Italy. Ah, what a life…

There's only one other bad guy I can think of who could have given Gotti a run for his money in the personal styling department – Babar. In South Beach, when he was the prince of the city (at least in his own mind), he would try not to overexpose himself. He would only go to monthly superstar soirées, which only the crème de le crème of the club scene would attend. This took an extraordinary amount of preparation (and more than a few ducats).

He'd ratchet up his workout routine as the big day approached so he'd be extra ripped. He also ramped up his tanning schedule – both indoor and outdoor – to ensure he achieved that perfect, deep-bronze hue. Then he'd get his hair cut by his favorite hairstylist, Ilona Scandulosa, followed by a mani-pedi, groin wax, herbal facial, and deep-tissue massage. All would be topped off with a shopping spree for a brand-new hipster outfit, including shoes. (If they weren't already platformed, he'd take them to his favorite cobbler to add a precious inch or two. As Marco says, "You can never be too rich, too tan, or too tall.") In short, he'd spend all day making himself look good, and all night making himself *feel* good.

Although *you* need not go to such aesthetic extremes, it is important that even as a struggling villain, you always be buffed to a high sheen and perfectly coiffed. Nary a shellacked hair should be out of place. My personal idol has always been Tony Manero in *Saturday Night Fever*, who spent two hours brushing his hair before hitting Disco 2000 in Bay Ridge. *Attica! Attica!*

Anyways, with his new wardrobe, South Beach penthouse, snazzy 5-Series, thousand-watt smile, George Hamilton-tan, and single-digit body fat, Marco was in like Flynn. He and his like-minded, high-flying criminal associates (drug traffickers, marijuana growers, ecstasy chemists, nightclub owners, British con men, Filipino gangsters, Latino playboys, top-notch strippers, superstar DJs, and high-class female escorts) had an absolute ball for eight straight years. They used to spill out of nightclubs at dawn, look and each other, and laugh, "When will the fun end?!"

Um, it ended as soon as the Miami Police Department slapped cuffs on Marco and sent his taut, overly-tanned ass to jail.

Cue Lucille Ball wailing at the top of her lungs: *Waaaaaah!*

Where were we? Oh yes. Why go to all this trouble to dress up, you dare ask? Because women will want to be with you, and men will want to *be* you. Crowds of admirers will follow you around like a tiny herd of caribou wherever you go – like Sam Malone's never-seen brother on *Cheers*. Once that happens, you can attach yourself to them like a suckling baby pig and slowly drain the life-blood out of them (financially speaking, of course). That should be the goal of every good gangster – fleece 'em while they're vulnerable.

¡Buena suerte! And remember, it's always better to look good than to feel good.

Lesson to Be Learned

If you're not a metrosexual, then by all means, insist on having one in your crew.

Fashions obviously change with the times, and the Mafia is no exception. In the early '90s, after John Gotti completely ruined the Mafia with his self-destructive grandstanding, the bosses issued new edicts about protocol and behavior. One of these concerned the new dress code. No longer could wiseguys wear flashy pinstriped or sharkskin suits or black leather jackets. No more camelhair overcoats or feather-festooned fedoras. No more shoes made from endangered species. No more open silk shirts and ostentatious chest hair. No more over-the-top displays of gold jewelry and diamond pinkie rings. In short, no more dressing like Johnny Boy, whose loudmouth was finally shut by, ironically enough, terminal throat cancer. He died in federal prison on June 10, 2002, at age sixty-one after a ten-year stretch.

Since then, the younger goodfellows have bedecked themselves in "Italian tuxedos" (Sergio Tacchini tracksuits) and spotless white designer sneakers. The older guys wear elegant slacks or pressed khakis and crisp polo shirts. Nothing flashy or loud. Gold watches and wedding bands only, with zero sparkle.

Yes, I know that mothballing your three-quarter-length black leather duster and matching *Breaking Bad* porkpie hat sounds utterly depressing. But look on the bright side – your new mode of dress can actually help you make money. Take Marco, for instance. When he started getting into more sophisticated white-collar crime, he needed to blend in and be immediately accepted by the country-club crowd in Bal Harbour and Palm Beach. This meant everything from eating and drinking at all the power hot spots in Miami to having Sunday brunch at the Ritz Carlton in Coconut Grove.

Marco studied how everyone in the sporting life dressed – from successful bankers to weekend wine connoisseurs. Then he hit Saks Fifth Avenue at Bal Harbour Shops and went hog wild. He stuffed his closet with beautiful and suave – but never flashy – Italian suits (Isaia, Zegna, Prada); Italian shirts and ties (Brioni, Armani, Hugo Boss); and *only* Salvatore Ferragamo shoes. For cocktail parties and yacht soirées, he'd wear navy blue Zegna sport coats, light-colored Gucci shirts, designer jeans or beige Prada slacks, and Ferragamo loafers.

Then he watched every single Cary Grant movie he could rent from Blockbuster until he could articulate and enunciate his speech precisely like him. If that's too boring for you mouth-breathers, I suggest you study how Doctors Frasier and Niles

Crane speak on *Frasier*, which you can binge watch on Netflix. Hannibal the Cannibal (Sir Anthony Hopkins in *Silence of the Lambs*) also speaks quite beautifully.

Fun Facts!

At one point, Griselda Blanco's three oldest sons – Uber, Dixon, and Osvaldo -- lived right next door to Kenny Gallo's father on Lido Isle. Small world, huh? The trio of bloodthirsty baby kingpins made a big splash along the OC's Gold Coast. They bought so many exotic cars at Newport Imports that the manager reportedly allowed them to use his own office as their international headquarters.

And did you know that John Travolta, who shed twenty pounds for the role of Tony in *Saturday Night Fever*, improvised the lines about his mother: "She hit my hair! I spent two hours brushing my hair and she hits it!" Or that Deney Terrio from *Dance Fever* was the one who taught him how to disco dance? Or that he's been a Scientologist since he was a TV star on *Welcome Back Kotter*? Or that he started out as an insipid pop singer with an appearance on *American Bandstand* before his TV stardom? No? Well, now you do!

Finally, did you know that Cary Grant, whose real name was Archibald Leach, dropped over one hundred hits of LSD in his day? That's right – he started dosing in the late '50s. In fact, in 2017, a documentary called *Becoming Cary Grant,* which touches on his acid trips, premiered at Cannes. He apparently enjoyed his trips far more than Whitey Bulger.

Shameless Namedrop

Many, many years ago, my friends and I rented a large suite at the Ritz Carlton hotel in Dana Point (south Orange County) to celebrate our high school graduation. There were many of us and we were making a hell of a racket. Around midnight, we heard a pounding on the door.

"Oh crap," I said, "it's probably the manager. See who it is."

My friend Phil looked through the peephole. When he turned back to us, he looked positively stupefied. "Uh, it's John Travolta."

I couldn't believe it. "You mean as in John Travolta from *Saturday Night Fever*, *Grease*, and *Urban Cowboy*?"

Phil looked at me as if I was an idiot. "Do you know any other John Travolta?"

"Well, open the fucking door!" someone barked out.

Phil opened the door and sure enough, there he was in the flesh. He was still thin back then and really, really, ridiculously good-looking. He was holding a bottle of expensive Bordeaux and a wine glass. Flashing his million-dollar smile, he said, "Hi, my name's John. I'm in the suite next door. I heard the music and was wondering if I could join you guys."

A roar went up from the crowd. Phil grabbed Travolta's arm, pulled him in, and that's how we adopted him for the night.

Can you dig it? I knew that you could!

Chapter Six – How to Behave Yourself as a Wiseguy (Part One – The Dos)

"To live outside the law, you must be honest." – Robert Zimmerman

Congratulations, tadpoles! You followed *Maestro* Martín's law to the letter thus far and now you've not only been noticed by the higher ups, but you've been put on record by an actual made guy. This means you have been officially recognized as an associate with a particular LCN Family – you're now on the books and will be operating under their umbrella.

Cue Ludwig van Beethoven's "Ode To Joy."

You've made it to the first rung of the organized crime ladder and the only way to go now is up, right? Wrong! You're now about to *Riverdance* down a Byzantine path laid with more land mines than Pol Pot's Cambodia. One false step and you're trunk music – stinking up your own Cadillac like Roy DeMeo.

Maybe five to ten percent of Mafia associates get tapped to become made men. The attrition rate is daunting but with a wee bit o' help from yer old Uncle R.M., you'll be swimming upstream in no time. *Grazie mille, San Gennaro!* I'm gonna tenderly hold your hand and guide you safely along the golden brick road.

Always Keep Your Word

I love that quote above from Bobby Dylan (his stage name). In fact, it's my favorite quote from anyone anywhere anytime about the criminal lifestyle. It perfectly encapsulates the mindset you must have when you become an outlaw. The wisdom Bobby D. was trying to impart was simple: if you're a criminal, you have only two currencies – your word and your rep, both of which are inextricably intertwined. This means you should never fuck anyone over (unless they deserve it, or unless you've been ordered to do so by the powers-that-be). And you should always mean what you say and say what you mean (unless doing so will bring you or your loved ones harm). Or as Texas-Vegas crime boss Lester "Benny" Binion once said, "Don't ever tell a lie – unless you have to."

Even the bloodthirsty Gaspipe, who (like Sammy Bull) started out as a true man of honor in the literal sense before succumbing to his own paranoid delusions (and, according to Gallo, a crack addiction!). Back then, Gaspipe believed that when you made a promise to another wiseguy and shook on it, your word was your bond – as important as any matter of life and death. And, indeed, he'd seen enough carnage growing up on the streets of New York to realize that going back on your word *could* quite possibly result in your doom.

Take Marco, for example: in all the years he was trafficking in illicit contraband, he never once shorted his suppliers by even a single dollar, nor was he ever late with his payments. He knew that if he ever did so, he could get away with it once or twice, but not a third time. He knew they would cut him off, either by not returning his pages or calls, or by simply air conditioning him. The trust he had carefully developed over time was his lifeline.

His relationship with Gallo is an example of how Marco lived and breathed this philosophy. One time they were in their super-secret storage unit in Costa Mesa with about $2 million worth of uncut Colombian bam-bam. Gallo's back was turned to Marco, who was armed. It suddenly occurred to Marco that he could easily put two in Gallo's brain, and he would be much the richer for it.

But actually, he knew he wouldn't. What kind of garbage murders his friend for money? (Uh, Nicky Scarfo, Sammy Bull, and Gaspipe, for starters.) Without friends in this world, you got nothing! Marco would never betray any of his friends, and he never did. Marco never gave a shit about his *actual* family because they never gave a shit about him. So Gallo and the rest of The Crew became his surrogate family, as did later the Love Tribe, as Marco's South Beach hipster crew called themselves.

Bottom Line: Some things in life are more important than money. Besides, if and when you finally wake up and realize you've thrown your entire life away by being a criminal, at least you can bullshit yourself by saying, "Hey, at least I was honorable."

You'll do a lot of bad shit in the Game (or as the Canadian Mafia calls it, the Milieu), so you'd better have a rigid code of honor to live by. Otherwise, unless you're a textbook psychopath, you will never be able to live with yourself way down the road (when it counts). You must have a strict set of self-imposed rules. You should never fuck over or otherwise hurt your friends, never rat on anyone (even if they're your enemy), and never harm innocent people, especially women, kids, and the elderly.

Marco's taken some hard falls in his life – thumps he could have easily avoided by flipping, but he knew he wouldn't be able to look himself in the mirror, knew he couldn't be a man if he didn't pay for his own sins: "I don't know if that's right or wrong; I just know it was right for me. To this day, I can still hold my head up wherever I go because I never put my shit on anybody else."

And so endeth the sermon. Draw your own line in the sand and never, ever cross it. That way, no matter what happens, you can still have dignity and self-respect. It's pretty simple, this credo, which is perfectly and poetically expressed by Cuban gangster Antonio Montana: "All I got in this world is my word and my balls, and I don't break them for nobody."

So don't make promises you can't keep, and always downplay everything you're doing. This is particularly important when communicating with your supervisor, whether you're an associate dealing with a soldato, or a soldato dealing with a *capodecina* (another term for capo).

What I mean is this: if you promise your immediate superior that you're going to pull down a big score Saturday night, he's going to expect you to deliver, at least, a ten-percent cut to him on Sunday. And with wiseguys, the chickens are not only counted before they're hatched, they're already plucked, skinned, and sold off to Foster-motherfucking-Farms.

Thus, if you get your boss all worked up about the score and you don't come through for whatever reason, he's going to be bitterly disappointed. Now I'm not saying keep it a secret from him, because if he finds out about the score before you tell him about it – *especially* if it works out – he's going to suspect you're holding out on him. As Jimmy the Weasel liked to say, "Fucking with people's money is the fastest way to get clipped."

So what do you do? Tell your boss about the score but, again, downplay the shit out of it so he'll have reasonable expectations. That way, if it doesn't work out, he'll think, "Aw, fuck it – I wasn't gonna make that much anyway." Conversely, if it does fall into place, and you come through with his end, especially if it's more than he expected, he'll freakin' love you.

It's gonna be a good summer!

Always Be Respectful

You'd be surprised how many nimrods commit the cardinal sin of disrespecting people who should not be disrespected. This is particularly important in prison, where respect and strength are the two most important commodities. If you are polite and respectful to everyone, especially the bosses, you, in turn, will be treated with respect. (How do you think Jimmy "the Gent" Burke got his nickname?) This applies to people outside the mob as well, especially women. Being respectful displays strength of character – an absolute essential in LCN. It's a proven leadership quality.

You should, of course, be particularly deferential to the older guys, who can make or break you in the Life. You might not know the decrepit geezer sipping espresso with anisette, but he might be a big-time shotcaller just in from Palermo to visit his cousin, *your boss*. Better to be safe than sorry, I always say.

Being respectful also means being friendly and nice to people, but don't be too chummy – you want to be seen as a serious guy. This doesn't mean you have to be a self-loathing, poison-spitting prick like Frank "Lefty" Rosenthal. Lefty probably never cracked a smile in his entire miserable life.

Unfortunately, however, people often mistake kindness for weakness. It's okay to be the class clown, always cracking wise and making everyone around you laugh — if and *only if* you occasionally explode into violence. Again, this will make everyone wary and frightened of you. People should never know exactly where they stand with you. Keeping 'em on their toes will make most of them think twice before trying to screw you later.

Be a Goodfella

Be and stay loyal to your friends. Help them and their wives, kids, etc. whenever you can, especially when your buddies are doing time. Loyalty, friendship, and trust go a long way in the mob, and are not easily forgotten.

FUDGE-THE-FEDS SECRET REVELATION #1

I'm going to reveal many secrets in this book that the FBI doesn't want you to know about. The first is that informants, if they're important enough, actually have a say in who they will and will not have to testify against. The feds want you to think that if you flip, you have absolutely no choice but to rat out everyone you've ever known for everything you've ever done with them. This is simply not true.

Take Gallo, for example. From age eighteen to twenty-one, he was working as a doper and enforcer for the Avila family. He was also a cooperating witness (or whatever they called it back then) for the FBI, as well as the Irvine Police Department, as part of a joint organized crime task force. He wasn't in any trouble at the time. Instead, he agreed to cooperate in order to protect and expand his own criminal interests, and to protect the members of his own crew.

In other words, he did precisely what Greg Scarpa, Whitey Bulger, and Bulger's crime partner Stephen "Stevie" Flemmi did. By making a Faustian bargain with the FBI, these criminals were allowed to rise to the top of the underworld *with the FBI's acquiescence, assistance, and complicity*. See, the FBI knows that the higher its snitches climb, the better intel they provide, and the bigger case it makes.

The revelation that the FBI allowed special informants to dictate the terms of their own cooperation deals would prove highly embarrassing for the Justice Department, the US attorney's office, and the FBI. So please don't tell anybody.

Gallo told the feds straight out that he would never flip against his friends – and he didn't. He never turned on the Avilas. During the first of two times he went under, none of his crew took a bust that was not directly related to something stupid they did. (For example, in early 1989, Clyde got popped after shotgunning the Turtle Rock, Irvine, home of one of Gallo's enemies because the getaway driver, crewmember Jeff A., ran a stop sign on the motorcycle they were riding.) True, many years later, Gallo flipped against his close friend, Lucchese soldier John Baudanza, but Gallo had agreed to do so before he ever met JB.

How could these guys get away with this? Because the FBI is willing to bend over backwards for certain canaries if it means catching bigger fish like John Gotti Sr. or Colombo street boss Teddy Persico Jr. See, big Mafia fish mean big headlines, which in turn mean promotions and raises for everyone involved.

Believe me, friends – the last thing the Justice Department gives a flying fuck about is justice. They only care about winning, regardless of the consequences and costs – for them, the ends always justify the means. And please don't give me that true believer bullshit – how do you explain the fact that half of all mob lawyers are former federal prosecutors? As a result, these crooks are able to protect their real friends.

And why do these informants do that? Out of loyalty, which should always be a two-way street. For example, Sammy's crew was steadfastly loyal to him because he was always there for them, through thick and thin. Indeed, several of Sammy's crewmates were so loyal to him, they even visited him in jail after he flipped. This sparked a heated debate among the Gambinos as to whether or not these guys should be smoked. They lucked out and got a pass. FYI, Sammy is still a venal, psychotic asshole.

****

Displaying loyalty to your boss is a key way to move up the Mafia ladder. Take hitman Frank "the Irishman" Sheeran, who was like a son to Rosario "Russell" Bufalino. Don Bufalino was the most powerful godfather in the history of *La Cosa Nostra* of whom the public is unaware. He had his own Family based in Scranton, Pennsylvania, and ruled that state, as well as large swatches of the East Coast, including much of New York, New Jersey, and Florida. He was even a member of The Commission, the not-quite-so-secret-anymore national ruling panel of the LCN. It's traditionally comprised of the New York bosses, as well as the dons in Philly and Chicago. Bufalino was so well respected, he spent three days of every week in the Big Apple hanging with the other *padrones*. He also had the final say-so in whacking Jimmy Hoffa, among making many other important LCN-related calls.

In his 1980 RICO trial, one of the first prosecutions under that statute, Sheeran was acquitted of murdering a 300-pound hustler named Robert "Big Bobby" Marino. Frank did, in fact, kill Marino on orders from Bufalino on February 13, 1979. In a rare moment of recklessness, Bufalino had ordered Sheeran to waste Marino without first doing his due diligence. If he had, Bufalino would have learned that Marino was a major loanshark who secretly worked for Bufalino's close friend, Philadelphia don Angelo Bruno

It was only after Sheeran had murdered Marino that Bufalino realized by doing so, Bruno had lost $80,000 he had on the street through the shylock. As a result, Bruno blamed Sheeran without knowing the Irishman had done the hit at Bufalino's request. But being the stand-up guy he was, Frank kept his mouth shut about Bufalino's orchestration, even when Bruno brought Frank in for questioning. Fortunately, Bruno was very fond of Frank, so didn't whack him for the loss. By the way, Bufalino did try to call off the hit after learning of Marino's connection, but Frank was already on his way to give the vic a dirt nap.

Wow, just like in the movies!

With Bufalino, loyalty truly was a two-way street – a rare trait for mob bosses, who typically view their minions as highly-expendable cannon fodder. Sheeran revealed that as a direct result of Bufalino's influence and power, no less than seven murder contracts had been rescinded against him.

Be Smart When Beefing with Other Mobsters

Beefing with other stone-cold killers is one of the fastest ways to get clipped in this business. One of the things that most annoys me about Hollywood is its portrayal of mobsters in a ludicrously false light. For example, in virtually every gangster film (including even the exemplary *Donnie Brasco*), you see one mobster screaming at and threatening another in front of a crowd of fellow gangsters with impunity. FYI, that incident did not appear in Pistone's eponymous book for the simple reason that it never happened.

Let me make this crystal clear so there's no misunderstanding: in real life, if Stone-Cold Killer A threatens, embarrasses, or otherwise disrespects Stone-Cold Killer B, *especially in front of other stone-cold killers*, then from that moment on, Stone-Cold Killer B's every waking moment will be spent obsessing over how to murder Stone-Cold Killer A. That's because on the street, your reputation is everything. Even if doing so (a sneak tip – an unsanctioned, off-the-record murder) is against the Rules of LCN, Stone-Cold Killer B will figure out a way to secretly kill Killer A. Thus, you should never disrespect another wiseguy, especially one who has no problem performing the Italian rope trick on your obtuse ass.

"But, Romster, baby," you moan, "what if I have a legitimate beef with another bad guy?" I'm glad you asked. Here's exactly how to handle a beef with another mobster: *con mucho cuidado, pendejo*. In *Donnie Brasco*, Pistone explains how he handled 6'3", 230-pound lunatic Anthony "Tony" Mirra (who murdered at least thirty people) after Mirra berated and humiliated him in front of other gangsters.

First, he had to ensure that when he confronted Mirra, they were alone. He had to ensure that Mirra saved face. So he told him something like, "Tony, listen – I know you're a made guy and I'm not, and that gives you a certain status on the street. But I'll say this one time and one time only – if you ever embarrass me in front of people again, I'm gonna get you, okay? It'll be when you least expect it, and no one will know what happened, understand? I'm not just some *schmuck* you can push around."

Mirra was quiet for a few moments, eyeballing Pistone, then simply shrugged it off with an it's-all-good smile. "I was just fuckin' with you, Donnie. We're good, babe."

Although the two tough guys didn't exactly hug it out, they made an uneasy peace. But from then on, there was tension between them. Mirra never forgot that Pistone had essentially threatened to murder him.

I have no doubt whatsoever that Pistone would have followed through on his threat to Mirra – he would have had to; otherwise, he would have been finished on the street. Nobody would have respected Pistone, and his deep-cover operation (the first of its kind) would be *finito*. No one would have feared him. Everyone would have ripped him off. But although he was a maniac, Mirra was no *boombots* – he knew that Donnie the jewel thief was a capable guy (capable of murder).

Kenny Gallo was also a master at dancing between the raindrops when it came to confronting another shooter. Gallo told me during one of our many interviews:

> You can never back someone into a corner. They'll have no choice but to attack you – either right then and there or later, especially if there's other people around. You always have to leave them an out so they can save face.
>
> I never threaten anyone or raise my voice or cuss at them. I never put my hands on anyone. I try to pull them aside to speak to them alone, and I talk to them in a respectful tone but in a way that shows I'm not messing around. Like, I'll say, "Listen, Joey, you've got a problem here. You ripped off so-and-so but so-and-so is with you-know-who. So you-know-who has asked me to talk to you like a man, okay? You gotta pay the money back and that's all there is to it." And that usually did the trick, and the guy paid back the money right away.

See, no need for threats or violence. If you have a no-fucking-around street rep like Gallo then the other shooter will do as *respectfully* instructed. And the other shooter will keep his dignity and maintain his own rep by proclaiming it was all a simple misunderstanding.

Let's turn up the heat a bit. How should you comport yourself when you're confronted by a violent psychopath – particularly one who is accompanied by a large number of other violent psychopaths? Again, *very* carefully, snowbunnies.

First and foremost, you must never show fear, even in the face of overwhelming odds. Gangsters are natural predators, and they'll smell weakness and fear a mile away. I'll let Marco explain: "When I walk in a bad neighborhood, especially at night, or down the cellblock tier, I show total confidence and strength. My eyes go dead-blank and my body language says, 'Don't even *think* about fucking with me 'cause I'm having the worst day of my entire life.'"

Like Clemenza instructed Michael, "Don't look anyone in the eye, but you don't look away either."

If you walk tall and carry a big stick – on the street, that's your itchy trigger finger and superior fighting skills; in prison, that's the uncomfortable katana lodged in your sphincter – then you'll be just dandy. Predators will simply move on in search of easier prey.

Second, you best think fast on your feet, my son. Let's look at one of Jon Roberts' most memorable New York moments in the early '70s. One of the marks he suckered, a big-time club promoter named Hampton, went squealing like a blubbering manbaby to then Gambino-associate John Gotti. He whined to Gotti that Roberts and his partner, fellow Gambino thug Andy Benfante, had stolen his restaurant. Since he was paying Gotti for protection, Johnny Boy felt obliged to step up.

Gotti sent word to Roberts about the beef and asked for a meet. In light of Gotti's extremely violent reputation, Roberts and Benfante should have requested a sit down that included their respective skippers. In his autobiography, Roberts claims he and Andy agreed to meet Gotti directly out of sheer hubris. But I suspect the true reason lay in the fact that they had not kicked up from this restaurant score; therefore, they did not want the brass to catch wind of their off-record gig.

And so a meet was set for the following day in the basement of a Brooklyn bar. Since they weren't entirely reckless, Roberts and Benfante came with a handful of well-armed heavies. Down in the basement, they faced off against Gotti and half a dozen cavemen, who were also strapped.

Gotti, of course, took Hampton's side. "Hampton's with me, and you ripped him off. That means you ripped *me* off."

Right on cue, twenty more swarthy ruffians squeezed down the stairs, surrounding Roberts and his band of merry men. Jon and Andy exchanged looks, perfectly understanding their predicament. If they backed down from Gotti now, they would be finished in New York. On the other hand, however, if they made Gotti look weak or threatened him in front of his men, he'd have no choice but to dead their asses right then and there. Nobody wants to die in a basement.

And that's when Benfante saved the day. Ignoring all of Gotti's goons, Andy moved closer to Johnny Boy and said, "Well, guess what? Your buddy Hampton is a fucking snitch for the FBI. So fuck him and his restaurant."

Gotti hadn't anticipated this, and wasn't sure if Andy was telling the truth. (Benfante was actually bullshitting, but would later learn that Hampton was in fact an informer. So there's that.)

"I'll check it out and get back to you," Gotti finally muttered with a poker face. See, no one would have expected Big John to defend a rat, least of all himself. And that gave him the out he needed to save face. As a result, Roberts & Co. were able to walk out of there, heads held high and restaurant intact. They shambled past Gotti's men without another word.

Be Smart When Attending Sit Downs

For you squares, sit downs are meetings held between two disputing mobsters and their Dutch uncles (Mafia sponsors), and are presided over by a seemingly neutral, high-ranking *Mafioso*. Despite the bullshit Hollywood shoves down your gullible throats, beefs between wiseguys do not typically end in violence. Because organized crime is just that –*organized* – so beefs are usually resolved peacefully via an old Sicilian custom that was perfected in the New World. The arbitrator's decision is final, binding, and non-appealable. These are serious get-togethers that are often a matter of life and death. Therefore, you need to behave yourself accordingly.

When you attend a sit down, never curse, raise your voice, move your hands around, or be anything other than utterly polite and respectful. Dial your shit *waaay* down, Spanky. Pretend you're a wayward schoolboy brought to the principal's office for a proper tongue lashing. Be perfectly contrite.

If alcohol is offered to you, politely decline. It's a ruse to see if you're weak and stupid enough to drink at a sit down. Ex-Chicago mobster Frank Calabrese Jr. told me that his father, Outfit capo Frankie Breeze, was a master manipulator who would always try to ply his adversary with booze because people under the influence will say things they otherwise would not.

He also told me his father would always let his adversary speak first at a sit down, so that he (Frankie Breeze) could adjust his own story accordingly. "Once the other guy talks, his story is out there and he can't take it back." His father would say things to rile up his adversary at a sit down. "People say the wrong thing and get themselves in trouble when they get hot."

Next, never bring *anyone* outside the Family to a sit down. This is an absolute *infamia*. Gallo illustrates this sacrosanct rule in *Breakshot* when describing an incident involving a sit down between Jimmy Caci, Louie Caruso, and Tommaso "Tommy" Gambino (godfather Carlo's nephew) at an LA restaurant. According to the Rules, they and only they should have attended the sit down.

Instead, Caruso brought along two monstrous bikers as backup. As soon as this hapless trio squeezed through the front door, Caci exploded from his corner booth and screamed, "Louie, you little cocksucker! Why the fuck did you bring these two *giant* cocksuckers! You know the Rules, asshole!"

As Gallo explains, Caruso had insulted Caci on multiple levels. Caruso had not only defecated on the divine Mafia rules, but had disrespected Jimmy by trying to muscle Caci with the bikers. Back in the day, Jimmy's own friends would have devoured him if he had shown even the slightest hint of weakness. Therefore, Caci took this affront as a declaration of war.

Needless to say, the sight of Jimmy foaming at the mouth sent Caruso and his two meatheads backpedaling in terror. As they exited the restaurant, Caci spat out a threat, "Show up again with those two cocksuckers, Louie, you fucking cocksucker, and I guarantee the three of you will be on your knees sucking my you-know-what!" Think candyass Caruso ever tried to pull that shit again?

Always Be Generous

Even though wiseguys will think nothing of blowing thousands of dollars on a single night's entertainment, they'll cheap out when it comes to cutting up a score. I swear, it's almost pathological. They can't help but chisel a few extra bucks from their own friends and associates when it comes to divvying up the pie. This is just plain dumb in so many ways, I don't even know where to begin.

When you take good care of your peeps, they will want to take care of you. It's an immutable law of the universe. Anthony Fiato had over a million dollars on the street, accumulating ungodly sums of vig – more money than he could possible spend. But with great wealth comes great responsibility. The way he treated his crewmembers hearkened back to the days of yore when his mentors – Boston *Mafiosi* Nicky Giso, Paulie Initso, J.R. Russo, and Larry Baioni – generously shared the spoils with their own men. Following their lead, Fiato always ensured that his own legbreakers lived in luxury apartments, drove new cars, wore designer duds, and had plenty of spending cash.

As Jimmy Caan would say, "Good f'you, Ant'ny."

Conversely, when you shortchange your partners, they will resent you and, if you do it often and long enough, will begin plotting your death.

In August 1983, Francis "Mickey" Featherstone was a feared killer with the Irish mob in Hell's Kitchen. (They were dubbed The Westies by the press after hearing the phrase coined by NYPD detective and Mafia expert Joseph Coffey – rest in peace, brother.) Having just emerged from prison, Mickey asked his boss James "Jimmy" Coonan for a small loan to buy a house. Jimmy, who was rolling in dough at the time, foolishly refused. In light of how many people Mickey had whacked for Jimmy, this was tantamount to an outright betrayal. Eventually, this led to Mickey flipping against Coonan, who went away for life.

At the very least, if you chisel your partners, you'll get a bad reputation on the street as someone who doesn't do the right thing, and you'll lose respect. Needless to say, if you short your bosses, they'll almost certainly throw a blanket over you. If you're particularly greedy, they'll literally shove a fistful of twenties in your anus (typically *after* they kill you). *Thanks, fellas!*

Finally, always remember that you have a certain image to maintain. Never be cheap with waiters or concierges; even if your meal or bill is comped, always leave a huge tip. And a wiseguy never asks for change when he pays with a twenty dollar bill, even if it's for a pack of gum. Cheap is cheap.

Remember, peeps – if you look like a bigshot, talk like a bigshot, and spend like a bigshot, then you'll *be* a bigshot.

Fun Facts!

Believe it or not, Sammy "the Bull" Gravano made the same demand as Kenny Gallo, i.e., that he wouldn't have to turn against anyone in his own crew. Ironically, one of the crewmates that he protected, Thomas "Huck" Carbonaro, was convicted years later of conspiracy to murder Sammy after he relocated to Arizona and was outed by a local newspaper. Sammy Bull was also able to cut out from his cooperation agreement Gaspipe, whom he knew had a nasty habit of shooting the innocent family members of racketeers who ratted him out.

Chapter Seven – How Not to Behave as a Wiseguy (Part Deux – The Don'ts)

"You're not a regular guy anymore – you just can't go into a bar and get drunk with the guys and kid around." – Nicky "Crow" Caramandi

Now that we've gotten the dos out of the way, let's talk about the shite you *shouldn't* be doing – not if your testicles wanna stay attached inside your scrotum. See, the mob is a zero-tolerance organization – rarely are second chances granted, or quarter given. It's not like the Japanese Yakuza, where if, say, you bang the boss's wife, you can get away with merely having a digit on your pinkie cut off – on your non-jerkie hand, no less. Now that's a sweet deal.

In Tokyo, you can actually see these guys hanging out at the posh nightspots, wearing exquisite $15,000 Matsuda suits, with their missing digits and distinctive lapel pins that advertise the name of their crime family. And all the young guys drive supercharged Nissan GTR Hurricanes. So freakin' cool.

Now before you read the rest of this chapter, I implore you to watch *Donnie Brasco*, which contains a veritable font of useful information about wiseguy don'ts. This is sagely imparted by Lefty Guns Ruggiero to Donnie, portrayed by Depp, who resembles the real life, six-foot-tall, 220-pound, muscle-bound Joe Pistone as much as my mini-dobie resembles *Cujo*. Let me put it to you this way: if Johnny Depp and I were cell mates, he'd be washing my underwear in the sink and singing me showtunes.

Don't cry for me, Argentina...

Never Use Public Transportation

Speaking of the Yakuza, I occasionally spotted them on the subways in Tokyo and Kyoto. I was surprised because in New York, wiseguys taking any form of public transportation – the subway, the bus, taxis, ferries, or those ubiquitous blue Citi Bikes – is strictly verboten. The Commission has updated this edict to prohibit Uber X, Uber Select, or anything less than an Uber Black Car. And God forbid you get caught riding a Bird scooter.

Again, mob guys have a certain image to uphold. This worked wonders for Gallo while he was wearing a wire against the Colombos because he could travel via subway without worrying about being followed by his fellow gangsters. He never ceased to be amazed by mobsters' allergy to the finest public transportation system in the United States.

Sorry, Kenny, but I can't really blame 'em. I tried to take the subway when I was in the Big Apple, like the more than three million people who do so every day. I even thought I could get used to the interesting décor on the walls, which resembled something akin to a Jackson Pollock canvas, assuming he used human blood instead of paint. I thought that reptilian prick Giuliani had cleaned this town up, but the subway still looks exactly as it did in 1978's *The Warriors*. To top it off, as I was waiting for my train, I heard a little girl – a tourist – say, "Look, Mommy – it's Mickey Mouse!" Turns out it was a giant wharf rat scurrying across the tracks. I got the fuck outta there and flagged down a human rickshaw.

Bottom Line: If you don't have your own car, you can only take a Town Car or SUV, a Mercedes sedan, a boat, or a horse (a Sicilian holdover tradition).

You Get What You Get and You Don't Get Upset

Aside from threatening another killer, stealing his money, or playing hide the *salsiccia* with his wife or daughter, the fastest way to end up with cement shoes in the mob is to complain about being passed over. (In *La Cosa Nostra*, advancement is known as getting your stripes.) This is universally considered to be sedition by the powers-that-be. It's the kind of fightin' words that can easily cause dissension in the ranks – and trust me, that will never be tolerated. No way, José – that shit gets nipped right in the bud.

During the '90s, Tony "the Hatchet" Chiaramonti was a feared and respected hitter for The Outfit. But when he got passed over for promotion to capo, he started whining to friends whom he naively trusted. Those pals ran straight to the bosses and informed them of his treasonous rumblings. To make matters worse, Chiaramonti began pressuring the higher ups for a larger slice of the video poker machines he was supervising and managing for them.

On November 15, 2001, Tony the Hatchet met with made man Michael "Mickey" Marcello at a restaurant in Cicero, Illinois, which happens to be Capone's old stomping grounds just outside Chicago. Marcello was going to make one last attempt to get him to shut the fuck up. Doubling down on his own idiocy and suicidal ideations, Tony shoved Marcello to the ground, cursed him out, then left. (Another inviolate Rule of the Mafia is that you can never put your hands on another made guy unless it's during a sanctioned hit.)

Five days later, on November 20th, Chiaramonti learned what happens in the mob when you beef against your superiors. He was walking out of a restaurant towards his new emerald BMW when he saw a Chrysler minivan screech to a halt nearby. Out jumped a burly man wearing a Chicago Bears jacket – it was another Outfit shooter, master jewel thief and hitman Ronnie Jarrett.

Jarrett chased Tony the Hatchet back towards the restaurant and – BAM! BAM! BAM! BAM! BAM! – shot him five times in the head, chest, and neck, wasting him. Jarrett got away clean.

We got a moron here…

Bottom Line: If you can't say anything nice about someone, don't say anything at all.

"Nevah Let Nobody Disrespect Ya"

Never let *anyone* piss on your fire hydrant. You must draw a line in the sand, and if anyone dares cross it, you need to drop the hammer. For example, in prison, when you're pussy on the hoof (fresh fish, for you *Shawshank Redemption* fans), and some joik-off steps up to you and demands your lunch money, what should you do? If you have to even think about it, you're as good as corn-holed, boo. Without even blinking, you should shiv that bad boy right in the throat and keep walkin' the line – calm and cool, baby.

The same principle applies to the street. Anyone who disrespects you – especially in front of others – is essentially declaring war. That person must be dealt with in such a way as to send out unequivocal warning signs to anyone else who thinks you might have gone soft.

Now I'm not saying go straight at the Fredo who crossed you. No siree, Bob. That is not the *Cosa Nostra* way, my friend. That is too on the nose, as they say in Tinsel Town. Instead, be sneaky deaky about it. In other words, don't get mad, get satisfaction.

In early May 1976, Roy DeMeo got bitch slapped by Joseph Brocchini, a made member of the Colombo Family (Roy wasn't yet made at the time). Rotund Roy left with a swollen face, a black eye, and a helluva bruised ego.

According to the Rules, no one – not even a boss – can kill a made man from another Family without the approval of that made man's own boss. But when Roy complained about the insult to his own skipper, Nino Gaggi, Nino simply made his usual gun sign with his thumb and forefinger, and instructed Roy to make it look like an accident. (Gaggi was the only man in the Mafia whom DeMeo would ever admit to fearing.) Roy and his Murder Machine crew of fellow mob serial killers didn't wait long.

Two weeks later, on May 20, 1976, Roy, Henry Borelli, Chris Rosenberg, and almost certainly the so-called Gemini Twins (inseparable best friends Anthony Senter and Joey Testa) burst into the office of Brocchini's used car dealership. Everyone was wearing masks but no doubt Brocchini recognized DeMeo's unmistakable penguin-ish girth. While the others handcuffed and blindfolded the employees, DeMeo and Borelli went into Brocchini's rear office and shot him five times in the head. Bye-bye, Brocchini.

Roy's crew ransacked the place to make it look like a robbery, and the local fuzz reported it as such. But everyone in the underworld knew what really went down, and now knew (if they didn't before, as Roy had been whacking folks since 1974) the price that even a made guy paid if you fucked with DeMeo. You *know* that was the last time someone put their hands on revenging Roy.

Like Father, Like Son (Not!)

Only a human shit stain would want their son to join the Family business. Who the hell would want to expose their beloved boy to the incomparable horrors of the Mafia, where the chances of being murdered, spending life in prison, or flipping are virtually guaranteed? Plenty of imbeciles, as it turns out. Joseph Massino virtually insisted that his men bring their own progeny into the *borgata* in order to ensure the men's loyalty.

When Junior got his button proud pappy John Gotti actually bragged about it to Genovese boss Vincent "the Chin" Gigante. Chin stunned Gotti with his now famous response to the news: "I'm really sorry to hear that."

That sure took the air out of Johnny Boy's sails – not exactly the high-five he was expecting. Gigante despised Gotti, and would later try to kill him with a car bomb, with Gaspipe's help. The Chin rubbed salt into that wound by proclaiming that he, personally, would never want to bring his own sons into the

Life. Gotti fumed all night. Ironically, Gigante would prove himself to be a hypocrite years later.

For some reason, the New York Families have always been bullish on nepotism, unlike The Outfit, whose more successful members traditionally sent their male heirs to law school, business school, and so forth; Frank Calabrese Jr. being an unusual exception. Similarly, you'd be hard pressed to name a single Jewish gangster from the olden days who brought their own kids into the biz. The same could also be said for Irish-American hoods.

Greg Scarpa Sr., for example, once admitted that he had stopped counting his murder victims after *fifty* – and that was well over a decade before he stopped killing with impunity (thanks to the FBI). When Greg Junior followed in his father's footsteps at age sixteen, he ultimately ran his own thirteen-member crew, which allegedly whacked fifteen mobsters between 1980 and the late '90s.

The younger Scarpa became a major earner in his own right, and eventually rose to the rank of capo in the Colombo Family on his own steam. He was personally linked to as many as two dozen murders by the FBI, including thirty-one-year-old Mary Bari, whom Junior held down while his old man shot her three times in the head on September 24, 1984. The Scarpas had allegedly acted on Feebie Lin DeVecchio's tip that Bari was an FBI informant.

In 1998, the younger Scarpa was sentenced to forty years in federal prison for racketeering and drug trafficking. As of October 2017, he was attempting to obtain a compassionate release based on the fact that he's dying of cancer. Virtually every crime he ever committed was at the behest or on behalf of his father. Greg Junior himself puts it this way: "This man ruined my life and the lives of my brothers and sisters, and he put a mark on my name that I'll have to live with forever. He was the Grim Reaper, but he was still my father."

As bad as that sounds, it ain't jack compared to what Big Paulie Vario did to *his* prodigal son, Lenny, who was the favorite of his three boys. Paulie adored Lenny and had big plans to turn him into a gangland prince. And so Paulie took Lenny under his wing, just as he had done with Henry Hill years earlier, and introduced him to the Life. Things didn't go quite as planned.

On July 20, 1973, Lenny, age twenty-three, received third-degree burns over ninety percent of his body after he botched an arson job at a construction company. Lenny's two associates dropped him off at a hospital six blocks away and fled.

Poor Lenny lingered in agonizing pain for almost three months, finally expiring in early October. A chip off the old block, he refused to identify his associates or provide the police any information about the incident. His family was forced to bury him in a closed casket.

Paulie was understandably heartbroken, but to Hell with him, right? He's the one that sent him out on that torch job in the first place. I never liked him anyways – he had an affair with Henry's wife Karen while Hill was in the can. Paulie also brutally beat with a baseball bat a female bartender with whom he was having another affair after she told his wife about it. Oh, and when he was twenty-one, he and a group of four other thugs were prosecuted and jailed for gang-raping a sixteen-year-old girl. What a swell guy, huh? Hope it's not too hot down there for you, Paulie.

Just Say No!

A major occupational hazard of working in the Mafia is alcoholism. Granted, booze is what *made* the Mafia. On January 17, 1920, the geniuses in Congress saw fit to pass the Eighteenth Amendment to the United States Constitution. Also called the Volstead Act, it banned the manufacturing, distribution, and use of alcoholic beverages. Literally overnight, a massive black market in illegal liquor was born. Everyone from moonshining hillbillies in the West Virginia Ozarks all the way up to Joseph Kennedy Sr., the kingmaker himself, got into the act. In Chicago, Al Capone personally controlled over a thousand speakeasies, generating an annual income of $100 million.

In order to cut down on competition, avoid costly violence, and maximize profits, the Prohibition-era gangs quickly organized. However, it would take another eleven years, until 1931, for Salvatore Lucania, a.k.a. Charles "Lucky" Luciano, to convene a summit in Chicago of the nation's most powerful Italian and Sicilian gang leaders. Together, they created *La Cosa Nostra* (as accurately depicted in the legitimately sublime HBO series *Boardwalk Empire*).

By the time Prohibition was repealed in December 1933 (after almost fourteen years), the Mafia was wealthy beyond belief and here to stay. So I find more than a trace of irony in the fact that alcoholism has been the downfall of many o' goodfella.

Drugs

Crack is whack so please apply Nancy Reagan's advice from preceding section and just get high on life. Nuff said.

Gambling

Gambling is the second-worst vice you can have in the mob. Yes, yes, I know what you're whining about now: "But, Roman, *baba* – gambling is the life-blood of *La Cosa Nostra*." Right you are, sir! So just remember one indomitable rule: *don't get high on your own supply.* Gambling will suck out your cash faster than it comes in, make everyone lose respect for you, and turn you into a sucker. The Mafia is for predators, not for prey, and when you become a degenerate gambler, you become just that – a target, a mark, a big. Time. *Loser.*

Now, many of you in the know will say that John Gotti was the worst degenerate gambler in the history of the modern Mafia, and you wouldn't be far off. It seems like virtually every book I read which mentions the Gambinos talks about what a horrible gambler he was, and how sick he was with this disease.

Gotti's gambling losses were indeed staggering. During one weekend alone, he lost $90,000. During one football season, he lost almost $200,000. And he'd routinely lose $50,000 a weekend on horse racing and other sports. But as the dearly departed Tom Petty used to sing, "Baby, even the losers get lucky sometimes." And so it was with Gotti, who once won almost a quarter-million dollars playing the numbers in Brooklyn, then lost it all shooting craps over a two-night period.

Another estimate had him losing over $5 million a year gambling – and you thought Johnny Depp was a profligate wastrel. It was this bottomless money pit that forced John to turn a blind eye to the heroin trafficking his entire Bergin crew became heavily involved in after he became boss, including his own brother Gene and best friend Fat Angie.

Two interviewed FBI agents both agreed John Gotti's immense hidden fortune is one of the great enduring Mafia mysteries. They estimated he had hidden away as much as $100 million before he went away for good in 1992. Guys, let me spare you the suspense – *there is no fortune. He blew every freakin' dime!*

At least Gotti's gambling addiction didn't get him killed, which was the case with Gambino soldier Edward "Danny" Grillo. He was a hard-luck ex-con bank robber and gunman, whom Gambino associate Dominick Montiglio met at Roy DeMeo's Gemini Lounge in Canarsie, where DeMeo and his Murder Machine slaughtered and dismembered as many as two hundred victims.

In early November 1978, bosses and capos from different Families, including the Gambinos' Paul Castellano and Nino Gaggi, used two crooked Brooklyn rabbis to host a casino night at their synagogue. It was a first-class affair all the way, with professional dealers and craps, blackjack, roulette, and other gaming tables. Nino put Dominick in charge of the House that night.

Unfortunately for everyone involved, Danny Grillo was gambling that night – with his life, as it turned out. Grillo bullshitted the craps pit boss into believing that Dominick had approved one hundred thousand bucks in markers. Big surprise – he lost it all, and had no means to pay up. He begged

Dominick to tear up the markers, and like a moron, Dominick tore up half.

But that still left Grillo on the hook for fifty grand. As his immediate superior, Roy DeMeo was responsible for Danny's actions. As equally idiotic as Dominick, Roy paid the debt and made Grillo promise to quit gambling forever. Grillo crossed his heart and hoped to die. Literally.

Exactly one week later, Grillo went to a high-stakes craps game in Manhattan and lost another $150,000 in markers. Amazingly, both Nino and Roy chewed his ass out, but let him live and even paid his debt (as a loan)! Once again, Danny promised to go on the wagon with the dice.

Then shit got *really* crazy.

Grillo was super desperate now that he had a 150-large shylock loan with Gaggi and DeMeo. Never a good thing. And the only way he thought he could pay it back was by – yup, you guessed it! – gambling. So to execute this brilliant scheme, Grillo somehow convinced his old pal, Westies' top man Jimmy Coonan, to borrow fifty thousand dollars from DeMeo, but to *not* tell DeMeo that he was borrowing it for Grillo! Can you believe Coonan actually agreed to this hairbrained scheme?

Amazingly, Coonan did. That same night, Grillo lost the entire fifty grand Coonan had borrowed from DeMeo. Grillo later tried to murder Coonan to cover his tracks, and Coonan, who caught wind of this plot, tried to whack him first – but Roy beat him to the punch.

After hearing about Grillo's latest subterfuge, on November 14, 1978 (less than two weeks since the ill-fated casino night), Roy murdered and dismembered Danny, then scattered his remains in the nearby Fountain Avenue dump (his favorite burial ground). On the day he disappeared, Grillo had been summoned to the Gemini Lounge by Roy. Grillo's wife later discovered that he had left home without his wallet and jewelry. Danny knew exactly what was about to go down but went anyways. *Jesus H. Christ!*

People, *please* let the story of Danny Grillo be a cautionary tale for all. Conversely, don't be a goddamn enabler like all the numbskulls above. Do your gambling-junkie pal a favor and just blow his fucking brains out when he's not looking. It'll save everyone lots of headaches in the long run, and, believe me, you'll be doing your bud a favor.

"Broads"

Finally – the ladies. Oh yes, the very reason Marco got into this crazy business in the first place. His *numero-uno* motivation for becoming a criminal. The babes. Or as Gallo would make fun of him by perfectly imitating his voice when Babar saw attractive females: "Dude, *chiiiiiiiiiiiiiiiiiiiicks*!"

Affecting Marco's unique *barrio*-surfer argot, Gallo would also call and make dates with women all over town. Of course, he forgot to tell Marco he had done so. They would then hit the clubs and run into these ladies, who would frequently toss drinks in a bewildered Marco's face. Gallo, of course, laughed his ass off. It took months before Marco finally figured it out.

Without a doubt, women have been the cause of wiseguys going to jail more than any other reason aside from their own stupidity. I love the line in *The Godfather*, "In Sicily, women are more dangerous than shotguns." Hell, Marco's first major bust was because a woman dimed him out to the coppers. And Gallo almost took a hard fall when he agreed to commit insurance fraud for his then wife Tabitha Stevens – a brush with the law that convinced him to join (for the second time) Team USA. He's the first to admit that he had lost his mind when he married her. Or as Marco blithely told me, "A porn star and a mobster – who would've thought it wouldn't work out?" It was a great wedding though, with every LA- and Vegas-based mobster in attendance. Babar, of course, flew in from Miami, frying his brains out on magic mushrooms.

So, gentlemen, if you absolutely insist on having Biblical relations with the fairer gender, for the love of God, never let them know *anything* about your business. Never! And never, ever get married. Marriage and the Mafia don't mix – and neither do kids. All they'll bring you is domestic strife and financial misery. Even Lucky Luciano once said, "People in our life should never get married." Follow the lead of the Russian *Mafiya*, whose members vow never to wed or sire offspring because the bosses know that love of family usually trumps loyalty and duty to the *organizatsiya*.

'Sides, wives and children are *hella* expensive. That's why Marco got snipped the moment he turned eighteen. Let's face it – even he admits he really shouldn't be breeding since mental illness is hereditary.

Oh yeah – whatever you do, don't shag another mobster's wife, girlfriend, or daughter. That's against the Rules, and will get you killed faster than ... well, to quote Omar "El Mono" Suárez, faster than a rabbit gets fucked.

Don't Be an Abusive Asshole

I'm gonna turn the mic over to Marco, who apparently is never at a loss for words or opinions about any particular subject.

"God, I hate bullies. Even now, I can't help myself if I see someone bullying a weaker person. I have to step up and tell that guy to kick rocks. And if he won't, or if he talks shit to me, then we're going to have a serious problem. I *never* back down." Which probably explains why he's had more stitches than Frankenstein's Monster.

This quasi-pathology apparently stems from the abuse Señor Falcón suffered as a child at the hands of his stepfather. Many mob guys I know feel the exact same way. They'll throw down at the drop of a hat with a bully. When Gallo lived in LA, in a gated fortress guarded by a pack of dogs and security cameras, he'd walk around with a boxing mouthpiece in his pocket just in case the opportunity to bitch slap a bully arose.

On the flip side, there is a veritable plethora of bullies in the mob, which attracts more than its share of sadists. If you're one of them, then trust me, everyone around you secretly hates your guts and prays daily for your premature death. And that's no way to go through life, son.

Look at that maniacal meatball Tommy D. Foxy Jerothe was looking to beat him up for physically abusing Foxy's younger sister, whom Tommy was bedding. Tommy should have been iced the day after he shot Foxy to death. John Gotti loved Foxy like a little brother after he discovered him as a homeless fourteen-year-old secretly sleeping in his backyard shed. Foxy was also Sal Polisi's best friend, and from all accounts, everyone loved him because he was such a great guy. He was a classy gangster who always treated women with respect and kindness. By comparison, Tommy physically and emotionally abused women.

The only reason Tommy D lived for more than another four years was because Jimmy the Gent, who was Big Paulie Vario's top earner and killer, loved Tommy so much. He had known DeSimone since Tommy Two Guns was five years old. Burke loved Tommy so much that when he was in his thirties, he began "dating" Tommy's fifteen-year-old sister, and would do so for the next twenty years.

But Tommy D sealed his fate by trying to rape Karen Hill while her hubby Henry was in prison. He then smacked her around when she rejected his drunken advances. Again, Karen had reportedly been having a secret affair with Paulie at the time, and Tommy's violent reaction was the last straw for him.

The point is, the second Paulie withdrew his protection, John Gotti and his crew rubbed out Tommy D after slowly torturing him over a long period. Paulie supposedly even drove Tommy himself to the fake induction ceremony where he was abducted. Many people, including Sal Polisi, had been dying to kill Tommy for many years because he was such an incorrigible bully.

Vario also wanted him gone because Two Guns Tommy had been ID'd as a Lufthansa robber and, therefore, could expose Vario's complicity in the heist. This was probably the real reason Vario finally gave the nod on ghosting Tommy, since DeSimone was disappeared on January 14, 1979. This was six months after Hill was paroled so it's unlikely Vario was still carrying on his affair with Karen. Not that Henry would have noticed as, even he admits in his book, he was then a hopeless heroin addict.

Lessons to Be Learned

Keep your flippin' trap shut about promotions or money or *whatever*. Never ever bitch about anything. Keep your melon-farming mouth closed and good things will happen to you, *ohkay*?

In fact, now that I'm on this subject, don't talk shit, *period*. If your precious ego gets hurt by someone, kindly swallow that bile and *quietly* plot your revenge. Aside from giving you the life expectancy of a mosquito, trash talking just makes you a downright a-hole. Even if you can get away with it because of your lofty status, just don't do it.

Look at that deadhead John Gotti Senior – he was the biggest backstabbing shittalker in the *history* of the Mafia. My God but this dense stooge couldn't keep his mouth sealed! FBI supervisory agent Bruce Mouw's Gambino Squad (until 9-11, the FBI had five separate squads in NYC – one for each Family) recorded Gotti calling the Colombos "Cambodians," deriding Lucchese bosses Vic Amuso and Gaspipe Casso as "the circus," and slagging off his own close friend and neighbor, Bonanno boss Big Joey Massino, as "the whale" and "a punk." Gotti even referred to diehard-loyal *consigliere* Joe N. Gallo as an "old fuck" and an "asshole, weak cocksucker."

Massino was thoroughly rattled when he heard his long-time Mafia ally stab him in the back when the feds played him the Gotti tapes. This was particularly shocking to him because he and Gotti were *compares* who had come up together in the mob. They rose up the ranks almost in tandem, becoming made at almost the same time. They were even neighbors in Howard Beach, Queens. Heck, Gotti's own crewmates, including Angelo "Quack Quack" Ruggiero, helped Big Joey dispose of the bodies of the three captains the Bonannos had whacked on May 5, 1981. In 1975, Joey and Johnny even jointly murdered Vito Borelli, a Gambino stooge who insulted Paul Castellano, as Massino himself testified to in court many years later.

Not cool talking trash about your homies, John. Not cool at all.

And John Boy, way to go for calling your lifelong bro and loyal associate Willie Boy Johnson – who was half Native American and half Italian-American, and who had whacked lots of people for you – a "nigger" and "half breed" behind his back. His FBI handlers were only slightly more enlightened, assigning Johnson the code name "Source Wahoo" after the Cleveland Indians' racist "grinning brave" mascot. By the way, Willie Boy was also John Alite's mentor in the mob.

This was one of the reasons Wilfred flipped against you, John. How ironic was it then that Walter Johnson, an African-American bank robber you were doing time with in Marion Federal Penitentiary – whom you actually called nigger to his face – beat the living shit out of you in front of a crowd of onlookers? Talk about poetic justice! And you know why nobody protected your doughy ass? Because you had no loyalty or respect from anyone. Plus, you had stopped paying the Aryan Brotherhood five grand a month in protection money. Not too bright, buddy. All the mobbed-up guys in the can with you *let it happen*. There were even guards watching! So, John, once and for all, for the record, "Ah, *bafangool* you!" Christ, I'm giving myself heart palpitations…

And it was Gotti's shittalking that convinced Sammy Bull to flip after federal prosecutors played tape recordings of John Boy trashing Sammy behind his back. Most infuriating for Samwise G. was Gotti blaming The Bull's insatiable greed for a rash of murders he had ostensibly committed on Gotti's behalf.

The fact that Gotti was actually telling the truth didn't figure into Sammy's decision to rat. Sammy's M.O. was to tell Gotti someone in the Family was talking shit about John-John. Gotti, who trusted Sammy implicitly and loved like a brother, would give the nod, and Sammy would then whack that guy *and take over his business*. This enabled Sammy to rival even Gaspipe as one of the top earners in the Big Apple Mafia at that time.

Next, if you have to whack someone who's unwhackable, make it look like an accident (a robbery gone bad) – the way Greg Scarpa had his own brother murdered in January 1987.

Paisani, remember to strip your stiff of all his valuables to make it look good. Coolio?

Oh, one last thing -- remember, kids, when you shit on everyone around you, their loyalty towards you will wane and render you vulnerable to well-deserved betrayal. Again, you cannot push people without them pushing back. *So don't push.* Look, what's the point of being in the underground empire without friends who love you? So be loveable. *Capisce?*

Fun Facts!

I may not be a big fan of Paul Vario, but I sure as heck am of Paul Sorvino's portrayal of him in *Goodfellas*. Sorvino, however, almost didn't end up on the silver screen in this role. After being cast by Martin Scorsese and Nicholas Pileggi (who co-wrote the script with Marty), Sorvino struggled for months in rehearsal to nail down Big Paulie's chilling, insidious character.

Three days before the film commenced shooting, Sorvino woke up in the morning determined to quit the film that very day. But when he went into the bathroom and looked at his reflection in the mirror, he knew he had it – that cold, dead-eyed, baleful glare of the real Paulie Vario. The black orbs of a stone-dead killer. And the rest is cinematic glory. Sorvino parlayed that thousand-yard stare into a brief but memorable role as a Chicago gangster in 1993's *The Firm*, starring Tom Cruise.

As for Vario's fate, thanks to Henry Hill's testimony, he received four years in the slammer for helping Hill obtain a no-show job after he was paroled from prison in 1978. Paulie subsequently received ten more years for extorting air freight companies at JFK Airport. On November 22, 1988, Vario's greatest fear was realized when he died at the Federal Correctional Institute (FCI) in Fort Worth, Texas, at age seventy-three as a result of respiratory failure. *Ah-choo!*

I realize that not everyone reading this book believes that the birth of LCN was a positive consequence of the Volstead Act.

However, I dare anyone to dispute the upshot of the following additional outcomes:

First, Prohibition enabled non-sex working women to socialize with men in saloons for the first time. Second, it inspired the invention of the cocktail, which masked the inferior taste and quality of rotgut booze that was so prevalent at the time. Hence, the expression "bathtub gin."

Not surprisingly, after the repeal of Prohibition, many of the major underworld liquor suppliers and distributors immediately went into legitimate business on a grand scale with their ill-gotten gains. For example, Joseph Kennedy Sr. became a major distributor with Haig & Haig Whiskey and Gordon's Gin. LCN founding father Frank Costello founded Alliance Distributors. And Canada's number-one bootlegger, Samuel Bronfman, founded Seagrams.

To paraphrase nineteenth century French novelist Honoré de Balzac, "Behind every great fortune lies a great crime."

Moving on…

The worst thing you can do in the mob is shit where you eat. When it comes to imbibing, this means you shouldn't drink too much around mob guys. Be like George Thorogood and fly solo at home, or else do it with friends outside the Life (if you have any, which you *should*).

"*Pourquoi, mon ami?*" you gasp. "But I love to get my swerve on!"

The reason is simple: drinking alcohol lowers your inhibitions, which loosens your tongue. It makes you say things you should never say – like talkin' trash about your colleagues and supervisors. Loose lips sink ships, Chatty Cathy. They can also get you whacked out in a heartbeat.

I once had the distinct pleasure of spending an entire afternoon with Frank Calabrese Jr. He told me that when his dad wanted to elicit information from someone he considered to be a threat, he would ply the guy with copious amounts of booze. Inevitably, the man would slip up and give himself away. By contrast, Frankie Breeze would drink sparingly, constantly watering down his Scotch (just like Nicky Scarfo when *he* was setting someone up for a hit).

Getting shitfaced can also spell your untimely demise in more visceral ways. Gallo, for example, became a teetotaler by the time he was twenty. Even though he went out clubbing almost every night of the week, he *never* drank, preferring to tipple only cranberry juice or Perrier. Nor did he partake of you-know-what. He explained it back then to Marco like this: "Dude, if I come staggering outside some nightclub wasted, one of my enemies can sneak up behind me and pop me in the head."

Finally, the Gambino made man who fired the fatal bullet into Tommy D's brain was Thomas "Tommy A" Agro, a close friend of Gotti. Agro also murdered Tommy's brother Anthony DeSimone several years earlier after Anthony had flipped against the Gambinos. Agro, a raging psychopath forced to take lithium, was going for a perfect trifecta by plotting the murder of the dead DeSimones' other brother, Robert. But Agro got popped just before doing so in 1984 for loan sharking, extortion, and attempted murder. Agro went down after baseball-batting an associate, Joseph "Joe Dogs" Iannuzzi, who flipped against Agro as soon as he was released from the hospital.

As I was saying, when you're a bully, guys will jump at the chance to rat you out and testify against you. Chicago capo Frank Calabrese Sr., who headed The Outfit's Chinatown work crew (hit squad), was so abusive to everyone that even his own brother, Nicholas "Nicky Breeze" Calabrese, and son, Frank Junior, testified against him. He went down for life.

First, Frankie Breeze had beaten the beejeezus out of two of his shylock clients so badly that they both ran straight to the FBI. Then, after Frankie Breeze welched on his promise to Frankie Junior to quit the mob, after a childhood of physically abusing him, and a lifetime of emotional abuse, and to stop murdering people, Junior turned against him. Finally, after learning his own brother had approved a hit on him, Nicky Breeze also switched sides.

In all fairness, however, Nicky Breeze likely would have done so even without learning of Frankie's fratricidal inclinations. On September 6, 1986, the Calabrese brothers set out to eliminate Giovanni "Big John" Fecarotta, an Outfit soldier who had been screwing up at work. Not the least of his fuckups involved the failed disposals of Tony Spilotro and younger brother Michael's corpses three months earlier.

That night, Nicky picked up Fecarotta in a stolen new Buick somewhere in Chicago on the false pretense that they were pulling an arson job on a dentist's office. When they pulled into an alley behind the office, Nicky made his move. He whipped out a .38 revolver, but not fast enough. Big John was expecting the play, so grabbed his gun hand. During the struggle, the gun fired twice; first striking Big John in the chest, then hitting Nicky Breeze's shoulder.

Fecarotta burst from the car and ran across a major boulevard, Calabrese hot on his heels. They both bled as they crossed, and Nicky barely missed being struck by a car.

But Fecarotta didn't make it – he collapsed by a bingo hall's front door, weak from blood loss. He tried to rise but Nicky grabbed him by his hair, yanked his head back, and – Pow! Pow! – put two in the back of his brain, killing him.

Nicky fled the crime scene on foot but accidentally dropped the leather golf gloves he had been wearing. Chicago PD arrived minutes later and quickly found the blood trails and gloves.

Eventually and inevitably, physical evidence tied Nicky Breeze to the gloves and blood, and ballistics testing to the murder weapon. But what finally convinced him to flip was the recording Frankie Junior had made of his father while they were both incarcerated. Frankie Breeze unwittingly confessed to approving his own brother's murder contract. The wire was hidden in Junior's Sony Walkman, which he would wear when they strolled the yard.

Chapter Eight – How to Distinguish Yourself as an Up & Coming Mafioso

"This thing is just shoe leather, elbow grease, and a little ass kicking." – Jimmy Caci

I am thus far cautiously optimistic about your progress, people – you've learned how to earn your street rep, to avoid being a total dick, and to even be a gangster's gangster. You've been accepted into a crew, and thus you've managed to climb to the second rung on your way to fame and fortune. But here comes the hard part: how do you come up? How do you break away from the pack and become a shooting (mob) star?

Anyone can learn how to knock folks out, or how to keep their mouth shut and laugh at their boss's stupid jokes. It takes a genuine *wunderkind* to be earmarked for advancement by the *padrinos*. This requires a combination of certain skills, characteristics, and tactics. Ah, where to begin?

Kicking Up

The number one way to rise above the human flotsam and jetsam at the local social club is to earn with both fists, and to kick up some of your earnings to your boss. (This can range anywhere from ten to fifty percent of your earnings, depending on how greedy your skipper is – though everyone cheats on their kick ups.) We'll get into making money down the road.

For now, however, let's focus on the importance of doing the right thing and lining your soldato or capo's pockets.

There is no greater utilitarian purpose to your pathetic existence than to enrich your captain – at least in his eyes. So all your energies should be focused on that singular goal. It matters not whether you like him, or even if you would enjoy nothing more than treating his unsightly melon like a piñata. What does matter is that even if you do not respect the man, you'd best respect the rank.

I'm impressed with Gallo's long-term proactive approach towards his Mafia bosses. Even if he was having a bad week, Gallo would always kick up the same healthy amount of cash to his sponsor. Gallo knew his boss would quickly come to rely upon this steady income, which in turn would bring Gallo closer into his orbit. Gallo would then slowly but steadily increase the weekly pay up so the guy would love him more and more over time.

See, by showing his boss what a reliable earner he was, Gallo made himself increasingly indispensable. This will pay dividends in two important ways. First, the boss will expose you to more lucrative scores and deals, and put you into position to get a larger percentage of those rackets. Bossman knows that the more you make, the more *he'll* make. That's what shortsighted, short-con, boot-licking mobsters out there just don't get. They simply fail to see the big picture.

Second, if your boss loves you, he will go to bat for you all the way during a sit down. He will lie, cheat, and even kill for you, so long as you keep filling his coffers. He'll tell you exactly what to say and how to behave yourself at the sit down. Even if you're clearly in the wrong, as long as your boss is more powerful than the boss of the disputing mobster, the arbitrator will almost always side with you and your boss. That's just the way it is – in the mob, he who makes the most money and carries the bigger stick gets to break the Rules, and sometimes even make them. *That's* the Golden Rule of Gangsters.

Bottom Line: Take care of your boss even better than you take care of your closest friends. In fact, regardless of whether you despise the egomaniacal prick, do whatever it takes to become *his* best friend.

That's how a cave-dwelling cro-mag like Tommy Bilotti got to be the Gambinos' underboss – he was Paul Castellano's *driver*, for Christ's sake. I mean, at the time Bilotti was upped, he was a capo who never even had his own crew. Okay, so maybe Bilotti isn't the best example, considering how things worked out for him in front of Sparks Steak House. *Mea culpa.*

Be a World-Class Brown-Noser

Commensurate with kicking up is kissing ass. It behooves you to make your boss feel good not only financially, but also emotionally. So how exactly do you go about becoming your boss's bestie? Very easily, assuming you have the necessary *chutzpah*. Emulate Marco's strategy when hitting on a woman: "Find out what kind of guy she likes, and *become that guy*." Simply brilliant.

Gallo was the greatest gangster suck up in the history of the LCN. It wasn't that he sucked up more than anyone else in the mob which garners him this unique accolade – it's that he sucked up *smarter*. Employing the skills he learned from Jedi Master conman Jerry Zimmerman, he became BFFs with both Eddie Garofalo Jr. and Teddy Persico Jr. He made himself essential by always being available to hang out, bounce around, and hit the town with them. Whatever they were interested in, so was he. He shared their every opinion, and subtly stroked their delicate egos. Basically, he became their favorite emotional-support human.

This was particularly true with Teddy, who had just emerged from a sixteen-year stint in prison after a drug bust. Since he had entered the can at age twenty-five, Persico was an emotionally stunted individual who needed to be handled with finesse. Gallo took care to always keep him in his comfort zone, only taking him out to local bars, clubs, and restaurants. He never annoyed him and was always helpful. By sticking to him like flypaper, Gallo gradually earned his trust.

Similarly, while wearing a wire for two and a half years against the Gambinos, G-man Big Jack Garcia used this technique against skipper Greg DePalma. Garcia learned how to emotionally manipulate DePalma by anticipating and understanding his ever-changing moods. Big Jack learned these subtle methods through his many years working undercover.

"But, Romie, boo-boo," you wonder, "won't it be a little obvious if I permanently insert my tongue into my boss's anal cavity?"

A valid question but the answer is *negativo*. Your boss will almost certainly be an arrogant, self-centered, bloviating gaslighter who thinks he's God's gift to organized crime. As a result, he will view your obsequiousness as merely confirming his own lofty opinion of himself. *Ta da!*

Get Yourself a Dutch Uncle

If you properly kick up and kiss ass, you will almost certainly acquire a sponsor in the mob who will help you reach your full potential. Conversely, to quote Anthony Fiato, "Without a sponsor, you're just another punk on your own." Goddamn right.

Every aspiring gangster needs a mentor to not only take him under his wing and show him the ropes, but to protect him when shit goes south. Virtually every major mobster has had a sponsor who helped him ascend the ranks of LCN. For example, John Gotti had Carmine "Charlie Wagons" Fatico, who taught him how to become one of the biggest hijackers in New York City.

Once you've learned and gained all you can from your sponsor or your sponsor dies (from causes natural or not), you should move on and find another sponsor. This should be someone who's higher up on the food chain than your original sensei. After Fatico passed away, Johnny Boy glommed onto powerful Gambino capo and future long-time underboss Aniello "Neil" Dellacroce, the scariest-looking mobster of all time – man, talk about crazy eyes!

Gotti and Neil were extremely close for many years until Neil's death from cancer at age seventy-one on December 2, 1985. His death paved the way for Gotti to dethrone Paul Castellano two weeks later. In fact, it was Castellano's stunning lack of respect in skipping Neil's funeral that served as the final straw for Gotti.

During their time together, Neil always protected Gotti and his Bergin crew in Queens. Again, after Gotti got crowned, he moved his HQ over to Neil's former social club, The Ravenite, in Manhattan. In turn, Gotti and his boys served as one of the Gambinos' two workhorse crews, which acted as the enforcement arms for the Family. The other crew being Roy DeMeo's Murder Machine in Canarsie – the two crews were deathly afraid of one another. Gotti loved Neil so much that he reportedly had a long-term affair with his illegitimate daughter, Shannon, and even had a child out of wedlock with her. Sorry, Mrs. Gotti, but you really shat the bed when you married Johnny Boy.

Anyways, make sure you spread the love around because nowadays, thanks to Joe Pistone, you need *two* sponsors to propose you.

Having a knowledgeable sponsor is particularly handy if you want to be a bloodthirsty killer. Nowhere in the annals of the American Mafia has there been such a symbiotic bond as that between a top button man and his eager-beaver protégé. The reason is simple: murder done well is both an art and a science, and it cannot be absorbed through mere osmosis.

One must be trained on how to take another man's life without getting caught. One must be carefully instructed on how to dispose of the body and clean up the crime scene.

This has always been the case with the mob's most prolific killers. During the late 1940s and early 1950s, young Nicky Scarfo was tutored extensively by Felix "Skinny Razor" DiTullio, then the most notorious hitman in Philadelphia. Later, DiTullio proposed Scarfo for membership. It was with Skinny Razor that Scarfo made his bones by committing murder for the first time at the mob's behest. He stabbed the victim to death, castrated the poor guy, and stuffed his private parts into his mouth. This was the corpse that Crazy Phil Leonetti unwittingly helped Nicky transport as a very young boy.

Tony "the Ant" Spilotro, of course, had Mad Sam DeStefano as *his* tutor. Al Capone had Johnny Torrio, Roy DeMeo had Nino Gaggi, Tommy Karate had Anthony "Bruno" Indelicato, Tommy D had Jimmy Burke, Greg Scarpa Junior had his dad, Nicky Breeze had his big brother, and so forth. You get the picture.

Become a Squealing Rat-Faced Motherhumping Rat

Truly sensational gangsters – those cosmically destined for greatness – always have an ace up their sleeve to give them an edge over everyone else. Flipping might be your ace. By becoming a wire-wearing rat-fink, you can shield yourself from criminal liability *and* simultaneously eliminate your enemies and competitors with the help of Johnny Law. This is especially true if your FBI handler is actually your crime partner, as was allegedly the case with Greg Scarpa Sr. and FeeBee Roy Lindley "Lin" DeVecchio. (Apologies to Joe Pistone and former federal prosecutor-turned-author Charles Brandt, who are both dear friends and staunch supporters of DeVecchio. No hard feelings, gentlemen?)

This was also the case with Whitey Bulger and Steve Flemmi, who were both TEIs (Top Echelon Informants) for the FBI's John Connolly and his rotten-to-the-core supervisor, John Morris. (How's prison in Florida, John?)

Hey, Mr. Morris, every day out of the can is a good day, huh? Do you see the delicious irony in your having become a professional "wine consultant" after you obtained immunity and ratted out Connolly, et al.? After all, it was Bulger and Flemmi who provided you all that expensive wine that you otherwise couldn't afford as an FBI agent. God, how I love to *schadenfreude!*

Bottom Line: By flipping, you earn a get-out-of-jail-free card. It's that simple.

FUDGE-THE-FEDS SECRET REVELATION #2

With your FBI ace-in-the-asshole, you can murder as many people as you want and, at most, face a baby-slap on the wrist.

A common misconception is that Sammy the Bull "only" murdered nineteen people, based on his testimony at Gotti's final racketeering trial, and based on the bullshit the feds fed us. I'm convinced he actually murdered *forty-four* people. These additional victims include Peter Calabro, a crooked New York City auto crimes detective who provided DeMeo inside info. Gravano hired Richard "the Iceman" Kuklinski to shotgun Calabro.

According to Sergeant Robert Anzalotti, an investigator with the Bergen County DA's Office in New Jersey, the feds were aware that Gravano had paid Kuklinski to murder Calabro, but still proceeded to work with Sammy.

Sergeant Anzalotti's partner, Detective Mark Bennul, and prosecutors in the New Jersey Attorney General's Office were also convinced that the Justice Department had turned a blind eye to The Bull's involvement in the Calabro hit.

In late February 2003, Kuklinski plead guilty to blowing Calabro's head off on March 14, 1980, as Calabro drove home through a snowstorm in his Honda Civic. The Iceman testified before a state grand jury that Gravano had hired him for the hit. Gravano, of course, denied any involvement, but the fact that he was never prosecuted by the feds lends some credence to the claims of Anzalotti, Bennul, and Kuklinski.

On February 24, 2003 (immediately after The Iceman's testimony), New Jersey state prosecutors indicted Sammy Bull for Calabro's murder. Gravano had been sentenced only five months earlier to a twenty-year federal prison term for trafficking ecstasy in Arizona. However, he caught a lucky break when Kuklinski croaked of natural causes on March 5, 2006, at age seventy – only several months before Sammy's trial was scheduled to begin. As he was the only witness, the murder-for-hire charges, which presumably would have carried a death sentence, were dropped against Sammy Bull.

Sammy was also a major drug dealer at the time he flipped against Gotti. Thus, he committed perjury by lying about the number of murders he had committed *and* his dealing, which he denied on the stand. Oh, and the FBI agents and federal prosecutors with whom he was working all apparently knew about these unpleasant indiscretions, but chose to look the other way for obvious reasons. I haven't yet figured out whether they also knew about Calabro's murder before they teamed up with Gravano, but give me some time.

Look, as you may have inferred from my subtle broadsides, I'm not exactly president of the John Gotti Fan Club (Senior or Junior). But even I believe Gotti Sr. deserved a new trial, with Sammy being excluded as a tainted witness. But no way would the feds allow that – too many careers were made on Sammy's broad back and Gotti's life sentence. The ends always justify the means.

In any event, Sammy served five years of easy time as a federal snitch in the so-called Valachi Suite, a spacious, two-room, well-apportioned cell with color TV and air conditioning at the federal penitentiary in La Tuna, Texas. Named for its initial occupant, canary Joseph Valachi, a Genovese made man, La Tuna is where the feds stash many of their prized songbirds. Sambo only had to serve five months for each of the nineteen victims he *admitted* killing.

Funny thing is that the feds never even needed his testimony – it was just icing on the prosecutorial cake since Gotti's own tape-recorded words alone would have ensured a RICO conviction and life sentence. Certainly, the combined testimony of turncoats Crazy Sal Polisi and Crazy Phil Leonetti would have sealed his fate. So fudge the feds – and why not? They certainly screwed the families of those nineteen murder victims, virtually all of whom had been executed as a direct result of Gravano's insatiable greed.

UNDERWORLD | 139

Immediately after his five-year bit, of course, good ol' Uncle Sam unleashed Sammy on poor unsuspecting Arizonians, whose children consumed the thirty thousand ecstasy pills he distributed statewide *every week*. *Way to go, Sammy!*

****

Greg "the Grim Reaper" Scarpa murdered at least seventy-five people in his three and a half decades as a TEI. DeVecchio even allegedly assisted Scarpa with at least five of these murders, including by providing him the secret locations of his enemies. He even once supposedly called off an FBI surveillance team so Scarpa could whack one of his targets during the 1991-93 Colombo War.

In March 2006, the Brooklyn DA's Office charged DeVecchio with four murders. This is long after a Justice Department investigation in the late '90s failed to turn up sufficient evidence to prosecute him for any crimes. In 1996, he had retired from the FBI with a full pension after thirty-three years of service.

However, charges were dismissed on November 1, 2007, during trial after *Village Voice* reporter and LCN true-crime writer Tom Robbins came forward. Robbins provided the judge with audiotapes of the key witness, The Grim Reaper's long-time girlfriend Big Linda Schiro, which had been made a decade earlier. These recordings indicated she had changed her story about DeVecchio's complicity. According to Schiro, she had not previously accused DeVecchio of the murders because she had been afraid of him.

DeVecchio walked away a free man to enjoy the rest of his retirement in Sarasota, Florida. However, I am convinced by the incredible detail and overwhelming evidence presented in Peter Lance's book *Deal with the Devil* that he was indeed guilty of conspiracy to commit numerous murders with Scarpa.

At the same time, however, I agree with Brooklyn DA Charles J. Hynes' decision to dismiss the case on the ground that Schiro's testimony was tainted beyond repair. Certainly, it cannot be reasonably disputed that DeVecchio was corrupt, as admitted by federal prosecutors in a 1995 trial that freed numerous mobsters on the basis of *his* tainted testimony and actions. Indeed, that DeVecchio was a thoroughly rotten federal agent who literally got away with murder is a widely-held opinion – one apparently shared by esteemed Eastern District of New York (Brooklyn) Federal Judge Edward Korman. He stated on the record during a 2012 court hearing regarding Greg Junior, "It was my view and remains my view that Lin DeVecchio provided information to Scarpa that got people killed."

Read *Deal with the Devil* for all the fascinating details regarding the Scarpas and DeVecchio, who co-wrote his own book, *We're Gonna Win This Thing*, wherein he protests his innocence.

FUDGE-THE-FEDS SECRET REVELATION #3

Kids, if you're worried about having to wear a wire in order to secure this ace up your sleeve, have no fear. First of all, no one will ever pat you down in the Mafia like the clueless wankers in Hollywood want you to believe. That simply isn't done. It would be a sign of utmost distrust, which in turn is a sign of disrespect, which in turn is a declaration of war. You see where this leads? That's right – a bloody Tarantino finale.

Now, granted, if mob guys *are* suspicious of you, they'll hug you, rub their privates against yours, and otherwise dry hump you to feel if you're wearing a gigantic Nagra recorder taped under your nutsack. But fear not, Halflings! Thanks to wonderful technological advancements, there is no longer such a thing as a wire. And there sure as hell is no longer a group of overfed agents drinking stale coffee and stinking up a surveillance van with blacked-out windows parked conspicuously down the street.

Instead, these days rats wear Rolexes with teeny-tiny MP3 recorders inserted into the battery area. And instead of a cramped, smelly van stuffed with days-old donuts and Radio Shack gadgets, the MP3 recorder remotely transmits to a digital recording device at the local FBI headquarters.

In other words, it is virtually impossible to detect a wire these days. Thus, you should have all your sit downs inside a Turkish bathhouse with everyone buck naked and sans jewelry. Or as Gallo suggests, when discussing sensitive business, everyone should be wearing nothing but hospital scrubs and slippers. Indeed, after Joe Pistone revealed himself as Donnie Brasco, the Bonannos became so paranoid about undercover agents, wannabes were forced to strip naked before they got straightened out in a formal induction ceremony.

Gallo wore a wire for eight years, beating Pistone's record by two. Every midnight, Gallo would go jogging in his Bay Ridge enclave. He'd toss his gold Rolie through the open window of a parked car and keep going. While he was taking his evening constitutional, an FBI agent in the car would switch out the MP3 recorder so it would have a fresh battery.

Authors Selwyn Raab and Larry McShane both confirm in *Five Families,* and *Chin*, respectively, that the FBI supplies its rats with these special Rolex wires.

See? Again, nothing to worry about. Keep in mind, however, that there's no way to stop the recorder – it tapes *continuously* for at least twenty-four hours. This means that if you don't want to capture your (real) friends on tape, you need to avoid them. This itself can obviously raise suspicions so be careful out there!

Corrupt Law Enforcement Officials

For those of you out there who are a bit squeamish about sucking the FBI's teet, try a more honorable route – do a switch a roozie. That means, of course, that you should make every conceivable effort to corrupt the coppers. Now this is considerably harder to do with FBI agents, who overall are infinitely more honest than your regular beat-walking flatfoots and gumshoes.

The best way to corrupt and bribe the popos is through gambling. Cops, like most blue-collar tough guys, love to gamble. Personally, I just don't get it – my brain simply doesn't release those neurochemicals that gamblers' brains do when they roll the dice or draw a card. Cops see gambling as a wink-wink vice, a relatively harmless pastime, particularly in this day and age of legal online gambling, state lotteries, and Native American casinos.

So as soon as one of these men in blue gets in over his head to a mob guy, then that mobster owns his dumb ass. This is how Roy DeMeo was so successful for as long as he was – he had cops, including someone in the local district attorney's office – feeding him top-secret information, such as when raids were coming down or the identity of informants. Lots of people (including innocent civilians) died as a result of this intel, but for Roy, it was just everyday business. Nothing personal.

This is why I highly recommend getting into gambling and loansharking – it's sure to ensnare not only cops, but also lots of other useful individuals.

Cops also like to drink a lot, and the more adventurous ones would hang out at the Gemini Lounge and place bets through Roy or his cronies. DeMeo was generous, not only with the drinks, but in paying attractive sex workers to rock these cops' socks off. And believe me, once these jokers experienced their first go-round with a pro, they lost their motherfucking minds. Just like Lefty Rosenthal did with his future wife Geri McGee (Sharon Stone in *Casino*). She was earning $500,000 a year as the top Vegas call girl in the '60s. Bill Roemer and Nick Pileggi both chivalrously omitted that little tidbit when describing her money-making activities in their books. And that's when Roy had 'em.

Henry Hill employed a similar if somewhat more lackadaisical approach to corrupting the law. Virtually overnight, his new bar in Queens, The Suite, became a mini-Costco for hot merch. All manner of shady law enforcement personnel, including cops, detectives, and even prosecutors from the local DA's office, came in to buy swag. More importantly, when the coppers and dicks went bar hopping, they routinely enjoyed a nightcap there.

And that's when the real soirée started. The bulls and flatfoots would party all night long at Henry's bar before staggering home at first light to sleep it off. Henry quickly grew tired of babysitting these barbarians so he would just hand them the keys to the bar. This magnanimous gesture made Henry and his crew exceedingly popular with the coppers.

This heady, combustible mix of players on both sides of the law, sprinkled with politicians, worked to everyone's advantage. These Runyonesque characters developed close friendships after debauching and gambling together for endless hours. Henry ensured there were plenty of happy sex workers on hand to satisfy even the most voracious appetites.

Soon, the good guys and bad guys became indistinguishable, with the two groups cooking up various schemes together. The lawmen tipped off the gangsters to imminent raids and ongoing investigations in exchange for cash and cuts from scores. The politicians even told them which areas in town were safe to plunder. As Henry wondered, "How could anything go wrong?"

How indeed! What a beautiful setup. My friends, I also think you should rent a party pad that the coppers can use to romance their *goomaras*. Stock the place with plenty of booze and food, and leave sugar bowls of various controlled substances lying about. In no time at all, the Man will be eating out of your hand.

Please take your sweet time cultivating these law enforcement relationships, but make sure you don't seem too cozy with them lest your bosses think you're feeding *them* info instead of vice versa. Try to always have someone with you when you meet with them so you have a witness to these encounters.

If you play your cards right, you'll slowly corrupt your mark, encircling, entangling, and then strangling him like an anaconda. (I can't think of any female law enforcement officials who have been corrupted by the mob, can you?)

Follow Whitey's lead in regard to John Morris – he started off with small gifts that eventually became more and more substantial (and incriminating). Morris was so incredibly stupid, he eventually took cash from him in order to fly out his mistress to be with him on an FBI business trip. John Connolly, who grew up with Whitey and his younger brother Billy Bulger in Southie, was in from the start so there was no need for this seductive routine with him.

Cops particularly like money since they make very little of it, and they will quickly grow accustomed to your cash gifts. Soon they will come to rely on them, especially if you wine 'n' dine them and expose them to the good life – just like John Morris. If you get really lucky, they might even start setting people up for murder, like Morris, Connolly, and their FBI predecessor, H. Paul Rico, did. Rico, who died of a heart attack in January 2004 while facing murder charges, *literally* shat himself when he was finally arrested three months earlier for the 1981 murder of Oklahoma businessman Roger Wheeler. This was the killing that led to Whitey and Steve Flemmi's downfall, and which was actually carried out by Johnny Martorano for $50,000 in "expenses."

If you get really, *really* lucky, they'll even do hits for you like the so-called Mafia Cops, former NYPD detectives and partners Louis Eppolito and Stephen Caracappa - or Fat and Skinny, as Gaspipe nicknamed them. Now those evil bastards were extremely useful, and better yet, sold themselves dirt cheap. Unfortunately, like typical blockheads, they murdered at least one innocent person in a case of mistaken identity. Specifically, a twenty-six-year-old telephone installer named Nicholas Guido (*not* the Nicky Guido they were trying to whack for Gaspipe), whom they obliterated on Christmas Day 1986. The City of New York was ultimately forced to pay $5 million to settle a wrongful death suit filed by Guido's elderly mother.

Louis Eppolito (son of Gambino *Mafioso* Ralph "Fat the Gangster" Eppolito) was also a two-bit actor, who briefly appears in *Goodfellas* as Bamboo Lounge crewmember Moe

Black's brother, Fat Andy. His one line – "How you doin', buddy?" – was enough to get him a coveted Screen Actor's Guild membership. Ironically, it was Big Lou's lust for fame that ultimately did him (and his crime partner) in.

The seeds for the Mafia Cops' destruction were sown twenty years before their conviction. In early 1986, Fat Angie Ruggiero was doing time with Irish-American gangster James "Jimmy" Hydell. Ruggiero hired Hydell to murder Gaspipe Casso, but reports differ as to whether or not John Gotti was behind the contract. Some say Gotti was not involved, and that the beef concerned Gaspipe shorting Ruggiero on a major heroin deal. Others claim Gotti was making a preemptive strike against Casso, whom everyone knew hated Gotti and vehemently disapproved of Paul Castellano's unsanctioned murder in December 1985. Whatever the reason, a shitload of money exchanged hands shortly thereafter when Hydell was released.

On September 6, 1986, Casso was sitting in his black Cadillac in a Flatlands, Brooklyn, parking lot eating an ice cream cone. Suddenly, a three-man hit team, including Hydell, pulled up in a Lincoln and – Pow! Pow! – opened fire, striking him twice in the shoulder.

Fortunately for Gaspipe, the hit car had pulled in too close to his Caddy, so the shooters couldn't open their doors wide enough to get out and finish the job. This SNAFU enabled Gaspipe to scramble out the passenger door and serpentine around the whizzing bullets into the safety of a nearby Chinese restaurant. He hid in its basement freezer until the police found him, shaking from the cold, blood loss, and rage.

Now it was time for payback. Casso reached out to all his underworld sources and ascertained Hydell's identity. Through his good pal Burton Kaplan, he contracted with the Mafia Cops to abduct Hydell. Eppolito and Caracappa had been working for Gaspipe through Kaplan since 1985, after Kaplan had made the connection while doing time with Eppolito's cousin, Frank Santoro. (Christ, how many *goombah* relatives did fatfuck

Eppolito have? So far, I'm counting a father, an uncle, and two cousins.)

Later that same month, in September 1986, Eppolito and Caracappa, a.k.a. the Mafia Cops, tracked Hydell down in Bensonhurst, Brooklyn, after first stopping by his house and getting the brush off from his mother, Betty Hydell. Flashing their gold detective's shields, they arrested Hydell at another location, drove him to a local auto body shop, and shoved him into the trunk of another car. They then drove him to a Toys "R" Us parking lot in Flatbush, Brooklyn, where they met Casso (for the first time ever) and handed him the car keys.

Casso then drove to a friend's home in Brooklyn, where he tortured Hydell in the basement over several hours until he gave up the names of his two co-conspirators, including Nicky Guido. Casso then finished him off with fifteen bullets.

Flash forward four years and many murders later, in late 1990, and we find Abbott and Costello retiring with full pensions and honors; Eppolito was the eleventh most-decorated officer in NYPD history. Big Lou immediately began writing his much-sanitized autobiography with journalist Bob Drury, who had no idea that his co-author and subject had murdered at least eight people for Gaspipe (and God knows how many for other mobsters). The book was published in 1992 as *Mafia Cop: The Story of an Honest Cop Whose Family was the Mob.*

Shortly thereafter, in 1992, Eppolito appeared on *The Sally Jessy Raphael Show* to promote his book. In her television audience that day was none other than Betty Hydell. To her shock, she instantly recognized Eppolito as the obese detective who had knocked on her door the day her twenty-eight-year-old son had disappeared. Fearing retribution, Betty held her tongue for another eleven years.

Meanwhile, in 1994, Eppolito moved to Las Vegas. The stick-thin Caracappa followed a year later and even bought a house directly across the street from Big Lou's. Also in 1994, Gaspipe flipped, plead guilty to thirty-seven murders (though probably killed twice that number), but remained incarcerated.

UNDERWORLD | 147

While doing hard time, Gaspipe happened to come across a copy of *Mafia Cop*. For the first time, he was finally able to put a name to the obese copper who had handed over Hydell eight years earlier. This resulted in *60 Minutes*' Ed Bradley (who was Johnny Martorano's childhood friend!) interviewing Gaspipe in prison in 1998. However, the show's executive producers couldn't substantiate Casso's claims at the time, and so the interview was not aired on CBS until April 2007. (Ladies and gents, you've gotta catch this fascinating episode on YouTube to get a clear picture of what a bonafide lunatic Casso is. He is truly the personification of evil. His eyes are dead black. Scary!)

In the fall of 2003, Betty Hydell finally came forward, sparking an eighteen-month investigation by a task force comprised of DEA agents and retired NYPD cops in the worst case of police corruption in New York history. During that time, Burton Kaplan also flipped against his former attack dogs, resulting in the Mafia Cops' arrest on March 9, 2005.

On April 6, 2006, Eppolito and Caracappa were finally convicted on all charges, and on March 6, 2009, were both sentenced to life without parole. Caracappa died in the clink eight years later of cancer, on April 8, 2017. Lou is still in stir, waiting for some Hollywood bigshot to turn his book into celluloid glory. He should have stuck to living off his pension and clipping coupons.

Be a Good Con Man

Mobsters with big brains rule the roost in *La Cosa Nostra*, and those who can convince others to do their bidding will always rise to the top of the Mafia dung heap. These talented individuals are master manipulators, and use their intelligence, charm, and charisma to acquire fame and fortune. I'm talking about being a world-class confidence man.

It is this razor-sharp mercenary instinct that allows these chosen few to soar head and shoulders above everyone else in the mob. It is these select individuals who are so highly valued in the Mafia that they have a special, direct connection to the boss himself. This means they don't have to report to any soldier, skipper, or even the sotto capo (underboss). And that is your sweet spot.

Now I'm not talking about fast-talking, slick dick, bullshit hustlers like Vincent "Fat Vinnie" Teresa, who laughably claimed he was the right-hand man of legendary New England Godfather Raymond Patriarca Sr. Nor am I referring to homicidal, high-rolling flim-flam artists like Nicholas "Nicky Crow" Caramandi, former soldier in Nicky Scarfo's Philly *cosca* (*borgata*). I'm talking about racketeers who exist on their own elemental plane – superstars who create their own one-of-a-kind rackets. Like caporegime Michael Franzese, college graduate and son of the legendary Colombo underboss John "Sonny" Franzese.

Recognize When You Are Being Tested and Pass Their Stupid Tests

Throughout your nascent career as a villain, your higher ups will test you in various ways, both large and small. (The Hells Angels call them mud checks.) You need to instantly recognize when you are being tested, and immediately rise to the challenge without question or reservation. By continually proving you are a good soldier who follows orders to the letter, your star will shine brighter and brighter. Don't worry, this grooming period shouldn't last more than three to five years, give or take.

Sometimes your boss will test your deference *and* subservience, as former New Jersey-based Lucchese powerhouse capo Anthony "Tumac" Accetturo learned early on. Mobster Anthony "Ham" Delasco once approached the then teenage Tumac in front of his fawning homies and ordered him to fetch an ice cream cone. Tumac was understandably embarrassed in front of his pals but realized that his obedience was being tested. Without hesitation, he ran and retrieved the ice cream. He knew that if he wanted to hitch his wagon to Delasco, he would have to completely submit to his will.

Sometimes your ability to keep sensitive intel in the vault (as *Seinfeld*'s Elaine liked to say) is tested. Gallo, for example, instantly realized Colombo big shots Eddie Garofalo Jr. and his uncle Manny Garofalo were testing him to see if he was Mafia material. Eddie told him that he and Manny had had a falling out to see if Gallo would relay info from Eddie to Manny. Manny then attempted to oh-so-subtly extract said intel from Gallo, who clammed up like a clam. Gallo understood that if he had disclosed anything at all, he would have been labeled a rat, and that would have been the end of his Colombo trajectory. Fortunately, however, Eddie's younger cousins had already tipped him off about the heartwarming father-son bond between Eddie and Manny. Needless to say, he passed their test with flying colors.

Gallo established the Colombo connection years before he moved to Bay Ridge when these younger cousins would visit other *Mafiosi* in LA. He made their acquaintance through mutual associates, then showered them with VIP nights on the town, as well as pharmaceutical cocaine and horny porn stars. Word quickly spread to their *paisans* back East that Gallo was the man to meet in SoCal!

Or your honesty may be tested, as John Gotti Sr. did with erstwhile associate James Cardinale when Gotti gave him a wad of what he said was $5,000 to exchange at the bank. When Cardinale did so, he discovered Gotti had given him $5,*500*, all of which he exchanged for larger bills and returned to Gotti.

Similarly, when Gallo was only fifteen and just starting out with the Avilas, they gave him specially prepared packages of cocaine and money to deliver around town. They had packaged the stuff in such a way that they would be able to tell if Gallo tampered with it; which, of course, he never did.

These tests are gradual but will increase in substance and significance so hang in there, baby – in no time at all you'll be doing real work. And that's when the fun really begins.

Fun Facts!

Ironically, it was Castellano's sanctioning of Roy DeMeo's murder that directly resulted in his own assassination. By 1979, Roy and his Murder Machine crew were raking in $200,000 *a week* via their international car theft ring – the largest in New York City's history. The cars were swiped off the streets of all five boroughs, loaded onto freighters, and shipped to Kuwait and Puerto Rico. Castellano was only too happy to accept his weekly envelopes from Nino Gaggi or, foolishly, directly from DeMeo himself.

That is until Big Paul learned that DeMeo was chopping people up left and right in connection with the GTA ring. This included nineteen-year-old Cherie Golden, who was the girlfriend of the crew's top car thief, John Quinn. By December 1981, three of Roy's crewmembers had been arrested for their roles in the car theft ring, including Vito Arena, who flipped.

This was all too much for Paulie, who gave Gotti and his Bergin crew the green light to whack Roy in early 1982. Gotti reluctantly accepted the contract but to his *goombata* privately said, "Fuck that – Roy's got an army of killers."

Gotti hemmed and hawed for a year, claiming to Big Paulie that he was trying his best to kill Roy but just couldn't catch him alone. But he helpfully suggested to Castellano that they outsource the hit to the Lucchese's Gaspipe Casso, who they knew worked closely with DeMeo crewmembers, brothers Joey and Patty Testa. Casso despised Gotti but agreed to do it as a favor for Gotti's *compare* Frank DeCicco, whom Gaspipe respected and liked. Casso's affection, however, didn't stop him from blowing up DeCicco with a car bomb on April 13, 1986, as payback for his involvement in the Castellano assassination four months earlier.

On the morning of January 10, 1983, Roy went to Patty's house in East Flatbush, Brooklyn, to talk shop and pick up some dough he was owed. The Gemini Twins, Joey Testa and Anthony Senter, were waiting for him. As Patty poured Roy an espresso, the Gemini Twins whipped out their semi-automatics. Roy instinctively raised his right hand to protect himself, catching the first bullet in his palm. But the other six slugs penetrated his face and skull, ending him and his nine-year reign of terror.

Castellano was thrilled, but Gotti even more so. Now there was no one to stop him and his crew from whacking the boss – something he would have never dared attempt while Roy was still alive. Castellano's main problem, aside from his insatiable greed, was his inability to see the long-term consequences of his actions or to empathize with the financial plight of his blue-collar soldiers. And even though it would take almost three more years after DeMeo's death, Big Paul would pay the ultimate price for this myopia on December 16, 1985.

See, Gotti knew that underboss Aniello Dellacroce would never have allowed him to move on Big Paul while Dellacroce was alive. Even though Aniello hated Castellano, he was a diehard Mafia loyalist who would never break the most sacrosanct Rule in the mob by killing the boss without The Commission's permission.

And hey -- did you know that Scarpa – and *not* Joe Valachi, as everyone mistakenly believes – was the first ever made man to flip, which he did two years *before* Valachi's famous 1963 public testimony? According to Peter Lance, Hoover took the information he gleaned from Scarpa, as well as from the FBI's nationwide, illegal wiretapping campaign (of which Bill Roemer was a major participant) as part of its Top Hoodlum Program. The feds then spoon-fed that info to the low-level Valachi in order to pump up the FBI's importance and budget. Do you really think a peabrained jag-off like Valachi would know the intimate structure, including all its members, of every major Mafia family in New York? *Puh-lease!*

Hell, even if you don't flip until *after* the FBI takes you down, you can still get away with a double-digit body count. Just look at Johnny Martorano, who *admitted* to murdering twenty people, including two innocent *teenagers*, one of them a *girl*. He only served an average prison time of eight months for each victim.

By the way, on September 18, 2017, Salvatore "Sammy Bull" Gravano, age seventy-two, was quietly released on parole after serving more than seventeen years of his drug-trafficking sentence. He will remain on federal parole for the rest of his life. To The Bull I would say, "Fool us once, shame on you. Fool us twice, um…."

Cue The Who's "Won't Get Fooled Again."

Moving on…

John "Sonny" Franzese Senior's other nickname is The Rock for his ability to do decades of prison time standing on his head – *four* decades, to be exact. Sonny joined the Colombos in the 1930s, and until his release following an eight-year stint on June 23, 2017, at age one hundred, Sonny was the oldest prisoner in the entire US federal prison system! He was ninety-three when indicted; consequently, he was also the oldest mobster ever tried for racketeering charges.

During the 1980s, Michael Franzese made more money than any other mobster in history, with the possible exceptions of Al Capone in the '20s and Anthony Peraino in the '70s with his *Deep Throat* skin flick phenom. Michael personally cleared over $300 million by brilliantly exploiting then existing legal loopholes to avoid paying federal and state sales taxes *vis-à-vis* a complicated daisy chain of gas stations.

He did so after muscling in on the Russian *Mafiya*'s ongoing operations and then expanding them. Michael was so successful that in 1986, *Forbes* ranked him as number eighteen on its list of the fifty most powerful *Mafiosi* in America. You can read all about Michael's exploits in his 1992 autobiography *Quitting the Mob*, including how he became a born-again Christian and motivational speaker. He now has a hit musical in Vegas called *Mob Story*! Well played, Don Franzese!

This sum does not even include the tens of millions he kicked up directly to Colombo boss Carmine "the Snake" Persico, who was amazed at the vast amounts of cash Michael was bringing in each week in grocery bags. Michael certainly came through on his promise to Persico "to bring you more money than you've ever dreamed of."

Nor does this sum include the $100 million he broke off to his junior partner Jerry Zimmerman, who many years later became Gallo's Jewish uncle in the mob. Jerry was a 300-pound teddy bear with a mind that worked at dazzling speed, amazing Gallo with its intricacy and deviousness. In *Breakshot*, he describes how Jerry taught him how to plant the greed seed in people.

First, it's critical that you act like 50 Cent in a rap video or even in his real, pre-bankruptcy life. This means swaggering into a hot club dressed like Lady Gaga in a fabulous head-to-toe ensemble (preferably with underlings trailing behind you, holding your cape, cane, and top hat). As you bulldoze your way to your roped-off VIP booth, make sure you stuff C-notes into the mouths of passing waiters. The bottle of champagne that's brought to your table should be so expensive that it merits its own parade, sparklers and all (like the way I celebrated my birthday at the Santa Anna Beach Club in Mykonos).

Now please note, this is *your* champagne, baby. For all the losers who flock to your table, pour them vastly inferior – but nevertheless expensive – swill. And shove plenty of shizzle dizzle up their hungry noses while they hang on your every word and periodically polish your watch and jewelry. You, of course, should abstain as doing drugs with, or even speaking to, these human canker sores, as it is utterly beneath you. In short, pretend you're Eddie Murphy in *Trading Places* when he goes to that shitty bar after getting bailed out of jail by the Duke brothers.

According to Gallo, this over-the-top, big-shot performance will draw easy girls, who, in turn, will attract all manner of suckers, whom you can then fleece at will. Just five minutes in your ecosphere should have them begging you to cut them in on whatever schemes you have going on.

When applying Zimmerman's greed-seed techniques to his own con games, Gallo required a more sophisticated approach as he was targeting high-net-worth Newporters. His favorite con partner was, of course, Babar, whom he describes in his book as a studly, stylish, and sleazy Latino playboy constantly hounded by rich, beautiful women.

In other words, Babar looked (and lived) the part of a big-time, flashy dope dealer and upscale gigolo. He also happened to be a compulsive braggart, which helped draw in even more suckers. Gallo would therefore use him as a buffer to run interference on all the wealthy wannabes in their orbit.

Then, after weeks of ignoring these salivating hangers-on, Gallo would finally grace them with his undivided attention. By that point, they were so desperate to get a piece of his pie that they would immediately agree to any opportunity, regardless of the terms. As predestined, these scams always ended in tears for the suckers and wads of cash for Gallo and Falcón.

Marco himself chimes in on this subject:

> Kenji and I ran this con game on many half-assed players and fake tough guys. One dickhead, an ex-banker cokehead we nicknamed 'Blinky' because of his eye which constantly twitched when he was high, was actually stupid enough to show us his safe where he kept all his cash, blow, and diamonds. He was also dumb enough to introduce us to his gigantic Rottweiler. This came in handy when Kenji and I broke into his house in Mission Viejo and robbed his safe – while Blinky was at a party at *our* house in Irvine. That was a good score.

Chapter Nine – How to Give and Take Tune Ups

"A little violence never hurt anybody." –
Benjamin "Lefty Guns" Ruggiero

Violence will obviously be an integral part of your organized crime career. The more you use it early in your profession, the less you'll have to employ it later on, since your fearsome reputation will already be firmly established. Thus, at this point, we should focus on the most rudimentary form of punishment: the good old-fashioned beatdown. We'll deal with the rough stuff later, once you've been properly acclimated to the concept of tuning someone up.

Before one can dish it out, however, one must learn to be able to take it. Marco, for one, was never the best streetfighter on his block, much less in his entire neighborhood. He was, however, a gifted *absorber* of beatings, particularly by groups of assailants. Now, if your childhood is filled with less-than-happy memories of physical abuse at the hands of your *paterfamiglia*, then you'll have no problem with this section.

See, when you get the *scheisse* beaten out of you on a daily basis, especially as a lad, you come to realize that what doesn't kill you actually does make you stronger. You'll learn that black eyes, bloody noses, and split lips heal quickly, and that in a few days, you'll be back to your old miserable self again.

Most importantly, you'll learn not to panic when you get punched in the kisser. Indeed, if this happens often enough, your body will produce less adrenaline with each beating. With any luck – as with Marco's Dade County crime partner Raul O. – someone will hit you in the face with a crowbar. Then, instead of crying like a baby, you'll spit your teeth at them like bloody Chiclets, then nearly decapitate them with their own car door. Now *that's* what I call grace under pressure.

I kid you not, gentle readers – keeping your composure when you are attacked and even seriously injured can make the difference between *la vida* and *la morte*. The most important thing you can do in such a dire situation is *think*. See, panic prevents your ability to think logically, which will impede your ability to escape or even reverse your unfortunate predicament.

Everyone experiences fear and pain, but what separates the wheat from the chaff is the ability to compartmentalize and even minimize those emotions. Take Marco, for instance – he's had the end of a claw hammer embedded in his forehead; a shard of broken glass rip open his right forearm, requiring sixteen nasty stitches; a surgical knife sliced his left thumb to the bone; taken a scalpel in the belly button; had a razor blade slice off the tip of his left forefinger; and even had his face split open with a telephone. These are just a few of the horrific injuries he's suffered during particularly vigorous encounters. And did he cry like Fyre Festival fraudster Billy McFuckface at his sentencing? Did he shit himself like a newborn? Damn right he did. Fortunately, Marco was successfully stitched back together after each incident and emerged with a stronger mindset. Speaking of which…

Adopt the Right Mental Attitude

It is imperative you develop the proper intestinal fortitude for violence. Only a tiny percentage of men can withstand a serious asskicking. Most tough guys will run as soon as they get hurt. But for the chosen few, the *true* tough guys, the more they are injured, the harder they will fight. Those men are extremely dangerous and, therefore, should be given a wide berth.

Nobody in the mob was as thoroughly indoctrinated on taking and giving a five-star asskicking like Jon Roberts. As a teenager, he ran with The Outcasts, a local gang who taught him the intricacies of inflicting and receiving corporal punishment. They took him down into a basement and pushed aside all the furniture, then attacked him with all manner of implements. This is how Jon learned how to withstand the physical and psychological rigors of violence. This is how he learned how to fight like a madman. What're friends for?

End the Fight ASAP

Strike first, strike second, and strike last: and strike with as much vim and vigor as you can muster. Practice on much smaller and weaker opponents before moving your way up to more evenly-matched adversaries. I suggest you start with the disabled, then kindly work your way up to senior citizens.

Also, the faster you administer your beatdown, the sooner it will be over and the less chance you'll experience problems. Jon Roberts' psychotic father taught him to hit his opponent with something hard to end the fight ASAP.

Most gangsters out there concur. Take Gallo, for example. His LA Mafia mentor Jimmy Caci was constantly worried about Gallo's fistfights, warning him that he was one punch away from a jail cell. He was particularly concerned he would kill someone in a brawl and do serious time.

Caci's fears were genuine, as Gallo always tried to end each fight expediently. He knew the longer the fight lasted, the greater the possibility he would be wounded or worse. He knew there were plenty of tough wannabes out there who were willing to take him on to establish their rep. But when they witnessed the brutality Gallo unleashed in combat, they tempered their ambitions.

The Iceman himself came to the same realization while still in his late teens. Kuklinski regularly got into bloody confrontations in South Jersey bars and pool halls. He never hesitated to utilize pool sticks, pool balls, or broken bottles on anyone who talked shit or welched on a bet. He knew all too well the sacred commandment: *he who strikes first and strikes hardest prevails.*

Stop reading, and go watch the 1993 Academy Awards Best Picture winner *Unforgiven*. I want you to pay particularly close attention to those scenes where Little Bill Daggett (Gene Hackman) gives a not-so-friendly welcome to out-of-town guntoters. As he's stomping the living daylights out of 'em, he's telling them, "This is for all them cowboys in Cheyenne and Kansas."

What Little Bill was trying to impart to his deputies was that through overwhelming force and ferocity, you'll avoid future confrontations. Like Daniel-*san* finally figured out, "You fight so you don't have to fight."

Hai!

In the alternative, follow former undercover fed Joaquín "Big Jack" Garcia's lead. Not unlike Kevin Weeks in Boston, Big Jack grew up street fighting and bar bouncing in the Bronx. In doing so, he learned that the best way to end a fight quickly and decisively is to punch the bastard in the throat.

Know When to Walk Away, Know When to Run

If I'm gonna fight somebody, I don't want to *think* I can beat them – I want to *know* I can. The flipside of this is knowing when to *avoid* a fight. I've seen fights where the losing party keeps coming back, regardless of the fact he's getting beaten to a pulp. It makes no sense – just raise the white flag, beg for mercy, and blow up his house after you heal up. That'll restore your delicate manhood in a single fiery explosion (preferably when he's not home).

It's important that you be able to size up a superior opponent and avoid escalating the conflict. For example, never fight someone with cauliflowered ears because that person is a hardcore boxer, wrestler, jiu-jitsu practitioner, or MMA fighter. I don't care if the dude is 4'10" and weighs a buck-ten soaking wet. That's how big one of Marco's old Muay Thai instructors was, and that little man (who'd been Thai boxing in Bangkok smokers since he was twelve) could break baseball bats with his shins.

The next best place to check is the hands. Gallo's, for example, are large, meaty, and covered in scar tissue – so please don't fight someone displaying these telltale marks of extensive combat. (And yes, Gallo's ears look like someone ran them through a wood chipper – a highly coveted merit badge among MMA fighters.)

Relax, everyone – the chances of you fighting someone at that skill level are infinitesimal at best unless you are incredibly stupid, outrageously drunk, or most certainly both. That's because professional fighters are by and large exceedingly peaceful individuals. In fact, they are among the nicest people I've ever met. This stems from the facts that (a) they have absolutely nothing to prove to anyone because they know they can destroy all comers; (b) they love what they're doing so they're naturally happy people; (c) they get their ya-yas out in the gym so they're exceedingly mellow on the street; and (d) since they don't drink, they snack on edibles so are probably high as a fucking kite.

I've even seen a drunken jackass at a bar challenge an MMA fighter to brawl. The MMA fighter just smiled and conceded that the drunk would win and so there was no need to fight. Of course, when this same drunken fool actually took a swing at the fighter, he knocked the doofus out with one punch – so fast that nobody else in the bar even noticed. The drunk simply collapsed in a heap. Now that's class, baby. Like Whitey Bulger, I've always been in awe of men with that kinda one-punch knockout power – Kevin Weeks sure as hell had it.

Jon Roberts agrees with this one-punch philosophy. He got to know Bruce Lee just before he became world famous, when Lee frequented Jon's Manhattan nightclubs. Even though Lee was small, he was in phenomenal shape. And Bruce's rep as a world-class martial artist preceded him. Jon would joke to his pals that someday he was gonna fight Lee, even though he was quite fond of him since Bruce was a friendly and humble guy. But after seeing his movies, Jon was relieved he had never taken him on. He realized Bruce was the real thing and he couldn't have defeated him, even with a baseball bat.

That's called wisdom, baby ducks. It takes a seasoned predator to know when he's outmatched. And there's no shame in it.

Oh, and if any of you smegma helmets out there doubt whether Bruce Lee was all he was cracked up to be, just watch his home movies on YouTube. You'll see him side kick the heavy bag in his backyard – he literally knocks it all the way across the friggin' lawn. Oh, and Bruce was only 5'8" tall and weighed 141 pounds in his skivvies. So don't judge a book by its cover.

Develop a Killer Instinct

One cannot fight at the UFC level without having *it*. This means that the nanosecond your opponent shows the slightest weakness, you strike. You do so without even thinking because it's an instinctive reaction, like muscle memory.

In most Hollywood crime thrillers or horror flicks, you always see the hero/ine subdue the antagonist, then stupidly turn their back on him. Inevitably, the bad guy pops up like a post-apocalyptic zombie and attacks the idiotic hero/ine *again*. This unrealistic bullshit chaps my ass as badly as watching celluloid thugs fire handguns sideways, gangsta style ('cause doing so diminishes your accuracy).

If you're ever attacked by a chainsaw-wielding maniac and you temporarily debilitate him, instead of running away, split his cranium open until his brains spill out like a horny octopus.

Undefeated streetfighter George Rowe throws in his two cents. He drove his pickup truck to his Vago brother Big Todd's house and arrived just in time to see Todd duke it out with a badass doper named Bigger Dave (or something like that).

Rowe saw Todd throw a right cross, which Dave easily slipped and returned with a beautiful right cross. CRACK! That bad boy perfectly kissed Todd's jaw. But before the Toddster licked the cement, Georgie was out of his Dodge Ram and sprinting towards dastardly Dave.

Now Dave was a fine boxer but no match for a professional MMA fighter like Mr. Rowe, whose first blow shattered Dave's third rib. The bone snapped in two and punctured poor Davie's lung. Dave collapsed to the pavement and cried for his mama. As Rowe explains, "Most people would have stopped right there, but not me. A street fight is no joke – you need to stomp your opponent 'til he stops moving."

And that's exactly what George did: he shit-kicked Big Dave until he went into convulsions and passed out.

Here, here!

Even if your assailant is not trying to kill you but merely intends to cause you grievous bodily harm, then use any means at your disposal to put him in the E.R. The closer he's clinging to the afterlife, the better. Why take any chances?

By the way, this killer instinct will really come in handy once you actually start *killing people*. More on that to come, saplings.

Fight Dirty

Again, only a blithering idiot fights fair. Never give your enemy an opportunity to take any advantage against you. Conversely, you should seek to instantly exploit any weakness or vulnerability on his part. I can't help but keep going back to Jon Roberts, whose book *American Desperado* goes into detail about how to dismantle another human being with everything from a baseball bat to a knife to a gun to your fists and feet.

> No matter what the other guy is doing, focus on his weak points. Take away his legs by kicking his knees. Take away his eyes by sticking them with your fingers. Work on his shins. Shins are very sensitive, and you can hurt a person real bad on his shins. And no matter what, always be kicking his balls. Use gravity when you fight. Punch down, not up.

In other words, fight like the Three Stooges!

Chapter Ten – Making Your Bones

"Once you pull that trigger, you can't take it back." – David "Fat Dave" Iacovetti

Oh boy, if any chapter in this book is gonna get me in trouble, it's this one. Committing cold-blooded, premeditated murder is the Mafia's Maginot Line. Contrary to popular belief, not everyone in the mob is a killer. Becoming one is not for all, and I won't hold it against you if it's not right for you. As Bonanno bigshot Joseph Massino once testified, "It takes all kinds of meat to make a good sauce. Some people, they kill. Some people, they earn, they can't kill."

But I will tell you this: aside from making big bucks, committing contract murders is the best way to ascend to the next rung on the LCN ladder. Case in point: the July 12, 1979, assassination of self-anointed Bonanno boss Carmine "Lilo" Galante at Joe & Mary's Restaurant in Bushwick, Brooklyn. As a result of this assassination, co-conspirators Dominick "Sonny Black" Napolitano and Joey Massino were both promoted to capo. Also, the imprisoned Philip "Rusty" Rastelli became the undisputed boss of the Family.

And traditionally, homicide – making your bones by doing heavy work – has been the primary prerequisite for formal induction in the Mafia.

Plan Meticulously

If you want to avoid getting caught, many hours of detailed planning are required to carry out a murder contract. A million things can go wrong and you only need one to dampen your day. Now I have neither the time nor the inclination to school you on how to avoid leaving forensic evidence behind at the crime scene. Fortunately, however, you can binge watch all nine seasons of *Forensic Files*. Suffice it to say that, ideally, you should wrap yourself up from head to toe in latex like a giant condom to avoid leaving evidence behind. Short of that, latex gloves are a must, a shower cap is advantageous, and plastic booties are most helpful.

Now let's move on to logistics. If the hit happens in a car, douse it with bleach first, then gasoline, and torch that fucker (preferably with the dearly departed still inside).

****

Before Gallo got mobbed up, he was one of the biggest cocaine traffickers in Orange County, as well as one of its most feared gangsters. Before breaking off to form The Crew, he worked directly for the Avila family. Led by the late Joey Avila, they allegedly *were* the biggest dopers in the OC. The main players were the three Avila brothers – Joey, Sal, and Sergio – who were all indicted in the infamous October 1977 Tahitian Connection cocaine trafficking case. They were charged with smuggling mass quantities of Peruvian flake to SoCal by way of Tahiti. Famous defense attorney F. Lee Bailey got them off.

On February 20, 1989, the Avilas' reputed top hitter, Eduard "Lalo" U., allegedly shot Gallo's top enforcer Clyde point blank in the eye with a .38 as he slept in a south OC hotel room. Naturally, Gallo and Marco decided to return the favor and permanently clip Lalo's wings.

When they were planning his murder, Marco felt absolutely confident that they would get away with it. After all, Gallo had extensive experience in military planning, strategy, and tactics. He obtained it from both military school and an allegedly corrupt Irvine PD undercover narcotics detective named Jerry H.

The plan, which they rehearsed multiple times, was simple, which is the way it should always be. They would meet Lalo at the Newport Beach hotel where he always stayed when he was in town, and take him out clubbing. Gallo would ride in Lalo's car with Marco following in his own. They'd drive up Bonita Canyon Road, which back then was rural and pitch black at night. Gallo would then have Lalo pull over, ostensibly so he could relieve himself.

Marco would then pull up behind them, kill the lights with the engine still running, and watch Gallo step out of the car. Gallo would then whip out his .380 Walther PPK and blast him – two kill shots to the head and two control shots to the chest. He'd then quickly wipe down the few areas on which he'd left fingerprints. Simultaneously, Marco would grab the gasoline bomb from his trunk that Gallo would have skillfully assembled earlier that day. Nothing like a massive explosion of petrol to eradicate any prints, fibers, or hair follicles. Then Gallo would simply hop in Marco's car and away they would go.

Gallo describes the end result of all this planning in *Breakshot*: Lalo disappeared, never to be seen or heard from again. Marco confirmed that Lalo stayed gone.

****

Plan your hit in reverse chronological order to ensure a successful escape. If you're gonna flee in a vehicle, then make damn sure you're intimately familiar with all the nearest freeway on-ramps, major intersections, side streets, drivable alleys, etc. Also be wary of closed-circuit TV cameras, which are posted under most major freeway overpasses, as well as security cameras from local businesses and ATMs. You'll obviously want to use a stolen car, preferably an older one that doesn't have an embedded GPS security device. Of course, you should switch the hot plates with a new set, which should also be stolen for this occasion.

Say what you will about Little Nicky Scarfo, but that homicidal, detail-oriented Gollum planned out his hits (at least the early ones) with military precision. For example, in preparation for making his bones, Phil Leonetti was thoroughly schooled by Scarfo, who cautioned him to never wear jewelry in case it fell off during the job. Nicky was concerned it might get traced back to Leonetti, either through fingerprints or the jewelry itself.

Little Nicky then had his nephew go over the escape route several times. Finally, Scarfo instructed him that as soon as he shot his man to throw the gun on a nearby roof. Phil did exactly as trained, and the December 16, 1979, hit on Vincent Falcone went off without a hitch. And with that, Leonetti took his first major step to getting straightened out.

Details and preparation, folks – it ain't freakin' magic!

Kill the Right Guy

Again, whacking the *right* guy can make you a *made* guy. My precious Mafia library is filled with these tales of pseudo-heroic derring-do that should inspire even the laziest couch potato to get off his ass. *Carpe diem*, bitches!

On June 17, 1957, in a scene that inspired the famous one in *The Godfather*, Francesco "Frank" Scalise was executed by two gunmen at an outdoor vegetable market in the Bronx. A gangster named Vincent Squillante, a.k.a. Jimmy Jerome, was responsible not only for Scalise's murder (on orders from then boss Albert Anastasia), but subsequently also for that of Frank's brother, Joseph Scalise. Joseph had suicidally bragged to everyone at Frank's funeral that he was going to avenge his death. Never telegraph your punches!

Anyways, Frank was young Nino Gaggi's *padrone* so it was only just that he avenge his (literal) godfather – Frank was Nino's father's cousin. This shit goes deep with the Italians, so Nino did the right thing.

In the Mafia, revenge truly is a dish best served cold. Thus, on September 23, 1960, more than three years after Frank's murder, Nino snuck up behind Squillante, plugged him in back of the head, dumped him in the trunk of a car, and drove off. Both Squillante and the car were demolished by a car compactor in a local salvage yard. Nino's reward: membership in *La Cosa Nostra* and the undying respect and admiration of his fellow mobsters.

Make Sure You Actually Kill the Fucker

The worst thing you can do when you go out to whack someone is to *not* whack them. In other words, ensure you actually *kill* your target. Obviously, if the guy survives and testifies against you, you'll do some serious time.

The Orange County, California, organized crime social scene back in the '80s was surprisingly cozy – all the players knew each other, and when they weren't devouring one another, they often worked together.

William "Bill" Carroll was a wiseguy who owned the infamous Mustang Club, a highly lucrative topless bar in Santa Ana. Carroll had done time in 1970 with LA capo Michael "Big Mike" Rizzitello, a.k.a. Mike Rizzi, who tried to shake him down for a piece of the joint. Carroll, who was already paying him $5,000 a week in protection money, foolishly refused.

On May 1, 1987, Carroll accompanied Big Mike, who was built like an NFL linebacker and had whacked a couple dozen people, and Mike's sidekick, Mafia wannabe Joseph Grosso, to a parking garage near South Coast Plaza in Costa Mesa … *at night*. Carroll even let Mike sit in the back seat while he drove.

Big surprise – after they parked, Grosso held down Carroll's legs, preventing him from escaping. Rizzi leaned forward and hissed, "This is for not letting us eat." BAM! BAM! BAM! He shot him three times in the back of the head with a .22. Carroll slumped forward, dead. Rizzi and Grosso got out and fled.

Except Carroll *wasn't* dead – he regained consciousness several hours later, permanently blinded, his skull looking like a crimson bowling ball. He staggered out of the car and stumbled around, moaning incoherently, arms outstretched, looking for a hug. The parking garage attendant told the police he thought Carroll was a zombie coming to attack him!

Poor Mike Rizzi, who was always a day late and a dollar short, was convicted of attempted murder and sentenced to thirty-three years in prison. He died there fourteen years later on October 26, 2005, dead broke and with no book or movie deal in place.

Lessons to Be Learned

If you're gonna do a job, do it right. Big Mike should've emptied his entire mag into Carroll's head, then he should've slit his throat just to be safe.

But at least Big Mike only got jail time for his fuck up. Plenty of dumbshits out there have ended up victims themselves after botching an important murder assignment. And it's almost always for something really stupid – like not ensuring the guy is *dead*. The failed hit on the legendary Ken "Tokyo Joe" Eto is a prime example of what can happen to you if you screw up a piece of work.

Before Kenny Gallo, the highest-ranking Asian-American associate in the history of the Mafia was Eto (who was also Japanese-American). For more than twenty years, Eto had been the most successful gambling kingpin in Chicago, working closely with and under the protection of The Outfit. He made tens of millions of dollars for himself and his bosses. This magical relationship began to sour when Eto was arrested in August 1980. Outfit bosses Tony "Joe Batters" Accardo and Joseph "Joey Doves" Aiuppa doubted that Eto would be a stand-up guy in the face of a lengthy prison stay. So why take chances?

On February 10, 1983, a few months before Tokyo Joe's trial was scheduled to begin, Outfit associate and ex-Chicago cop John Gatuso had Eto pick him up. They then picked up another Outfit thug, loanshark and bookie Jasper "Big Jay" Campise, ostensibly to drive to a high-level meeting with the brass to discuss trial strategy. They never made it.

Gatuso, who was sitting in the back seat behind Eto, pulled out a .22 and – Pop! Pop! Pop! – drilled him thrice in the noggin. Believing he was dead, Dumb and Dumber jumped out of the car and fled. They should have done what Outfit hitters are trained to do – slice his carotid artery to ensure he bleeds out.

Miraculously, the bullets – as .22s are wont to do (especially if you pack the gunpowder yourself, as these nitwits inexpertly did) – never penetrated his skull, and Eto survived. The first call he made when he regained consciousness in the hospital was to the FBI, and, boy, did they come a-runnin'. Fifteen Outfitters went down as a result. Fortunately for Gatuso and Campise, the bosses were in a forgiving mood and merely fined them for their mishap.

Just kidding, Moo-Moo!

Five months after the botched hit, on July 14, 1983, the decomposing bodies of Gatuso and Campise were found – where else? – in the trunk of a car in a suburban parking lot west of Chicago. They had been beaten, stabbed, and strangled – which, of course, they should have done to Tokyo Joe.

As for Eto-*san*, he entered WITSEC and lived in Georgia until he passed away on January 23, 2004, at age eighty-four of natural causes. He used the surname Tanaka, which is also the name Gallo used after entering the Program. The FBI apparently gave Gallo the same surname as a winking homage to Tokyo Joe.

Use the Right Ammo, Numbskulls!

How *did* Messrs. Carroll and Eto each survive three slugs in the melon? .22-caliber bullets, *bambino*. Any mob guy will tell you that if you're going to do someone up close, use a .22. The main reason is that once the round penetrates the skull, the bullet will rattle around like Ricky Bobby at NASCAR and turn the brains into mush. This, in turn, will ensure death. At least that's the prevailing logic. The other two reasons: it's a relatively quiet firearm, and easy to conceal.

True, that happens *most* of the time. But much of the time, however, a .22 round – which is a small projectile – will merely bounce off the skull and create a non-lethal groove around the brain, or, alternatively, simply bounce right off.

Ergo, if you're going to use a .22 peashooter (which is the least noisy gun you can use, and the most adaptable to a silencer), make sure you plug each of the target's eyeballs. This will guarantee a massive hematoma. Otherwise, empty the entire mag into him. Or better yet, if you have the stomach for it, give him a Colombian necktie. Just be careful if you do that 'cause slicing someone's throat may very well douse you in a firehose of *sangre*.

And by the way, with a .22, you can easily make a silencer at home by stuffing an empty two-liter plastic soda bottle with newspaper, which you attach to the barrel with duct tape. Then practice at home by shooting into thick phone books. That's how Gallo practiced when he was too lazy or busy to go to the range or desert. But this only works with a .22 – anything else is too powerful.

Alternatively, for upclose work, according to Philip Carlo's *The Ice Man*, Richard Kuklinski preferred .38 Derringers. They were small, easily concealable, and particularly deadly at close range when loaded with dum-dum bullets. This book was made into the decent 2012 film *The Iceman*, starring Michael Shannon as Kuklinski and Ray Liotta as Roy DeMeo. It's worth catching.

DeMeo supposedly hired Kuklinski to commit numerous contract murders that were too sensitive to be done by *Mafiosi*. I liked the movie but take issue with the fact that DeMeo's real-life henchman, Chris Rosenberg, refers to The Westies as such. No one in the mob ever called them The Westies, but instead the West Side mob or the Irish mob. Sorry, folks, but I'm a stickler.

Please take care that your ammo is *not* defective. Firing duds can make a simple hit far more complicated and disgusting than you ever imagined – and that kinda thing will give you nightmares. Just ask Frank Cullotta. Cullotta describes his assignment from Spilotro to murder stool pigeon Sherwin "Jerry" Lisner.

On October 10, 1979, Cullotta knocked on the front door of Lisner's Vegas pad, ostensibly to discuss his recent testimony before a federal grand jury about Spilotro and Cullotta's criminal activities. Lisner welcomed him inside his home, explaining that he told the grand jury nothing of consequence. As soon as Lisner turned his back, Cullotta slid out a .22 revolver and – POP! POP! – banged him in the cranium.

Under typical circumstances, Cullotta would have used a silencer. But for some reason, he didn't have one that day. So in a misguided attempt to minimize the noise of the gunshots, he used half-loads, meaning that he had emptied half of the gunpower from each bullet. But Cullotta failed to realize the obvious: half the gunpowder means half the firepower.

So after popping Lisner in the head, Sherwin merely turned around and asked Cullotta, "What the hell are you doing, Frank?" He then took off running through the kitchen with Cullotta in hot pursuit. POP! POP! POP! POP! Frank shot him four more times in the head. Amazingly, Lisner still didn't go down, and even made it all the way into his garage.

As Lisner hit the button to open the garage door, Cullotta brained him with the revolver, then dragged him back into the kitchen. He then grabbed an electric cord from a water cooler and tried to strangle poor Sherwin, but the cord snapped!

Folks, I gotta be honest – at this point in the story, I'm not sure whom to feel sorrier for, do you?

Cullotta paused to catch his breath while Lisner stared up at him, gasping, wondering what was next. Frank grabbed a butcher knife off the counter and prepared to saw off his buddy's head. Suddenly, Cullotta's accomplice Wayne Matecki (who had been waiting outside in their car) entered the house. Taking in the kitchen scene, Matecki picked up Cullotta's revolver off the floor and loaded it with six more half-loads.

Not wanting to miss out on the action, Matecki grabbed a seat cushion and tried to smother Lisner. "Die, die, die!" Wayne screamed. But that little fucker just wouldn't listen – he was like the Energizer bunny!

Cullotta then shoved Matecki aside and fired directly into Lisner's eyeballs, finally killing him. The kitchen looked like that blood-filled hallway from *The Shining*. Cullotta hadn't worn gloves since it would have tipped his mitt to Lisner, so he had taken care not to touch any surfaces. But he was concerned about leaving fingerprints on Lisner's body. So with Matecki's help, he dragged it out to the backyard and heaved it into the pool. Cullotta knew the water and chlorine would erase any forensic evidence.

After tidying up a little, the two killers went back to Cullotta's nearby condo, where Frank showered with Ajax to scrub away any residual blood traces. Meanwhile, Matecki cut Cullotta's clothes up into strips, placed them into multiple garbage bags, and tossed them in the desert. He then took a taxi to the airport and caught the next flight back to Chicago.

Later that same night, Spilotro picked up Cullotta for a late supper. After hearing the details of the grisly killing, Tony the Ant said, "I never want to talk about this ever again." And they never did.

Who's up for Sizzler?

It's rare that a single man can terrify an entire Mafia family, but it does happen. I've seen it with Jimmy Burke, Roy DeMeo, and Greg Scarpa Sr., to name a few. But Anthony "Bruno" Indelicato takes the cake – he terrified at least *two* Families, as did Gaspipe. His father, Alphonse "Sonny Red" Indelicato, was murdered with two fellow capos during the so-called *Cinco de Mayo* Massacre on May 5, 1981, after a failed power struggle to take over the Bonanno Family.

Both the Bonannos and the Gambinos (who had disposed of the bodies) were quaking at the retaliatory shit storm they knew Bruno could unleash. He was a coke-addled maniac who, less than two years earlier on July 12, 1979, had murdered Bonanno drug czar Carmine Galante, then the most feared man in the Mafia. Bruno was convicted of that murder – one of the most infamous in LCN history – in late 1986 and sentenced to forty-five years. But for some reason, he only served twelve years before being released in 1998.

Bruno was also a gun nut and mentor to Tommy Karate. Bruno was such a scary guy, he dipped his bullets in cyanide so if he even merely nicked his victim, his target would die a slow, agonizing death.

What can we learn from Bruno (who eventually made peace with the Bonannos)? Don't take chances, bruh.

Don't Leave Incriminating Evidence Behind

Circling back, yes, I realize this is a total no-brainer but I would be sorely remiss if I didn't mention the number-one rule in committing a homicide – *don't leave evidence which can lead back to you.* Look, if the majority of you would-be killers out there weren't such flippin' mooks, I wouldn't even have to go there. But you are, so I will. (No offense, mooks.)

Hopefully you've taken my advice and become an avid fan of *Forensic Files*. I'm assuming you have and therefore will avoid what would otherwise be an insufferably technical discussion. Instead, let us simply emulate Vincent James Flemmi, a.k.a. Jimmy the Bear, who was a proficient hitman for the Boston family and brother of Stephen "the Rifleman" Flemmi. He was so feared during the '60s that when his photo appeared in the local papers, the photographers insisted they not be credited for the pics.

By 1965, the FBI had attributed at least seven murders to Jimmy the Bear, including a beheading he had committed in 1963 after being released from one of his many stints in prison. He shot the victim (someone he had recently done time with) after an argument in a Dorchester saloon where the vic tended bar. Jimmy decapitated the man because he was concerned the bullet in his skull could be traced back to him. Then for good measure, he burned the entire bar to the ground. Jimmy was most definitely bat-shit crazy but he wasn't entirely stupid.

Don't Leave Incriminating Evidence on *Yourself*

When you discharge a firearm, gunpowder residue will get on your hands, your clothes, even in your hair. Therefore, you should discard your clothing and gloves when you do a hit. Ideally, you should burn said items (and, if you can manage it, your victim's corpse as well). Take a brisk shower afterwards and thoroughly shampoo your hair. You might even consider shaving off your hair just in case. If anyone asks, just tell them you're moving to the Orient to become a Shaolin monk. What the hell do they know – you'll be lammin' it anyways.

Also, Gallo recommends washing with Neat Feet, a harsh foot scrub that allegedly crooked cop Jerry H. taught him to use every time he discharged a firearm during a crime. This product erases all traces of gunpowder residue.

You should also carry a book of matches with you in case the paraffin test comes back positive. The match triggers a false positive on the test. Then you can claim you were taking a massive Cleveland steamer while the cops were banging down your door, and so you had lit a match out of professional courtesy.

Finally, Nicky Crow emphatically suggests that you should rinse a gun in vinegar after you use it in a murder. With all due respect, Nick, how cheap (and foolhardy) can you be that you'd keep that firearm after a job? How the heck is vinegar going to change the rifling marks on the bullet after it's fired from the subject weapon?

Always Use a Revolver

Use a revolver instead of a semi-automatic when smoking someone. Semi-autos will often jam on you, meaning that one of the bullets gets caught as it rotates up the magazine as you're firing. The revolver, by contrast, has no mag and therefore it is impossible for its bullets to jam.

It is also impossible for a revolver to accidentally discharge. Thus, it boggles my mind that actor Mickey Rourke was able to escape prosecution for allegedly shooting his then wife, model and actress Carré Otis, in the mid '90s. She claimed Mickey's .357 Magnum "accidentally" went off in her purse when she dropped it and shot her in the shoulder.

Oh puh-lease!

Coincidentally, around that same time, Mickey was reportedly arrested for slapping her around. Hmmm...

Aside from not actually killing the target, using a semi-automatic pistol is the second-worst way to foul up a hit. In 1991, Vic Amuso and Gaspipe Casso, who were then both in the wind, put a hit on crew chieftain Peter "Fat Pete" Chiodo. They considered him disloyal for taking a ten-year plea in the now-legendary Windows RICO case without first clearing it with them. When you take a plea like this, you'll be forced to admit on the record that you're a member of a Mafia family, which is a big no-no in the mob. Your admission can be used as evidence of the existence of that Family against other *Mafiosi* in subsequent prosecutions. The fact that Fat Pete had been one of Gaspipe's closest friends and biggest moneymakers for many years didn't factor into the murder equation.

Then acting boss Little Al D'Arco delegated the hit to his son Joseph, who had proven his mettle and aptitude in a previous contract killing in LA.

On May 8, 1991, Joseph D'Arco (who by that time had been made as a result of the DiLapi job) and fellow fuck-up hitman Frank Giacobbe ambushed Fat Pete at a Staten Island gas station. Giacobbe stumbled out of their work car, tripped, and accidentally discharged the 9mm pistol in his hand. Chiodo, instantly alerted to the peril, immediately drew his own *pistola*. Giacobbe regained his footing, and accompanied by young D'Arco, charged full speed ahead, guns blazing.

Cue Wagner's "Ride Of The Valkyries."

They plugged Chiodo a dozen times in the arms, legs, and torso. Chiodo backpedaled furiously, firing off five shots of his own, though none found their mark. (You see now why target practice counts?) He finally fell onto his back, looking like the world's largest In-N-Out Double-Double smothered in ketchup.

D'Arco stood over him to deliver the coup de grâce, but then his own 9mm jammed! He desperately tried to work the slide to no avail. So instead of grabbing Fat Pete's pistol and finishing the job (which would have been the height of irony), Joseph panicked, ran off like a total wuss back to the car, and drove off with Giacobbe.

Thanks to Chiodo's Walmart-shopper physique (400-500 pounds at the time), none of the twelve bullets penetrated any vital organs. He lived, and he sang, and eventually Vic and Gaspipe were convicted largely as a result of his testimony, and sentenced to life. Chiodo was the first made man (much less capo) in the Luccheses to flip, followed shortly thereafter by Al D'Arco and son.

In case you're wondering, Henry Hill – the first major Lucchese *associate* to ever flip – couldn't be made was because he was half-Irish on his father's side. Same for Burke, who was one hundred percent Irish.

I probably should have mentioned this earlier but it used to be that in order to be formally inducted into the Mafia, both your parents had to be Italian or Sicilian. Then John Gotti Sr. changed that Rule so that only your father had to be such. He did this to get Gotti Junior made because Junior's mother, Victoria Gotti, was of Russian descent.

Subsequently, the Mafia changed the Rule again so that you could get badged if even only your mommy was Italian. Nowadays, because of attrition and gentrification, I'm pretty sure you only have to like Italian food.

Lessons to Be Learned

Always use a wheel gun or at least have one as a back-up piece. And don't go on hits with blockheads who are gonna trip over their own dicks and accidentally discharge their firearms.

Don't Bring Stupid People with You on the Hit

Speaking of ignoramuses, let's talk about 'em some more. When you go out on a murder assignment, you are literally entrusting your compatriots with your life. Again, all kinds of stuff can go wrong, and as you saw from the previous example, often do. Think of it as Murphy's Law for Murderers. So you'd better have someone who's a tried and true stone-cold killer with you.

This is particularly important in California, which has the felony-murder rule. This means that if someone is accidentally killed during the commission of a felony, even if it's your own crime partner, they *you* can be charged with first-degree murder. This is true even if none of you had any intention whatsoever of hurting someone. For example, let's say you and your colleague try to rob a bank and a guard blows your pal's head off. You might be facing life for *his* murder. Very uncool – just like that B.S. three strikes law in Cali. Conversely, you need a cool cat with you who's not gonna panic and kill innocent bystanders.

One of the dumbest hitmen in the annals of New England crime has to be Brian "Balloonhead" Halloran, a hopeless alcoholic and cocaine addict. Balloonhead was his actual nickname. On October 13, 1981, In Town (Boston LCN) hitman Francis "Cadillac Frank" Salemme was dispatched by godfather Jerry Angiulo to brace local cocaine trafficker George Pappas for not kicking up enough. Unfortunately for all parties, four decades earlier, Balloonhead's mother had shat him out in a Southie nursery ward. This less-than-fortuitous event somehow culminated with Cadillac Frank bringing him along as extra muscle that night. This makes no sense whatsoever since even Whitey Bulger had a healthy fear of Salemme, not to mention the rest of the Boston underworld.

So these three Mouseketeers met at a greasy Chinatown eatery at three in the A.M. to slurp down MSG-infused egg rolls and tepid tea. After this last supper, the waiter, a man named Soon Yen Chin, placed the check on their table and left. He did so only moments before the conversation became heated enough for Balloonhead to whip out his sidearm and – BANG! – blow Pappas' right eyeball out of its socket. The orb exited through the rear of his skull, along with most of his cerebellum. Frank and Brian took their fortune cookies to go.

The Boston homicide dicks examining the crime scene found a set of car keys on the table for a white Buick Regal parked down the street. They discovered the Buick had been rented from a local National Car Rental – in Balloonhead's own name, no less. And on the same set of keys was another – it belonged to Halloran's apartment. Are you starting to fathom why he was called Balloonhead?

Halloran was so indescribably stupid that later, even after he knew Whitey was looking to whack him as a witness to the 1981 Roger Wheeler-murder conspiracy, he went into one of his favorite bars. Afterwards, his pal Michael Donahue – a regular citizen in the wrong place at the wrong time – offered to give him a ride home. As soon as they left the bar, Bulger machine-gunned both of them to death.

Don't Telegraph Your Punches

You know how in the movies gunsels always spout off cool lines like "Michael Corleone says hello" just before they whack some poor slob? Yeah, please don't do that. In real life, you're just giving your victim a heads up.

The most infamous flub of this nature happened on May 2, 1957, when Mafia founding father Frank Costello was targeted for death. Other bigshots sent a young up and comer named Vincent "the Chin" Gigante to do the job. In preparation, Gigante spent several months target shooting to perfect his accuracy. Too bad it didn't help.

On the night in question, Chin (*sans* disguise, though he had gained sixty pounds to alter his appearance) ran past the doorman into Costello's Manhattan apartment building. He charged towards Costello with his .38 revolver in hand. Revealing his dramatic flair, Chin yelled, "This one's for you, Frank!"

Costello instantly veered his head to avoid what he knew was coming next. BLAM! Gigante fired one round, which, thanks to the head jerk, merely grazed Costello's scalp. Without emptying the other five chambers into Costello's temple, Gigante simply spun around, fled the building to a waiting car, and escaped. Thus, the doorman got a good look at him coming *and* going.

That wasn't the end of Gigante's cosmic blundering. Because these birdbrains had double-parked directly in front of the building, the doorman was able to jot down their license-plate number. Turns out the work car had been purchased only two weeks earlier and was registered to – hold your breath! – one Vincent Gigante.

As a result, the previously anonymous Gigante was now on the cover of every paper in the country, sparking a nationwide manhunt to track down his lamming ass. And while he was on the run, the police put incredible pressure on his wife and mobbed-up brothers, Mario and Ralph. Way to go, Chinster!

To this day I'm befuddled as to why he wasn't whacked. Good thing for the Genoveses he wasn't 'cause he turned out to be their most successful and powerful boss ever. Go figure.

Seriously, folks – it is truly amazing that Gigante was not murdered for his spectacular faux pas. Perhaps it was because even this botched attempt achieved its intended purpose – Costello immediately retired from the mob and permanently withdrew from the public eye. Apparently there were no hard feelings, as years later, famed mob attorney Frank Ragano spotted Costello and Gigante dining amicably together in the Volcano (LCN's nickname for NYC).

Nevertheless, Gigante forever more became a public figure, permanently losing his anonymity, which unless you're an egomaniacal buffoon like Al Capone, Tony Spilotro, or John Gotti, should be your most cherished asset.

Don't Kill Indiscriminately

If there's one thing that really gives contract killers a bad name, it's savages who go around killing lots of people who don't need killing – namely, *innocent* people. At Whitey Bulger's trial, Johnny Martorano admitted to murdering twenty people but claimed he was still an honorable man because he only killed as "favors" for his friends. He testified that he would happily accept "expenses" or "tips" after doing a job, like the fifty grand he got for murdering Roger Wheeler in 1981. But since he refused financial remuneration *beforehand*, as he explained to the jury, he was still a good guy. You can imagine how that went over.

Now I happen to kinda like Martorano, who by all accounts was a loyal and fun-loving guy, though he wasn't the brightest bulb on the Mafia Christmas tree. But recklessly spraying bullets at carloads full of people tends to result in senseless murders.

There were at least several innocent people The Executioner "accidentally" slaughtered. On March 8, 1973, The Hill was looking to whack rival gangster Alfred "Indian Al" Notarangeli. That night, the bartender at Notarangeli's restaurant, thirty-year-old Michael Milano, had stopped at a light shortly after getting off work. Unfortunately, Milano, who both resembled and emulated Notarangeli, was wearing a black leather overcoat like Indian Al's *and* driving a brown Mercedes identical to Notarangeli's. Milano wasn't alone – riding shotgun was Diane Sussman de Tennen and in the backseat was her boyfriend Louis Lapiana, who had just started bartending at the restaurant.

Martorano emerged from the darkness, spraying the front seat first, then the back. Milano was hit by four bullets and would die three hours later. Sussman de Tennen caught one in the arm but would live. Louis Lapiana also survived but was rendered a quadriplegic for the rest of his life.

Ah, heck – no sense crying over spilled blood or severed vertebrae. As Martorano nonchalantly told his biographer Howie Carr in regards to this incident, "Shit happens." Notarangeli himself was finally killed by Martorano on February 21, 1974.

But you'd think Martorano would have learned from the *identical* mistake he had made only five years before in early 1968. That night he set out to kill an African-American leg-breaker named Herbert "Smitty" Smith for slapping around Stevie "the Ladykiller" Flemmi. Ever the loyal friend, on January 6th, Martorano ambushed Smith as he sat in his snow-covered Mercury sedan in Boston's Roxbury neighborhood. But as Johnny prepared to do what he does best, he suddenly realized there were two other people with Smith. His solution: shoot first and give a fuck (or not) later.

He shot all three occupants to death in three seconds: Smith in the front seat, nineteen-year-old Elizabeth F. Dickson next to him, and seventeen-year-old Douglas Barrett in the back. Dickson and Barrett were also African-American, as were many of Martorano's other victims.

Way to go, Johnny! Kill 'em all and let God sort 'em out, I always say. Women, teenagers – it's all good, am I right, *compadre*? Fuck it – walk it off.

And *this* is who the FBI made the second-best rat deal of all time (second only to Sammy Bull's). Johnny only served about eight months for each murder, or a total of eight years of his original twelve-year sentence. That's how bad the feds wanted Whitey Bulger.

Oh, and remember my earlier revelation about the feds making sweetheart deals with snitches? Well, Johnny's deal allowed him to only have to testify against Bulger, Flemmi, and John Connolly. (FYI, Connolly's fellow FBI agents despised him so much for his blustering arrogance, Bulger ass-kissing, and ridiculous Mafia-inspired outfits, that they nicknamed him John Cannoli.) Thus, Martorano was able to protect all his old pals from The Hill.

At trial, Martorano smugly chuckled on the stand at the amazing deal his lawyer had secured for him. Now that's a damn fine attorney. And a goddamn shame for the families of those innocent victims, whom the government merely viewed as collateral damage. What the hell – I mean, they're only *people*, right?

Ironically, in the end, the feds got nothing for their devil's deal with Martorano. The jury at Whitey's 2013 trial was so disgusted with Martorano's indifferent callousness towards his victims and appalling self-righteousness that they didn't believe a word he said. As a result, Whitey wasn't convicted for *any* of the eight murders Martorano tried to pin on him.

Wear a Disguise

Nobody these days wears disguises when they go out on hits. Apparently, it's not considered *de rigueur* to hide your appearance, regardless of the obvious benefits of doing so. I'm sorry, but it seems to me that avoiding having eyewitnesses identify you is vastly preferable than having to later hunt down and kill those very same eyewitnesses.

Accordingly, we should look back to the days of yore when old-school mobsters, to take care of business, dressed in drag (Colombo capo Dominic "Donnie Shacks" Montemarano and Genovese associate Donald "the Greek" Frankos), as priests (LA Family shooter Pat "the Priest" Prieta), and even Hassidic rabbis (Stephen Flemmi and Frank Salemme).

At the very least, you should always wear a wig – is that too much to ask? Doing so certainly served Whitey Bulger well when he gunned down Balloonhead Halloran and his bystander pal, Michael Donahue. Indeed, on that occasion, wearing a wig actually resulted in an innocent person being charged and prosecuted for the brazen double murder.

Specifically, during that May 11, 1982, hit, Whitey wore a brown Afro wig, which made him look a lot like a local hoodlum, Winter Hill associate Jimmy Flynn. And that's exactly whom Halloran mistakenly identified as his killer to the police in his last dying breath. Flynn was quickly arrested and prosecuted, but fortunately was found not guilty.

Don't Farm Out Your Wet Work

If you want a job done right, you better do it yourself – especially if you're given a murder contract. This final note doubles back to my earlier rule about not working with dolts on such assignments.

In 1980, Little Nicky Scarfo wanted to give a receipt to union leader John McCullough. He wanted Raymond "Long John" Martorano (no relation to Johnny in Boston) and Martorano's brother-in-law, Albert Daidone, to do the hit. But instead of doing it themselves, Long John and Albert hired Willard Moran, a low-level drug dealer from South Jersey, to carry out the job. And on December 16th, that's just what Moran did.

Long John really screwed the pooch on that one. Mafia protocol dictates that Martorano should not have outsourced the killing because he was personally given the contract by the godfather himself. Even worse, he shouldn't have gone outside the Family to do so. Instead, he should have simply asked Scarfo to lend him another shooter to help with the job, if necessary. Even worse, Long John delegated the hit to a complete imbecile who was bound to bring heat back on everyone involved in the plot.

And bring heat he did. That same night, Moran the moron celebrated the hit at a dive bar with his equally idiotic pals. They bought round after round of shots, and even had the bartender toss a shot into the sink for the deceased while they all loudly toasted his demise. Unfuckingbelievable.

The barkeep and other patrons who were there that night later testified about Moran's antics, and the one-hit wonder was ultimately convicted of first-degree murder. Sealing Moran's fate was the fact that the van he had rented for the hit was traced directly back to him. In lieu of cooking in Pennsylvania's electric chair, he flipped against Martorano and Daidone, who were also convicted of first-degree murder in 1984. Both were sentenced to life in prison.

Gee whiz, am I the only one who thinks these stooges are exactly like the hilariously bumbling hitmen played by William Hurt and Keanu Reeves in the classic 1990 comedy *I Love You to Death*? Honestly, people this moronic should not be allowed to walk the streets.

Fun Facts!

In 1992, while serving time in federal prison for the 1979 Carmine Galante hit, Bruno married Jimmy the Gent's daughter, Catherine Burke. Indelicato met her while she was visiting Bruno's fellow prisoner, Gotti crewmember John Carneglia (one of Paul Castellano's assassins).

Six years later in 1998 (two years after Burke died in captivity), Bruno was released. He moved in with Catherine in the Howard Beach home she had inherited from The Gent. Bruno thereafter reportedly gained access to the millions of dollars Burke had stashed away from the Lufthansa Heist.

Bruno allegedly squandered most of it gambling and living the good life (the *very* good life, apparently). Easy come, easy go?

Unfortunately for Bruno, *la dolce vita* only lasted about eight years. In February 2006, he was charged with the 2001 murder of Bonanno associate Frank Santoro. Frank had threatened to kidnap one of the sons of Bruno's good friend, then capo Vincent "Vinny Gorgeous" Basciano. Again, Santoro was Mafia Cop Lou Eppolito's cousin. In August 2008, Bruno plead out to lesser charges and was sentenced to twenty years. *Sigh.*

As for Catherine, I wonder how she feels today about the fact that both her father *and* husband were two of the scariest guys in the history of the mob – and two guys who just couldn't stop committing crimes regardless of the Lufthansa millions they were sitting on. Please don't be this stupid, greedy, or crazy!

Hey, did you know that Mickey Rourke was friends with John Gotti Sr. and even showed up at one of his trials so the jury could see them shaking hands in a sympathy ploy? The same goes for actor Anthony Quinn, who played Neil Dellacroce in the 1996 HBO film *Gotti*.

Also, you should know that after Joseph D'Arco flipped, he admitted to the FBI that in early 1990, Gaspipe (through Little Al) had ordered young D'Arco to travel to Hollywood to hunt down Lucchese soldier-turned-rat Anthony DiLapi. On February 4th, Joseph caught DiLapi unawares in his apartment garage and shot him to death. Gaspipe had gotten DiLapi's location from the Mafia Cops, with Burton Kaplan once again acting as intermediary. Even more unawares, however, was the US Attorney's Office, which had given Joseph blanket immunity for all his crimes when he and his father flipped in late September 1991. The feds didn't know at the time that Joseph had committed several contract murders. *Oops.*

Finally, know this: Jimmy Flynn portrayed the Boston judge who sentences Matt Damon's character to jail in the 1997 film *Good Will Hunting*. How's that for irony? Kevin Weeks, who stood as the lookout during the Halloran-Donahue killings, must have been grinning ear-to-ear when he first saw the movie. Even more so when he watched from his usual booth at Southie's now-famous L Street Tavern – the one repeatedly shown in the film – as Damon and Ben Affleck accepted their Academy Award for Best Original Screenplay.

Chapter Eleven – How to Properly Dispose of Dead People

"No body, no crime." – Roy DeMeo

On second thought, I'm thinking *this* chapter might get me into the most trouble. I can practically hear the Bible-thumping rabble screaming, "For the love of sweet baby Jesus in his little holy baby manger, why oh why on God's green Earth would you tell people how to dispose of corpses?! You are a horrible person who will burn for all eternity in the Hellfires of damnation!"

Um, I can't really dispute any of that. (A brief pause here while I spit on myself three times – *ptu, ptu, ptu*!) For all those whom I've offended, I apologize wholeheartedly, unequivocally, and without reservation. Jimmy the Weasel would simply shrug and say, "Whaddayagonna do – it's just one o' dem t'ings."

So let's chop it up for reals. It is *always* a good idea to get rid of your murder victims' carcasses in order to avoid unpleasant legal complications. If there's no body, the police will rarely make a concerted effort to find the victim. With a little luck, they may even believe he took it on the lam. And let's face it – cops aren't exactly going to break their backs searching for a missing non-celebrity criminal, especially if it's a person of color.

Regardless of his character flaws, Whitey was no dunskie – he had a high IQ and meticulously planned his crimes. He knew that leaving bodies in the streets was bad for business because it results in headlines, stokes the public's ire, and guarantees investigations. As a result, he changed The Hill's M.O., which previously celebrated dead bodies as trophies of war to be gloated over.

Thus, after murdering rival gangster Paul McGonagle in 1974, Whitey took a no-body, no-case approach to his murder victims (which during his long criminal career easily numbered above forty). He simply made them *poof!* disappear, mostly through burials; or as he liked to say, "putting 'em into the ground." That way, no one else would ever know for sure the victim was actually dead. This decreased the likelihood of an investigation, or more than a cursory one if indeed one commenced.

Again, with a little luck, the coppers would simply assume the victim was in the wind, fleeing some crime or beef as crooks often do. It also lessened the chances of the victim's more violent friends and family members from seeking retribution.

But I know what you're thinking: "Roman, I *create* the bodies – I don't *erase* the bodies!" Well, it's time to step up your game, killas. So put on your thinking caps and pay close attention – there'll be a pop quiz on this later.

Doin' the Houdini

One of the best ways to dispose of your corpse is to, uh, turn one large piece into six smaller pieces – four limbs, a head, and a torso, to be exact. Use a bone saw! You then dispose of those pieces in a place where they will never be found. Like the old Fountain Avenue dump by the Belt Parkway. Bad news: the dump is no longer there – but there are plenty more dumps and landfills in the five boroughs, so no worries, mate.

This is where Roy DeMeo and his crew scattered the remains of several hundred unfortunate souls amidst seven thousand tons of refuse. When the task force investigating Roy found out he had done so, they didn't even bother searching for body parts due to the virtual impossibility of finding these needles in the haystack, or of identifying the victims from mere bones (since no DNA technology existed back then).

Admittedly, very few people have the stomach for this kinda thing. However, by disappearing your victims like this, your chances of detection are greatly diminished. It was the favorite method of Roy DeMeo, Tommy Karate, Jimmy Coonan, and Eddie "the Butcher" Cummiskey.

Tommy Karate had an effective, if slightly distasteful, methodology. He'd strip and toss the body into the tub, then run a hot shower so the water would wash away the blood. Meanwhile, he would strip off his own clothes, fold them neatly aside, then climb into the tub.

He would dismember the victim into six parts, separating the head and limbs. Two of his associates would haul in a huge, empty trunk. Pitera would toss in the blood-drained body parts, finish showering himself, then step out and dry off. He would always ensure there was no residual blood nor gore in the tub before he shut off the water.

After dressing, Pitera and his associates would haul the trunk out to Tommy K's car and toss it into the trunk. They would then drive out in darkness to his favorite burial ground, the William T. Davis Wildlife Refuge on Staten Island. This federal-government-protected area was completely devoid of people at night (aside from other *Mafiosi* burying their own victims).

Using a flashlight, Tommy would guide his associates deep into the bird sanctuary, then direct them to dig a deep hole with shovels. Finally, they would shove the trunk into the grave, cover it with dirt, leaves, and twigs, then happily skip back to their car.

This was virtually the same process as the infamous Gemini Method, perfected by Roy DeMeo and his Murder Machine. It worked like this: the victim would enter the Gemini Lounge, expecting to do business with Roy or one of his minions. After entering, Henry Borelli or one of the Gemini Twins (Anthony Senter or Joey Testa) would approach with a big smile and handshake. Then, suddenly, Roy himself would glide out of the darkness like Bela Lugosi and shoot the unwary victim in the head.

But before the cadaver could hit the ground, Roy's quasi-adopted son Chris Rosenberg would pounce, wearing only silk underwear and gold chains so as not to stain his designer threads. He'd immediately stab the vic in the heart multiple times to slow the bleeding. At the same time, Roy or another of his ghouls would wrap the stiff's head in a thick towel to staunch further bleeding.

The crew would then wrap the body in a heavy tarp, drag it into a nearby bathroom, then hang the corpse upside down in the shower, slit the throat, and allow sufficient time (forty-five to ninety minutes) to allow all the blood to drain. Meanwhile, they'd send out for pizza, pasta, or hot dogs (seriously!). This was such a common occurrence that mobsters would often enter the Gemini and see corpses hanging from the shower if the door was left open.

Roy, a former butcher's apprentice, would then dismember the corpse, wrap the six pieces in large trash bags, then have his henchmen discard the remains in the Fountain Avenue dump. Easy peasy. Just remember that when you "Houdini" or "disassemble" someone (phrases The Westies popularized), there will be quite a bit of blood, so please take all necessary precautions.

****

Sometimes even the mere *threat* of dismemberment can bring positive results for your budding criminal enterprise. In the early '90s, Gallo and Marco believed that one of their crew, Victor C, had ratted them out to the Orange County Sheriff's Department's organized crime unit. The deputies had raided one of their safe deposit boxes at an Irvine bank and seized $80,000 in cash.

So when Victor walked into their house in Irvine, they jumped him, bound him with duct tape, and dragged him into the guest bathroom. Victor's eyes almost popped out of his head when he saw that the carpet was covered in plastic. He certainly didn't need to see the assortment of serrated knives, electric turkey carvers, and rusty hacksaws on the sink to realize what they had in mind. But thanks to the sight of this cutlery, it didn't take long to get the truth from Victor. He was actually innocent: it was another guy in their crew, Darren, who had ratted them out. Gallo took care of *him* post-haste. By mere happenstance, that occurred on the very hour Victor turned twenty-one.

Cue Altered Images' "Happy Birthday."

In any event, Victor miraculously bounded out of the house, hands and feet still duct taped, after Marco paused to check out his hair in the bathroom mirror. He and Gallo were forced to tackle Victor outside in broad daylight in front of stunned neighbors. As they duct taped Victor's mouth and dragged him back into the house, they smiled and called out to the onlookers, "Nothing to worry about, folks – just a fraternity prank!" The relieved citizens went back to their mundane lives. And yes, Victor is still alive and well, thank you very much.

****

Uber is super-handy for transferring body parts across town. They'll pick up packages from you and deliver them wherever you want for the same price as a regular ride-share. Please ensure that your pieces are thoroughly drained of bodily fluids, then shrink wrap them in plastic using a foodsaver machine from Costco. Finally, wrap everything in heavy butcher paper, seal them into FedEx boxes, and gussy them up like birthday presents. *Voila!*

Marco used to use that same Costco machine to vacuum seal scores of pounds of high-grade BC bud that he would smuggle in from Vancouver, Canada, into Seattle, and from there to Miami. This was, of course, before 9-11 when you could hand your suitcases filled with drugs, cash, or body parts to baggage handlers at the ticket counter. You could also buy last-minute, one-way tickets in cash without having to show ID. However, vacuum sealing your items absolutely guarantees no human will be able to smell the contents.

****

When doing the slice n' dice, always use a razor-sharp fillet knife to remove all tattoos, noticeable scars, and birthmarks from your homie's body parts on the off-chance someone finds one of his pieces. One of The Westies' victims, Mafia super-shylock Charles "Ruby" Stein, was identified by a medical examiner when his torso washed ashore on Brooklyn's Rockaway Beach in 1977. Stein had recently undergone open-heart surgery.

Similarly, before you separate your man's head from his torso, kindly remove all his teeth with dental extractors or serrated-edge pliers to avoid identification through dental records if his pumpkin surfaces. Failing that, smash the poor bastard's teeth to smithereens with a ballpeen hammer.

Further, please consider removing your guy's genitalia, lest he be identified by his spouse, lover, or favorite sex worker. It's not like he's going to be needing his twig and berries for anything anyways. And whatever you do, for God's sakes, do not keep the head (or *any* body parts) in your freezer to show off to your friends during cocktail parties. That's just downright reckless, not to mention creepy. If you do find yourself keeping your victim's trophies (like Gotti crewmember Charles Carneglia and serial killer Tommy Karate), then you should see a qualified mental health professional.

Putting 'Em Six Feet Under

Marco, you have the floor, *monsieur*.

> I'm not a big fan of burying people. First of all, you have to perform hours of manual labor, something I hate even more than working a real job, which I've had to do to get my fucking

P.O. off my back. Dude, I can't believe people actually do that shit all day *every day*! It, like, takes up most of your time. Second, you always have to worry about the dead dude's body being discovered. Those fucking cadaver dogs can smell a body ten feet deep. Or one of the other diggers could rat you out down the line.

This is precisely what happened to Tommy Karate, who's now doing life, having miraculously escaped the death penalty.

As Marco indicates, a major drawback of burying someone is the amount of time it takes to dig a hole deep enough to prevent animals from digging up the corpse, or from some hikers stumbling across it. Every minute you're out there shoveling dirt is going to be terrifying. This means that even the tiniest sound can spook the stuffing out of you so badly, you could blow the entire caper.

This is what went down when Tony Spilotro and his younger brother and criminal sidekick Michael were buried in an Indiana cornfield in 1986. They had been beaten and strangled to death in a suburban Chicago basement sixty miles away by a dozen of their friends, including Nicky Breeze, who testified in 2007 that Tony was refused a final request to say a prayer. For the record, their murders did not go down as depicted in *Casino*. Nor was Frank Cullotta present at the time, as also depicted therein. (Hey, I wonder why Frankie Breeze wasn't in on the hit since he was then The Outfit's top hitter.)

In early June 1986, The Outfit brass tasked Giovanni "Big John" Fecarotta, one of the Spilotro brothers' killers, with a very important mission: to bury deep Tony and Michael in north Indiana. To assist him, Fecarotta handpicked a crack team of imbeciles consisting of Albert "Caesar" Tocco, Dominick "Tootsie" Palermo, Albert "Chickie" Roverio, and Nicholas "Jumbo" Guzzino. The F-Team loaded the two unsightly stiffs into a work van and drove off.

It was just after midnight when our merry band arrived at an isolated cornfield. They parked their van, spilled out like circus clowns, and began to dig a single grave big enough to hold both Spilotros. After digging only a few feet, they heard a car pull up nearby. Thinking it was Five-O, they collectively shat their silk undies and blindly scattered. Turns out it was just teenagers looking to steal marijuana plants from a nearby field. Tootsie, Chickie, and Jumbo (they even *sound* like clowns!) returned to the gravesite. Meanwhile, Tocco wandered around, hopelessly lost in the vast cornfield with no idea how to get back to the macabre party. Had he been an astronomy aficionado, he could have simply followed the North Star.

No big whoop 'cause it was pretty much over anyways. Despite realizing there was no law enforcement threat, the inane clown posse was still rattled so they only dug another foot before tossing in the two bodies. After splashing a few inches of dirt over them, they clambered back into the van, leaving poor Tocco to find his own way back.

And unfortunately, that's just what he did. He managed to find the local highway, then marched his blood-drenched hide several miles up the interstate to a roadside emergency phone booth. He called his sleeping wife, Betty, and had her drive all the way out to pick him up. Seriously, where *does* the mob find these geniuses?

Tocco was so pissed off at the debacle, and particularly about his friends bailing on him, that during the entire drive home he spilled the beans to his wife. He talked about the murders, the participants, and other juicy details about the subsequent comedy of errors. Betty would eventually testify against her husband about all of this – the first wife ever to do so in *Cosa Nostra* history. So much for spousal immunity. I can't really blame her since Albert was such a degenerate crook, he even cheated when playing Tic-Tac-Toe *against his own daughter.* So says Betty.

Less than two weeks later, on June 23, 1986, a farmer noticed a patch of turned-over dirt at the edge of his cornfield. Thinking it was hastily-buried poached game, he called the Indiana Game Wildlife Agency. The GWA sent out a biologist who immediately discovered the decomposing bodies, which were clad only in underwear. He, in turn, called the local sheriff's department, which dispatched a couple deputies, who then called the FBI office in Chicago.

The stiffs' dental records scored a match. (Remember what I told you about removing teeth?) Ironically, it was Tony and Michael's own brother, Dr. Pasquale "Pat" Spilotro, a highly regarded local dentist (and law-abiding citizen unfairly maligned by the feds), who identified them through their x-rays.

On September 6, 1986 (three months after the bodies were unearthed), Big John Fecarotta was shot to death by Nicky Breeze Calabrese outside a bingo parlor in the Windy City. Again, it was the physical evidence tying Nicky to this murder that led to him flipping against his own brother, Frankie Breeze, as well as the rest of The Outfit in the now-famous Family Secrets trial. The defendants were convicted of Fecarotta's murder, the Spilotro brothers' deaths, as well as fifteen other killings, thanks to the combined testimony of Nicky Breeze and his nephew, Frankie Junior. So, ironically, one could say that Tony Spilotro had reached out from the grave to exact his posthumous revenge against the men who had executed him and his brother.

Things didn't fare much better for Albert Tocco, who fled to Greece to escape RICO charges in 1988. The FBI lured him out of hiding by using his own son as bait. Trusting Tocco was extradited home, convicted, and sentenced in 1990 to over two hundred years in prison, where he died sixteen years later.

In 1991, his compatriot Dominick "Tootsie" Palermo was convicted of extorting protection money from northwest Indiana bookmakers. Alas, he, too, croaked in the joint fifteen years later in 2006 (the same year the angels flew away with Tocco).

Not sure what happened to Albert "Chickie" Roverio or Nicholas "Jumbo" Guzzino. I heard they got hired as trapeze artists for Cirque Du Soleil in Vegas.

Speaking of Dr. Pat Spilotro, it took him twenty years to avenge his brothers' murders. It must have been a bittersweet experience since it entailed working closely with the federal government, an entity he undoubtedly despised.

In the early '80s, the IRS began investigating the good dentist for alleged criminal and civil violations. In 1986, the same year as his younger siblings' killings, Pat was indicted in the Northern District of Illinois for two counts of filing false tax returns. He had allegedly failed to report miniscule amounts of interest on savings accounts held in the names of his *twelve* kids. But for his fraternal relationship with Tony the Enforcer, Dr. Pat would never have been investigated, charged, or prosecuted for this bullshit. Bill Roemer agrees.

Thank Zeus, Dr. Spilotro was acquitted of all charges in November 1986 by a Chicago jury. Over a period of five years, the Department of Justice had assigned half a dozen IRS agents, FBI agents, and prosecutors to bring down Dr. Pat. The cost to American taxpayers was in the millions.

Bottom Line: If the G can't get you, my budding buttons, they'll go after your family – even if they're completely innocent. The United States Department of Justice can be a petty, vindictive leviathan.

Fortunately for the feds, Dr. Pat wasn't as spiteful as they were. Two decades after shelling out God only knows how much money to defend himself against the bogus tax case, he helped the FBI nab Outfit Godfather Joey Lombardo. It was common knowledge that Joey had been intimately involved in the squashing of Tony the Ant – a fact that did not escape the wily dentist. An abscessed tooth presented an opportunity to finally even the old score.

As of January 2006, Joey the Clown had been on the run for nine months from the Family Secrets RICO indictment of The Outfit brass. But that month, Joey made a secret appointment to have his tooth treated by Dr. Spilotro in his suburban Park Ridge office. Amazingly, for the last twenty years, Dr. Pat had continued to treat Chicago mobsters in the hopes of gleaning the names of the perpetrators. I wonder if he charged them.

Anyways, Dr. Pat clandestinely treated Lombardo for the tooth (after hours, of course), then made a second appointment to repair The Clown's bridge. As he testified at the 2007 Family Secrets trial, while treating Lombardo again, Spilotro pressed him for details about his brothers' murders. "He said, 'Doc, you get an order, you follow that order. If you don't follow the order, you go too.'"

Thanks in large part to Pasquale's testimony, Lombardo and fellow Outfit *padrino* James Marcello were convicted and sentenced to life in 2009.

Anyways, make damn sure you pre-dig your hole several days before you clip your man, as this will expedite the actual burial process. Then carefully cover it up (but *not* fill it in) in such a way that you'll be able to immediately tell if someone's disturbed it. I suggest leaving a $50 bill on top, held in place by a rock. Then, on the day of your magic act, come by, and if it's still there, you're good to go.

Barring that, in order to save back strain and blisters, follow San Diego gangster Frank "Bomp" Bompensiero's lead. His shtick was to convince the victim they were going to do a murder together but needed to dig the hole first. Bomp would then bring his associate out to the woods and have the poor bastard dig the hole by himself, claiming a bad back. Then Bomp would have this brainiac drop down into the hole to see if it was deep enough.

"How's this, Bomp?" the clueless sap would ask as he stood in the hole.

"Just fine," Bomp would bark, then – BOOM! BOOM! – blast him twice with a 12-gauge shotgun. Bomp would laugh his ass off whenever he relayed these stories to Jimmy the Weasel over frosty brews and cigars.

Next, walk the route to your predetermined (and hopefully pre-dug) grave at least once or twice at night to ensure you know how to get there. You don't want to be stumbling around in the dark with all that dead weight, especially if rigor mortis sets in. The last thing you want is a hernia from lugging a dead body.

Also, always douse your stiff with plenty of quicklime or lye to dissolve it. Make sure it's not the kind of lime that's used in fertilizer as that will create the opposite intended effect and actually preserve the body. This is what happened to Arthur "Bucky" Barrett.

In August 1983, Whitey Bulger and Steve Flemmi murdered him for failing to kick up from a major bank heist three years earlier. Afterwards, they buried him in the basement of a house owned by Winter Hill associate Pat Nee's brother, Michael (a civilian who knew nothing about the killings or burials). They nicknamed the house the Haunty because of several other bodies they buried there, including Flemmi's twenty-six-year-old girlfriend, Debra Davis.

Several years later, on Halloween no less, 1985, Whitey and Stevie had Kevin Weeks and (allegedly) Pat Nee dig up Bucky and the others because the house was going to be sold. When he did, Weeks discovered that the body had been mummified – i.e. perfectly preserved.

As you can imagine, this was a nauseating endeavor since the bodies were all in various states of advanced decay. One of the victim's heads popped off in Weeks' hands as he was trying to move the corpse. He puked his guts out.

Nasty! Stupid is as stupid does, people. Don't let this happen to you.

Finally, another major drawback of planting your stiff in terra firma is the fact that even if you have to disinter them for some reason, you're certain to leave behind tiny bits of bone that will lead to their identification through DNA analysis. Look, I'm not trying to rain on your homicidal parade but someone has to lay out the realities of the murder game. If it was easy, everyone would do it.

By the way, just in case you weren't one hundred percent convinced that Whitey and Stevie were total assholes, please note that within a decade of Bucky Barrett's disappearance, both of his sons chose death by suicide on different occasions – by jumping in front of the same speeding train. Talk about collateral damage. Thanks again, FBI! I sure hope all that carnage, all those murders, suicides, and destroyed families were worth Whitey and Stevie ratting out boss Jerry Angiulo.

Take 'Em for a Cruise

Dumping your subject's carcass in the water is my second-favorite disposal method. You take a boat out on the ocean and simply dump him – the blood draining from his wounds will turn him into instant fish food. Try to go out past the three-mile international water line, if possible, for jurisdictional purposes. It's just good seahorse sense. You can even make a day out of it – bring a big cooler stuffed with cold beer and tasty snacks, maybe even go fishing.

The best part about this method is that you can bring your victim along while he's still breathing. Hell, you might just be giving him the best day of his soon-to-be short-ass life, what with the fishing and all. Then, after you finally get bored, just as he's reeling in a big bass, simply put down your Corona Light and – BAM! – plug him and chuck him. It's easy enough to wash away all the blood, gore, skull fragments, and brain matter with a hose.

Keep this in mind, however: unless you sufficiently weigh down your buddy, the bodily gasses will inflate the stomach, lungs, and other internal organs, and cause him to rise to the surface. He might even wash ashore, and next thing you know you have a *Weekend at Bernie's* situation on your hands.

No siree, Bob, you want that sumbitch to stay put in Davy Jones' locker. The only way to do that is to slice 'im open from cock to nock, and preferably the chest cavity as well. Use a clavicle spreader for the latter, which you can buy at any medical supply store in the surgical tools department. That will not only prevent those annoying bodily gasses from forming, but will also facilitate a chum-feeding frenzy from whatever fish come by to feast on your friend. You might even get lucky and attract some cool sharks. No selfies, please!

Yes, I am painfully aware of how disgusting all of this is. But the alternative – *not* slicing 'n' dicing your man – is simply unacceptable. One hundred percent guaranteed, he's going to pop back up like a bad penny.

And so it went with John "Handsome Johnny" Roselli on August 7, 1976, when the fifty-five-gallon oil drum his body had been stuffed into bobbed to the surface in Florida's Biscayne Bay. That occurred even though heavy chains had been wrapped around the drum. The FBI was able to identify him from a partial fingerprint. His murder remains unsolved to this day and caused his *compare* Jimmy the Weasel endless heartache and sorrow.

The same thing happened in 1977 when Jimmy Coonan and Gambino soldier Edward "Danny" Grillo murdered Ruby Stein. The duo ventilated the shylock so Coonan could take over his book of debts and Grillo could wipe out his own considerable loans to Stein. Even though they chopped him up, placed him into numerous garbage bags, and dumped him in New York's East River, his torso washed ashore. This created a splitting migraine for Coonan because Stein was a major loanshark for the Gambinos. Even Coonan admitted he had screwed up by not splitting open Ruby's prodigious belly before taking him for a dip.

Still, not for nothing, but the currents around Ward's Island in New York (particularly in the area known as Hell Gate) are quite strong and will wash the various pieces of your *amici* down the East River and out to the Atlantic.

A final note: one murderer I interviewed told me that when he lived in Texas near the Gulf of Mexico, he would wrap his victims' corpses in heavy chains to weigh them down, and then wrap those "packages," as he called them, with chicken wire. That way, the fish could nibble the victims down to the bones after he dumped the packages into the Gulf.

Who's up for Red Lobster?

Dissolve Your Buddies in Acid

This is an exceptionally effective method of disappearing your vics. Charles Carneglia was the younger brother of John Carneglia, one of John Gotti's most trusted shooters and a made man with the Gambinos. Charles, however, was not respected at all as he was mentally disturbed, a diehard alcoholic, and a hopeless drug fiend. In fact, the only reason he finally got made (thirteen years after his brother John got *his* button) was because of his only talent – disposing of the Gambinos' victims by submerging them in barrels of corrosive acid. This is how Gotti disappeared John Favara, the neighbor who accidentally killed Gotti's twelve-year-old son, Frank, in March 1980, after Frank darted out into the street on a mini-bike.

Anyhoo, Carneglia would put the bodies (which were typically *not* intact) into steel barrels. After a few days or even a week, he would dump the barrels into the ocean or simply pour their contents into a sewer drain after the bodies had turned to slush. The Mafia is not exactly an eco-friendly organization, I'm sorry to say. C'mon, guys – we can do better!

I don't recommend this method, however, as nowadays buying the type of chemicals you'll need (sodium hydroxide or potassium hydroxide), particularly in the necessary quantity, will draw the attention of the Department of Homeland Security. But just so you know, chemical supply companies and metal plating companies stock these types of chemicals. And you can still buy this stuff without much hassle in Eastern Europe and South America, so if you can figure out how to smuggle them back to the States, you're golden. Then you'll be the envy of all your pals!

Cremation (My Personal Favorite)

If you plan on doing the whack-whack on more than a handful of people during your career in organized crime, you should buy a funeral parlor or some other business that requires a crematorium or furnace. Veterinarians often have their own crematoriums to dispose of dogs they put down – so maybe get one of those guys on your payroll. That way you can simply shove in your cold bodies and be done with them – no mess, no fuss.

Afterwards, you'll want to scatter the ashes, of course. This is precisely what one mid-twentieth century gangster did in Newark, New Jersey. I am referring to Richie "the Boot" Boiardo, who had prudently installed a crematorium in the back of his mansion. Many an enemy found themselves toasting inside it like a wood-fired pizza in a brick oven.

If you lack the necessary wherewithal and commitment to become a mortician, then I suggest you follow the advice of John "the Nodfather" Franzese. Sonny, a.k.a. The Rock, was once caught on a wire in the mid oughts bragging about having bagged dozens of bodies. On the same FBI tape, he can be heard discussing his favorite method of corpse disposal: chop up the body into small parts inside a plastic kiddie pool, then microwave them until they become dry enough to grind up in a commercial-grade garbage disposal. Rinse thoroughly when done. Kool Moe Dee? Or you can always use a burn barrel – that's a fifty-five-gallon drum into which you stuff your pal and douse with gasoline.

If You're Gonna Do It, Do It Right

I'll end this chapter on a cautionary note. As important as it is to properly bump off your man (i.e., actually flatlining him *and* getting away with it), it is equally imperative that you competently dispose of his mortal remains. Because if you don't, you may very well earn yourself a spot right next to him in the burial pit. Case in point: the 1984 murder of the Bonanno Family's Sicilian heroin heavyweight, Cesare "the Tall Guy" Bonventre.

Bonventre was a capo with a fearsome reputation for violence (with twenty-five notches on his belt), and was the leader of the Sicilian faction of the Bonannos – all were killers *and* major heroin dealers. And so rival skipper Big Joe Massino naturally came to view him as a threat. Massino was also miffed at Bonventre for not kicking in to Massino's escape fund while he was on the lam in the Pocono Mountains. This forced Big Joe to pay for his own Colgate and Charmin.

On April 16th, Bonanno associates Salvatore "Good Lookin' Sal" Vitale and Louis "Louie HaHa" Attanasio Jr. – nicknamed for his habit of bursting into laughter whenever he heard about someone's murder – picked up Bonventre. They were tasked with bringing him to a meeting with briefly-out-of-prison-but-otherwise-total-loser-of-a-boss Philip "Rusty" Rastelli at a glue factory in Wallington, New Jersey. As Vitale drove the car into the factory, Attanasio – BANG! BANG! – fired into Bonventre's skull. Vitale later got his wings for doing this hit.

Bonventre miraculously survived ... for a few more seconds, and rolled out of the car after briefly struggling with his two killers. Attanasio – BANG! BANG! – plugged him twice more, finishing the job. Bonventre's corpse was heaved into the trunk of the car. Associate Gabriel Infanti was given explicit instructions to make the body disappear forever.

One week later, Infanti met with Vitale and told him he had chopped up the body and dumped the pieces where they would never, ever be found. "Never, ever" lasted about one more week.

On April 17, 1984, the feds stumbled across three fifty-five-gallon drums in a warehouse in Garfield, New Jersey, while searching for stolen goods. They made the grisly discovery of what turned out to be Bonventre's disassembled remains.

Several days later, Infanti met again with Vitale, blamed the screw up on another underling, and promised to delete him. That kind of pass-the-buck B.S. might fly in a big corporation but it doesn't cut the mustard in the Mafia. As a result of his gross incompetence and deceit, Infanti was murdered by Bonanno soldiers Louis Restivo, Good Lookin' Sal, and none other than Tommy Karate himself.

Lessons to Be Learned

If you insist on burying your frenemies, I suggest planting them in state wildlife sanctuaries like the ones on Staten Island. The federal government protects them from development and limits the number of people who can visit them, as well as the areas people are allowed to hike therein. This drastically reduces the chances of someone stumbling upon you while you're digging your hole. The last thing you want to do is dig another hole. As Tony Spilotro in *Casino* warns, "You could be out there all fucking night."

This way, you never have to worry about going back to dig up a body if some a-hole decides to build a condo complex on your personal burial ground. Remember that famous scene in *Goodfellas* when they have to dig up William "Billy Batts" Bentvena, a.k.a. William Devino? "Here's an arm, here's a leg, here's a wing!" That'll give you the heebie jeebies big time.

Fun Facts!

On June 12, 1970, as depicted in *Goodfellas*, Tommy D and Jimmy the Gent murdered Billy Batts in Henry Hill's bar, The Suite. The whackadoodle went down only three days after Bentvena was released from prison after doing six years on a dope trafficking conviction. Billy Batts, who got badged in 1961, was a protégé of Charley Wagons Fatico and close friend of John Gotti Sr.

The film also accurately shows Tommy and Jimmy killing Billy following the "get your shinebox" insult. However, this was merely a pretense – Burke had already planned on murdering him since he had taken over Batts' shylock book while he was in prison and had no interest in giving it back.

Also, after exhuming Billy Batts' half-decomposed corpse from its Connecticut grave, the fellas drove it in Henry's Pontiac to a New Jersey junkyard where it was crushed in a mechanical compactor. As the sole living witness to the murder and excavation, Henry's word was not enough to justify a murder prosecution against Burke.

I'm certain there was a major sit down between the Gambinos and Paul Vario over Batts' mysterious disappearance. But Vario never once lost a sit down due to his powerful status within the Lucchese *borgata*. And so, because the Gambinos couldn't actually prove Jimmy did it, he got a pass. Tommy D's penance for the murder would have to wait another eight and a half years.

Hey, did you know Whitey's disgraced younger brother, former Massachusetts state senator Billy Bulger, lived next door to the Haunty when each of these murders occurred and, incredibly, reportedly, still lives there today.

Chapter Twelve – How Not to Get Busted

"I thought it would never end." – Nick "the Crow" Caramandi

Now I know y'all are chompin' at the bit ta git to the makin' money part but safety comes first. Before we start delving into various types of crime, my first priority is keeping you baby vipers out of the pokie. Now I don't mean to sound condescending or disrespectful 'cause I got nothing but love for youse, but let's face it – my mini-dobie has taken dumps with higher IQs than your average criminal. So it's my job to help you avoid the common mistakes these dimwits make, because the longer you're free, the more you earn. So I'm sorry if I've offended your delicate sensibilities or ruffled your silky feathers. Let's hug it out.

See, most wiseguys live only for the moment and never think about their future. My friends, that's *all* you should be thinking about, *capisce*? Don't you want to emulate Marco and retire someday to a country where they only speak Portuguese? Sure, the HIV rate there is a bit higher than he'd prefer, and the street urchins will literally chop your hand off to get to your Rolex, but the beaches are awesome!

Cue Stan Getz's "The Girl From Ipanema."

Keep Your Big Trap Shut

My God, how many times do I have to drill this through your thick skulls?!! Never, *ever* talk out of school, people. I know how much you're dying to brag to your loser friends about all the scores you've pulled down, the bodies you've buried, and the women you've conquered, but *just don't do it*.

Most mobsters suffer from what I diagnose to be a compensatory façade. They attempt to overcompensate for their glaring insecurities and profound self-loathing by boasting about their criminal prowess and penis girth. Maybe see someone about that? But please, if you trust in your Uncle Roman, in no time at all, you'll have *other people* doing all your bragging for you. And that's when you've made it, baby. Let *others* sing your praises because when you do it yourself, it's downright tacky.

So my number-one rule for staying out of the slammer is to never talk about anything illegal you do with anyone unless it's absolutely necessary, such as when your boss wants a report. Look, you never know if your social club, home, office, car, or what-have-you is bugged, or if your friends are wired up. You should assume that everything you say is being recorded at all times. A little paranoia in that department is a good thing, *okay*?

This is particularly true when it comes to murder, which, as you know, has no statute of limitations. So listen to what our *goombah* Johnny Martorano once said: "If you're gonna kill someone, either do it or shut the fuck up about it. Because the walls have ears." Or as Joey Massino testified at the 2011 trial of Bonanno acting boss Vincent "Vinny Gorgeous" Basciano, "Once a bullet leaves that gun, you never talk about it."

Don't be like John Gotti, who bragged to Crazy Phil Leonetti that he was the one who had Paul Castellano whacked, and then lied to Phil and Nicky Scarfo that The Commission had sanctioned the hit. And so Leonetti testified against him.

****

Now let's take a brief look at what happens when you pound your chest, rattle your saber, and bark at the moon about your spectacular exploits. Once again, we need look no further than our favorite bungling bad guy, John Gotti.

On December 28, 1972, Irish-American gangster James McBratney murdered Carlo Gambino's nephew, Emanuel "Manny" Gambino, after a botched kidnapping. McBratney did so even though Carlo had already paid $100,000 for his nephew's release. (However, other wiseguys claimed the godfather refused to pay the ransom because doing so would have endangered all the other members of his *famiglia* – and *that's* why young Manny was snuffed.)

Needless to say, Gotti and his men could barely contain their glee when they got the nod from the don himself to exact revenge.

Less than six months later, on May 22, 1973, McBratney was drinking at a really shitty Staten Island bar. In waltzed Gotti, Angelo Ruggiero, and Ralph "Ralphie Wigs" Galione dressed like the gangsters they were: no masks, no nothing. They did, however, flash a badge and handcuffs, and informed McBratney he was under arrest.

Despite his obvious lack of intellectual acumen, McBratney wasn't buying it and ran for the door, all 6'3" and 250-prison-muscled-pounds of him. Gotti and Ruggiero pounced on him like hyenas on a lion, but he somehow managed to shake them off. Then, just as McBratney was tasting sweet daylight, Ralphie Wigs saved the day. He stepped forward and – BAM! BAM! BAM! – blasted McBratney in the head.

Larry, Moe, and Curly then fled the bar and immediately began bragging to anyone and everyone who was interested that they had done the hit. In case you were wondering, this was a textbook sloppy shooting. Carlo Gambino's explicit orders had been to snatch McBratney and bring him back alive to he could be tortured until he gave up the names of his accomplices.

Even worse, eyewitnesses from the bar picked out all three stooges from photo lineups, and Fat Ange was promptly arrested. Ralphie Wigs had nothing to fear since his own crewmates whacked him shortly thereafter. They stuffed his body into the trunk of Sal Polisi's rental car while Sal was obliviously vacationing in Florida on Gotti's dime. What the hell is it with these guys and car trunks? As for Johnny Boy, he was forced to lam it for the next eighteen months. This slapstick routine continued unabated until Gotti bragged to his pal Willie Boy Johnson (the loyal henchman whom Gotti backstabbed) not only about the deed itself, but about his own current whereabouts.

Willie Boy informed the FBI, who immediately arrested Gotti as he sat playing cards in a Mafia social club. That's certainly one of the most ingenious hiding spots I've ever heard of for a lammin' wiseguy – hide in the last place they'd expect, right?

****

Even if you're not bragging but simply discussing business, your loose lips can still sink ships. In the mid '70s, FBI agent John Larson overheard Jimmy Fratianno telling some fellow mobsters at a restaurant near Palm Springs that he wanted "a piece of the porno." The feds wisely deduced from this phrase that Jimmy wanted to shake down pornographers in the LA area.

As a result, in 1977, the FBI set up a sting with a fake porno company called Forex, with several undercover agents pretending to be unconnected bigshots who sold their product in South America. Sure enough, Mike Rizzitello attempted to shake them down, despite warnings from Jimmy the Weasel *and* Anthony Fiato, who both smelled a rat. Consequently, Big Mike went off to do a nickel (five years) in the slam and got a bunch of other LA mobsters into hot water.

Notably, the "tip" on Forex came from long-time secret informant Frank "Bomp" Bompensiero, then an LA Mafia capo based in San Diego. Bomp's own handlers, Special Agents Jack Armstrong and Jack Barron, had Bomp spread the word about Forex even though they knew the mob would whack him as a result.

And that's what transpired on February 10, 1977. Bomp was shot to death by associate Tommy Ricciardi with a silenced .22 handgun while standing in a Mission Beach phone booth, down in San Diego, talking to the new boss of the LA Family, Dominick Brooklier.

Notably, Rizzi's attempted extortion of Forex was described in both Ovid Demaris' *The Last* Mafioso, and *The Animal in Hollywood*. In fact, Mike Rizzi was a close friend of both Fiato and Fratianno. So why are there no substantive mentions of Jimmy the Weasel in Anthony's book and vice versa? Call me, we'll talk about it.

Never Talk on the Phone, in a Car or Anywhere You Regularly Hang Out

"Eventually, everybody gives themselves up over their phones," Henry Hill once said; ironic, considering it was a wiretap on his home phone that brought him down for good in 1980, and led to him flipping. Thus, you should never have a landline in your house, office, or business. With the ubiquity of cell phones, that's not even uncommon these days. Shit, I haven't had a landline in over a decade.

And when you use your cell phone (preferably an untraceable burner), get one with a digital scrambler. Even then, only use it to make an appointment with someone to meet later. And even that brief conversation should always be in code. Never leave voicemail messages.

If you really wanna be super-duper-squeaky-sneaky, use only a series of whistles over the phone like Vincent Gigante, or make animal sounds like Whitey Bulger and Kevin Weeks. For example, Weeks would ribbit like a frog when he wanted to meet Whitey in a certain park that displayed frog sculptures. Hell, indigenous people in the mountains of Mexico have an entire language based on whistling called *Mazateco*.

This may sound crazy and I agree – crazy like a *fox* – but here it is: you and your entire crew should become fluent in sign language. That way you can communicate freely when talking about sensitive stuff, as long as Johnny Law can't see your finger movements. Signing (specifically, in American Sign Language) is surprisingly easy to learn and it'll drive the feds nuts. Recent scholarly research in Sicily identified a village that had developed a secret sign language to outsmart Greek invaders as far back as the fourth century BCE.

You can also try writing things down on paper and then burn the paper when you're done, as recommended by former Special Agent Joseph D. Pistone himself in *Donnie Brasco: Unfinished Business*, wherein he discusses all the stuff he couldn't in his original book as a result of then ongoing investigations.

That same concept applies to using Microsoft Word on a laptop. You and your pals (assuming they can actually read and write) can sit next to each other and type out what you need to discuss. As long as you don't save the draft, *no problema.*

Also, you should never text anything even remotely incriminating, and, again, only in code and only to set up in-person meets. Nor should you ever e-mail each other anything. In fact, there's no need to do so because you and your guys can share the same Gmail account. As long as you all know the password, you can simply leave messages for each other in the DRAFTS folder. That way you never leave a trail as you would even if you deleted your e-mails, and even if you emptied them from your TRASH folder.

Keep in mind that the feds can always scrub your hard drive to find any and all incriminating stuff you've ever saved or e-mailed. If you're gonna play the Game, then you'd better be a chess grandmaster.

Better yet, follow the lead of Canadian mobsters, who are either compatriots of the Sicilian Mafia or the Calabrian 'Ndragheta – the latter arguably being the most powerful Italian crime syndicate in the world, eclipsing even the Naples-based Camorra. By 2012, Canadian *Mafiosi* had ceased using encrypted Blackberries, and began communicating via ultra-secure messaging systems like WhatsApp and Viber. Criminals had also began using the Dark Web to facilitate communications and transactions.

These days, I suggest using disappearing-message aps like Wickr, which leave no digital trails. Or try PGP, a highly secure and private chat service that automatically encrypts all of your messages. Or send carrier pigeons.

And under no circumstances should you ever use social media – anything you write gets saved in the Cloud, whatever the fuck that is. I'm slightly technophobic. In the Mafia, you'll have all the friends (and enemies) you'll ever want so there's absolutely no reason for you to be Tweeting, Facebooking, Snapchatting, or Instagramming.

Finally, you should always have your cell phone locked. The least impregnable are iPhones. And God bless Apple (even if the fuckers pay *zero* US taxes) because they'll tell the G (the US government) to pound sand when it demands that Apple unlock iPhones. Just keep in mind that the feds employ top hackers for such purposes, and their super-geeks are able to hack bad guys' iPhones from time to time.

Bottom Line: Don't get careless, and don't be lazy. Learn from other fools' mistakes because you can't live long enough to make them all yourself.

Keep a Low Profile

Commensurate with staying mum is flying low and avoiding the radar. God knows proper villains love flyin' high, livin' large, and rollin' deep. But take it from me, Kemosabe – it's much more prudent for you to dress down, drive a nondescript car, and live in a modest home.

This is precisely what Tony and Nancy Spilotro did when they first moved from Chicago to Vegas in 1971. They initially kept their heads down, buying a single-story, ranch-style house in a solidly middle-class neighborhood; buying Chevrolet Monte Carlos; and enrolling their son in the local Catholic school, where Nancy joined the PTA. Tony even coached his kid's Little League team. Too bad for Tony (and the rest of Las Vegas) that he didn't stay that way.

Gotti, notably, continued to live in the middle-class neighborhood of Howard Beach in a modest house even after he became boss. Of course, I ascribe this relatively humble abode more to his all-consuming gambling addiction than any desire to be low-pro. After all, this was a guy who traveled around with more *paparazzi* than wiseguys (which is why his enemies could never get close enough to whack him out).

Lessons to Be Learned

Keep those cards close to your vest, baby ballers. Those who need to know will know, and those who don't and try to mess with you will be told to chill out *or else*.

Walk and Talks

The American Mafia, in addition to sit downs, has also perfected the art of the walk and talk. These involve two or three wiseguys walking abreast around the neighborhood, talking shop in *sotto voce*, and covering their mouths to thwart lip readers. I'm all in favor of these, but just be careful 'cause the feds have high-tech bugs they plant in parked cars, as well as long-range parabolic microphones. They can even mic alley walls, which they can remotely activate.

To counter that, I suggest taking Uber or Lyft to a random spot, hopping out, then meeting your pals to do a walk and talk in *that* neighborhood. Better yet, do walk-talks in foreign countries, like Big Joey Massino and Vito Rizzuto, the late leader of the Sicilian *decina* (branch) of the Italian-Canadian Mafia. Or do boat-talks like Gaspipe Casso, where the engine will drown out even the most sensitive wire. Swim-talks (again, no Rolexes) would be my personal fave.

Be Proactive When It Comes to Counter-Surveillance

You should routinely photograph strange cars in your neighborhood, jot down their license-plate numbers, then stake out the local police or sheriff's department to see if any of these cars emerge therefrom. If you lazy-ass, gold-bricking, feather-bedding, lolly-gagging, pud-stroking *jamooks* out there think that would be boring, try picking up trash on the freeways or serving meals to homeless people (it's called community service).

You should also hire a legitimate electronics expert to regularly sweep your home, office, and cars for bugs. I highly recommend SoCal's Joe D., who uses serious NSA-quality, state-of-the-art equipment that even the feds rarely have access to. As an added bonus, Joe also performs polygraph exams on people, which will come in handy if you ever suspect one of your men has betrayed you.

Tony "the Little Guy" Spilotro was the heavyweight champion of counter-surveillance experts. Remember in *Casino* when he opened the infamous Gold Rush, a two-story jewelry store done up in a Wild West motif, located near the Strip? He brought in The Outfit's electronics and bomb-making whiz Ron DeAngelis to sweep the place for bugs (which he regularly flew back to Vegas to do).

DeAngelis also installed a half-dozen scanners with specialized crystals. He placed one for every federal, state, and local law enforcement agency trying to take down Tough Tony. This included the FBI, the Vegas PD, the Clark County Sheriff's Department (before the police and sheriff's departments merged into Metro), the Nevada Gaming Control Board, and even the IRS. Not once did the feds or coppers catch Tony on a wire, or in any other way for that matter. As a result, he enjoyed a stellar fifteen-year run in Sin City.

Never Keep Contraband in Your Own Home

No brainer but worth mentioning all the same: live your life as if you're going to be raided at any moment.

During Junior Gotti's last major bust in 1995, the feds found $348,000 in cash in his basement. They also discovered a list of all the mobsters who had given various amounts of cash to him as wedding gifts for his 1990 nuptials: the fact that Sammy Bull only gave him $7,500 underscores the secret loathing Gravano had for the spoiled shit. Even worse, Baby Huey also kept a list of proposed members for induction in the Family. All of this was used as evidence not only against him, but against many of the people on those lists in subsequent criminal prosecutions.

The entire Mafia gave a collective eyeroll and exasperated groan when the word spread. Gotti Baby was so dense that he intentionally kept the wedding registry with the cash (which he used as an ATM and regularly replenished with ill-gotten gains). This way, if he *was* raided, he'd be able to explain the source of the money. Not sure what he was thinking by keeping the proposed membership list down there. What a freakin' *stunad*.

Now this is stupidity on an almost Shakespearean level (tragedy or comedy – take your pick). This overwhelming evidence of his status in the mob convinced Baby Gotti to take a plea on the day before his trial, thereby admitting to loansharking, illegal gambling, extortion, and income tax evasion. In September 1999, he was sentenced to six years and five months in federal prison and was forced to pay a $750,000 fine. *Ouchie!*

Finally, gangsters always need ready access to cash so always keep guns, drugs, and currency locked in heavy safes that are bolted down in other people's homes (though never keep *dinero* and dope in the same place). These should be guys whose rent you pay and whom you trust. Guys who are total squares – straight-A college students who have nothing to do with the Life. None of them should have any idea what's in the safes, much less how to open them. That way, even if the police raid the dude's house, he can't be forced to open the safe.

Don't Get Emotionally Attached to Your Guns

Guns are like condoms – you should use 'em and chuck 'em, preferably in a place where they'll never be found. (And also, of course, it's better to have them and not need them than vice versa.) You can always get others, perhaps easier than you think. If you have some money in your pocket and you're white or Asian, you can simply go to a gun show and buy a bloody howitzer if you want.

Seriously, back in the day, Gallo would buy entire arsenals at these shows. There, a monster truck aficionado will sell you, say, a semi-automatic assault rifle, then direct you to the front parking lot where his brother Mordecai will sell you the kit to convert it to fully automatic. Then his two cousins in the rear parking lot, Billy Bob Joe and Jebediah, will sell you a suppressor and illegal, armor-piercing ammo. One-stop shopping, baby boy. God bless America and the Second Amendment. *Yee-haw!*

Cue Arthur "Guitar Boogie" Smith's "Dueling Banjos".

But don't even bother going to these events if you're Latino or, God forbid, African-American – in all the years Marco attended these shows with Gallo, he never saw one of either. These good ol' boys don't take too kindly to people of color at "their" events. Fortunately for Marco, those damn conquistadores had raped all his *mestizo* ancestors and that's why he automatically passes for white. Indeed, growing up in the *barrio*, his nickname was *wedo,* Spanish slang for "white boy."

A final note: don't waste your precious time filing down the serial numbers on your weapons – that doesn't work anymore 'cause the boys in the crime lab will easily enough raise those shorn digits with a special acid.

Drive and Park Evasively

Every self-respecting gangster knows how to drive like a fiend, but the extraordinary criminal will spend the time, money, and effort to actually take evasive driving courses. There are a million techniques to shake a tail (the Mafia calls it drycleaning) – whether it's the police or your enemies – and they all work if properly executed.

For example, Gallo was always trying to avoid tails. He would roar his custom smoked-gold ZR-1 passed a hundred MPH on the freeway. He'd then suddenly veer to the shoulder and slam the brakes. If anyone was following, they'd bomb right past him; otherwise they'd blow their cover. He'd also blast the wrong way up one-way streets, kill his lights when driving at night, and fly across four lanes on the freeway to exit before whipping around and heading back onto the freeway in the opposite direction. With sidekick Marco in tow, it was like *The Fast and the Furious* – picture hip, multi-ethnic, muscle-bound gangsters and plenty of snappy dialogue.

You should also drive around a random block several times, stop at green lights, blast through red ones, and even switch cars to dryclean your tails. Illegal U-turns are equally handy. And always be checking your rear-view mirror.

Still, cops are not stupid, especially feds, who will use up to half a dozen cars in tandem, relaying back and forth, dropping off and shooting ahead of you so you don't make them. They're especially good at these techniques when they have a surveillance helicopter. But police birds and spotter planes are easy to shake – all you have to do is drive through any airport where there's restricted airspace. The coppers will have no choice but to drop off, and TSA is never going to give even the feds the right to invade their air space.

That's when you should park, get out, run through a few terminals, and emerge to another waiting car. Which brings me to a related subject: parking. Big indoor malls are the best – dump your ride in the parking structure, zig-zag through the mall using elevators and escalators, dash through a department store or two, then find your second car. The possibilities are endless.

Big city office buildings with rear exits that lead into alleys, for example, are also wonderful escape mechanisms because the cops will rarely have more than just the entrance covered – they simply don't have the manpower. Popping in and out of subway cars is also a nice touch. When in doubt, simply recite the following mantra: *run, Forrest, run*!

By the way, if you are driving around with contraband, or even if you're a little buzzed, always use Waze to avoid cop cars. Also keep in mind that the Man can track you through your cell phone even if it's turned off, so if you don't want to be traced, remember to take out the battery and leave it at your mom's house.

That's pretty much it, gang. Make Papa proud. Oh Christ – and please don't forget to occasionally check for GPS trackers under your car.

Don't Do Stupid Shit

Stupidity as much as sheer laziness gets you canned more than tuna. I mean, let's be frank, shall we? The vast majority of criminals out there should not be criminals. They should be working as *baristas*, stocking shelves at Target, or delivering for Postmates. Take Marco for instance: "If I wasn't so fucking stupid, I'd never have even jaywalked and would have been worth ten times what I am now. But no, I had to be the big man, buying drinks."

Enough about Marco. Let's look at people are who are truly dumb, dumber, and dumberer. There is certainly no shortage of whacky Mafia hijinks for us to peruse. We can start with Nicky Scarfo's underboss Salvatore "Chuckie" Merlino, who was arrested for drunk driving in the mid '80s. He was so shitfaced that he actually tried to bribe the arresting officer with a fake gold Rolex and $400 in cash while he was being booked at the station. Unfortunately, the old Chuckster was caught on videotape and now faced ten years in prison for attempted bribery of a police officer instead of just a few hours in a holding cell.

Chuckie's almost-as-braindead brother Lawrence "Crazy Larry" Merlino was also facing time after getting trashed at a wedding and making terrorist threats (a felony) to a Philadelphia cop (a *huge* felony).

Cue Social Distortion's "Prison Bound."

Similarly, Scarfo's one-time top killer Nicholas "Nick the Blade" Virgilio did three years in the slammer for getting drunk and threatening to kill someone at an Atlantic City casino. Are we seeing a familiar pattern here (aside from the fact that Little Nicky drove all his men to drink)? Try to keep up, please.

FYI, kiddies, at least in California, it's only a crime if you threaten to actually *kill* someone or inflict great bodily injury (GBI). That's why you should always use oblique language when trying to scare someone, preferably movie dialogue like "Boy, I'm gonna rip off yer head and shit down yer neck!"

Or how about Tommy DeSimone, who took off his ski mask long enough to be identified by witnesses during the Lufthansa Heist? Fortunately for Tommy D, Gotti and his boys whacked him before he could be arrested.

Even Joseph Massino, who by all accounts was one of the sharpest mobsters in the Big Apple, caught his first federal case as an up-and-coming soldier when one of his men, Raymond Wean, got pinched after hijacking a semi-truck. Big Joey was driving the spotter car at the time, but instead of driving away from the scene, he returned for some inexplicable reason and was arrested. *D'oh!* Fortunately, Massino was found not guilty at his trial (after convincing the jury that he just happened to be driving by at the time). Still, what a giant pain in the ass and wallet.

And what about Roy DeMeo's cousin, Murder Machine crewmember Joseph "Dracula" Guglielmo? He was busted as the wheelman on a bank job because he was too embarrassed to tell his associates that he didn't know how to drive stick. So when the robbers hightailed it out of the bank with the loot and jumped into the getaway car, Dracula was unable to lurch more than a few feet before it stalled and died.

Top runner-up prize for all-time stupidest pinch goes to Joey D., a connected Boston burglar. For six straight nights, Joey D. conducted surveillance on a huge, single-story furniture store. Finally, on the seventh night, he climbed up to the roof and cut a hole through the main showroom's ceiling. He misjudged his timing, lost his balance, and crashed through the ceiling onto the showroom floor. He was shocked to find himself surrounded by startled shoppers – Joey D. didn't realize the store stayed open extra late on Saturday nights.

But the number-one stupidest bust, which resulted in an eight-year prison sentence and an end to his good times, goes

UNDERWORLD | 217

to one of my favorite not-always-so-wise wiseguys, Colombo associate Crazy Sal Polisi. (Polisi's truly the horniest gangster in Mafia history – he'd sometimes get six hummers a day from six different sex workers!) As "Sallie *Ubatz*" explains in his autobiography, *The Sinatra Club*, one of the prosecution's key pieces of evidence in his bank robbery case was a surveillance-camera photo of him from the Franklin National Bank.

The image showed the robber wearing a fake wig, a fake mustache, and a white, Damon-knit turtleneck sweater. Polisi's lawyer Mike Coiro persuasively argued that the disguise prevented a reliable identification of the robber. He also argued that the only eyewitness was the head teller, who was so freaked out that she literally pissed herself during the robbery.

But suddenly the prosecutor leapt to his feet, pointed to Sal at the defense table, and yelled, "Look! He's wearing the exact same sweater as shown in the surveillance photo!"

Sure enough, being the genius he was, Polisi was wearing that very same Damon-knit turtleneck in court! It took less than half an hour for the jury to find him guilty, and about the same for the judge to give him an eight-year bid in Lewisburg federal penitentiary.

Th-th-th-that's all, folks! Which, according to John Alite, is what Baby Huey once said to a guy he had just stabbed in a Queens bar as he watched him bleed to death.

Fun Facts!

John Gotti Sr. was clearly the inspiration for Joe Mantegna's "Joey Zaza" character in 1990s deplorable *Godfather III*. Coppola admitted he only took the helm on that unmitigated disaster for the $5 million paycheck. At the time, he hadn't had a hit in years – since 1979's *Apocalypse Now* – and his Napa Valley winery was on the verge of bankruptcy. Looking back now, I wonder if he thinks it was worth it to besmirch his cinematic legacy. FYI, his winery is booming nowadays. Every weekend huge herds of tourists from the Midwest regularly squeeze out of their bus and stampede the place. *Saluté!*

You should never announce to the world that you paint houses (with your victims' blood) or do your own carpentry (dispose of their bodies). These are the terms for special work (contract murders) coined by Frank "the Irishman" Sheeran. The one smart thing that Frank "Frankie Breeze" Calabrese Sr. did when he was coming up was to keep his reputation as a talented contract killer on a need-to-know basis. He preferred that most people think of him merely as a loanshark.

Similarly, Sheeran was such a prolific assassin that he once clipped a guy in Chicago, then immediately flew by private plane to Puerto Rico, where he eliminated two other men that same day. At no time did the pilot look back to see whom he was transporting. Yet ninety-nine percent of the people who knew him thought he was just a big-time Teamsters official, which he was, thanks to his close friends Jimmy Hoffa and Russell Bufalino.

Next, to return the favor for giving them the sit down and walk-talk traditions, the Italian-American Mafia gave their Sicilian brethren the concept of The Commission. In mid October 1957, LCN founding father Joe Bonanno traveled to Palermo (the capital of Sicily) to work out a major international heroin distribution network. The Bonannos have always been notorious junk dealers, and were even booted from The Commission for many years following the twin debacles of Joe Pistone and the 1984 Pizza Connection heroin bust. Ironically, this expulsion enabled Massino to escape the 1986 Commission RICO case, which brought down most of the bosses in the other Families.

To ensure that all the big Sicilian bosses got to wet their beak and to ensure peace between the Mafia clans in dividing the smack spoils, Bonanno suggested that they follow the LCN's example and form their own board of directors. With the help of Lucky Luciano, who had been deported to Sicily eleven years earlier, the Sicilians agreed and formed the *Cupola*, which remains active to this day. Bonanno left *that* out of his autobiography, including his direct involvement in causing a massive heroin epidemic in the United States, resulting in thousands of overdose deaths. Thus, one could argue that Bonanno killed more people than any other mobster in the history of America.

People always thought Gotti Senior was so slick with his jaunty quick-step as he hopped around the neighborhood during walk-talks. That hitch in his step was due to the toe he lost years earlier when he worked on a loading dock. This is one of the reasons you should never get a straight gig – it's downright dangerous. Writer Selwyn Raab, however, claims he lost his toe in a different scenario. . And it's true – for many years Gotti avoided bugs by hoofin' it. However, for the last several years he got downright lazy.

Instead of doing walk-talks, Gotti simply slipped into the Ravenite Social Club's hallway. Or, for more substantive meetings, he used an upstairs apartment owned by Nettie Cirelli, the elderly widow of a Gambino soldier. It took a while for the feds to figure this out because all they initially knew was that the voices of Gotti and his men would occasionally vanish from the hidden bug in the Ravenite's main room. Thus, the monitoring FBI agents (the legendary Bruce Mouw's famed Gambino squad) knew Gotti was leaving the social club for sensitive conversations. But they couldn't figure out where he had gone since he wasn't leaving the building as he had previously done several times a day, often with Sammy Bull holding an umbrella over John and his ego.

As a direct result of this ego, it never occurred to Gotti that there could be stool pigeons in his crew who would give away his two "secret" meeting places. In fact, the FBI had at least *five* of them who regularly hung out at the Ravenite.

Cue UB40's "Rat in the Kitchen."

Johnny Boy had such a gaping mouth that he openly made incriminating remarks to Baby Huey (the derisive nickname everyone in the New York underworld gave Junior) when the younger Gotti later visited him at the United States Penitentiary in Marion, Illinois. Big Papa did so despite the fact that he was well aware that all calls in the visiting areas are monitored and recorded.

Lessons to Be Learned

Gentle people, let's take a page out of Gotti's book and remember that the gangster's greatest enemy is his own complacency and arrogance. Never, ever drop your guard or get lazy. There will be plenty of time to chill when you're in the Bahamas celebrating a big score or, if you're a *gavone*, in the can. Ain't nothin' to do in the big house but catch Zs, lift weights, and polish your bishop.

Also, never underestimate your *own* stupidity. Just look at Paul Vario, who, by the mid '70s, was facing half a dozen federal and state criminal cases (not merely *charges*). Many of these resulted from conversations he had had in a junkyard trailer with a detective pretending to be a corrupt cop. Both the trailer and the detective were wired up. Even more embarrassing were the recordings played in open court of Vario bragging to the detective that he was so cautious about being recorded that he didn't even have a phone in his house. Once again, my precious peeps – stupid is as stupid does.

Shameless Namedrop

In 1990, only days after *Goodfellas* came out, I was hanging out at the old Nicky Blair's bar on Sunset Boulevard – a local Mafia favorite – when I saw Joe Pesci sitting all by himself in a corner booth. Nobody knew who he was yet but I went over and introduced myself, complimenting him on his incendiary performance as "Tommy *DeSimone*". He was surprised that I knew the character's real last name because he only goes by "Tommy" in the film (and is identified as "Tommy DeVito" in the credits).

Next thing you know, he invited me to sit with him and we hung out for a little while, talking in-depth about the real-life mobsters portrayed in the film. Turns out he grew up with tons of wiseguys from back East. I congratulated him on his overnight success. He laughed and said it had only taken him twenty years to make it. What a lovely man.

By the way, did you know that Joe Pesci's Oscar acceptance speech for Best Supporting Actor in *Goodfellas* was the sixth shortest in the Academy's history? All he said was "It's my privilege, thank you." He later admitted that he hadn't prepared a speech because he didn't think he had any chance of winning!

Did you also know that Pesci, who grew up in New Jersey, was close friends with the real Tommy DeVito, a petty crook, as well as with Frankie Valli? Pesci actually introduced DeVito and Valli to singer/songwriter Bob Gaudio – a portentous meeting that resulted in the formation of The Four Seasons. True! This magical alignment launches both the magical Broadway play and the insipid 2014 film *Jersey Boys*, in which Pesci is named and depicted as the matchmaker.

Chapter Thirteen – How to Deal with Rats, Undercovers, and Witnesses

"Three can keep a secret if two are dead." – Hells Angels motto

I know I've said this once or twice before but this time I *really* mean it: *this* chapter is going to jam me up more than any other. No sense pussy footin' around, so let's just dive in headfirst... Without a doubt, the biggest threat facing the Mafia today, aside from gentrification and atrocious films like 2018's *Gotti*, is the proliferation of informants and undercover officers and agents. I'm going to explain how to deal with these insufferably annoying cretins.

FUDGE-THE-FEDS SECRET REVELATION #4

I learned this neat little trick from Gallo, who learned it from Irvine PD undercover narcotics detective Jerry H., who learned it from the FBI. If you suspect someone is an informant or an undercover cop or agent (a UC), simply tell them you want them to provide you a gun so you can murder one of your enemies. That's all there is to it. "Oh Roman," you cry out, "you got some 'splaining to do!" Ah, indeed I do, little piglets.

No law enforcement official – even a long-term, deep-cover agent like Joe Pistone – can *ever* legally provide a weapon that he knows, or even has reason to believe, will be used in a murder (or for *any* reason, for that matter). Doing so would make him an accessory to murder and perhaps even a co-conspirator, even if they don't know the identity of the putative victim.

Aside from landing the po-po in the hoosegow, it would subject his law enforcement department or agency to a wrongful death lawsuit, not to mention decades worth of horrendous publicity. As if the FBI needs more of that, right?

In the entire history of *La Cosa Nostra*, no honest fed or cop has ever *legitimately* provided a firearm to a mobster.

Similarly, if the individual you're suspicious of *is* a rat, if *he* provided you with a murder weapon, the entire case would be blown to smithereens. His FBI handler and the handler's supervisor would both be fired and lose their precious pensions, as well as those cushy post-retirement gigs in the private sector. In fact, it would blow *every* criminal case in the works, past and present, based on that rat's cooperation.

Bottom Line: If the suspect won't cough up a gun, you know he's either a rat, an undercover, a chickenshit, or a criminal who's so pathetic he can't even rustle up one measly gat. In other words, this individual should be *persona non grata*.

Uh, by the way, I'm not saying you should go out and actually *kill* someone if the guy does cough up a gun – that's bad karma. It's just a test, Einstein. Christ, don't take me so fucking literally. Finally, if he does give you a rod, ensure the firing pin hasn't been removed and that it otherwise actually fires real bullets.

FUDGE-THE-FEDS SECRET REVELATION #5

Conversely, assuming your suspect is an informant and not a cop or agent, *you* should provide *him* a firearm for safe keeping. Outlaw motorcycle gang informant, convicted felon, and hardened ex-con George Rowe provides a rather illuminating vignette. One fine day, Big Roy Compton, the P (president) of the Hemet Vagos chapter, produced a Czech-made pistol he had shown Rowe the previous year. Roy told George he would sell it to him on one condition: Rowe could not resell it. Roy was worried it could fall into the wrong hands and somehow come back to bite him in the ass. (No doubt it had been used to shoot someone.)

George promised and the deal was done. Rowe then took it to show his ATF handler, John Carr, who photographed it, sealed it in an evidence bag, then told him he was taking it back to the local ATF office for processing. Special Agent Carr ignored George's protestations that Roy might suspect he was a snitch if he was unable to produce the gun upon request. Carr explained to him that under no circumstances could the ATF allow one of its informants – particularly a violent felon like Rowe – to possess a gun.

See? No fucking way will your informant-suspect be able to keep a firearm on hand for extended periods of time – *especially* if he is a convicted felon. So just do what Big Roy did – give a pistol for the guy to hang onto for you. Then, a couple weeks down the road, ask that fucker to cough it up. If he can't, and comes up with some bullshit excuse, then you'll know where you stand.

Trust me, a gun cannot be provided to a confidential informant due to the DOJ's extremely restrictive guidelines. No law enforcement agency is ever permitted to authorize a CI to participate in any act of violence or even such a *potential* act. Fact is, federal agents cannot legally provide firearms to even their most trusted informants, nor can feds be involved in the sale of a silencer or even ammunition.

FUDGE-THE-FEDS SECRET REVELATION #6

Alternatively, tell the suspect you want him to travel with you to a foreign country to commit a major crime – to pull off a big heist, dope deal, or whatever. It's just a ruse to see if he'll come along. Federal agents (excepting the DEA and CIA) typically only have jurisdiction to operate in the United States.

Thus, it would be extremely difficult and complicated – albeit not impossible – for a FeeBee to get permission to travel to a foreign country on an undercover operation.

Jay Dobyns is an ATF Special Agent who went undercover for two years to infiltrate the Hells Angels in the early oughts. A member of an outlaw motorcycle gang, the Solo Angeles MC (motorcycle club) once directed him to go to Tijuana to meet with the Solos' leader. According to Dobyns, no one short of Jesus Christ himself could give ATF agents permission to leave American soil. Those special agents' jurisdiction did not extend to Mexico or any other foreign country. Indeed, as he points out, foreign American agents conducting clandestine operations in another country without permission could result in an international incident.

As Dobyns clearly indicates, it would be virtually impossible for that person to get permission *overnight* to do so, particularly if the suspect requires that permission from the host country's government. So tell the suspect you want him to fly out with you *tomorrow* to do the heist or whatever. If he claims his passport is outdated, then *check his bleedin' passport*.

This isn't quite as foolproof against informants, who may or may not be authorized to commit certain crimes in foreign countries by the FBI. But most likely they're not, though they may do so anyways to avoid your suspicion. But if they do commit unauthorized crimes, this will jeopardize the case against you.

By the way, bumping off one of your associates in, say, Mexico, drastically increases your chances of getting away with it since Third World countries don't have the same law enforcement resources or technology we do. Besides, if by some fluke you do get busted in such a foreign locale, you can usually bribe your way out of trouble. Just sayin'.

'Course, the downside is that if you can't, you'll end up doing time in a *Midnight Express*-type hellhole. Just read George Anastasia's *Gotti's Rules*, which includes a gut-wrenching account of John Alite's two years in the most horrendous prisons in Brazil (which are apparently the worst in the entire world). If reading that *and* watching the 1992 film *American Me* don't scare you straight, then by God, nothing will. (Maybe this book?)

Anyhoo, you can actually follow through on this out-of-the-country ploy fairly easily if you live in SoCal. Simply drive down with the suspect to the Tijuana border, park in one of those city-sized parking lots on the US side, walk through the turnstile across the border into T.J., take a cab to Avenida Revolución, pop into any pharmacy, buy some anabolic steroids or Valiums or other illegal pharmaceuticals, strap them onto your suspect's body with duct tape, and force him to smuggle it back across the border. If he's cool, he'll do it. If not, let him find his own way home, never to contact you again. Cool? *Cool.*

Finally, don't work with anyone who hasn't spent at least two years in prison (and *puhlease* verify they actually did so). This seems like such an obvious rule to thieve by that I can't even justify calling it a fudge-the-feds revelation. Now in truth, I've never heard of an undercover fed or cop actually going to jail, much less to prison, to establish his criminal bonafides. However, the relatively short-lived, late 1980s TV show *Wiseguy* (which launched creepy Kevin Spacey's career) as well as the 2006 flick *The Departed* have made me downright paranoid. But no way in Dante's inferno is a copper gonna spend significant time in a jail just to make himself known.

Fuggedaboutit!

Counter-Surveillance

If you think one of your homechickens is a stoolie or UC, then have the suspect followed 24-7 for a couple weeks. If you see him meeting with cops, agents or prosecutors, or going into the local federal building, then he needs to be chopped. Here's how this technique might play out:

In November 1979, Chicago hitman Billy "Chopper" Dauber was indicted for trafficking guns and drugs after he tried to move a big load of dope to an undercover narc. Selling *los drogas* is a big no-no in The Outfit, which doesn't just pay the typical Mafia lip service to its prohibition against slinging illicit substances. South Chitown bigshot Albert "Caesar the Fox" Tocco was understandably concerned that the Chopster might not want to do thirty years.

But Tocco didn't climb up the Mafia ladder by being rash or foolhardy. He had veteran soldier James "Jimmy the Duke" Basile follow Dauber around the clock. Sure enough, Basile hit paydirt after a few weeks of constant surveillance when he caught his man secretly meeting with law enforcement officials.

On July 2, 1980, an Outfit hit squad comprised of Frankie Breeze Calabrese Sr., Ronnie Jarrett, Gerry Scarpelli, and William "Butch" Petrocelli moved on Billy. They followed Dauber and his wife Charlotte, who was in the wrong place at the wrong time with the wrong husband, after they drove away from the Will County Courthouse. They had just attended a hearing on Dauber's gun-and-dope case.

The Daubers noticed the work van speeding up behind them so Billy put the pedal to the metal of his muscle car and roared away. Frankie Breeze also slammed on the gas, and a neck-in-neck car chase ensued for ten miles along a major highway. Frankie Breeze finally swung in front of the Daubers' car, forcing them into a ditch. Scarpelli jumped out of the van, ran over to the car, and blasted the unfortunate couple with his shotgun. The van was later set afire.

Bottom Line: If you don't plan on whacking your guy even if you do find out he's a rat, and you want to keep your investigation a secret from the rest of your crew, hire a reputable private detective to follow the dude around. Or just hire my friend Joe D. to conduct a polygraph on him. If Joe tells you that the guy's answers "clearly indicate deception," then take him to your kennel and sic the dogs on his ass. Then you'll find out what's what.

Be on the Alert for Telltale Signs of Finkdom

If you find that your suspect often appears nosy or intrusive – you know, asking questions about things that are none of his business – then he might be a rat or UC. No self-respecting racketeer sticks his nose into things that don't concern him because he knows nothing good will come of it. *Au contraire*, he knows that he'll develop a reputation for being a Nosy Parker. Only someone incredibly stupid, desperate or compromised will do this.

Also, beware of old pals who suddenly pop up after having been gone for extended periods of time, immediately trying to rejoin the fold. Those of you who have seen the masterful 1990 film *State of Grace* starring Sean Penn, Gary Oldman, and Ed Harris (loosely based on The Westies) know of which I speak. But forget the movies – this actually happens in real life.

In late 2003, Bonanno capo James "Big Louie" Tartaglione began secretly working for the FBI. He returned to NYC on the pretense of wanting to help the Family sort out some of their administrative problems. He went directly to the Family's three-member ruling panel while wearing a wire. However, then capo Vincent "Vinny Gorgeous" Basciano smelled a rat, suspicious of how Big Louie had suddenly returned from Florida to hang out with his old pals, despite knowing that doing so would violate his parole.

On January 18, 2004, Tartaglione attended a meeting with the ruling triumvirate at a diner. Vinny Gorgeous tasked soldier Dominick Cicale with conducting counter-surveillance on the diner. After spotting several suspicious-looking government-issued vehicles in the parking lot, the sharp-eyed Cicale paged Basciano with a pre-arranged beeper code. At that point, Basciano wisely moved the foursome's conversation away from anything incriminating.

Two days later, the feds swooped in and arrested a bunch of Bonannos for RICO violations, including most of the top brass. But not Vinny Gorgeous, who never said dick around Big Louie. Needless to say, the remaining Bonannos were gripped with paranoia. Even Basciano started forcing his underlings to strip to their underwear during meets to ensure no one was wearing a wire.

The same thing happened to former Bonanno capo Vincent Asaro when his cousin Gaspare Valenti suddenly popped up in New York after living in Vegas for fifteen years. Valenti was dead broke and only flipped for the money, receiving as much as $6,000 a month from the FBI to wear a wire against Asaro. Valenti's cooperation resulted in Asaro being indicted in January 2014 and tried in October 2015 for allegedly participating in the 1978 Lufthansa Heist. He was also prosecuted for the December 6, 1969, murder of informant Paul Katz. Fortunately, the jury didn't believe Valenti, the sole witness, and Asaro was acquitted, much to the G's humiliation and chagrin.

Oh snap, motherfucker – Suh-NAP!!!

Notably, Henry Hill never alleged to Nick Pileggi in *Wiseguy* that Asaro had been involved in the heist. Indeed, Hill reportedly told author Daniel Simone, while they were working on their book, that Asaro had *zero* involvement in Lufthansa. And based on those in the know, Jimmy Burke personally strangled his hijacking partner Paul Katz with a dog chain after learning from a corrupt police officer that Katz had flipped against him.

****

Incidentally, I don't loathe *all* federal prosecutors, only those who trample on defendants' civil and Constitutional rights to get what they seek most: trial wins, glory, and promotions. I always liked and respected Edward McDonald, the former Assistant US Attorney who ran the Eastern District Organized Crime Strike Force (in Brooklyn). He flipped Henry Hill (and many other mobsters), and convincingly played himself in *Goodfellas*. By all accounts, McDonald was a straight shooter who was impeccably honest in prosecuting the Mafia.

I'd also like to give a shoutout to Miss B., a former Southern District of New York Organized Crime Strike Force prosecutor who also retired with honor and respect. One of the reasons

I like Miss B. so much was her approach to dealing with mobsters: treat them with respect and they will do the same to you. Never lie to them, never bullshit them. This makes perfect sense, because as a prosecutor, you want to establish a good rapport with all potential flippers. Miss B. agreed with me that *Mafiosi* as a rule don't hate the feds, who are simply doing their job. In other words, gangsters typically don't take investigations and prosecutions personally.

Hell, while I'm on this roll, I'd like to express my admiration for the following federal prosecutors: James D. Henderson, former federal strike force US attorney for the Northern District of California (San Francisco). He was also the former LA Organized Crime Strike Force chief who turned Fratianno. And to Walter Mack, AUSA for the Southern District of New York (Manhattan), as well as chief of the Southern District's organized crime unit, I say, "Respect!"

These are the types of feds that deserve our admiration and praise.

Alas, the same cannot be said for Diane Giacalone, who was directly responsible for the August 29, 1988, murder of Willie Boy Johnson. In 1985, Giacalone, a federal prosecutor for the Eastern District, brought Johnson's stellar sixteen-year run as an informant for the FBI and NYPD to a screeching halt. She threatened to out Johnson in a RICO trial unless he copped a plea and testified against his boss, John Gotti Sr. Willie Boy refused, having been promised by both the FBI and the NYPD organized crime unit detectives that he would never have to testify in open court if he just continued providing them information. (Willie was paid quite handsomely to do so.)

Willie Boy begged Giacalone not to out him because he knew it would mean a death sentence. She refused, but Johnson, apparently out of some residual loyalty for Gotti, again rejected her deal. As a result, she revealed his informant status in court over the protestations of numerous FBI agents and even other federal prosecutors (namely from the Southern District of NY, which had its own RICO case brewing against Gotti).

Writers Gene Mustain and Jerry Capeci explain in *Mob Star: The Story of John Gotti* how the FBI believed Giacalone was seeking a late-stage fix for what she knew was a weak case by pressuring Johnson to testify. The authors barely conceal their disdain for Giacalone, who they point out could have easily prosecuted Johnson in a separate case and thereby kept his informant status a secret. This would have maintained the integrity of the FBI's Top Echelon Informant program.

They point out the fact that two key FBI bosses from New York, Thomas Sheer and James Kossler, even attempted to get the Justice Department brass in Washington, DC, to back down Giacalone. Unfortunately, however, her two direct superiors, Eastern District US Attorney Raymond J. Dearie and his underboss Susan Shepard, backed her play. Even worse, the DOJ punted the final decision to the glory-hungry Dearie, who gave Giacalone the thumbs up.

During a bail hearing for Willie Boy, in recounting to the judge how she had been warned by the FBI that Johnson would be murdered if his informant status was disclosed, she admitted, "It is an assessment with which I cannot disagree."

Again, Giacalone was desperate for Johnson's cooperation because she – and many other AUSAs – believed she had a less-than-airtight case against Gotti. As many insiders predicted, she lost spectacularly. Her seven-year investigation and six-month trial resulted in a not guilty verdict in March 1987, despite the combined testimony of rats James Cardinali, Salvatore Polisi, and Matthew Traynor.

In all fairness, however, it didn't help Giacalone that juror George Pape had been bribed. Supposedly, the prosecutors were aware of Pape's bribery because of the Ravenite Social Club bugs and mobster-pillow talk heard from a female informant. However, the feds apparently didn't want to share this information with Giacalone because they knew she would out them as well! Regardless, it was this courtroom victory against Giacalone that earned Gotti the "Teflon Don" moniker.

And instead of going on to fame and glory, she apparently suffered a nervous breakdown. She quietly resigned several months after the trial and got a job working for the local transit authority.

Cue Gene Autry's "Happy Trails."

I also place blame for Johnson's murder on Giacalone's boss, Andrew Maloney (who replaced Raymond J. Dearie during the trial, and who became US Attorney for the EDNY after the trial), for approving her big reveal. He ignored the pleas from both the FBI and the Eastern District Strike Force, and fully backed Giacalone and co-prosecutor Gleeson.

But don't worry, Diane, Raymond, Susan, Andy, and John – the Mafia is eternally grateful to all of you for helping them extract a painful sixteen-year thorn from their side. Among many other major busts, Johnson had been credited for ratting out the infamous Pleasant Avenue Connection heroin ring, including the Bergin crew's participation therein, as well as Gotti himself after he whacked James McBratney. Wilfred had also tipped off the FBI in the mid '70s about Paul Vario conducting business in his junkyard trailer, which lead to the feds planting a mic and consequently sending Big Paulie off to jail in Operation Gold Bug.

Johnson was apparently the Forrest Gump of Mafia informants – always in the right place at the right time. Oh, did I forget to mention that Johnson was committing murders for the Gambinos the entire time he was an informant? Par for the course, the FBI simply chose to look the other way.

By the way, Giacalone was so shameless that she claimed to the jury that one of the reasons she despised Gotti so much was that as a fellow lifelong Ozone Park resident, she had been forced to walk by the Bergin as a young girl and see the mobsters openly cavorting there. One small problem – it was later revealed that the Bergin didn't even exist at the time!

The Tapatío Test

If some newbie in your crew claims he did time in the California prison system, it's fairly easy to check out if you have decent connections. It's not like the federal prison system where you can run the inmate's name on the US Bureau of Prisons' publicly available website. (To locate a federal inmate, simply type in his/her name at https://www.bop.gov/inmateloc/)

But if you don't, and if for some reason you're not able to confirm or deny his claim, simply ask him what he thinks of Tapatío sauce (that's salsa picante, a.k.a. Mexican hot sauce, for you Midwesterners). If the guy says he loves it or hates it or something like that, then you're back to square one. But if he asks you what it is, blast him in the fucking face right then and there! Give him a motherfuckin' Moe Green special right in his spying eye.

That's 'cause in Cali, whether you're doing your initial ninety-day intake in Chino or serving an all-day sentence (life) in the SHU (Secure Housing Unit) at Pelican Pay (where they keep all the prison-gang shotcallers), the bulls serve Tapatío *with every goddamn meal*. All my Cali brothers behind bars out there know *exactly* what I'm preachin' about. Much love, homies! Keep ya heads up!

Compromise the Suspect

I want to take this opportunity to clear the air on a few things, dispel a few urban myths that are just that – myths, as in fiction, as in *not true*. First, an undercover cop does *not* have to admit to you that he's such if you ask him. This is one of the most inane things I've ever heard, and I have no idea where this bullpucky came from. Show me the criminal statute or police operations manual that purports to make this statement. What a crock of *caca*. Was it in a movie?

Equally ludicrous is the nonsense that a narc can't do drugs when he's undercover. I know where we can trace this line of malarkey – one of my all-time favorite shows, *Miami Vice*. In real life, unless you already have a rep for being a teetotaling health nut, turning down a line of cocaine from a bad *hombre* á la Sonny Crockett could mean your *ass*. Hell, Jerry H. snorted more Tijuana talcum powder than anyone Marco had ever known. One time Marco and Gallo came home at seven A.M. from an all-night after-party and found Jerry (who lived in their condo complex) waxing *Marco's* car!

Real narcs are more like John Leguizamo's DEA agent character in the 2016 flick *The Infiltrator*. He encourages his partner to do whatever it takes to convince the crooks that he's one of them: shag a stranger, do a line, whack someone, whatever it takes. That's exactly what they'll do (okay, maybe not the whacking part).

Christ, even Joe Pistone admits in *Unfinished Business* that he committed numerous major felonies during his six years undercover, including hijackings, armed robberies, and assaults. I agree with him that he had to do so in order to maintain his cover. Cheers, Joe! Mad respect!

So how do we deal with all this? Again, having your suspect engage in crimes of violence will absolutely torpedo any ongoing investigation. I'm not saying have the guy whack someone – maybe just make him zap someone's testicles with a cattle prod. Joaquín Garcia will tell you the same thing. According to Big Jack, no FBI agent can ever allow physical violence to occur in his or her presence. Even a simple beating in such circumstance could easily nuke an ongoing investigation or prosecution.

Threaten the Wife of Your Suspect's Handler

Every serious gangster has at least one cop or fed who has a hard-on for him. You know, some a-hole who jerks off at night as he fantasizes about busting your evil ass while his wife contentedly snores and flatulates next to him. And I'll bet you dollars for donuts that this self-flagellating goober is working very closely with the suspected rat or narc in your crew.

So here's what you do, fine fellas: sidle up next to your suspect at the bar, buy him a few drinks, and start talking about how you're planning to whack your archnemesis's spouse. Throw in a few salacious details so it seems like you're dead serious, and you're on your way, my friend.

Now if your suspect is merely a rat, he may or may not report this to his handler. However, I'd bet good money he'll beeline right to the hard-on and spill the beans about your insidious plot just to earn brownie points. So make sure you have your trusted crewmembers follow the suspect after he leaves you, and to monitor his calls, if possible. He'll probably have a pop-up tent in his pants at the thought of passing on this big news, so he might not even try to shake your guys' tail. Or slap a GPS tracker under his car and tail him that way.

Better yet, provide him and all the other guys in your crew with iPhones so you can *always* track their movements online.

By contrast, if your suspect *is* an actual undercover police officer or federal agent, then he will mos' def' run straight to your archnemesis and bring him up to speed. Failing to do so would get him fired, to say the least. Now once that happens, it'll only take a matter of days, or even mere hours, for your archnemesis to make his move. He'll directly approach either you or your boss with the warning that if you harm a hair on his precious wife's head, he will bring the entire weight of his department or agency upon your heads. He'll be so pissed!

And just like that, this doofus will unwittingly show his ass and reveal the identity of the rat or narc in your crew. *Am I genius or what?*

Okay, I want to clarify something at this juncture: I'm not *theoretically* opposed to you taking your rat-fink crewmember out for a short, one-way walk into the woods. However, under no circumstances should you ever murder a cop or federal agent. It's straight up against the Rules of *La Cosa Nostra*, and for good reason – doing so would bring so much heat on your Family that it would literally force it to cease doing business (at least for a while). More importantly, it would absolutely ensure your own demise.

This is precisely what happened to Colombo Family associate, and member of Greg Scarpa's comically-named but seriously deadly Wimpy Boys crew, Costabile "Gus" Farace.

On February 28, 1989, Farace murdered undercover DEA agent Everett Hatcher during a cocaine buy. Farace had previously done time for kidnapping and brutalizing two sixteen-year-old gay boys, whom he forced to fellate him, and one of whom he murdered. Why this animal was ever released from prison is beyond me.

Unfortunately, Agent Hatcher's bumbling back-up team members lost track of him on the way to the buy-bust on Staten Island. As a result, Farace was able to shoot Hatcher in the head three times, killing him. Not cool at all.

A nine-month nationwide manhunt ensued with Farace being placed on the FBI's Ten Most Wanted list. The pressure from the DEA and FBI brought all Mafia business in New York to a screeching halt. When you kill one of their own, the feds will stop at nothing, legal or illegal, to bring you in, dead or alive. And rightly so, in my opinion. And this is precisely what they told the bosses of all five LCN families in the Big Apple: bring him to us either vertical or horizontal.

So the contract went to Farace's best friend, Lucchese associate John Petrucelli, who just couldn't bring himself to kill his buddy. So the mob killed *him* instead, and then sent Farace's uncle, the Grim Reaper himself, Greg Scarpa Sr., to burn Farace on November 17, 1989. However, according to Gallo, the actual shooting was done by James Galione, Mario Gallo, and Louis Tuzzio – presumably at Scarpa's behest. For once, I applaud Scarpa's homicidal actions.

Personally, I think only a *strunz* would kill a narc or UC – the guy's just doing his job, doing what he thinks is right. It's nothing personal, just business. A rat, on the other hand, was once your friend and is exploiting that friendship to destroy your life in order to save his own. He deserves whatever he has coming to him, with few exceptions .

Denial is Not Just a River in Egypt

This may seem to be a slight non-sequitur but bear with me. I've noticed a certain phenomenon among very scary mobsters: they believe they are such badasses that nobody they know would dare rat them out. This terribly vexes me because how the hell are you gonna exact vengeance against a rat once he's been pulled out by the FBI and thrown into WITSEC? Indeed, as of 2019, in the entire eighty-eight-year history of *La Cosa Nostra*, no such *federally*-protected witness has *ever* been murdered (though Sammy Bull came close).

Both Anthony "the Animal" Fiato and Anthony "Gaspipe" Casso are prime examples of this self-delusion. In the early 1980s, Fiato began to suspect that his house had been bugged and that one of his loanshark customers was a rat. As he explained to his biographer, his sixth sense told him someone in his inner circle had gone bad. Nevertheless, he refused to believe that any of his crime partners would ever turn against him. For example, his pal Robert "Bob" Kessler, who lived just down the street, was dropping food and gifts off at Fiato's condo almost every day. Fiato knew that Kessler knew that Fiato would whack him in a heartbeat if he ever flipped against him. But Bob did and, of course, nothing ever happened to him.

In May 1990, Gaspipe fled to escape the imminent Windows RICO case. While on the run for thirty months, he trusted his drug-dealing partner Burton Kaplan with numerous financial transactions. Burtie was also tasked with ferrying Casso's wife, Lillian, for secret rendezvous in various motels in New Jersey, where Casso was living with an old girlfriend. This was an awful lot of trust to put in someone as slimy as Kaplan, but Casso believed Kaplan feared him so much he would never flip on him. And when Casso demanded that he deed the Cassos' half-a-mil house back into Lillian's name, Kaplan did just that.

On January 16, 1993, Kaplan drove Lillian up to a (final) get-together with Gaspipe at the Rockaway Mall in New Jersey. The next day, an FBI/SWAT co-op team raided Gaspipe's secret love nest in Mount Olive, NJ, where he was laying low with his ex. Casso was in the shower at the time – the last time he'd ever be able to take one without worrying about dropping the soap.

Thus, because he foolishly trusted Kaplan, Gaspipe is currently going on twenty-seven years (as of 2019) in a maximum-security/Level-Five federal prison with no end in sight. And, of course, he never got his house back. Casso would eventually admit to Philip Carlo that trusting Kaplan was one of his biggest mistakes ever.

And poor Lillian's fate? She dropped dead of a heart attack on her kitchen floor twelve years later, in February 2005, after being hounded mercilessly by Gaspipe's old criminal associates, who were trying to get at the fortune he had stashed away. She had never forgiven Anthony for cheating on her with his ex.

Lessons to Be Learned

Friends, don't bullshit yourself that you're so all-powerful and omnipotent that none of your bros will ever screw you over. So keep your friends close and your enemies closer. I'm dropping pearls here, hatchlings.

Plata o Plomo

Witnesses are a major pain in the ass because they are *civilians*, which means you can only prevent them from testifying against you by one of two ways: *plata o plomo*. This is a term favored by Colombian *narcotraficantes*, particularly *El Jefe* himself, Pablo Escobar. It translates to "silver or lead," meaning that you offer your witnesses two choices: a bribe or a bullet. Since we're not savages for God's sake, we always encourage them to go with the former. Use your words, people!

And if they're too stupid and/or civic-minded to accept that, then to Hell with 'em – the Earth's overpopulated anyways. In other words, if it comes down to having to choose between you and them, then I say *adiós, pendejos*! Send flowers to their widows if it makes you feel better. (JK! Not funny? My bad.)

This sounds like a simple concept, but just as with making your bones, anything and everything can go wrong when eliminating witnesses. However, if you just follow a few simple rules from your old Dutch uncle, Don R.M., you should be as sound as a pre-Brexit pound.

Don't Be a Tightwad, You Cheap Bastard

You might get lucky and be able to pay only a relatively modest amount to escape a conviction, or even prosecution, depending on the severity of your crime, as well as the nature of your relationship, if any, to the victim.

Take Andrew "Good News" DiDonato, for starters, who shot someone for the first time in 1983. That day, he was riding around at dawn after an all-nighter with future mob lawyer Joseph "Jo Jo" Corozzo Jr. He was the nephew of Andrew's boss, Nicky Corozzo, and the son of Gambino *consigliere* Jo Jo Senior.

> Jo Jo was driving his father's Mercedes. I was in the passenger seat and starting to nod off. A friend of ours was in another car and Jo Jo started playing a game of chicken. But some other guy was on the road with his girlfriend. This guy got pissed off, and him and Jo Jo exchanged words and obscene gestures.
>
> When we stopped at a light, this guy pulled up behind us. In the rearview mirror, Jo Jo saw him get out of his car and start running up the passenger side of our car. Jo Jo hollered at me, "Wake up, Andrew! Wake up! Shoot him, Andrew! Shoot him!"
>
> I looked in the side mirror and saw this guy coming up toward my door. He was carrying a Bowie knife. I lowered the window and pulled my gun. When he grabbed my door handle, I shot him in the groin area. He dropped to the pavement and Jo Jo took off.
>
> Jo Jo Senior found out which hospital the guy was in and sent two of his men to see him. His wound wasn't life-threatening. They gave him ten thousand dollars. If he didn't take the money and wanted to cooperate with the police, they told him his wound would become fatal. He took the money and that's the last I heard of it.

Escaping an attempted murder charge for ten grand was admittedly an easy break for Andrew. The fact that two

Gambino killers made this lowball offer *possibly* influenced the victim. But you can't expect to get lucky like this more than once, if ever. This is why I suggest putting aside a little nest egg for yourself for this type of rainy day. Plus, if it doesn't work out, you can always use that golden parachute to lam it.

Be on the Alert for Opportunities to Bribe Jurors

On March 13, 1987, John Gotti was acquitted in AUSA Diane Giacalone's RICO trial. It wasn't until Sammy Bull flipped years later that the public learned that juror George Pape had been bribed to vote not guilty, thereby guaranteeing Gotti a hung jury. But for the sharp eye of one of Gotti's men, Kevin McMahon, however, Gotti would have missed out on the next five years of freedom.

During the trial, which McMahon dutifully attended every day, he would walk to his car in the court's parking lot. At the end of one fateful day, he saw Pape get into his car and drive off. But not before McMahon clocked his license plate. Consequently, Gotti's men were able to track down where he lived.

Gotti's good luck turned downright extraordinary when his men learned that Pape knew Bosko Radonjich. Bosko was the Yugoslavian gangster who would soon emerge as the new leader of The Westies after Jimmy Coonan went down for life the following year, in 1988.

Those of you well-versed in mob lore are aware that the Gambinos and The Westies had a symbiotic relationship going back to the late '70s when Roy DeMeo first courted them. To seal the deal, on May 13, 1977, DeMeo gave Coonan an early Christmas present by murdering rival Irish mob boss Michael "Mickey" Spillane (no relation to the famous writer). Since he was a teenager, Coonan had wanted to kill Spillane for smacking around Coonan's father over a bad debt. It was this unholy alliance that resulted in Roy finally getting his button from Big Paul Castellano (who despised Roy for his *braggadocio* and bloodlust).

And so a deal was struck. Pape wanted $120,000 but Sammy Bull got him down to 60Gs. The cash was then funneled through Radonjich. Pape should have held out for the full 120 'cause he certainly earned it: he actually convinced the other eleven jurors Gotti was *innocent*. Thus, instead of merely securing a hung jury with an all-but-guaranteed second trial, Gotti was able to saunter out of court a free man to greet his legions of fans and reporters.

Hilariously, Gotti's old lawyer, the comically bombastic and obnoxiously abrasive Bruce Cutler, still brags on his website that Gotti's acquittal was due to his own legal genius. However, he conveniently omits the salient facts about Pape, who was convicted of obstruction of justice five years later in 1992 and shipped off to federal prison.

Cue The Doobie Brothers' "What A Fool Believes."

As for McMahon, Gotti couldn't have been happier with him. That is, except for the minor matter of a back then teenage McMahon having loaned Gotti's twelve-year-old-son Frank the mini-bike on which he died (again, by illegally darting out into the street on March 18, 1980). But according to John Alite, McMahon was making so much money for Gotti dealing drugs that Gotti gave him a pass. In any event, Gotti told people that McMahon was his lucky charm. He even had McMahon sit next to him on Gotti's boat as a precaution against tipping over. Go figure.

Dispatch Uncooperative Jurors Only as a Last Resort

Murdering innocent people, including recalcitrant jurors who refuse to accept your bribe, will prove to be a highly distasteful enterprise. So instead of going straight to the *plomo*, try to ramp up your intimidation tactics gradually.

On March 25, 1986, assault and robbery charges against Gotti were dropped after the key witness against him, refrigerator repairman Romual Piecyk, suffered a bout of temporary amnesia. (You grey-balls out there might recall the next day's famous giant headline in the *New York Post*: "I FORGOTTI!")

The common misconception is that Piecyk decided not to testify against Gotti (who punched Piecyk and stole $400 cash from him over a parking dispute) due to Gotti's recent notoriety. After all, Gotti had whacked Castellano only four months earlier, *after* the alleged assault.

But that's not the whole story. Gotti's crew terrorized Piecyk in the months leading up to the trial, including repeatedly calling him at home and threatening to kill him, cutting the brakes on his van, following him around the neighborhood, and once even literally kicking him in the ass. Bruce Cutler also shamelessly (and laughably) takes credit for this victory on his website.

Or maybe Piecyk was just a whole lot smarter than John Favara, the utterly clueless neighbor who accidentally ran over Gotti's boy. Favara couldn't take a hint, despite the repeated threatening phone calls to his home, the spray painting of his car with the word MURDERER, or even the grieving mother attacking him with a baseball bat! His other neighbors alternately begged and chastised him for not moving. He finally put his house on the market but inexplicably continued to live there in the meantime.

Then, on July 28, 1980 (one week before escrow was set to close), a van pulled up as he exited his workplace. According to both John Alite and fellow flipper Kevin McMahon, two burly men jumped out, including Fat Angie Ruggiero, who clubbed Favara and tossed him into an unmarked utility van. He was then driven to a warehouse, where he was tortured and chainsawed. Taking a page out of Al Capone's book (who was on vacation in Florida during the infamous 1929 St. Valentine's Day massacre), the Gottis were also in the Sunshine State at the time. Or so say their hotel receipts.

If you so desire, you can just skip the witness-intimidation foreplay and go straight to the happy ending. Like Gallo, who once dissuaded a witness from testifying against him by blowing up his father's car in La Verne, California. Why mess around if you're pressed for time and need immediate results? Plus, Gallo didn't even have to kill the witness. I call this a win-win.

Similarly, Andrew DiDonato never had to stoop so low as to snuff the life out of a material witness. During the summer of 1985, DiDonato came to the aid of his crewmates Anthony Gerbino and Michael "Mikey Y" Yannotti. The noble cause: dissuading an eyewitness who had spotted the duo heisting a car from cooperating with the fuzz. This witness turned out to be a military recruiter.

And so Andrew strolled into the recruiter's office on the pretense of enlisting. After what must have been the longest half-hour of his life, Andrew lured the recruiter outside. BANG! BOOP! PAP! DiDonato and fellow crewmember Mario jumped the poor schmuck, beating him with fists and a lead pipe. They then promised they would kill him if he didn't keep his mouth shut. It worked like a charm and the fellas dodged a bullet. What're friends for?

Sometimes, however, there's just no way of getting around it, such as when a witness against you is in protective custody. In such an instance, I understand the need for decisive and definitive action. It is what it is.

Example:

In 1937, Mafia founding father Vito Genovese was charged with murdering one of his business associates, Fernando Boccia, three years earlier, after a witness, cigar salesman Peter LaTempa, came forward. Don Genovese prudently hopped on the next steamer ship to *Italia*, where he laid low for the next eight years. The Italian authorities finally buckled under US pressure and deported him back to America to stand trial.

Genovese's power had not waned while he was away; my gut instinct tells me he was shipping heroin over. LaTempa was being held in the Brooklyn jail in protective custody. Only days away from testifying against Don Vito, he was given what he thought was medicine to alleviate a painful gallbladder. Instead, it was enough cyanide to kill a team of Clydesdales. Or at least enough to silence LaTempa forever. God bless the

NYPD in the good ol' days! All charges against Genovese were dropped.

Lessons to Be Learned

When in doubt, whack 'em out – assuming, of course, all else fails. Now go forth, children – as Basil King, a nineteenth century Canadian clergyman and writer, famously said, "Be bold and mighty forces will come to your aid." No, Nietzsche did *not* coin that phrase.

Fun Facts!

After Jimmy Burke extinguished Paul Katz, he buried him in the basement of an Ozone Park home. More than forty-three years later, on June 18, 2013, what was left of his disinterred remains were discovered following an anonymous tip from a reliable source. This was thirteen years after Burke cashed in his own chips in the pokie.

The tipster was Gaspare Valenti, who testified he had heard about it from Asaro. Asaro allegedly had not only helped Burke dig the original hole they stuffed Katz into, but also moved the body - allegedly with the help of his son Jerome Asaro. They allegedly did so on Burke's orders shortly after he had been arrested in 1980 for fixing the Boston College basketball games.

Katz knew it was likely his meeting with Burke that night would be his last. He told his wife Delores that if he didn't return in fifteen minutes, she should call the police. Ignoring her pleas not to go, he stepped outside his home and was attacked by Burke, who had been waiting in the darkness like the Grim Reaper (Greg Scarpa or the other one – take your pick).

Finally, force your suspect to cough up his cell phone records. You'll see the same number pop up over and over again – that'll be his handler or, if he's an undercover cop or fed, his supervisor. Or it'll be an unlisted number. Question your man and run down those leads.

Vago snitch George Rowe almost got busted from his fellow outlaws in this very manner. Vago shotcaller and cold-blooded psycho Big Roy Compton ordered several Vago brothers to check Rowe's phone records. Hundreds of calls to his ATF handler were contained therein. Amazingly, the brothers bought his explanation that the calls were to his uncle.

Chapter Fourteen – How Not to Get Whacked

"Every day above ground is a good day." –
Detective Mel Bernstein, Miami PD

As far as you're concerned, this is the most important chapter in this book. After all, what's more important than breathing (without a ventilator)?

Always Take Basic Security Precautions

I hate to be the bearer of bad news, guys, but according to Marco, "The Life ain't all about crack and chicks." In the Game, you will make mortal enemies, whether you are aware of them or not. As a result, in addition to constantly being conscious of not getting busted, foremost on your addled brain should be your personal well-being.

To wit, suppose you have a meeting but you're worried the attendees may come dressed, what Old West gunfighters called well-heeled – that means *armed*, for you cityslickers. Well, you should try to meet them in an airport lounge so everyone has to pass through metal detectors.

After falling out with Junior Gotti in 1994, John Alite disappeared from their mutual stomping grounds in Queens. Alite thereafter insisted on meeting Junior at the Aqueduct Racetrack in Jamaica, Queens. He knew Gotti and his boys would have to pass through a magnet-o-meter that would ring an alarm if anyone was carrying a gun or metal weapon.

Another rule of thumb: never sit in the front passenger seat. *Never.* Johnny Martorano called it the death seat. He should know.

Vary Your Routine

If there's only one survival tip that you take away from this chapter, it should be this: *never be predictable in your movements.* I'll provide a perfect example in the guise of Frank "Lefty" Rosenthal.

On October 4, 1982, Lefty did the same exact thing he did at the same exact time every night. At 8:30 P.M., he walked out of the Tony Roma's restaurant in Las Vegas, having just finished eating dinner with the same group of friends with whom he always ate at the same table.

He got into his 1981 yellow Cadillac Eldorado, which was parked in the same spot where he parked every night, and turned on the ignition. For all you Scorsese fans, you know what happened next: KA-BOOM!

Cue Jigsaw's "Sky High."

The one smart thing Lefty did at this moment was to leave his car door open when he fired up the Caddy – an old habit he learned from The Outfit. By doing so, the blast was partially deflected.

Someone (perhaps it was an Outfit hit, perhaps it was ordered by Tony Spilotro) had stuck C-4 plastic explosive under the car. The blast shot the roof sixty feet skyward and shattered the windows of all the cars in the parking lot, as well as in the rear of the restaurant.

Lefty jumped from the car, his clothes on fire. Unfortunately, he survived, although he did receive several severe burns and broken ribs, and had car parts embedded in his emaciated, albino physique.

You might not be as lucky as Lefty, who by sheer serendipity had recently purchased that particular Caddy model – a 4,000-pound behemoth that, for the first time ever, had a welded steel plate under the driver's seat for added suspension. This plate prevented Lefty from being turned into a charcoal briquette, not that anyone besides his kids would have given a crap since he was such a condescending, arrogant prick to everyone.

John Alite adopted the exact opposite of Lefty's suicidal routine during his cold war with Junior Gotti. He stopped hanging out at all the Mafia social clubs he typically frequented, as well as his favorite bars, clubs, and restaurants. He went to great lengths to avoid having any set schedule or clockable movements. He refused to show up to meetings scheduled by Gotti, and would only meet at the last minute at a time and place of his own choosing. Killing a cold-blooded killer can be downright frustrating if your target stays on point.

Similarly, after Andrew DiDonato had a falling out with Nicky Corozzo and Mikey Y, he always wore a bulletproof vest and carried multiple firearms. He never showed up on time for appointments, if at all. If he told someone he would drop in on them on Tuesday morning, he'd instead come by on Thursday night. Nobody knew where he was or where he would be.

Bottom Line: A moving target is always harder to hit.

After Gallo and Marco dispatched Lalo for allegedly murdering Clyde, they knew there would be immediate – and possibly fatal – blowback. They went out with a bang, hitting all of their favorite clubs in Newport and partying like Kanye and Diddy. Even Gallo drank and snorted a little Peruvian flake that night, if Marco's not mistaken. Marco knows he sure as hell did.

And then they simply went underground. Gallo had presciently planned for this day for many years. He had never let Sal Avila, Lalo U., or any of their men know where he and his own crew lived. They certainly knew everywhere else the boys hung out and partied, but Gallo and Marco immediately stopped going to those places. They switched gyms and stopped going out to clubs and bars.

Sure enough, the night after Lalo went bye-bye, the boys started getting calls and pages from everyone they knew who worked at their favorite nightspots. They got word that carloads of really scary-looking Mexican guys were coming around asking for them everywhere. Never did find them though.

It all comes down to proper planning, foresight, and discipline. Don't be a self-destructive *schlemiel* like Brian "Balloonhead" Halloran by going back to your favorite hangouts when you know there's a "green light" on your ass.

Don't Embarrass the Boss

A no-brainer, right, but if it didn't need to be explicitly stated, then I wouldn't state it. *Never make the boss look bad.* Like the ignoramus who made fun of Gambino Godfather Paul Castellano's Big Bird-like nose – he ended up pushing daisies one week after ridiculing him to other mobsters. The victim was one Vito Borelli, a gangster who went belly-up at the meaty, manicured hands of Big Joey Massino and John Gotti Sr. Here's another example of what happened when someone else made Castellano look bad.

In the late '70s, Mafia Cop Lou Eppolito's uncle, Jimmy "the Clam" Eppolito, and Jimmy's son Jim-Jim were both Gambinos, with the dad being a capo and the son a soldier. Jim-Jim had set up a phony national charity campaign called the International Children's Appeal, which was supposed to raise money for starving kids worldwide. It was a total sham. Not only did Jim-Jim skim every dime (with help from his crime partner, convicted forger John Ellsworth), but he used it as a front to launder proceeds from his drug- and gun-trafficking endeavors.

Being the consummate con man he was, Jim-Jim even managed to wrangle the support of President Jimmy Carter's wife, Rosalynn, as well as from Senator Edward Kennedy. The whole shithouse went up in flames when *20/20* exposed the five million dollar million fraud, and identified Jim-Jim and his father as being members of the Gambino crime family.

Big Paul made up his mind to eradicate father and son before the first commercial break. See, Dim-Dim had been explicitly warned not to associate any politicians with his fake charity because Castellano knew it would bring bad publicity.

On October 1, 1979, the duo took a ride to Coney Island with Nino Gaggi and Roy DeMeo. (Would *you* ever get in a car with DeMeo???) Nino and Roy shot them multiple times in the head at point-blank range.

Adios, muchachos!

Always Kick Up

Always do the right thing and take care of everyone who needs taking care of, not least of whom will be your boss. Holding out on your kick ups is a surefire way to end up with a wire around your neck. This applies even if you don't have a direct supervisor, like Gallo's good friend Herbert "Fat Herbie" Blitzstein (who Marco confirmed had attended Gallo's wedding to Tabitha Stevens at Caesar's Palace in Vegas). Herbie was a major loanshark in Vegas and had been one of Tony Spilotro's closest confidantes, going all the way back to The Chi with him in the '60s. After Tony found himself dead and buried in 1986, Herbie decided he didn't need to answer to anyone in the mob and so kept all his lucrative shylock proceeds to himself. Big mistake.

The problem with him doing so was he no longer had any protection. Since he was not a violent man, and did not have violent friends (aside from Gallo, who was too far away in Brooklyn to help him), Herbie became an attractive mark for the Milano Family.

On January 6, 1997, two LA Family associates, Peter Caruso and Alfred Mauriello, executed him with three bullets to the head in his own condo. They then stole uncut diamonds worth over $65,000, Rolex and Cartier watches, twenty-five pounds of gold bullion, and over $100,000 in cash. Everyone involved got in big trouble but that didn't help poor Herbie, who should have known better.

Where There's Smoke, There's Fire

The Mafia is just like the jungle – the denizens who reside within its confines can feel deadly vibrations rippling through it like wind across leaves – it's subtle but unmistakable. The more attuned you are to this energy (which the Chinese call chi), the better your chances of survival.

Andrew DiDonato told me that the reason he lasted so long on the street, and why he never got whacked, is because he had a hyper-sensitive antennae that would vibrate whenever danger was near. For example, when a potential adversary was speaking to him, he would pay close attention to what was *not* being said. He was an expert at reading between the lines, interpreting people's body language, and vibing off them. This kind of sixth sense only comes after you've been on the street for many years, but just know that you *can* develop it.

In prison, if you're gonna get your ticket punched, people will walk away from you or otherwise try to stay as far away from you as possible. You can feel the tension crackling in the air like static electricity when someone's about to get shanked. But that's due to the fact that everyone is in such a relatively confined space. On the streets, the warning signs will be subtler so you need to be more attuned to them.

If you're marked for death, which usually means your own boss has given the okay to make a move on you, the first warning sign will be the commencement of a whisper campaign against you. This is where people start saying negative things about you behind your back, like, "Be careful with Joe – he's no good," or "Joe's gone bad."

Fortunately, more often than not, somehow, someway word will get back to you, and that's when you should get the hell outta town. You'll need to lay low until you can find out exactly what's going down and why. You might get lucky and be able to squash the beef. I wish I could give you more specifics, but this kinda stuff goes down on a case-by-case basis.

And just like in prison, when your closest friends start avoiding you and stop returning your calls, you know your number's just about up. (The *carnales* in the Mexican Mafia prison gang, a.k.a. *La Eme,* describe it as "going into the hat.") Your bros will start coming up with excuses about why they can't come over for a playdate or go out bouncing with you, so be on the alert for that.

A less common telltale sign is when someone who would normally never borrow money from you suddenly hits you up for a sizeable loan. This should tip their mitt because thanks to me, you should now know that your buddy has no intention of paying you back.

For example, before murdering loanshark Frank Sidone in 1980, Philadelphia's short-lived boss, Phil "the Chicken Man" Testa, borrowed $50,000 from him. Then, ironically, when gambling kingpin Frank "Chickie" Narducci later planned on whacking *Testa*, Chickie tried to borrow $50,000 from *him*. (Not too subtle, guys – a little originality goes a long way.) This play was particularly obvious because Chickie was a multi-millionaire who needed fifty grand like I need dance lessons.

Another danger sign is when your crewmembers stop cutting you in on scores or otherwise start reducing your income flow.

In the mid '80s, Charles "Charlie White" Iannece was Nicky Crow's closest friend and crime partner. However, after Nicky went down for his final big bust, Charlie stopped sending Nicky's wife his share of their illegal enterprises. For the previous five years, they had shared equally in everything, cutting up millions of dollars (and, of course, kicking up a healthy share to Nicky Scarfo). But suddenly, Charlie started pleading poverty and feeding Nicky's wife a line of B.S. like, "There was a misunderstanding" and giving her only pennies on the dollar. For example, one time he gave her a $500 payment instead of the $8,000 he owed The Crow.

Bottom Line: No one sees much sense in paying good money to a dead man.

Finally, watch out for the death traps, da Vinci. After Henry Hill's big 1980 drug bust, he was understandably on edge since selling dope was a big no-no for Paul Vario. Jimmy Burke told him he wanted to meet to discuss the case, and suggested a bar on Queens Boulevard owned by their pal Charlie the Jap. Henry had never heard of it. In twenty-five years of running together, in a thousand bars they had drank in, and more than five years together in the pen, Jimmy suddenly wanted to meet him in a strange bar.

Hill's danger antennae shot up like R. Kelly's little soldier at the sight of a pre-pubescent girl. His fears were confirmed when he drove by the bar. It was exactly the kind of place Burke had used for innumerable hits in the past – it was owned by one of Burke's crew, and had a back entrance with rear parking lot hidden from the street. "That way you could take a body out of the bar with no one seeing," Hill explained to Nick Pileggi. "So no fucking way I'm goin' in there."

Instead, Henry showed up announced at Burke's sweatshop. Jimmy was clearly surprised and nervous, uncertain what Hill was up to. Thinking quickly, he asked Henry to go down to Florida to whack informer Bobby Germaine Jr. – the first time Burke had ever asked him to commit murder. Henry knew that trip to Disney World would be a one-way ticket. Henry agreed, taking Germaine's address, but that was the last time Hill saw Burke on the street. Henry Hill might have been a goof, but he was a master of self-preservation.

Don't Rip Off Other Gangsters

If you play with fire, eventually you're gonna get burned – it's simply one of those immutable laws of the universe. This means don't screw over guys who won't hesitate to kill you if you do so. One fine example hearkens back to the birth year of *La Cosa Nostra,* 1931, when certain Irish-American gangsters apparently didn't get the memo that there was a new sheriff in town.

During the mid 1910s, Southie residents and Irish-American gangsters, brothers Frank and Steve Wallace, founded the Gustin Gang. Thanks largely to their political connections and fearlessness, the Gustins rose to prominence during the Prohibition era and came to dominate the Boston underworld.

But they got too greedy and started posing as Prohibition agents to hijack booze shipments from other criminal groups. One too many of these heists involved bootlegging trucks owned by a new breed of gangster – the Italians. In New

England, they were fewer in number but no less fierce – or as they say in *La Eme*, *"Somos pocos pero somos locos"* ("We're few but we're crazy."). More importantly, they were far more disciplined, organized, and cunning. And they most definitely did not like to get buggered senseless in this manner.

On December 22, 1931, Frankie Wallace and his lieutenant, Bernard "Dodo" Walsh, were called to the North End for a sit down with the Italians, who were led by one Joe Lombardo. But instead of delicious gnocchi and fruity Chianti, Frankie and the aptly-named Dodo were met with a hail of bullets from two hitmen at the meeting site (a building on Hanover Street). It would take another four decades before Irish bad guys (The Hill) would challenge the Mafia's monopoly in Beantown.

Stay Close to the Boss

The flipside to not embarrassing the boss or shorting him at Christmas (when the capos give him envelopes to express their fealty) is to stay Velcroed to him. By spending as much time as possible with your superior, especially if he's the head guy (easier done in smaller Families), then you'll be able to predict his mood swings. This, in turn, could prolong your lifespan.

Between 1984 and 1986, Nicholas "Nicky Crow" Caramandi spent as much quality time as possible with Little Nicky at Casablanca South, his mansion in Fort Lauderdale. It was precisely for this reason Caramandi survived the bloodbath that Scarfo unleashed during that time. Scarfo died in prison on January 13, 2017, at age eighty-seven, after doing more than thirty years.

By spending so much time with the psychotic Scarfo, The Crow was able to truly understand how the homicidal godfather's addled brain worked. At every opportunity, Caramandi kept mum and studied Scarfo's every move and decision. By doing so, Nicky Crow was able to predict Scarfo's volatile mood swings and thereby stay on his good side. This paid long-term dividends, much to Scarfo's chagrin, including even when The Crow fell out of favor.

Don't Shag Married Women (Especially Other Wiseguys' Wives)

Marco used to put the stones to lotsa married ladies without giving it a second thought. Then one time, when he was in his early twenties, this burly construction worker found out he was playing hide the *chorizo* with his wife. She was a beautiful blonde, whom Marco used to warn, "Brace yourself, baby – I'm gonna do to you in five minutes what your people have been doing to mine for five hundred years. *Viva la raza!*"

So the huffy hubby called Marco and promised that if he didn't stop treating his soulmate like an amusement park, he would have no choice but to send him to Hell. Marco would not have hesitated to blow this guy's head off if he saw him coming up the driveway. However, he realized that if the guy caught him slipping, *Marco* would be the one sucking on the business end of a .45.

Marco made a vow right then and there that he would never mess around with a married woman again, and he never did. It was purely for survival, not out of some antiquated chivalrous notion. Marco realized that some men out there will go insane with vengeance if they are cuckolded, and will stop at nothing to put you in a pine box. See, when you shag a man's wife, he doesn't think about jail, numbnuts – all he thinks about is killing your dumb ass.

This is definitely true when it comes to mobsters – a painful lesson that Jon Roberts had to learn the hard way. Sometime in the early '70s, he found himself having a hot, torrid affair with Marie, the forty-something-year-old wife of Luigi, a major trafficker with the infamous Pizza Connection Sicilian heroin ring (which operated from 1975 to 1984, importing $1.6 billion worth of pure Turkish wholesale *babania*). We're talking up-against-the-wall-*9½ Weeks*-Binobo-monkey-sex, baby. Indeed, during coitus, Marie was so limber that she could actually smoke a cigarette – with her toes!

Still, Jon knew he was playing with fire, and, boy, did he get burned. As even Jon himself had predicted, he was pile-driving

Marie (or vice versa) at her apartment when Luigi and his gun both came home early from work.

Roberts jumped off the bed and streaked towards the door. He tried to give Luigi a high-five as he passed him on the way to the living room, but the old fart had no sense of humor. Instead, he shot Jon in the back. The bullet struck his coccyx, shattering the bone and splintering his intestines, before tearing through his pancreas and stomach.

The force of the blast knocked him to the ground. The white-hot agony was so excruciating, Roberts was certain he had been paralyzed. Blood squirted out of both ends, and bile came from his nose. He mercifully passed out from the pain.

Adding insult to injury, Luigi dragged him down multiple flights of stairs and dumped him on the sidewalk in the freezing snow. Mercifully, a pedestrian spotted Jon and called an ambulance. By the time he reached the E.R., randy Roberts had slipped into a coma. When he finally awoke, he started screaming – the pain was even worse than when he had been shot.

Jon's uncle Sam from the Gambino Family dropped by for a visit. "If you ever fuck another made guy's wife again," he promised, "I'll personally chop your balls off for ya."

Thanks to Jon's powerful Mafia protectors, he wasn't killed for violating this Rule. However, it was one of the reasons he was ultimately forced to flee New York with nothing but the cash in his pocket. Miami, of course, beckoned.

Bottom Line: So, if you want to keep your own upside-down fruit bowl attached to your precious nether region, leave the *forbidden* fruit alone.

Amazingly, however, when Greg Scarpa Sr. caught his common-law wife, Big Linda Schiro, humping their eighteen-year-old grocery delivery boy, Larry Mazza, Scarpa not only didn't kill him, but actually adopted him into his crew. And the best part of all? The kid was allowed to keep bedding his wife! Now that's what I call a Dutch uncle, Santa Claus, and the motherf'ing Easter Bunny all rolled into one!

Cue theme from *Happy Days*.

As previously indicated, if and when you finally get your wings, at your formal induction ceremony, you will be told the most fundamental Rules of *La Cosa Nostra*. First and foremost, there is the penalty-by-death prohibition against sleeping with another member's wife (or daughter).

The zips (Sicilians a.k.a. Siggies) brought this tradition with them over from the Old Country for good reason. The Mafia chieftains there learned centuries ago that nothing ignites an interclan war quicker than infidelity. So pretty please, with sugar on top, keep Mr. Snake in his cage.

"Never Let Anyone Know What You're Thinking"

Don Vito Corleone was a very wise man indeed. Whether or not you're aware of this fact, whenever you voice your opinion about any particular subject, those around you will judge you. That's because human beings are a vile, repugnant species who more than deserve the imminent zombie apocalypse.

If you're a civilian, B.F.D., right? But if you're in the mob, your big mouth could land you in trouble that you might not even see coming. And that's the worst kinda trouble to have. So whenever anyone asks you where you stand on a particular issue or how you feel about a certain individual, you should simply shrug and grunt noncommittally. Stay neutral, baby – like Switzerland (Nazi gold notwithstanding).

In late August 1976, Jimmy the Weasel told his beloved friend Tony "Dope" Delsanter about how Chicago boss Joey Aiuppa slyly tried to gauge Jimmy's reaction to the murder of Jimmy's other BFF, Johnny Roselli. As he explains in *The Last* Mafioso, Jimmy had flown into the Windy City to talk to Joey Doves to discuss Fratianno's possible return to The Outfit. They both took a seat in Aiuppa's social club while his massive goons loomed in the background.

Aiuppa waved his short, stubby index finger in the air as if he was trying to recall something. "Hey, Jimmy, d'you hear about that guy they found in that barrel down in Florida. You know, what's his name?"

Aiuppa eyeballed Jimmy to read his expression. Fratianno stared right back. "That was Handsome Johnny, so what?"

"Just wondering what you thought of that. No big deal."

No big deal, my ass, Jimmy had thought at the time. As he explained to Tony Dope, "That cocksucker Aiuppa knew Johnny and I were like brothers. He's lookin' to see if I'm gonna want payback against whoever clipped him. I ain't stupid, you know. I say the wrong thing, Aiuppa's gonna clip my wings right then and there."

"So what'd you say?" Delsanter asked.

"I just shrugged and said, 'Whaddaya gonna do – it's just one o' dem t'ings.'" Aiuppa studied him for another moment, then smiled and poured Jimmy another espresso with anisette.

The same thing happened to Gallo after his first mentor Joe Avila was slain on May 8, 1987 (just before Gallo's nineteenth birthday). Joey's murder had been perfectly orchestrated by an evil septuagenarian – an old-school dinosaur-gangster named Michael "Big Mike" Marvich, the Avila family's only legitimate rival when it came to moving major weight. Indeed, the DEA estimated that Marvich's organization was raking in $50 million a year by the mid '80s.

Anyways, Joey made the mistake of flexing with a *real* gangster. Although Joey had allegedly put plenty of guys into the ground, he was more of a playboy than a do-or-die mobster. That's no critique of the man, who was truly one of a kind, a legend even in his own time. (During the '70s, Joey and Sal – who both looked exactly like a young Julio Iglesias – owned the infamous Animal Farm. This was a huge ranch in Costa Mesa where party animals from all over the world – from movie stars to Hells Angels to Tim Leary and his Brotherhood of Eternal Love – used to hang out for days on end, tootin' nose candy, smoking Afghani hash, and dropping Orange Sunshine.)

Joey should have realized his own limitations. He should have understood that he was facing a superior predator. If Joey was a velociraptor, then Big Mike was T-fucking-Rex. But Joey couldn't help himself. Not only did he start knockin' boots in early 1985 with Marvich's gorgeous, blonde, thirty-eight-year-old girlfriend Cathy Lawrence, but he "borrowed" $200,000 from her. It was, of course, *Marvich's* money. Big Mike calmly asked for the money back and requested that Joey back away from his lady, but Joey just laughed in his face and even threatened him. Big mistake.

Joey should have already learned this lesson several years earlier. One day, his crew had been hanging out at the Balboa Island location of the Avilas' popular El Ranchito restaurant chain. A man walked in and asked for Joey. When the dull-witted hostess pointed Joey out at the bar, the guy walked up and said, "This is for fucking my wife." He then smashed a full tequila bottle across Joey's face. The guy calmly walked out, followed by Lalo, who shot him multiple times in the back. Joey had to undergo reconstructive plastic surgery as a result.

Remember when I said revenge was a dish best served cold? Nobody ascribed to this credo more than Marvich, who waited several more years before finally making his move. Ironically, it was Joey himself who set this final act in motion. One day, he had Gallo and the Avilas' second-favorite shooter, Elroy, break into the Santa Ana law office of Marvich's attorney, Roger (who later became Gallo and Marco's criminal defense attorney). Gallo and Elroy broke into Roger's safe and stole fifty kilos of uncut Medellín Cartel cocaine, which Roger was holding for Marvich.

Like the Machiavellian puppetmaster he was, Marvich didn't get mad – he got satisfaction. Unbeknownst to Joey, none other than Medellín Cartel founding father Gaviria Gacha Gonzalez, a.k.a. The Mexican, had fronted Marvich the fifty keys. This was the same druglord who had allegedly been supplying the Avilas. Marvich seized this opportunity to kill two birds with one stone: obtain his pound of flesh from Joey and simultaneously make the biggest score of his life. You see, those fifty keys were the tail end of a mammoth 500-kilo load The Mexican had fronted Marvich, who had already sold the first 450 bricks and was about to ship those millions back to Colombia. Instead, Marvich called The Mexican and told him that Joey had stolen *all* 500 keys.

So The Mexican sent a hit squad north. As Joey was driving home from his Balboa Bay restaurant at midnight, two helmeted men on a 250CC Honda motorcycle pulled up next to Joey's black Porsche (vanity plate: BBBBBAD). BRRRRRRRRRRP! They sprayed him with a fully-auto MAC-10. Joey was gone.

At least Marvich allowed Joey to breathe as long as he did. Big Mike's girlfriend's punishment came shortly after Joey threatened him. According to *The O.C. Weekly* reporter Nick Schou:

> On March 29, 1985, Catherine Lawrence died of a gunshot wound to the head at Marvich's Costa Mesa house. Police ruled the shooting a suicide, and the coroner's report provides no evidence of any struggle or foul play. But Kenny Gallo insists that Marvich murdered her in her sleep because she had loaned $200,000 to Avila. Furthermore, Gallo claims, Marvich suspected her of having an affair with Avila, even going so far as to hire an investigator to spy on her.

Gallo explained to me what actually happened, based on his insider's knowledge (including, presumably, from Detective Jerry H.) – a story which Marco confirmed Gallo had contemporaneously relayed to *him*.

That night, Marvich and Cathy went to sleep as usual. At some point, one of Marvich's henchmen crept into their bedroom. As instructed by Big Mike, the intruder put a .357 Magnum to Cathy's head as she slept and blew her brains out. After altering the crime scene to make it appear to be a suicide (including leaving the murder weapon behind), the killer escaped undetected.

The next morning, Marvich, who was then in his late sixties, woke up and calmly phoned the police to report his wife's "suicide." When the incredulous detectives questioned how he could have slept through the gunshot, Mike simply shrugged and replied, "I'm old – I'm hard of hearing." There were no arrests.

So shortly after Joey's murder, Marvich summoned Gallo to his large, comfortable but surprisingly modest two-story home on a bluff in Costa Mesa. Marco's not sure why Gallo brought him along. He suspects Gallo thought Marvich would be less inclined to murder two teenagers, as opposed to just one, in his own home in broad daylight. Marco admits that he was so stupid, he just thought it would be like super cool to hang out with the most notorious gangster in Orange County – a man who did his first prison stint (for bank robbery) in 1948! And a man who, according to Gallo, had his girlfriend's ex-husband, Jerry Lee Lawrence, murdered and left in the trunk of his own car at the Ontario Airport in June 1984 after he had threatened Marvich!

Anyways, Marvich was without a doubt the scariest human being Gallo and Marco had *ever* met, and both had known many dead-eyed killers. He was a large, hulking, powerful man even in his ripe old age, with hands that Gallo describes as being the size of catcher's mitts. His eyes were as flat and dead as a great white shark's. As Gallo and Marco sat in his living room, he asked Gallo what he thought about Joey's murder.

Marco recalls feeling all the oxygen escape the room like a space vacuum. Gallo was quiet for a moment then said something like, "He's gone. Nothing's gonna change that so I don't have a problem with it." Just then, a gigantic peckerwood – maybe 6'5", 300 pounds of rock-hard prison muscle – lumbered down the steps towards them, barefoot, wearing only blue-jean overalls, and crude prison ink sleeving massive, bulging arms.

"This is CQ," Marvich said, bemused. "He's into some heavy shit."

Gallo and Marco could only exchange furtive glances, hoping their collective throat gulps didn't echo too loudly in the carpeted living room. After a bit more small talk, including Gallo's assurances that neither Sal nor Sergio Avila would seek reprisal against Marvich, they were allowed to leave.

Strangely, Gallo and Marvich actually became somewhat friendly thereafter, and Gallo even brought Marco over a second time. But there's no doubt that Colin "CQ" Quick would have eaten them as a light snack had Gallo said the wrong thing.

Lessons to Be Learned

So remember, ducklings, never share your opinion about anyone or anything, regardless of how benign it may seem. And in case you're obtuse, this lengthy anecdote contains numerous other lessons to live (and die) by so take heed, young squire, lest you become a *part* of history instead of a maker *of it*.

Don't Do Stupid Shit

There are no shortage of ways to die by virtue of your own stupidity in the Mafia. All it takes is pissing off the wrong people – the kind of people you do not want to piss off. Henry Hill provides the following suicidal scenario: in the '60s, the eighteen-year-old son of one Johnny Mazzolla began sticking up mob-connected card games and bookies. The young genius was warned numerous times but failed to take heed. (Studies have shown that the frontal lobe of the brain has not yet fully developed until about age twenty-five, thereby resulting in poor decision-making and failure to understand consequences.)

Since those admonitions didn't take, the local *Mafiosi* then tried warning the elder Mazzolla. Indeed but for the mob's respect for Johnny, the kid would have been vacuum-sealed immediately. But as it turned out, baby Einstein disregarded papa's pleading and continued robbing away. He never saw his twentieth birthday, dying of a broken heart caused by two bullets pumped into it at close range. The thoughtful killers wanted to allow his family to have an open casket.

If you're particularly simple-minded, you don't even have to screw with mobsters to get liquidated. All you have to do is travel to a red state and *not* mind your manners. Case in point: DeMeo crewmember Vito Arena, the Mafia's only openly gay hitman to date.

In early 1991, he was released from prison, having completed a short sentence after testifying against the mob.

Hard up for cash, he went back to a life of crime. This time, however, instead of stealing cars and occasionally snuffing people, he hit rock bottom and began robbing liquor stores and gas stations in the south. Does it get any more PWT than that?

On February 15, 1991, Vito learned the hard way that you don't mess with Texas. On his last day on Earth, he robbed the wrong Piggly Wiggly at gunpoint in Houston. He would've gotten away with it except as he was waddling out the door, he suddenly realized he needed some cassette tapes for the long drive back to his fleabag motel. So he rotated his prodigious girth and headed back. The clerk pulled out a .357 Magnum and – BOOM! – blew his head clean off. *Oh snap!*

Vito never could resist Springsteen – it was The Boss's cassette tapes he first demanded when he flipped (after having his boyfriend/crime partner Joey moved into the cell next to his own).

Don't Do *Incredibly* Stupid Shit

It's hard to imagine doing something more self-destructive than threatening to expose the illegal activities of powerful Mafia bosses. But that's precisely what Jimmy Hoffa did after he was released from prison in the early '70s following a labor racketeering beef. Hoffa was furious that the mob had replaced him with Frank Fitzsimmons as head of the International Brotherhood of Teamsters. Hoffa had been warned countless times until Russell Bufalino and other LCN shotcallers had finally reached the end of their patience.

On July 30, 1975, Hoffa disappeared, never to be seen again. Twenty-eight years later, in 2003, the mystery was finally solved, thanks to a deathbed confession from Frank Sheeran. As told to author Charles Brandt in *I Heard You Paint Houses* (which was what Hoffa said to Sheeran when they first met), Sheeran drove Hoffa to a nondescript house in a Detroit suburb on the pretext of a meeting to work things out with the mob. Hoffa completely trusted Sheeran as they were best friends, so he didn't think twice about walking ahead of Sheeran into the house.

As they went upstairs and entered an empty room, according to Sheeran, Hoffa spun around and tried to flee, believing both of them had been set up and were about to die. It never occurred to Jimmy that Sheeran had set him up. And that's when Frank blew open the back of his best friend's head.

Sheeran got away with it – and, again, Hoffa's disappearance remains officially unsolved to this day – but it ruined his life. Afterwards, he became a slobbering drunk and eventually chose death by suicide many decades later in an old folks' home by starving himself. Despite the other four dozen people he had wiped out (not to mention the scores he had killed during World War II, including Nazi SS guards at Dachau), The Irishman had a heart of gold.

Lesson to Be Learned

As Sal Vitale once testified, "Only your friend can hurt you."

The stupidest thing you could possibly do in the Mafia, the one sure-fire way to seal your own doom, is to burglarize and ransack the house of your own godfather. That's exactly what Outfit associate and grandmaster jewel thief John Mendell did to Anthony "Tony" Accardo in the late '70s.

Mendell was what you call a high-line pro – a highly-skilled, sophisticated thief specializing in cash, diamonds, and jewels. For some reason, Chicago used to breed these types of rare criminals the way Charlestown in Boston produced bank robbers and armored-car thieves in the '70s and '80s. (And *not* in the '90s, as depicted in the bitchin' 2010 flick *The Town*, which is a chillingly accurate portrayal of Irish-American gangsters in Beantown back then. Director Ben Affleck even got the haircuts right.)

On December 21, 1977, Mendell and his one-of-a-kind crew (aside from the two Bypass Gangs operating at the same time in NYC) pulled off a daring score at one of Chicago's largest and oldest jewelry stores. In fact, the cops and the press called it the biggest jewelry score of the decade, with the take exceeding $1 million in cash, jewels, and furs. Mendell was the top alarm expert in the Midwest and so was able to circumvent owner Harry Levinson's complicated system.

There was just one slight problem: Levinson was an Outfit associate who operated a lucrative sports book and loansharking operation on the DL. Even worse, he was a very old and dear friend of Tony Accardo, a.k.a. The Big Tuna, the most powerful Mafia don west of Russell Bufalino. This was a guy who got his other nickname, Joe Batters, by beating people to death with a Louisville Slugger for Capone in the '20s. He was even alleged by Bill Roemer to have been one of the shooters in the 1929 St. Valentine's Day massacre in the Windy City.

As a result, Levinson's store was strictly off-limits to criminals. The first person he called on the Monday morning after the break-in when he discovered his store in shambles – even before the police – was Accardo. Within days, Accardo's lieutenants were giving Mendell a stern dressing down. If Mendell hadn't been so valuable to The Outfit, he most definitely would have been sleeping with the *branzini*. So instead, all he had to do was give up the entire score, which he personally delivered to Accardo's mansion in River Forest, an upper-class Chicago enclave filled with elegant, stately homes.

But Mendell just couldn't let it go. He was furious that he had been forced to give up one of the biggest scores of his life, one that had taken months of planning. And so he did what can only be described as the most monumental blunder in the history of LCN.

He waited a few days until Accardo and his wife left for their winter holiday in Palm Springs, and then he and his crew broke into his mansion to retrieve the loot. They also planned to take whatever other goodies they could find – and knowing the Big Tuna, there were plenty. However, they would miss the $400,000 in cash Accardo had stashed in a hidden safe.

And on January 6, 1978, that's exactly what Mendell and his men did. They bypassed an alarm system that was so intricate, every mobster in the Midwest knew only one regional gang could have done it. The identity of the burglars couldn't have been more obvious if Mendell had left his business card at the scene. And that's when the most infamous cycle of retribution in the history of *La Cosa Nostra* commenced...

Exactly nine days after the burglary of Accardo's mansion, on January 15th, Mendell disappeared off the face of the Earth.

Five days later, on January 20, 1978, the first body was found. It was that of Bernard Ryan, slumped over the wheel of his 1976 Lincoln Continental on a side street in the western suburb of Stone Park. He had been shot four times in the back of his head, and his throat had been slit ear to ear.

On January 31, 1978, Steve Garcia was found in the trunk of a rental car in the parking garage of Chicago's Sheraton O'Hare hotel. His throat had also been slit, and he had been repeatedly ice-picked in the torso.

Four days later, on February 4th, the corpses of ex-Chicago police officer Vincent Moretti and Donald Renno, a.k.a. Donald Swanson, were found in the backseat of Renno's Cadillac in the southwestern suburban parking lot of Esther's Place restaurant. Their gullets had been slashed. But Moretti, who as an Italian should have known better, had been traipsing around town wearing Tony Accardo's favorite gold cuff links! So he had also been brutally beaten, and his killers had castrated him and stuffed his penis in his mouth. But not before he had been disemboweled and had his face burned off with a blowtorch.

Cue Buster Poindexter's "Hot Hot Hot."

On February 20th, thirty-six days after he disappeared, Mendell's bloated carcass was found in the trunk of his 1971 Oldsmobile, which had been parked in a South Side neighborhood. He was frozen stiff, half-naked, and hog-tied. He too had been ice-picked numerous times in the chest, but had died by strangulation from the nylon rope that had been tied to his own feet as he struggled to free himself. And he had a trench-deep nick in his neck, but who knows – he could've cut himself shaving. His body revealed signs of torture.

And the hits just kept on comin'!

On April 14th, Johnny McDonald's corpse was discovered in a West Side alley. He had multiple bullet holes in the back of his skull and neck and, of course, he had an extra smile cut into his windpipe.

Cue Queen's "Another One Bites The Dust" – c'mon, you know you were waitin' for that one!

On April 26th, Robert "Bobby Toggs" Hertog's body was found playing trunk music in his car, which had been left in the parking lot of a Chicago supermarket. He had been shot in the back of his head, as well as his throat.

Finally, on October 5, 1978, elderly Sicilian Michael Volpe, the longtime caretaker at Accardo's mansion at the time of the burglary, also vanished. He was never seen or heard from again, and is presumed to have been murdered. He probably shouldn't have flapped his gums to the federal grand jury investigating the preceding string of murders.

And the entire time, Tony Accardo and his cherished wife were chilling in their luxury condo at the Indian Wells Country Club.

Lesson to Be Learned

Don't do *anything* any of these galoots did. (I mean, really – walking around town with The Big Tuna's favorite cuff links???)

Fun Facts!

Accardo's exclusive Indian Wells enclave had been built by the father of Marco's high school girlfriend and junior prom date, Laura.

Laura once allegedly hired Victor C. (the guy who bounced out of Gallo's house) to kill Marco after she found out he had shagged another babe in that very same enclave? Fortunately, she didn't know that Victor was a sleeper (Mafiaspeak for a secret member) in Gallo's crew. Victor went straight to Gallo with the plot, and the three of them cut up the five grand in cash she had paid him.

"What can I say," Marco explains, "I was a disgusting pig. Maybe I still am? Fuck it – at least I tip well."

Chapter Fifteen – Extortion, Loansharking, and Debt Collection

"Don't kill the golden goose, or even one that just lays the occasional egg." – Marco "Babar" Falcón

Finally! If you've made it this far, then you're ready to graduate to the proverbial Big Time. You're ready to start earning with both fists, *paisan* – you're ready to be an earner. But before we start, your favorite Uncle Roman would like to take this brief respite to give you a manly yet heartfelt shoulder-bump-hug. I'm proud of ya, Padawan – you've kept yourself alive and free.

Okay, enough already – don't get all misty-eyed on me. Man up now – you're about to matriculate from Mafia kindergarten to LCN elementary school. Thus, we begin with the most basic of all the mob's meat-and-potato rackets: extortion, loansharking, and debt collection, which are all intertwined.

The Joys of Loansharking

Baby, baby, *baby* – one of the first rackets you should jump into immediately, if not *the* first, is motherf'n' loansharking, boyo. This is where having an organized crime family behind you comes in super handy.

For you clock-punching do-gooders out there, when you get made, you are *not* handed a bag with a million dollars. On the contrary, taxpayer – instead, you are thrust out into the cold, cruel world and told not only to fend for yourself, but to make enough money to kick up to your capo. Barring that, you might as well get your massage therapy license and start giving happy endings to accountants on their lunch break.

Yes, I realize this is a sobering thought – actually having responsibilities and deadlines and so forth. But before you curl up into a fetal position in the corner and cry for your mommy, I'll lay this on you.

Your capo will loan you a decent chunk of change to put on the street in the way of usurious (illegal) loans. And the interest rate to your capo will typically be only one percent per week on the principal. He'll either be loaning you his own money or borrowing it from *el padrino* himself at one-half of one percent per week (0.5%).

So then *you* go and loan out that same money to various losers and degenerate gamblers, charging from two-and-a-half to five points per week, depending on the size of the loan and your relationship to the customer. The money will come tumbling in! Indeed, the only other traditional racket where you can accumulate wealth as quickly as loansharking is slingin' dope.

The Mafia also comes in handy dandy here 'cause you've got the entire weight of your organization behind you if broke dicks refuse to pay you. This presents excellent opportunities to beat mo'fos up *and* feel good about doing it. In addition, like drug trafficking, your customers will soon refer other suckers to you, thereby commensurately increasing your loan pool. Plus, in order to pay off their Third World-type debts to you, they'll tip you off to scores and heists.

Schwiiiiing!!!

Loansharking Basics

I am painfully aware that not all of you merry pranksters reading this are familiar with the fundamentals of issuing usurious loans. Again, these are loans that carry a higher-than-legally-allowed interest rate. In New York state, it's anything above twenty-five percent. I'm gonna let Andrew DiDonato take the spotlight on this.

> Here's how shylocking works. Interest is based on the point system. One point equals one dollar of interest on every hundred dollars borrowed. That's a weekly payment. For example, a six-thousand-dollar loan at three points means a hundred eighty dollars a week in interest. If I got the money from Nicky Corozzo, he'd get sixty dollars and I'd get a hundred twenty. I charged different points depending on the size of the loan. More points on small loans because there was less money involved and they got paid off quicker.
>
> There were less points on the larger loans because you didn't want to choke the customer with interest. If I had a real good customer, I'd sometimes give him a knock-down loan. For every four weekly payments, two went for interest and two came directly off the principal. There was good money in shylocking.

That's putting it mildly. FYI, knock-down loans are typically large loans that are paid off in pre-scheduled, pre-determined installments with the interest rate already built in.

One of the things I despise most about the federal government is its pernicious hypocrisy. To wit, loansharking is illegal but insanely high interest rates on credit cards are not. Nor are pay-day loans and negative amortization subprime mortgages. WTF??? The game is rigged, baby. Hell, if I were king of the world, I would have imprisoned every CEO involved in the 2006 collapse of the American real estate market, which resulted in ten million families losing their homes to foreclosure. You tell me who's doing the most damage. Awright, awright – I'll get off my self-righteous soapbox.

Additionally, always schedule your pick ups for the same day each week with your customers (though vary your routine to avoid being clocked). This way there's no misunderstanding about when they're supposed to pay you.

Finally, try your best *not* to keep records, as this kind of incriminating paperwork will obviously be used as evidence against you if you get popped. In other words, work on your memory skills, Poindexter. Every night, before you choke your iguana or roll over on whatever *guidette* who's temporarily stomaching you, re-memorize all your shylock loans. *Ju can do it, mang!*

Oh, and for you illiterates out there, the term "shylock" first appeared in William Shakespeare's comedy *The Merchant of Venice,* written circa 1596. Shylock was a character who loaned money to people at a high interest rate and, if they failed to pay, would demand a pound of flesh.

Never Make Death Threats

My penultimate take-away rule from this chapter is, as I've indicated, *don't make death threats.* When you threaten to blow someone's head off to collect on a debt (particularly an illegal one), then you might be rewarded with a felony conviction and five-year prison stretch. Even worse, extortion is one of the twenty-seven enumerated predicate acts for a RICO charge, which, as you know, can send you away for the big bitch (life).

Marco is painfully aware of what ensues when you are charged with extortion because his big mouth once landed Gallo in hot water (one of many times). In 1990, Gallo pulled off a major score by ripping off some Colombian dopers' stash house in Costa Mesa. He then enlisted Marco's help to sell off the twenty kilos, roughly a cool half-mil wholesale back then. After doing so, they invested some of the money in a nightclub-sushi bar in south Orange County.

Gallo's old friend Jack Rausch was a Colombian distributor who worked directly for Pablo Escobar's trafficking network, and who did a dime in the federal pen for the privilege (after he was busted with 550 kilos). He describes their hangout, Genesis nightclub and sushi restaurant, in his autobiography *From the Cartel to Christ*: "I had been hanging around at a sushi bar in Lake Forest and those guys were into guns and all kinds of mischief. I wouldn't be surprised if the heat on me had come from them."

Marco explains how the extortion beef went down.

> We bought the club from this sleazy, half-assed Turkish fraudster who called himself 'Antonio' and drove a red Ferrari. It was a great place for The Crew to hang our hats and party with all of our friends and business associates. Some cool dudes who went to high school near us, Zack de la Rocha and Tim Commerford, had their band Rage Against the Machine play their first professional gig ever at our club. All the gangsters in south O.C. would hang out there – and all the pigs had it under surveillance. I pretty much got laid on a nightly basis.

Cue Bruce Springsteen's "Glory Days."

Marco adds, "Antonio was a piece of human cockskin so he fucked Kenji over somehow. I don't even remember what it was about. Is this being recorded, by the way?"

A life-threatening message was left on Antonio's answering machine, which seemingly produced the desired effect. Antonio told Gallo he had the money he owed him, but when Gallo went to collect, he was swarmed by the Newport Beach PD. Gallo was charged with felony extortion and spent a week in the Orange County Central Men's Jail before the judge granted him bail.

Fortunately, the charges were eventually dropped when Gallo's lawyer Roger was able to prove it wasn't Gallo's voice on the tape – it was Marco's! So thanks to Marco, Gallo had to spend a week inside. Please don't be this dense, people. As with some of Gallo's other enemies, Antonio mysteriously disappeared thereafter, never to be seen or heard from again. According to both Gallo and Marco, Clyde had been staking out Antonio's waterfront home with a sniper rifle in the weeks before Antonio evaporated.

So instead, talk around the subject of the outstanding debt, and be extremely subtle about your threats. See, although in

California you need to actually threaten someone's life or threaten them with GBI in order to get charged with making a terrorist threat, there's an exception for extortion. All you have to do is threaten to use force when collecting on a debt to catch a felony case.

That's why I admire Gallo's approach to making explicit threats back in the day – *he didn't*. Instead, he would simply say, "You don't owe me a thing. Your debt is wiped out. Have a blessed day."

Now this downright freaked out the debtor, who knew Gallo would never let himself get hosed like this. They also knew of his fearsome reputation, which included running over not one but *two* enemies with his car in the span of only three years. The second incident resulted in an attempted murder charge. It didn't take long for these blithering idiots to conclude that Gallo was wiping out the debt because he was going to wipe *them* out. Even the most dimwitted debtor quickly coughed up the dough.

Gallo provided another example of a related and equally effective technique that worked with Michelle Braun, the proprietress of Nici's Girls. Remember, this was the escort service Tiger Woods regularly (and, again, allegedly) used for his $10,000-a-night sex workers – even though he was such a tightwad, it pained him to spring for even a Subway sandwich for his own mistress. He also showed his cheap ass when he failed to pick up a dinner check with a group of Navy SEALs who had spent their entire day training with him, including allowing him to fire their exotic weapons and expensive ammo. What a total dick.

Alas, I digress. At one point, Braun failed to pay ten grand owed to Gallo's ex-wife, VHS goddess Tabitha Stevens, who was also working as an escort for her. Gallo remained friendly with her after the divorce, and so did her a favor. He decided to kill two birds with one stone, as his other porn star pal, Dayton Raines, was owed $8,000 from Braun. But Michelle refused to take his calls.

Gallo then proceeded to Plan B. A little amateur sleuthing uncovered the names, addresses, and phone numbers of all her immediate family members. His first call was to Michelle's father. Gallo was pleasant and friendly, and asked him to please let her know that he was trying to reach her. The next day, Braun wired him the full amounts owed. Gallo calls this technique "extortion light" – making the target aware that you know where his or her family members reside.

Like Teddy Roosevelt said, "Walk softly and carry a big stick." Or was it "Wield an iron fist in a velvet glove"? Whatever – you get the picture, happy ass.

Know Your Customer

I shall now explain the symbiotic relationship between being a bookmaker and loansharking: bookmaking automatically leads to shylocking. As a result, you must develop an innate sense of whom you can and cannot lend money to. This translates into you *not* loaning money to someone who's going to run to the cops or feds the moment you slap him around, or even merely threaten him. Believe me, *boychik*, this happens far more often than you'd think.

Sal Polisi provides the cautionary tale of Stanley, a Big Apple bus driver who just couldn't stay away from the ponies. Polisi explained to mobster Big Funzi that Stanley had a delicate constitution and therefore should not be manhandled or even threatened if he fell behind on his vig payments. Sally Boy even warned him that Stanley's cousin was an FBI agent.

So what did Funzi do? Yep, you betcha – he threatened to hurt Stanley after he failed to make the weekly vig. And so Stanley ran straight to his cousin. Big Funzi went away for a nickel stretch in the federal pen.

Need I mention that you shouldn't shylock to relatives of FBI agents?

Dealing with Recalcitrant Debtors

Just because I told you not to threaten your customers doesn't mean you shouldn't put the smack down when they tell you to fuck off on pay-up day. *Oh hell-to-tha-no!* You should take that rebuff as a personal affront to your good name. No, siree; if that happens, you should definitely pound them like a mallard duck. Trust me, once the word gets out that you have a zero-tolerance policy on welchers, people will beg, steal, or borrow to pay you. And that's how it should be.

If you are particularly energetic, you may even want to follow Anthony Fiato's lead. His crew inflicted violence on a daily basis on deadbeats who owed money, bookmakers who refused to kick up, or bar and restaurant owners who balked at paying for protection.

No one could claim Fiato was lazy – he even collected on Sundays. For example, one morning he staked out a degenerate gambler who had lately been dodging his vig obligations. The Animal found him chowing down early on the Sabbath at a North Hollywood taco stand. When the target saw Fiato approaching with a baseball bat, he dashed into a nearby Catholic church for sanctuary. It didn't work – Fiato charged in and brained him right in the middle of morning mass before a packed congregation.

As he explains in *The Animal in Hollywood*, he wanted to ensure that none of his victims believed they could ever find sanctuary from him. This methodology worked wonders – as soon as the target regained consciousness, he paid up in full.

Fiato describes a similar incident in early 1980. One his loanshark customers was TV star Vince Edwards, who played Dr. Ben Casey on the 1961-1965 hit series *Ben Casey*. Unfortunately, Edwards was also a hopeless gambing addict. Even worse, he was a hopeless gambing addict who refused to pay his debts. When Fiato tried to collect, Edwards told Fiato to go fuck himself. The Animal cratered his face with a pair of brass knuckles and doubled him over with a knee to the groin. Gasping for air, Edwards somehow managed to unclasp and hand over an expensive watch. Fiato pawned it and cleared the slate.

Oh, yes – get that skrilla! Now that is straight up good, clean fun, kids.

Lessons to Be Learned

The following are words to live by: don't take shit from *anyone*. If some *strunzo* gives you lip, give him a knuckle sandwich. And if he fights back, or God forbid strikes you first, give him a Folsom Prison-style beatdown, which Frank Sheeran did on the following occasion.

> I had this one guy who I made a loan to avoiding me. I couldn't find him anywhere. One night I caught up with him playing cards in a bar. I told the deadbeat to get up from the card table. He was my height but outweighed me. He got up ready and threw a punch at me, and I decked him. He came up with a chair in his hand, and I snatched it away from him and proceeded to beat him to a bloody pulp and left him unconscious on the floor.

Try Not to Kidnap or Kill Your Deadbeats

Jon Roberts had a highly effective if somewhat controversial method of dealing with his insolvent loanshark clients – he would grab and take them to a secret location in NYC. This was an apartment rented specifically for this purpose. He and an accomplice would strip them naked, tie them to a chair, and beat them. The poor bastards would then be allowed one phone call. The person on the other end of the line would then deliver the money to Jon's associate at a nearby coffee shop. Roberts would then let the victim leave.

JR was lucky none of these deadbeats ratted him out to the FBI, which would have subjected him to a kidnapping charge – a maximum life sentence. And if you're facing life, then you might as well kill the fucker so he doesn't testify against you.

But if you're gonna kill the guy, he won't be able to pay you. See where this circular logic leads? That's right, genius – in a *circle*.

That's why I say *don't* kidnap these fools because they're your livelihood. Don't be a sadistic psychopath like Boston hitman Joseph "the Animal" Barboza. He *wanted* his shylock customers to default so he would have an excuse to kidnap, torture, and murder them. That's just downright unpleasant and asshole-ish.

For your own edification, you might like to know that Barboza was not only the first gangster to enter WITSEC, but the first to murder someone while in the Program. After relocating to Santa Rosa, California, he was rumored to have murdered as many as ten more men before he himself was finally put to sleep by four shotgun blasts to the chest in San Francisco on February 11, 1976.

In the immortal words of the Bard himself: *Goodnight, sweet prince.*

Bottom Line: If you need to slap the dude around to get his attention, then do so, but for God's sake, don't *hurt* the guy. I call it tough love – put the fear of God into him but please don't send him to Valhalla. You'll never get paid if that happens.

Bust Outs

As I indicated earlier, I am not a big fan of the bust out. Why squeeze out pennies on the dollar from your debtor when you can become his business partner, and have both a permanent and legitimate income stream? This will help you with both the IRS *and* your P.O.

Jon Roberts observed his gangster-father's own short-sightedness in this regard. One time, his dad loaned money to the owner of a successful hardware store in New Jersey. When the man failed to repay, his father took it over. But instead of continuing to operate the business, he sold off all the merchandise at a steep discount. He did the same with the store itself, then burned it down for the insurance money before he transferred title to the new, unsuspecting owner.

This perplexed young Jon, who saw his friends' business-owning fathers living in large houses in good neighborhoods. He could not fathom why his own dad couldn't simply continue running the business as the previous owner had.

Fuckin' A! For all you schmucks out there, imagine how your depressing hand-to-mouth lifestyle would be concurrently improved if you had a dozen of these involuntary partnerships. As a loanshark, Nino Gaggi, for example, had secret ownerships in many lucrative businesses, including a restaurant and a pornographic VHS counterfeit-production and distribution company. Nino was *rich*, bitch, and so should you be. Nothing's too good for my peeps.

Rolling It Over

Most Mafia loansharks advise rolling over all the proceeds (the interest, the vigorish, the juice) on your loans instead of simply spending or doing something else with the vig. This way, your principal – the money you have out on the street – continues to accumulate like an avalanching snowball. Sal Polisi is one of these advocates. He claims that the first rule of loansharking is to put everything you earn back into the business.

Now this business strategy makes perfectly good sense unless something goes wrong – and something *always* goes wrong. If you get whacked, the mob will absorb all your outstanding loans and your family will be left with nothing. Or you might fall out of favor with your boss for whatever reason, and once again, your loans will be re-appropriated.

See, in the Mafia, what's yours isn't necessarily *permanently* yours. There are plenty of festering genital warts out there like Little Vic Amuso and Gaspipe Casso who will murder their own men so they can absorb their loanshark books, and justify it by labeling them rats, traitors, or thieves.

Alternatively, you could get busted and go to prison. Guess what *always* happens, even if you're in good standing with your Family? Bingo – we have a winner! That's right, your scumbag boss will make up some bullshit excuse as to why all your money mysteriously evaporated. For example, he'll claim that no one wants to pay now that you're on a chain gang. All your dough goes right into that prick's pocket.

In case you're wondering, all that B.S. about the Mafia taking care of you when you go away to college is just that – total bullshit. All your friends and bosses will screw you in a heartbeat and steal all your cash. Expect your wife to go on welfare and food stamps if you haven't made arrangements beforehand. Still wanna join?

So what to do, what to do? Follow my simple rule: only roll over *half* of your vig back on the street, and wisely invest the other half. That way, no matter what happens, you'll still come out way ahead of the Game, even if you get screwed over down the road or if the IRS seizes all your assets. The IRS did just that to Gambino skipper Gregory DePalma after his 1999 bust for extorting Scores strip club in Manhattan. They seized his mansion, cash, luxury cars, furniture, art collection, and jewelry.

A final note: with a little prudent fiscal management, your long-suffering wife won't have to turn tricks, groom pets (like Karen Hill), or warm your boss's futon while you're away just to put food on the table (also like Karen Hill).

Fun Facts!

Kenny Gallo's UC work with the FBI eventually resulted in Braun pleading out to two felonies: money laundering and violating the Mann Act (for transporting women across state lines for the purpose of prostitution). She received six months of penthouse detention and three years probation, and had to surrender substantial assets to the G. Presumably, she got this light sentence by ratting out some of her clients to the FBI.

But you can't keep a good woman down, and you can't keep Michelle Braun down either. After paying her dues to society, she married wealthy businessman Jeffrey Berk. With his financial backing, she started an online company called Privé Porter, which specializes in middling extremely expensive used purses. For example, in 2016, she middled a record-setting Hermès Birkin bag that sold for almost 300 grand! Her sales in 2017 exceeded $20 million, enabling her to buy a five-story townhouse in Manhattan. *Bravo!*

CHAPTER SIXTEEN – SHAKEDOWNS

"You can't pick up a rattlesnake without expectin' ta get bit." – Marco Falcón

This is precisely what it sounds like – you shake down some assclown who's stupid enough to voluntarily enter your poisonous orbit. Then you suck him in like the Death Star tractor beam and bleed him like a stuck pig. You think I feel sorry for, say, semi-legit crumbs who do business with the mob and then get burned? What'd you expect – they're *mobsters*! The only reason you got involved with these people in the first place is because you are a greedy little piggy. *Oh, oh, ohhhhhhhhhhhhhh!!!*

Aside from generating significant income streams, shakedowns will also allow you to rid yourself of the competition. Thus, yet again, having an army of bloodthirsty killers behind you really works to your advantage when it comes to shaking down weaker people. In the underworld, might makes right. It's social Darwinism in its most primordial form – the law of the jungle reigns supreme.

For all you wusses out there who are offended by this admittedly primitive worldview, I say this – gargle me, you tea-bagging wimps! Even the skinniest girly-men out there – regardless of age – can become badasses after six months of daily Brazilian Jiu-Jitsu training. So have at it and stop whining.

Shaking Down Groups of Criminals

If you have a solid, true-blue gang o' hard, pipe-hittin' homies behind you, then put these fine gentlemen to good use. Have them go around town, grab every unconnected crook, and threaten to delete them unless they start paying you street tax.

I'm serious, that's all you have to do – scare these pansies silly by breaking a few heads. Believe me, everyone will fall into line as long at least one of the guys in your crew is a no-fuck-around, cold-blooded, DTK psycho. That evil bastard will be the indispensable lynchpin for this racket. (In Nicky Corozzo's crew, that man was Michael "Mikey Y" Yannotti; in Paul Vario's, it was Jimmy Burke; in Jimmy Coonan's crew, it was Mickey Featherstone.) The dividends will be astounding – enough to keep your entire crew well fed and (in *faux* French accent) *'appy as 'eeppos. Sacré bleu!*

Three mobsters stand out as having been the most effective in shaking down *groups* of criminals without reprisal, thereby generating ungodly sums of moola. I'll start in ascending order, beginning with our third place finalist, Anthony "the Animal" Fiato.

Anthony first came to Hollywood in the '60s when his father got a job as a bartender at the Villa Capri, when Anthony was a teenager. After his introduction to the mob in La La Land, Fiato eventually returned to Boston where he hooked up with In Town (again, the Boston LCN Family, then run by long-time boss Gennaro "Jerry" Angiulo). After years working the street, building his rep as a leg breaker, and even making his bones, Fiato returned to LA in the mid '70s.

This time, he set up shop in Beverly Hills, took one look around, and realized he had found the promised land. By this point, the LA Family was just a ragtag group of broken-down valises who couldn't hurt a fly. Aside from Mike Rizzi and Jimmy the Weasel (who was on his way out at that time), there was absolutely nobody who could stand up to Fiato. (Hell, even Rizzi once backed down from him.) And so he did what comes naturally to a hungry predator – he feasted on all the weaker creatures in his poaching grounds.

But he couldn't do it alone as there were simply too many freelancers ripe for defrocking. So he put together a core group of eight or ten linebacker types who loved to put the hurt on guys who thought they were hard. Eventually, Anthony's much younger brother Larry joined the crew and became invaluable muscle who loved dental work (knocking teeth out) as much as his big bro. Together these brawny barnstormers became known as the Gangster Brothers.

Anthony and crew chased down unconnected crooks from the San Fernando Valley to the South Bay, chewing up and spitting out anyone who got in their flight path. Anthony left the LA Milano crime family alone as they were part of a much larger network that could call on, say, Chicago, to send torpedoes in to deal with Fiato if he disrespected the local *borgata*. Since Rizzi went off to prison to do a nickel on the Forex sting, and the Weasel had flipped years earlier, Anthony essentially became the de facto Godfather of Los Angeles.

As a result of these relentless, systematic blitzkrieg tactics, everyone else soon fell into line, cutting Anthony in on everything from scores to dope deals to bookmaking operations. And bet your ass the milquetoast Milanos stayed the fuck out of his way and didn't dare ask for tribute.

Without any competition, he and his partner Robert "Puggy" Zeichick became the biggest loansharks in town. Some days Anthony didn't even have to leave his home to make tens of thousands of dollars. Puggy, Larry, and other crewmembers would drop by his posh Beverly Hills condo and dump big bags of cash on his kitchen table. Now that's what I call working from home.

No great scheme goes off without a hitch, and Anthony's hostile takeover of Tinsel Town was no exception. However, this consisted mainly of minor rebellions that were quickly suppressed with a little perfunctory bloodletting. Notably, the LAPD organized crime detectives (the famous Gangster Squad) suspected him of committing a dozen murders but were never able to charge him with even *one*. Anthony's brains certainly matched his brawn.

Anthony talks about his shakedown of Jack Catain, a veteran LA wiseguy who enriched himself over the previous four decades – a tough guy who had the gumption to flex at Anthony As he explains in his biography, he wanted to shake down Catain for $100,000. But every time he tried to set up a meet, Catain would dodge him.

He finally managed to lure Catain to the Polo Lounge at the world-famous Beverly Hills Hotel through a mutual acquaintance, Harry Guardino. But the wary Catain showed up with a bodyguard who resembled an NFL defensive end. The three men sat down in a corner booth occupied by the Gangster Brothers, Anthony and Larry.

Tony the Animal introduced himself to Catain, who immediately began nervously scanning for the nearest exit. In response to the request for a hundred grand "loan," Catain stammered and muttered something about not being able to help him out. This clearly incensed the Animal, but before he could flex, the bodyguard condescendingly patted his hand and told him to chill out.

After saying something about how he and his brother bury all the so-called tough guys in town, Anthony jammed a fork deep into the football player's cheekbone. He had been aiming for his eyeball! The big man squealed like a howler monkey as blood squirted out of his face and all over their table.

Pandemonium erupted at the neighboring tables as women screamed and men shuddered with horror. Larry rose to back down a few would-be heroes but otherwise, that was the end of the fanfare.

The end result: a week later, Catain coughed up $50,000 as tribute to the new king and closed up his own shop. What the hell – a bird in the hand, right?

Second-place prize for greatest shakedown mobster of all time has to go to Whitey Bulger. After finishing his nine-year federal stretch for bank robbery in 1965, he moved back home to Boston and fell in with the Winter Hill Gang, an Irish OC crew (with the exception of the Flemmi brothers and Johnny Martorano). Within weeks of his triumphant return, Bulger partnered up with Steve Flemmi, who was already partners with Martorano (and was already a TEI). Along with Howie Winter, the gang's original leader, they went out and imposed a street tax on all the unconnected bookies in the greater Boston area.

The plan was freakin' ingenious, if I understand it correctly. They fanned out their minions all over the Boston metropolis to bet heavily with every bookie they could find. If they won, they collected the winnings and then bet again. If they lost, they simply told the bookie to go jump in a lake.

In the latter scenario, Whitey and Stevie simply sat back and waited. If someone from In Town showed up to collect, they paid up, claiming it was all a misunderstanding, and scratched that particular bookie off their list. If no one from the Boston LCN showed up, Whitey and Stevie (or sometimes it would be Winter or Martorano) would relay the good news to the bookie: he would now have to give up fifty percent of his profits to them or end up at the bottom of Boston Harbor. Oh, but he still got to keep all the losses – Whitey and Stevie weren't interested in those. As Fiato liked to say, in on the scores, out on the beefs.

By the mid 1970s, the money from this racket was rolling in. During football season, The Hill was netting $75,000 a week. These gangsters had never seen so much money in their entire hardscrabble lives. First, everyone was buying new Caddies and Lincolns, then it was nice houses, and then it was boats. And it was all because of Whitey, who spent nine miserable years thinking about how he was gonna be a mob star when he got out.

Whitey eventually became the leader of The Hill after Howie went off to prison on a federal horse-racing beef. He soon expanded this shakedown racket to include all criminals who were not associated with In Town. Again, the Boston *Cosa Nostra* was run by Jerry Angiulo, the second-most powerful *Mafioso* in New England – second only to Godfather Raymond Patriarca Sr. in Providence, Rhode Island. *His* LCN family was known as The Office; nearby Buffalo's LCN *decina* was called The Arm.

Murders and beatings kept everyone in line, but as with Fiato and the Milanos, Whitey was smart enough to know not to mess with the North End-based mobsters. He knew that even though they were comparatively weak, New York and its armies of shooters were only a few hours' drive away.

The scheme worked like a charm and the millions poured in (even after Martorano lammed it to Florida in 1979 for sixteen years – almost as long as Whitey's own storied run from the fuzz). The success of the operation was due in no small part to Kevin Weeks' reputation as the toughest streetfighter in Southie. That, and the fact that a handful of unfortunate souls disappeared on his watch. They shook down every doper in town and continued doing so with the bookies, who, despite having The Hill for fair-weather partners, also made large fortunes.

Weeks claims Whitey refused to extort pimps since condoning prostitution was beneath him and Stevie. But clearly, molesting teenager girls and strangling women was not. But I'll bet you anything the venal duo took money from both pimps and sex workers but failed to give Weeks his cut.

Ironically, it would be these very same bookies who would ultimately spell doom for Bulger and Flemmi. As with the infamous 1957 Mafia conference in Apalachin in upstate New York, the investigation sparked when a Massachusetts state trooper noticed luxury cars double-parked outside a bar. Eventually, every one of the bookies rolled over on Whitey. As a result, he was forced to go on his sixteen-and-a-half-year hiatus after being tipped off on the pending indictment by FeeBee John Connolly, who, in turn, had been given the heads up by his supervisor John Morris. Flemmi, being the low-brow knucklehead he is, shrugged off the warning and stuck around until he finally went down weeks later, never again to taste freedom.

In the underworld, every sweater unravels with a single thread.

Perhaps you're wondering why Whitey doesn't get my top prize if he made so much money shaking down other crooks.

Weeks estimates Bulger made *tens of millions* over the twenty-five years he was with him. This second-place relegation is due to the fact Whitey still had to steer clear of the Boston Family. That's why that scene is such a joke in the otherwise excellent 2015 film *Black Mass* – no way would Whitey beat up the nephew of Jerry Angiulo, who still had several killers in his crew and ready access to many more. Weeks told one reporter the exact same thing – the scene was bullshit because Whitey would *never* fuck with Angiulo.

My number-one all-time greatest Mafia shakedown artist award, then, has to go to Tony "the Ant" Spilotro. When he arrived in Sin City in 1971, there were no other serious bad guys around to challenge him. With the help of Frank Cullotta, as well as alleged ice-cold killers Wayne Matecki, Ernie Davino, and Lawrence "Crazy Larry" Neumann, plus thirty or so other pals from Chicago, they imposed a citywide street tax on every pimp, pusher, sex worker, bookie, loanshark, burglar, card cheat, scamster, flim-flam artist, hustler, and grifter in town.

Those who refused to go along ended up in the desert outside Vegas since it was against the Rules back then to leave bodies around that town. Tony murdered six crooks in his first six months, and quintupled the city's homicide rate during his first five years. Aside from Griselda "the Godmother" Blanco, who moved from New York to Miami in the mid '70s to escape a drug trafficking indictment, no other gangster has ever single-handedly doubled a major city's homicide rate upon his (or her) arrival. Even Al Capone needed time to ramp up his body count after he inherited the Windy City from his retired boss Johnny Torrio in 1925. Indeed, both Blanco and Tony each maintained this one hundred percent murder spike for over a decade in their respective cities.

Who says criminals are lazy? Tony became Las Vegas' first true godfather. His predecessors Moe Daltiz and Johnny Roselli never involved themselves in street rackets or murders while they served as The Outfit's eyes and ears there. Like

Tony, however, both courted the media and publicity, and were replaced by The Outfit as a result.

Fortunately for Tony, the bosses back in Chicago were so oblivious (including his legendary capo and future Outfit boss Joey "the Clown" Lombardo) that Tony had the run of the place. He made millions – more money than he had ever dreamed of making. The best part was he didn't have to kick up any of his loot to the old timers back home. All of this, of course, is accurately depicted in *Casino*. No doubt his failure to share the spoils hastened his premature demise though.

Targeting Specific Businesses

Let's narrow our focus, little guppies. We've seen how guys like Whitey can shake down all the bookies in town, but what about other industries? Nightclubs that aren't mobbed up are always ripe for the picking. No one excelled at this more than Jon Roberts during his NYC Mafia glory days from the late '60s to the mid '70s. He had learned from his father's mistakes and so typically kept the same owners in place whenever he and his best friend and mentor, Gambino soldier Andy Benfante, took over a nightclub.

By doing so, they not only took a hefty cut of the cover charges and bar take, but also profited by having the club purchase the liquor from their own Mafia-affiliated suppliers. They even used their own friends to work the front door and provide security. I'm sure their peeps were selling coke there.

Their methodology for these hostile takeovers was quite simple and effective. They would send in their hard-ass pals into a club, who would then pick fights with other customers. Then, when the bouncers tried to stop them, the thugs would pull out their heaters and threaten to shoot them. After raising a little more hell, the troublemakers would then leave.

A few days later, Roberts and Benfante would approach the owner. "I hear you're having problems with your club. We can help!" By 1969, Roberts' twentieth birthday, they had taken over half a dozen clubs in this manner.

John Alite did the same thing with valet concessions in Philly and Florida. After conducting his due diligence, he was amazed to find that the mob had not infiltrated these highly profitable, all-cash businesses. In the parlance of the mob, they were wide open. And so he and his gun-toting pals simply muscled their way in, first taking over the industry in Tampa, Florida, then doing the same thing in South Philly. Anyone who stood up got the tar beaten out of them, and particularly obstinate prospective joint venturers simply disappeared. In less than a year, Alite expanded to South Jersey and Atlantic City, taking over concessions at upscale shopping malls and so forth.

Alite was thereby able to claim whatever he wasn't skimming as legitimate income to justify to the IRS his high falutin' lifestyle (and he lived *well*). Even better, he was able to launder all his proceeds from his drug trafficking, bookmaking, and loansharking rackets through the valet concessions.

It was almost too good to be true. In fact, it was. This shakedown racket ultimately landed him in federal prison after he fled a RICO indictment obtained by the US Attorney's Office for the Middle District of Florida in Tampa.

Bonanno Family psycho Tony Mirra (who Joe Pistone said was the scariest mobster he ever met) used a subtler approach for his vending machine business, which netted him 20Gs a month in the mid '70s. Mirra simply sauntered into a new business, identified himself, and suggested that the owner install one of his machines. If the owner knew who he was, a deal would be struck right then and there. If the owner didn't know him and balked, Mirra would say, "Okay. Ask around about me down on Mulberry Street. I'll see youse tomorrow."

Sure enough, twenty-four hours later, Tony would return. The owner would now be singing a different tune. *Madonn!* In all five boroughs, Tony Mirra was *known*.

In that same vein, Gallo imposed his own will against competing dopers in Irvine, Newport Beach, and Corona del Mar while he was still in high school. You either stopped selling dope in his backyard or you got a "date" with Greg

B., a superstar athlete and martial artist, and the only African-American member of The Crew.

Greg was six feet tall and tipped the scales at 230 pounds of shredded muscle. He loved to fight more than anything and was damn good at it. Greg was a legend among fellow varsity players at even the toughest schools behind the Orange Curtain. Other players – even those bigger than him who were mythical tough guys in their own right – knew never to mess with Greg. According to Marco, Gallo would pay Greg to attack the competition.

> And when I say attack, I mean no fucking foreplay or funny banter or nothin'. He'd just straight out charge at the dudes like a bull and beat the fuck out of them. I mean, you almost felt sorry for these guys. The toughest white boys in town would run like deer at the sight of Greg. Sometimes just for fun, if the dealer still wasn't being as cooperative as we'd like after a beat-down, Kenji would tell the guy that he was going to pay Greg to rape him right then and there. He was joking but you've never seen money appear so quickly!

Marco continues with his rose-colored recollection during one of the numerous times he called me from his SAT phone (apparently he has a lot of free time on his hands).

> If you were a wrecking crew, then all of us would go after you – sometimes we'd roll a dozen or more deep, all shit-kickers. Man, those were the absolute best of times! We'd fuck up entire water polo teams at house parties. If no one was biting, we'd put on the *Saturday Night Fever* soundtrack and start disco dancing in the living room. That always started a fight.

I asked him if Gallo's crew ever beefed with hardcore gangbangers (not to be confused with gangsters, who are primarily money-oriented as opposed to being merely turf-conscious). Marco laughed. "We never had any interest in going after the Chicano gangbangers in Santa Ana 'cause they didn't compete with us, and our paths never crossed until after high school. That was a good thing 'cause they'd shoot or stab you in a heartbeat."

Lessons to Be Learned

Know your limits, people – respect the boundaries. *You mess with the bull, you get the horns!*

Anyways, Gallo would always first try to rob these unsuspecting boobs so he could kill two birds with one stone. The looks on the marks' cherubic faces when he stuck his .380 Walther PPK in their ribs and stole their ounces of coke, pounds of weed, or sheets of acid was priceless. This is what happens if you're unconnected and unprotected, sweet pea – never forget it.

Targeting Specific Individuals

Okay, now that we've learned how to dominate specific rackets and even take over entire towns, it's time to laser-focus on fiscally attractive, high net-worth individuals. Once again, I turn to Whitey, who was the *capo di tutti capi* of shaking down rich dudes, including shady civilians. If they ever complained to the FBI, John Connolly would just scare them off by telling them that they'd have to immediately enter WITSEC for the rest of their lives! Man, what a racket, huh? Thanks, Uncle Sam! Let's hear it for Team America!

On August 2, 1982, Whitey sent Johnny Martorano down to Florida to whack John Callahan in an attempt to cover their tracks on the May 27, 1981, Roger Wheeler hit. Callahan was the sleazy accountant who brought Whitey, Flemmi, and Martorano on board to whack Wheeler. Callahan feared that the multi-millionaire would uncover the huge sums Callahan had embezzled from World Jai Alai, a major sports betting company Wheeler had purchased in 1978. (Johnny felt just terrible about the killing because Callahan was one of his closest friends. Thank God he somehow managed to find the inner strength to get over it.)

Anyways, Johnny shot Callahan in the back of the head with a .38 snub-nosed and stuffed his body in the trunk of a Cadillac at Miami Airport. He then tossed his wallet in a super shady bar in the Cuban part of town so the cops would think it was a drug deal gone bad. Which, in fact, they did.

Within days of his body being discovered, Whitey and Stevie began approaching every one of Callahan's shady and even not-so-shady business partners. They informed the former partners that Callahan owed them big money and that his debt was now theirs to repay. Since Callahan was quite possibly the crookedest CPA in Boston, there was no shortage of people to extort. Sometimes these partners simply handed over keys to safe deposit boxes. Whitey and Stevie were all heart; they even tried to shake down Callahan's widow before offering their deepest condolences.

Martorano was amazed at how much money they grabbed with this scheme. He even ran into one of Callahan's former business partners, who confirmed he had coughed up half a million dollars to them!

****

An excellent offshoot of this single-victim shakedown racket is the murder-for-hire con. If you have a rep as a proficient executioner, half-assed wiseguys will try to hire you to waste their business partners, wives, whomever. Unless they're undercover cops, I highly recommend you take their money. Simply pocket it, then tell them to piss off – who the fuck are they gonna run to? You're the scariest guy they know!

But don't be a jughead like Richard "the Iceman" Kuklinski. He got popped by talented undercover ATF agent Dominick Poliferone on December 17, 1986, on a murder-for-hire beef. Kuklinksi was sent away for six life terms and died in prison after doing twenty-five years. Couldn't have happened to a bigger, more humorless asshole: Kuklinski used to physically abuse his long-time wife Barbara so brutally that she had at least two miscarriages. He also once tore the door off a woman's car for inadvertently cutting him off in traffic, with her young daughter in the back seat. Total dick.

Anthony Fiato illustrates how this scheme works. One fine day, cocaine dealer Russ Hampshire approached him about offing his partner, who was snorting up their profits. Fiato told him he'd think about it. He then sent his associate Harvey Ross to buy a mini tape recorder at Radio Shack.

Fiato then set up another meet with Russ. But instead of going himself, he sent Harvey. Unbeknownst to Russ, Harvey surreptitiously recorded his dumb ass as he blathered away, confirming that he was willing to pay Fiato $50,000 to have his partner clipped, with half upfront.

Sure enough, Russ coughed up twenty-five large. Fiato and Harvey then met again with him, this time at the old Tail O' the Cock on La Cienega Boulevard's Restaurant Row. As instructed, after the trio were seated, Harvey took out the recorder and played the tape for him. Russ was understandably shocked. Fiato blackmailed him right then and there for the other twenty-five grand, and continued doing so for the next two years until Russ pled poverty.

Whitey and pals pulled the sorta reverse con, creating these opportunities out of whole cloth. They would target rich folks, clandestinely create a problem for them, and then solve that problem for a hefty sum. For example, they would approach a mark and inform him that someone had put out a contract on him. To calm the terrified individual, they would graciously offer to rescind the contract for anywhere between $50,000 and $500,000, depending on the mark's financial status. They would even put the vic on a payment plan, if necessary. Not once did the mark fail to pay.

Cue *Mighty Mouse* theme: "Here I come to save the day!"

****

For a modern twist on this Killers 'R' Us scam, you should emulate the Hells Angels hitmen who fleeced Ross Ulbricht of hundreds of thousands of dollars in fake murder-for-hire plots. In early 2011, Ulbricht (twenty-seven at the time) started a website on the Dark Web, which is a separate Internet that's not indexed by search engines and which can't be tracked by law enforcement. He called it the Silk Road and used it to connect thousands of drug dealers around the world with tens of thousands of buyers. Total sales ultimately exceeded $1.2 billion. Ulbricht's commissions, paid via Bitcoin, amounted to $100 million.

The products were also purchased with Bitcoin so the transactions were anonymous, and shipped in the mail from anonymous or fake return addresses. The participants used a free software and web browser called Tor, which allows users to invisibly access the Dark Web. Check out the web page "How to Install the Tor Browser & Stay Anonymous" at https://wildleaks.org/install-tor-bundle-stay-anonymous/. Also, try TorChat or PGP, which offer highly secure and encrypted chat systems and messaging platforms.

Supergeek Ulbricht, who operated under the pseudonym the Dread Pirate Roberts (watch the 1987 cult classic *The Princess Bride* and you'll understand), finally got busted in February 2015. He was sentenced to life without parole. If he had retired after only two years and disappeared, the amount of Bitcoin he had earned by then would have been worth hundreds of millions today.

Maybe he shouldn't have kept a diary? Maybe he shouldn't have told his girlfriend about the site? Maybe he shouldn't have been living in the US and, instead, in a non-extradition-treaty country? Maybe he should have hired an expert computer programmer to properly cover his tracks? Maybe he shouldn't have used his real email address when he first went on a forum to anonymously promote the Silk Road? Maybe he should have invented a time machine, catapulted himself into the future, read this book, and teleported the fuck back before he launched his site?

Eventually, the site (which he named after the ancient Chinese trade route started by the Han dynasty in 206 BCE) enabled and facilitated sales of poisons, weapons, ammo, silencers, human organs, and even murder. Or *fake* murder, as it turned out for Ross.

In 2013, Ross recruited some tech-savvy Hells Angels through the site. He hired them to murder a thief who had scammed him online for a princely sum and was now attempting to extort him for more. Ross paid them $150,000 in Bitcoin for a clean hit.

Within a week, the outlaw motorcycle enthusiasts e-mailed him a photo of the dead man. Unfortunately for Ross, however, the would-be extortionist had previously told four friends about the fact that Ross was the secret owner of the site. No biggie though 'cause the Angels agreed to eliminate the pesky foursome for half a mill more, which Ross promptly paid. Well, at least he got a group rate. Ross memorialized these payments and murders in his computer diary!

The FBI, after taking down Ulbricht, could find no evidence whatsoever that the Hells Angels – if indeed that's who they were – had killed anyone, much less these five individuals. Apparently, the Dread Pirate Roberts had been hoodwinked. As Bomb Voyage would say, "*Incroyable!*"

By the way, I looked up Ross on the federal Bureau of Prisons inmate locator website and found the following info.

ROSS WILLIAM ULBRICHT
Register Number: 18870-111
Age: 33
Race: White
Sex: Male
Located at: Florence - High USP
Release Date: LIFE.

Holy shit! This is the United States Penitentiary Administrative Maximum Facility in Florence, Colorado. Florence is the only federal supermax (Level Six) prison in the US, which makes it the highest-security prison in the country. According to Wikipedia, "It is unofficially known as ADX

Florence, or the Alcatraz of the Rockies. It houses the male inmates in the federal prison system who are deemed the most dangerous and in need of the tightest control."

Christ, Ulbricht's doing time with guys like Aryan Brotherhood supreme leaders and founders Barry Mills and Tyler Bingham; foreign terrorists Zacarias Moussaoui (convicted of the September 11th attacks), Ramzi Yousef (mastermind of the 1993 World Trade Center bombing), and Richard Reid (that asshole Shoe Bomber); domestic terrorists Ted "the Unabomber" Kaczynski, Eric Rudolph (1998 Olympics bombing in Atlanta), Terry Nichols (1995 Oklahoma City bombing), and Dzhokhar Tsarnaev (the Boston Marathon bombings). Some of Our Friends are in there too, including Outfit Godfather James Marcello and former Bonanno boss Vincent Basciano.

Ross is apparently under lockdown twenty-three hours a day. I sure hope he has Roku or Apple TV. In May 2013, *Mother Jones* magazine ranked ADX Florence number one of the ten worst prisons in the United States. Robert Hood, the warden of ADX from 2002 to 2005, admitted to *The New York Times Magazine* reporter Mark Binelli, "This place is not designed for humanity. It's twenty-three hours a day in a room with a slit of a window where you can't even see the Rocky Mountains. It's not designed for rehabilitation. It's a clean version of Hell."

Someone please send Ross a care package! I bet he wishes he took the original ten-year plea deal the US Attorney's Office offered him. With good time, he would've been out in eight and a half.

Sigh. I forgot what I was talking about. Moving on, people...

Fun Facts!

The Mafia's traditional edict against murdering within Las Vegas' city limits also extended to non-LCN gangsters. Even the legendary crime chieftain Lester Ben "Benny" Binion *usually* followed this rule. But before I illustrate, I'll enlighten you about Benny's background. Many of you know him as the sole owner of Benny's Horseshoe, the famous Glitter Gulch casino that popularized poker worldwide (particularly Texas Hold 'Em) with the annual World Series of Poker tournament. But I dare say that most of you have no clue what he did beforehand. So I'll tell you.

Benny was a rough-and-tumble good ol' boy from Texas who dropped out of school after the second grade. However, through guile, cunning, street smarts, viciousness, charisma, and a larger-than-life personality, he rose from a lowly moonshiner in 1920 to king of the Dallas rackets by the early 1940s. He surrounded himself with steadfastly loyal local politicians and law enforcement officials, as well as a small cadre of bloodless killers. Benny himself put plenty of enemies into the ground with his trusty .45 six-shooter – hence his nickname The Cowboy.

Did you know that NASCAR fans could form rigidly stratified organized crime syndicates? Crime knows no color or creed, babes. Did you also know the origins of NASCAR can be traced back to moonshiners, who super-charged their Fords to outrun Prohibition agents? After the repeal of the Volstead Act in 1933, former moonshiners began racing each other for sport and coin.

Benny's extraordinarily good fortune took a downturn when The Outfit came to Dallas and turned the tide against him. Wisely seeing the writing on the wall, in December 1946, he packed his custom Cadillac with one million in cash and his two favorite Tommy gun-toting killers, and made a twelve-hundred-mile beeline to Vegas. He arrived just in time for the ill-fated grand opening of Bugsy Siegel's Flamingo Hotel and Casino on December 26th.

Always one to easily make friends in low places, Benny became *compares* with such Mafia luminaries as Siegel, Meyer Lansky, and Moe Dalitz. He was eventually ranked a Top Hoodlum by Hoover himself until Benny became a secret FBI informant. Even Tony Spilotro wouldn't dare fuck with The Cowboy. The Ant once backed down in a confrontation over one of Binion's friends who refused to act as an insider in one of Spilotro's poker room scams.

Also, Jimmy the Weasel testified that he had committed a contract murder for The Cowboy, strangling Binion's former bodyguard Russian Louie Strauss in 1953 for sixty thousand dollars. In his own defense, Binion famously told the press, "Tell them FBIs I'm still able to do my own damn killings." This off-the-cuff boast helped cost him his casino license with the NGCB.

Back to the no-bodies-in-town rule. In December 1967, an unidentified man came to Benny Binion with information about a plot to kill Binion's son Ted, who had gotten caught up dealing drugs. The plotter was Marvin Shumate, a lowlife crook and cabbie who was a close friend of young Teddy. Ted was also a drug addict and constant source of disappointment for Benny. Someone apparently did murder him more than two decades later, on September 17, 1998; his live-in girlfriend Sandy Murphy and her secret lover, Rick Tabish, were eventually acquitted of his murder. Teddy's sister Barbara, who was also a hopeless dope fiend, died by suicide in 1977.

The Cowboy meted out his own brand of frontier justice. Several days later, Messy Marvin's bullet-riddled corpse was found at the base of Sunrise Mountain, east of Las Vegas. Homicide detectives suspected Benny had ordered the hit but could never muster the evidence to arrest him.

Binion, who died of natural causes at eighty-five on Christmas Day 1989, was such a rootin', tootin' badass that he and he alone was allowed to break this rule without the slightest repercussion from the "dagos" (his term). This incident involved William Coulthard, a former FBI agent and state assemblyman. In the summer of 1972, Coulthard was practicing real estate law. He also happened to be the majority owner of the Horseshoe's downtown lot. It was at that time Binion's lease expired.

Negotiations for a new lease took an ugly turn. On the afternoon of July 25, 1972, Coulthard left his downtown office, took the elevator to the third floor of the adjacent parking garage, and climbed into his Cadillac (what else?). He turned on the ignition, sparking the four sticks of dynamite that had been placed directly beneath the steering column.

KABLOOEY!!! The massive fireball engulfed the Caddy, as well as five other neighboring vehicles. Coulthard died instantly. The FBI was also certain Binion had ordered this murder but could never prove it.

Speaking of the FBI, on November 6, 2008, John Connolly was convicted of second-degree murder for his role in the Callahan homicide. He can thank Flemmi and Martorano, who both testified that Connolly had tipped them to the FBI's investigation of Callahan for the Wheeler hit. Connolly was sentenced to forty years in state prison. He had already spent six years in the federal pen on a ten-year racketeering stretch stemming from his hijinks with Bulger and Flemmi. He was released three years later in May 2011 from the FCI in Butner, North Carolina. He was immediately transferred to a Florida state penitentiary to begin serving his state term.

But lo and behold, on May 28, 2014, a three-judge panel of the Florida Courts of Appeal overturned his murder conviction by a vote of two-to-one. They found that his forty-year sentence was unduly harsh in light of the fact that he didn't pull the trigger himself. Connolly danced an Irish jig in his cell, thrilled that after a dozen years in a cage, he was finally about to get his life back.

Alas, twas not to be. The other seven judges on the appellate court were none too pleased about the prospect of Connolly going free. On July 29, 2015, the full court voted six-to-four (so close!) to reinstate the murder conviction. They found irrelevant the fact that he wasn't the triggerman since he was a principal conspirator. Big John won't be eligible for release until 2021, when he'll be a spry eighty-one years old. Easy come, easy go, Don Cannoli.

Postscript: Connolly was also directly responsible for the murder of FBI Top Echelon Informant Richard Castucci, an associate of the Patriarca Family, after Big J tipped off Whitey and Stevie to Castucci's status. On December 29, 1976, Bulger and Flemmi lured Castucci to an apartment in Somerville,

MA. As Castucci was counting out money, Johnny Martorano emerged from a bedroom, snuck up behind him, and – BLAM! – shot him in the head. The three killers then rolled up his corpse in a sleeping bag and stuffed the package into the trunk of Castucci's own Cadillac de Ville.

Fortunately for The Hill, Connolly deflected the FBI's investigation for the murder away from them and onto the Boston LCN. Good ol' Zip (the nickname Whitey gave Connolly in reference to their previously-shared Southie zip code) was truly the gift that kept on giving (and killing).

On June 12, 2009, a federal judge ordered the feds to pay $6.25 million to Castucci's family for his wrongful death.

CHAPTER SEVENTEEN – HEISTS AND SCORES

"God, I love this shit – I love it." – Little Nicky Scarfo

Man, oh man, oh man, oh *man*! Without a doubt, taking down scores and pulling off heists is the most exciting and fascinating thing the Mafia does. This is where *La Cosa Nostra* truly shines – bold, brazen, beautiful. Just like Brooklyn itself and all its denizens (excluding the gentrifying yuppie scum with their Volvo SUVs, Peg Perego strollers, and Petunia Picklebottom diaper bags). The sheer audacity and spectacle of these crimes is as breathtaking as that ugly baby on *Seinfeld*. Damn, I don't even know where to begin.

It goes without saying that pulling off these bad boys requires a tremendous about of time, discipline, patience, intelligence, and planning. Preparation, preparation, preparation – executed with military-like precision and maximum efficiency. Only the best of the best hoodlums participate in these kinds of activities, and to them, I tip my ostrich-plumed fedora.

Think Outside the Box

MINIMUM VIOLENCE, MAXIMUM CREATIVITY – make that your mantra, fellas. Do the unexpected. Surprise is the most important element when taking down a score or pulling off a heist. When you catch your marks off guard, they will usually roll over for you like a little puppy. Combine that with a miniscule taste of pain, the faintest whiff of death, to quell any heroic delusions from bystanders who've watched *Die Hard* too many times.

Personally, I propose smashing a would-be Mighty Mouse on the bridge of his nose with the butt of your 9mm GLOCK 19. This will shatter the cartilage and spray blood like a Yellowstone geyser. That will freak everyone else out and cower them into submission.

Hey, have you noticed how in the movies you always see one character hitting another in the face or head with a gun, knocking them unconscious, and leaving no mark? This is pure hogwash – when you hit someone with a gun, it's like striking them with a hammer. It'll splinter bone, rip flesh, and quite possibly kill the person. And there will always be a great deal of blood. That's why I think the only flawed scene in *Goodfellas* is when Henry hits Karen's neighbor in the face a half dozen times with his .38 snub. In real life, the dude's face would have required a hundred stitches and extensive plastic surgery.

Anyways, pay heed to this innovative heist Frank Cullotta pulled off on December 28, 1964 (talk about a Grinch!).

Cullotta and five fellow ski-masked brutes (including the gang's leader, Paul "Peanuts" Panczko) forced their way into the rectory of the Divine Savior Catholic Church in the Chicago suburb of Norridge. They then tied up the two parish priests, donned their garb, and waited.

Soon enough, an armored Brink's truck pulled up in front of the rectory. The gang knew the truck was arriving to transport the church's Christmas collection to the bank – the last of forty-seven stops on that day's route.

When one of the armed guards knocked on the door, the two "priests" let him in, then knocked him unconscious, and tied him up too. They quickly stripped his uniform, then one of the other robbers slipped into it, went outside to the truck, and knocked on the door. The driver – exhausted from the long day and distracted by his newspaper – glanced in the side-view mirror, saw the uniformed guard in the darkness, and let him in.

BING! BAM! BOOM! The driver ate a knuckle sandwich and went sleepy time. He too was hogtied. The rest of the gang clambered in, and off they drove to nearby Westlawn Cemetery, where they had stashed a work car. They unloaded $285,000 in cash and got away scot-free. They drove to Cullotta's home in nearby Franklin Park to divvy up the loot. The Outfit brass, who had sanctioned the score, got $70,000, so each robber netted $35,833. It was this score that propelled Cullotta into the Major Leagues of Crime. From then on, he was an official Mafia associate.

Cullotta later testified, as soon as the gang entered his home, "We were all jumping around like little kids that we pulled it off." It would take another eighteen years, until he flipped, that the case was finally solved. Of course, the statutes of limitations had long expired, as had most of the participants.

As a devout Catholic, Bill Roemer (who wrote about this heist in one of his five excellent books on The Outfit) was understandably horrified, not least of all because every member of the robbery crew had been baptized as bambinos.

For additional inspiration, I'll refer you to Bob Deasy. As a UC with the Ontario Provincial Police in Canada in the oughts, Deasy once investigated a string of high-profile burglaries executed by an Eastern European gang. These ex-soldiers were hitting Costcos and Home Depots all over the province.

What set these crooks apart was their discipline. While in the service, they had been trained to stay still for many hours. So during the day, two of the former commandos would enter the store and find a secure place to hide up in the rafters (though how they got up there was anyone's guess).

Later, after the store had closed and all the employees had left, a third gang member would cut the alarm located on the store's exterior. They knew this would bring both the cops and the store manager, who would all enter and search the place. Finding no one inside, nor any sign of a break-in, the manager would invariably blame birds that frequently nested in the rafters for setting off the motion detectors.

Then, after the cops and manager split and the coast was clear, the two crooks would descend from their perch, peel open the store's ATM with tools they found inside, and make their getaway.

Precision and Timing

Taking off a moving vehicle such as an armored car requires impeccable timing and pinpoint precision. It requires endless dry runs and relentless practice. Think of it as if you're an actor being filmed by a perfectionist director (preferably one who's not going to masturbate in front of you). You might have to do as many as thirty takes before you finally nail it. Pulling off a moving heist also requires a gigantic set of *huevos* so you'd better be damn sure neither you nor anyone in your crew is going to freeze up when it's go time.

The adrenaline rush from committing a serious crime can be so intense that it can actually debilitate you, or at least hinder your movements. One time, Gallo wanted to blow up the BMW of this hoser who, with his wrecking crew (The Punkers), had jumped him. They cracked him over the head with a beer bottle, giving him a concussion. This made Gallo hopping mad.

Several days later, as soon as Gallo was able to get out of bed again, he set his nefarious plan in motion. At two in the morning, he and Marco parked their car in an adjoining tract-housing development in Irvine. They then snaked through the pitch black cul-de-sacs and greenbelts, and came upon the Beemer. Gallo placed the carefully pre-prepared gasoline bomb on the hood, extended the fuse, then handed the lighter to Marco.

Marco later said, "Dude, my hand shook so badly from the rush that I couldn't even get the thing lit. Kenji took the lighter from me in disgust and lit the fuse, calm as can be. He never let me live it down. Trust me, though – the next time I did something that intense, I was ready for the adrenaline shock. Anyways, we hauled ass out of there. It was a sixty-second fuse with a back-up wire, so it wasn't until we got back to our ride that we heard the BOOM."

The massive explosion lit up the sky with a blinding light. The blast blew the 3-Series straight into the air, and shattered windows on every house and car on the block. You can read all about The Crew's summer of 1989 car-bombing campaign against their favorite rival wrecking crew in *Breakshot*, as well as on the front pages of *The Orange County Register*.

By the way, many years later, Marco and his Miami Love Tribe flew to Vegas to hang out with Gallo and his mobster pals at the annual porno convention, a.k.a. the Adult Video News (AVN) Awards. Gallo was celebrating his nomination as Best New Director of the Year (though he admits his highly-profitable films were terrible, always garnering limp-penis reviews).

On their first night, around three A.M., Gallo, Marco, and friends were rolling their brains out on E. As they were stumbling down the hallway of the Hilton hotel on the Strip, who do you think they ran into? You're right, The Punkers! And guess what happened? Wrong! Instead of attacking one another, they hugged each other like long-lost brothers. They partied all night together, reminiscing about the good old days when they used to beat the crap out of each other. Fortunately, nobody mentioned the car bombs, which would have been awkward. Go figure.

Bottom Line: You always want at least two or three well-seasoned veterans on your heist crew. They will calm the younger and less experienced teammates, and provide a steady, guiding hand.

Sally "*Ubatz*" Polisi describes how to do this kinda thing the right way in the so-called Five Families Score that went down in 1974. The heist involved one member or associate from each of the five New York *borgatas*, including himself, Foxy Jerothe, Tommy DeSimone, and some Bonanno soldier named Roundy (probably not his Christian name).

First, of course they followed and clocked the Brink's truck for a couple weeks. On the big day, it showed up right on the dot, riding low and heavy from all the gold bullion and coins it was hauling.

Sally drove the lead car with Tommy literally riding shotgun and Foxy in back. He smoothly passed the armored car and pulled in front of it. Meanwhile, Roundy, in the chase car, pulled in behind the truck, slowing down to ensure no other cars behind interfered.

The caravan smoothly exited on the Van Wyck Expressway. Tommy and Foxy pulled down their ski masks, checked their weapons, and Sally slammed on his brakes. This forced the truck to jam its own brakes, but it was too close and plowed into the back of their car. Thank God it was still operable.

Tommy leapt from the car, swung back around to the passenger's side of the truck, and aimed his double-barreled blunderbuss at the two guards in the front seat, who placed their hands against the windshield. Foxy suddenly pulled open the driver's door, shoved the driver over, and got behind the wheel. At the same time, Tommy hopped in on the passenger side.

Incredibly, an NYPD patrol car pulled up next to them at the light, but the cop was so terrified by the sight of the armed robbers sandwiching the two hostages that he simply froze. (Just like in *The Town*!)

Sally pulled away in the lead car, and Foxy followed him onto the Long Island Expressway. The caravan exited in Elmhurst and parked on a side street. The hostages were quickly handcuffed and ushered into the back of the chase car. Roundy then followed Foxy in the truck to the drop, which was a large warehouse in Queens. Meanwhile, Sally dropped off the drivers in Jamaica, Queens, unlocking their cuffs and giving them a hundred dollar bill each for their trouble.

Back at the drop, a not-yet-made John Gotti and his capo Carmine Fatico divvied up the take with the other gang members. The haul was stupendous: dozens of silver coins were jammed into shiny one-gallon paint cans, and gold bullion bars were stacked inside black five-gallon drums. As Sally explains, "It was freakin' bootyful!" He later had his share of the gold bars melted down, then sold them for ninety-eight percent of their value. He ended up with almost half a million cash from their historic Five Families Score.

Well done, Sally, but you gotta admit – you're lucky you didn't total your car when you got rear-ended by that truck.

Keep Your Shit Together When Shit Goes South

When the doo-doo hits the fan, you need to stay cool as Vanilla Ice. In fact, many if not most heists go awry simply because the crooks panic.

In June 1980, Big Joey Massino and Dominick "Sonny Black" Napolitano plotted a truly inspired home-invasion robbery. The plan was to break into the Manhattan penthouse of Princess Ashraf Pahlavi, the twin sister of the deposed Shah of Iran, Reza Pahlavi, and steal millions in cash, jewelry, and other goodies.

While Sonny Black waited in the getaway car, Bonanno associates Raymond Wean and John "Boobie" Cerasani entered her building by posing as deliverymen carrying an air conditioner. The clueless concierge unlocked the door and let them in.

And that's when everything went sideways. Wean whipped out his gun but stood too close to the concierge. The latter threw up his hands in terror, accidentally hitting the gun and causing Wean to shoot *himself* in the other hand. The adrenaline was so high, and the blood so plentiful, the bumbling burglars thought they had shot the concierge. They screamed and fled. So did Sonny Black, who drove off after hearing the gunshot, leaving the two meatheads to find their own way home.

WTF???!! Do you have any idea how big a score that would have been?! The Princess of Iran?! She and her evil twin had raped and pillaged their country for billions of dollars in the '70s while their people starved, so imagine how much loot the robbers would have gotten. The Pahlavis and their parasitic brood had fled their homeland only one year earlier so they were ultra flush.

So how could these Mafia numbskulls have turned this embarrassing fiasco around? Well, back then they didn't have

DNA-testing technology so Wean should have wrapped up his hand with duct tape to stop the bleeding. Then he and Cerasani should have forced the security guard at gunpoint up to the Princess's penthouse. After hearing a knock on the door, she would have looked through the peephole, seen the guard, and opened up. Merry Christmas! *Salam! Haleh shoma chetor ast?*

The rugs alone would have been worth tens of thousands. *Each.* And the kilo-sized tins of beluga in the fridge? *Sale noo mobarak!* We're talkin' the good, grey stuff from the Iranian side of the Caspian Sea, not the inferior black eggs from the Russian side. Ah, what's the use? I need a break...

Tipsters

Tipsters are the Mafia's Godsend. These are other crooks or quasi legit or even totally straight citizens who point out, and sometimes even lay out in detail, the scores for you. Sometimes it's in exchange for an equal share of the pie. So if you need four guys on the score, you'd typically divvy it up into six slices: one for each of the heisters, one for the tipster, and one for your lieutenant (capo). Sometimes it's simply to pay off gambling or loanshark debts – again, this is one of the best reasons to get into those rackets.

Although tipsters are indescribably valuable, mobsters don't respect them because they're too weak to do the job themselves. As Henry Hill liked to crow, "They have no balls." Okay, fair enough, Henry – but if they had the *cojones* to do it themselves, they wouldn't need you, and that leaves you out. So stop bitching.

In the book *Wiseguy*, Henry Hill describes an infamous heist that took place on October 16, 1979, at the Manhattan penthouse of cosmetics queen Estée Lauder. According to Hill, one of his friends from Lewisburg federal prison, William Arico, had joined a crew that specialized in robbing wealthy people, either at five-star hotels or their palatial homes. One of the crewmembers, Robert "Bobby" Germaine Sr., got hot tips on scores from a high-class female furrier and clothing designer who was intimately familiar with the layouts of her wealthy friends' homes.

One of these friends was none other than Estée Lauder. So that night, Arico, who was dressed as a chauffeur, bullshitted his way both into her building *and* swank pad. After tying her up at gunpoint, he let in his confederates – Germaine, Bobby Nalo, and a few other gangsters. They got away with well over one million in jewels, which Henry Hill claims he personally fenced.

Interestingly, Henry apparently never mentioned anything to Pileggi about actually being *part* of the home-invasion crew that night. However, according to a January 25, 2014, article in the UK's *Daily Mail*, GOODFELLAS MOBSTER HENRY HILL TOOK COSMETICS QUEEN ESTÉE LAUDER OUT FOR DRINKS AS HIS 'CREW' ROBBED HER NEW YORK CITY TOWNHOUSE (written by an unnamed reporter), Henry told author Daniel Simone that he *was* part of the break-in team. In fact, he claimed he had charmed Estée Lauder so much that during the robbery, he took her out for drinks and got her personal phone number! Does that make any sense whatsoever?!

Crazy Sal's primary source for heists was gambling junkies who paid off their debts with valuable intel. These degenerates would tip him off to valuable shipments coming into New York's JFK Airport. Polisi and his crew would then hijack the trucks. Alternatively, the tipsters would leave doors and cargo bays unlocked, which also made for easy pickings. Sometimes they even steered the gangsters to competitors' payroll deliveries, or to diamond and gold deliveries in Manhattan's Diamond District on West 47th Street. Sally's crew would jump the couriers and relieve them of their goods.

In fact, he and Foxy Jerothe specialized in ripping off couriers and jewelry stores in the Diamond District. None of these would have been possible without give ups (inside tipsters). It worked like this.

Sally and Foxy would don UPS uniforms and follow the courier. One morning, for example, Sal followed Foxy on a motorcycle while Foxy tailed, on foot, a Hassid jeweler carrying a briefcase full of diamonds. Foxy pulled down his ski mask and grabbed the man's briefcase as Polisi pulled the bike over to the curb. Foxy hopped on, and off they took. They made big money off those scores.

So God bless degenerate gamblers! Without these total losers, there would be far fewer opportunities for scores. Thanks to gambling, otherwise ordinary, law-abiding citizens are transformed into willing criminal accomplices.

Factory and plant foremen are excellent sources for tips so do whatever you gotta do to hook 'em and crook 'em. They'll draw outlines of the building for you, lay out your ingress and egress, clock the security guards' routines, and tell you where to find the loot.

Like the April 1967 Air France score at JFK: the night watchman Robert "Frenchy" McMahon gave Henry Hill the inside scoop on how to walk in and out of the cargo building with $480,000 in cash. The haul also included $300,000 in gold, jewels, and precious gems. This score catapulted Hill into the big leagues of the underworld.

However, *Goodfellas* skips over what I think is the most fascinating element of this score: how Henry obtained from "Barney," the midnight shift security guard, a copy of his only key to the vault where the loot was kept. This was money from American servicemen stationed in Europe that was being sent back for depositing in US banks. (Christ, Scorsese completely left out the entire Lufthansa Heist! It makes sense though as virtually the entire movie is told from Hill's perspective, and he was not directly involved in the actual heist.) Air France worked like this.

Henry found out Barney was a horny bastard who loved porn mags. Frenchy took him out drinking, and eventually introduced him to a high-priced escort, whom Henry paid to screw his brains out on several occasions. During one of these trysts, Henry managed to borrow Barney's key long enough to make a copy and return the original.

On the night of the robbery, Henry and Tommy D followed Frenchy's instructions. They walked into the cargo building at midnight when Barney was having his lunch, loaded up their giant, empty suitcase with packages of cash, and strolled out. Even though Barney knew Frenchy had somehow gotten the key from him to make a copy while he was with the escort, he couldn't report this to the police because he would have lost his job and pension!After the score, Henry and Tommy gave Jimmy Burke the entire haul. To hold them over until the loot could be properly divvied up (following Paulie's $150,000 end), he gave them $15,000 each. Being the *mamalukes* they were, that night the duo went out to celebrate at The Improv in Manhattan. They ended up meeting, partying with, and shagging two attractive secretaries, who were actually sex workers on the make. The next morning, Henry and Tommy woke up to find the ladies gone – along with their thirty grand!

In order to forget the strumpets' scam (and to create a pretense to explain their sudden windfall), several days later, the dumbfellas took their wives and kids to vacation in Las Vegas. They even rented extra rooms and flew their mistresses out to surreptitiously join them. Somehow, the boys still managed to find the time to lose another ten grand each playing craps. Easy come, easier go?

Greatest Mob Heists of All Time

All you wannabe heisters reading this can benefit from taking a closer look at these famous scores, which I'm listing in no particular order. These are just off the top of my head, so if you want to pull my coat to other great heists, then e-mail me, post on my website, or throw up the fucking Bat-Signal.

The Pierre Hotel Robbery

On January 2, 1972, in the wee hours of the morning, six tuxedoed men exited a black limousine, with the point man dressed as the chauffeur. They strolled into the lobby of Manhattan's world-famous Pierre Hotel. Over the next several hours, the crew handcuffed and blindfolded two dozen hotel employees and entering guests, rifled through the hotel's safe and scores of safe deposit boxes, and got away with more than three million in cash, as well as at least one million in sapphires, diamonds, brooches, necklaces, and bracelets.

Legendary Lucchese shotcaller Christopher "the Tick" Furnari bankrolled the heist. The actual robbers were seasoned crooks: Bobby Comfort, Sammy Nalo, Alfred "Flounderhead" Visconti, Donald "the Greek" Frankos, Nick "the Cat" Sacco, and some other dude whose name escapes me (but who no doubt is nicknamed after some creature in the animal kingdom).

Some accounts claim the haul was as much as $28 million but this seems a bit farfetched. So for now I'll stick with the $4 million, which still puts this heist as the biggest US hotel robbery of all time (as listed as such in the Guinness Records).

For more details about this heist, check out Daniel Simone's new book *The Pierre Hotel Affair*. I haven't read it yet but it's at the top of my list. And who knows – maybe after I do, I'll change my mind about the size of the score.

The French Connection Heroin Theft

Amazingly, only two days after the Pierre Hotel robbery, on the other side of the same town, a much quieter but equally lucrative score went down – once again, orchestrated by the Luccheses. What is it about this city?

Cue Frank Sinatra's "New York, New York:" "*Doobie, doobie, doo…*"

On January 4, 1972, a mobbed-up NYPD narcotics detective named Joseph Nunziata walked into the evidence room at the Office of the New York City Police Property Clerk. A few minutes later, he walked out with 44 kilos (96.8 pounds) of pure heroin with a wholesale value of $4.4 million.

This was the smack seized a decade earlier as a result of an investigation by NYPD narcotics detectives Eddie Egan and Sonny Grosso.

The two narcs had stumbled upon the so-called French Connection heroin ring, which imported the opium poppies directly from Turkey to Marseille, France. The poppies were then manufactured by French chemists into the highest-grade heroin, and smuggled into the US by Corsican gangsters working directly with Lucchese heavyweights. The ring supplied most of the heroin consumed in the US during the '50s to the early '70s, and was responsible for America's first major heroin epidemic, as well as thousands of overdose deaths. The network even surpassed Joe Bonanno's international ring for US heroin dominance.

At the time in 1962, it was the largest heroin seizure in American history. Detective Nunziata, who conveniently blew his own brains out shortly after the heist, was reportedly connected with Lucchese trafficker Vincent Papa Sr. In turn, Papa reported to Lucchese drug baron Angelo "Little Angie" Tuminaro.

On the basis of the street value of the drugs, $70 million, it was the biggest robbery in American history – *ever*. Of course, the police pull these "street value" numbers out of their asses because they guarantee big headlines. So as a rule of thumb, automatically slash that number by at least half.

The Lufthansa Heist

Jesus H. fucking Christ – was is it with these damn Luccheses?! These brilliant bad boys are like the Bernie Madoffs of the mob. Yes, as you know, once again, they masterminded another extravagant heist.

The Lufthansa Heist went down at JFK Airport on December 11, 1978. Almost six million dollars was stolen – five million in cash and $875,000 in jewelry, making it the largest cash robbery in US history at the time.

Henry Hill and Jimmy Burke got the tip from Martin "Marty" Krugman. He told them that each month, millions of dollars in untraceable currency from monetary exchanges made in West Germany by American servicemen and tourists would arrive via Lufthansa Airlines. The money was then stored in a vault at JFK. In other words, it was pretty much the same dilio as Henry's Air France score eleven years earlier.

Krugman got *his* tip from JFK employee Louis Werner, who owed him for gambling debts. Werner was instrumental in the planning of the heist, even explaining where the robbers should park. Better yet, he provided Krugman a key to the vault, a diagram of the building, and identified where each Lufthansa employee would be at the time of the robbery. Krugman would later be sentenced to fifteen years for his role – the only person ever convicted for the heist.

Using a van to transport the cash and a crash car, Burke sent along as the gunmen Thomas DeSimone, Joe Civitello Sr., Louis Cafora, Angelo Sepe, Tony Rodriguez, Joseph M. Costa, and his own eighteen-year-old son, Frank James Burke.

Anyhoo, just after three A.M., the masked, armed robbers overpowered two guards, then rounded up the other eight employees in the cargo terminal. They then lured in and jumped a third guard who had the only combination to the vault. Thanks to Werner, the gang knew all about the safety systems in the vault. This included the double-door system, whereby one door had to remain closed in order for the other to be opened without activating the alarm.

After examining the cargo manifests, the robbers removed forty parcels of cash. The entire robbery took only 64 minutes. The rest is history.

Gaspipe's $10 Million Jewel Heist

O.M.G. *Again* with the mama-mia-humpin' Luccheses!!! The *stugats* on these guys! It's no secret why Gaspipe, who was actively courted by all Five Families, chose them over the others, despite the fact that they were the smallest *borgata*. He knew they were the sharpest tools in the *Cosa Nostra* shed, the biggest moneymakers. Indeed, for decades the Lucchese crime family averaged one million dollars profit per year for each made man – one hundred million annually in *net* proceeds. Big money back in the '60s, '70s, and even the '80s when the Luccheses were at their peak of power and prestige.

Anyways, in the '70s and '80s, Gaspipe ran an insanely successful heist crew known as the Bypass Gang, for their skill at bypassing complex alarm systems. They're not to be confused with the gang of the same name which also pulled off major scores in the same town during the same time for the Colombos' Greg "the Grim Reaper" Scarpa. You have my permission to be confused though, 'cause the two gangs regularly shared members, and Gaspipe and Scarpa were close friends who often worked together in scores, drugs, and almost certainly murders. They also allegedly shared the intel provided by Scarpa's FBI handler, Lin DeVecchio. Gaspipe's crew was so successful that Michael Mann used it as inspiration for *Thief*.

In the early 1970s, Gaspipe's crew would meet every single day to strategize and plot out their scores. (The Bypass Gang was actually owned by Lucchese *consigliere* Christie "Tick" Furnari, who bankrolled and approved of every heist, with Gaspipe reporting directly to him.)

Gaspipe's primary tool was a magnesium bar (as seen in *Thief*), which was a long metal rod that burns at over 3,700° Fahrenheit. It was so hot it could burn through any type of metal or steel safe. With the bar, they were able to plunder millions of dollars in cash and goodies from warehouses, airports, jewelry stores, Wall Street firms, gold refineries, and banks.

His secondary tool was a highly-customized work van, which had pitch black, bulletproof windows which provided a false view of depth. If anyone tried to open the van with anything but the actual key, such as a lockpick or slide hammer, the locks would jam shut.

The interior was even more impressive – it contained a mini-fridge for food and drinks, a chemical toilet, a cot, blankets, pillows, and binoculars.

So here's what they did: they would park near the bank, and one of the gang would lock it up, then walk away so any witnesses would think it was empty. But two other members would hole up inside for days, if necessary, to conduct surveillance on the target bank. The spotters would take careful notes of everything, from the surrounding vehicle traffic to the schedules of the cleaning crew, including the license plate numbers of their cars.

At some point, Gaspipe and Junior Maguire would show up in the middle of the night to temporarily switch out the bank's front door lock. They'd take the original lock back to the van, where they would use a locksmith kit to duplicate the key, and then they would return and reinstall the original lock.

With their key, they'd then enter the bank and take photos of everything important, including the alarms and the vault. They would develop the photos in their own dark room, then tack them up on a wall in proper sequence to be studied. And then the Bypass Gang would gather to plot out the score. They would even buy an identical alarm system so they could practice dismantling it.

On the big night, they'd enter the vault, bypass the vault's alarm, and burn their way into the safe with the burn bar. Once inside, they'd first grab all the cash laying around, then use tools like hammer locks and crow bars to pop open as many safe deposit boxes as possible. That's where the real treasure lay: diamonds, jewelry, watches, gems, gold bars, drugs, bearer bonds, and, of course, cold hard cash.

According to the late great Philip Carlo, the Bypass Gang's biggest score was a ten million dollar haul from robbing a Chemical Bank in Manhattan's Canal Street jewelry district. Casso told Carlo, "It was an experience of a lifetime. It's a wonder drug. An amazing high every time you punched another safe deposit box. No one box is the same.'"

Amen.

Fun Facts!

Bobby Germaine Sr. was one of the robbers who pulled off the infamous 1972 Pierre Hotel heist. In 1978, Germaine got his son Bobby Junior a job doing maintenance at Hill's house. What Henry didn't know was that the eighteen-year-old Bobby was dealing weed on the side. In January 1979, young Bobby got popped by the Nassau County Narcotics Division. He immediately flipped on Henry, whom he had overheard making drug deals on his home phone.

Bobby later ratted out and testified against his own father. So Dad ordered a hit on Bobby, who was shot to death in 1980 (apparently by Lucchese associates and Robert's Lounge crewmembers Angelo Sepe and Anthony Stabile). According to Hill in *The Lufthansa Heist*, Jimmy Burke was involved in the murder to protect his own culpability as the financier of Henry's tri-state drug operation. It was the biggest in Nassau County up to that point, involving large amounts of cocaine, heroin, marijuana, and amphetamines.

As a result of Bobby Junior's cooperation, the Nassau County DA was able to obtain a wiretap order on Henry's phone, which resulted in Henry going down three months later. And the rest is history.

Speaking of history, and for those of you whom give a flying fuck, Messrs. Egan and Grosso were portrayed by Gene Hackman and Roy Scheider, respectively, in the 1971 classic *The French Connection*. The film went on to win the Academy Award for Best Picture in the same year as the heist.

Did you know that in the early twentieth century, Jewish gangsters dominated the drug business in New York? In fact, the slang term for heroin, *smack*, derives from *shmeck*, which is the Yiddish word for *smell*. Similarly, Marco's wealthy Jewish homeboys in Beverly Hills used to call the cocaine he sold them *shney*, which means *snow* in Yiddish.

CHAPTER EIGHTEEN – HIJACKING

> *"What Jimmy really loved to do more than anything was to steal."* – Henry Hill

If you're unfamiliar with the pure, unadulterated euphoria of hijacking an eighteen-wheel Mack truck stuffed with easy-to-sell consumer goods, then you clearly haven't lived – or at least seen *Goodfellas*. I'm obviously thinking about that glorious sequence ending with Tommy D sticking his gun in the driver's face, taking his place in the driver's seat of the cab, then firing his *pistola* into the air. *Yaaahoo!* What could be more fun that? Not much, my easily-impressed friends.

Now, if you *haven't* watched the movie, then why are you reading this book? I'm sure you all agree Scorsese was robbed of the golden statuette in 1990; although, in all fairness, who doesn't love *Dances With Wolves*? (I know what you're thinking: white bish knows how to say "soldier fort" but forgot her own fucking name? And how come her hair's always super-teased out like Mötley Crüe when all the Lakota Sioux women have perfectly braided tresses? And why is she the only woman in the tribe sporting hairy pits? Finally, what's the deal with Kevin Costner's super poofy *Joe Dirt* mullet? I mean, where the fuck did he find a blowdryer on the prairie???)

Hijacking requires extensive mob connections. In New York, for example, freelance hijacking is absolutely *verboten*. You'd have to be suicidal to commit a crime that constitutes poaching on *La Cosa Nostra*'s hunting grounds. And even if you did manage to swipe a truck, who are you gonna sell the merch to? Everyone knows everyone in this Game, so you best not step on any toes.

Hijacking is also most definitely a team sport – you need a solid, tight-knit crew to take off a big rig. You need two guys to commandeer the truck, and overpower and tie up the driver (unless he's in on the score, which is the case half the time). One guy drives while the other keeps an eye on the driver. Uh, please make sure your man actually knows how to drive a semi – you don't want to stall out and get popped like Roy DeMeo's braindead cousin Dracula. You'll also need one guy to drive the crash car, and another dude waiting for your team in the getaway whip.

You'll also need a whole network of tipsters and inside men, such as warehouse foremen, dock stevedores, trucking company owners looking to hurt the competition, and, especially, truck drivers.

Then you're gonna need a drop – typically a pre-arranged warehouse where you take and unload the rig. Hopefully your Home Depot A-Team is standing by to take care of all the heavy lifting. Finally, you'll probably need fences to middle the swag for you, unless you have the direct wholesale contacts to unload the merch yourself. It's all about teamwork, guys – work with me here!

Bottom Line: Hijacking requires more logistics and networking than any other activity in the mob. So you need to be a good team player.

The Exultant Joy of Hijacking

Hijacking is as close as you're ever gonna get to the nirvana-like bliss of robbing a stagecoach in the Old West – unless, of course, you got your head blown off by a shotgun-riding Pinkerton detective. (Did you know that the Pinkerton Detective Agency eventually morphed into the FBI?) Nobody – and I mean *nadie* – loved hijacking in the entire history of the mob as much as Jimmy Burke. It was in hijacking where Burke truly shined – he was quite possibly the number-one hijacker in all of New York. Even though he had a crew standing by in each drop spot, he would insist on being the first one to rip open the crates, packages, or boxes in each truck. His face would light up with sheer joy, the sweat running down his face giving him an angelic glow. Henry Hill told Nick Pileggi that he had never seen Burke happier than when he was ripping into these trucks – he was like a little kid on Christmas morning.

This is no lie – even though Jimmy was a millionaire with an army of hijackers and unloaders working for him in warehouses all over Brooklyn, he loved being a hands-on guy. He loved it more than counting money. He even loved it more than murdering people.

Give Ups

When possible, hijack rigs where the driver is in on the score and knows what to do when the time is right. These are usually connected guys who have verifiable experience doing give ups (also called gimmes), so they know the drill. Sometimes you pay them a flat fee; sometimes it's a percentage. The plus side is the absence of violence and the exponentially increased likelihood that you're gonna get away with the hijacking. The downside should be equally obvious – not much fun or excitement. But as I always say, *cabrón* – better to be safe than to involuntarily smoke a pickle in the joint.

That brings to mind the very first day of one anonymous mobster's first prison stay, who described it to me as follows...

> I was nervous as hell, especially when I first entered my cell and met my cellie – a giant bear of a man everyone called *El Oso*. He seemed friendly enough. He rolled off the lower bunk and stood up. Shit, that *vato* was *huge*.
>
> He smiled and said, "Welcome to your new home, *ese*. This is your first time in the pen, right?" I told him it was and he said, "Cool. So you wanna be the wife or you wanna be the husband?"

I almost pissed my pants right there. I told him, "*Definitely* the husband."

He smiled again and said, "Excellent! Get on your knees and give your new wife a blowjob."

Bring Along All the Necessary Accoutrement

If it's not an inside job, then you'd better bring along all the crapola you're gonna need – guns, gloves, ski masks, duct tape, handcuffs and keys, and a bottle of water (in case you're stuck somewhere waiting for a while after you take off the rig). You'll also need walkie-talkies (leave your cell phones at home so the coppers can't trace your movements when you go on your run), bleach and rags (to wipe away any fingerprints and hair fibers from the truck), and large, empty Snapple bottles (for relieving yourself if you're stuck waiting a while).

According to hijacker extraordinaire Sal Polisi, Foxy Jerothe was in charge of bringing all their equipment, including Smith & Wesson handcuffs. The cuffs were to keep the driver quiet and under control once they moved him to the hotski (stolen work car). They would tell the hostage the cuffs were police issue so he wouldn't panic. That way, the cops could use their own keys to unlock the cuffs once the hostage was rescued, as opposed to having to saw them off his wrist. This eased his apprehension. You never want to give your target cause to panic.

And just so you know, even Joe Pistone always came strapped when doing a hijacking. That's called armed robbery, baby. Good luck getting the FBI to approve that nowadays. What can I say – Mr. Pistone was a trailblazer.

What to Do with Those Insufferable Hostages

I would loathe dealing with hostages – they're always an unknown factor, and it's with them where things typically go sideways on you. The key is control, control, control. Make darn sure you've got them covered and immobilized at all times lest they hop away, like Victor C. did when Gallo left

Marco alone with him in their bathroom. Sure, later the boys all shared a hearty laugh about that escapade (okay, so maybe Victor didn't find it quite as amusing). But at the time, it was downright embarrassing. In Marco's own defense, he says that back in those days, he spent an inordinate amount of time staring at his own reflection in mirrors. As he explains, "If you don't love yourself, no one else will."

In any event, have a plan for what to do with these guys when you're done with them. You should always drop a hostage truck driver off in a strange neighborhood where he won't know where to go for help. Back in Polisi's day, most drivers were white, so he and Fox would drop them off in Harlem. If the hostage was Puerto Rican, they'd drop him off in the middle of an all-white suburb on Long Island. Sal would copy the pertinent information from the man's driver's license and give him a hundred bucks for his troubles after securing his promise to misidentify them. Finally, Polisi and Foxy would ditch the hotski and go back to Sal *Ubatz*'s social club to divide the spoils.

Speak to your hostage in a calm and soothing manner. Let him know that you are a seasoned pro who only employs violence as a last resort. And you obviously want to take the SIM card out of the hostage's phone as soon as you grab him. But mail it back to him after you do so – no sense being a dick, right? Oh, and always give him five hundred to a thousand bucks in cash for his trouble – it's good karma.

Getting Rid of the Evidence

Leaving incriminating stuff behind is a big no-no, partner.

After the hijacking and unloading were completed, Jimmy Burke would always douse the truck with bleach. This would eradicate any finger- or footprints, as well as any chance a canine could sniff out any evidence. Jimmy's associates would then drop the truck off in an industrial area, where it would fit in with the locale.

Burke was always one step ahead of the law. In an attempt to deter hijackings, the trucking firms began painting huge white letters on top of the trailers so police helicopters could easily identify and track the vehicles. As soon as Jimmy the Gent caught on, he began pouring black tar across the letters.

Always Be Looking

You should constantly be on the lookout for new opportunities to expand your hijacking business and contacts. Few men in the Mafia have ever matched the schmoozing skills of Gaspipe, or his grasp of these opportunities.

During the 1960s and '70s, Anthony Casso was constantly looking to pull down new scores, particularly hijackings. He made it a point to befriend truck drivers, who would give up their loads in exchange for $10,000 in cash. The exchange would take place at a prearranged location, the driver simply handing over the keys. The drivers would blame the crime on masked, armed bandits to throw the coppers off. Casso would wholesale the loads to fences connected to one or more of the Five Families at a huge profit.

Gaspipe knew that these trucks were loading up their goods at the Brooklyn docks. He saw that he could maximize his ROI by working directly with the guards who watched over the piers. These were the men who controlled everything that entered and exited the secure docks.

By corrupting the pier guards, he was able to hijack two or three trucks every week. He became so busy, he enlisted the help of his good friends, remorseless killers Junior "the Irishman" Maguire and Frank DeCicco.

Gaspipe's operation was so smooth and professional, he never had to resort to violence. You see how Gaspipe thought outside the box? Strive to go straight to the top of all of your illicit endeavors. I mean, why fudge around?

Up Your End Game

As in life, in the hijacking game, you should always know where you'll likely end up and try to improve on *that*. Now, if you are as imbecilic as I suspect many of you are, you'll probably store the stolen rig in some warehouse indefinitely until you sell off your merch piecemeal. That takes way too much time and will draw far too much heat. On top of that, your customers will know you're desperate to sell your swag so they'll lowball you.

Now if you wanna score more fruit (Signore Polisi's term for money), you should already have buyers lined up in advance. So if you swipe a semi crammed with fresh seafood, for example, then you should already have a dodgy Red Lobster manager lined up to take your entire load.

Better yet, take customized orders and then target the trucks hauling those particular items. *Please* tell me some of you are already way ahead of me and have reached the same conclusion. Even a garbage can (brokester) like Benjamin "Lefty Guns" Ruggiero figured out this was the best way to go.

Lefty Guns had a contact on the Brooklyn docks who provided him cargo manifests. He was thereby able to pre-sell his stuff by taking special orders for the merchandise on those manifests. This not only maximized his profits but minimized his exposure since he was able to immediately unload the swag.

I mean, even *Lefty* figured this out! And here was a guy who was so dense, he actually went willingly to a meeting where he knew he was almost certain to be whacked (for bringing Pistone into his crew). Lucky for him, the feebies swooped him up on the way to the meet and threw him in the pokie for thirteen years. They only let him out of prison in 2005 on a medical discharge so he could croak from cancer (and not of his prick, as implied by the film).

Where were we? Right, cut out the middleman, Einstein. Joe Pistone writes about Vinny the Fence, who sold his swag from hijackings and burglaries every weekend at a flea market booth he rented. By doing so, he doubled his profits. In the drug world, that's called seed-to-street.

Speaking of Mr. Pistone, I have a very minor bone to pick with him. In *Unfinished Business*, he claims that the top hijacking crews in the Big Apple during the early to mid '70s were those of Big Joey Massino, Dominick Napolitano, and

John Gotti. Collectively, these crews were taking off eight trailer trucks a day.

Okay, I totally agree that those guys were at the top of the hijacking game at that time, but what about Paul Vario's crew? I mean, Jimmy Burke surpassed any other mobster in New York when it came to hijacking. Indeed, by 1970, Jimmy the Gent had the run of JFK Airport. And he most definitely had more drop-spot warehouses than anyone else in the city.

Stop and Smell the Roses

Don't let the adrenaline, fear, and excitement distract you from thoroughly searching all the packages during your hijacking (and in any robbery, for that matter). You might just miss out on the biggest score of your life. Just listen to the tale of a circa mid '70s hijacking caper that involved the theft of ninety-eight mailbags. They were being transported from an air force jet to a US post office depot at JFK.

At that time, the four masked, armed hijackers were from Gambino capo Carmine "Charley Wagons" Fatico's crew, including brothers John and Charles Carneglia.

The Fatico crew forced the driver at gunpoint to lie on the floor of the cab while they drove the truck to their home turf in Queens. There, they transferred the mailbags to a bakery truck, which they drove to Brooklyn. Unfortunately, they failed to thoroughly inspect all the mailbags, which contained a whopping three million dollars in cash and bearer bonds, concealed in generic packages. As a result, their take was a relatively miniscule one hundred grand.

Let that sink in, my lovelies. That would have been the biggest score of Charlie's life. Not his brother John's though, 'cause he became a big-time heroin dealer worth millions. By the way, John's getting out soon after serving more than thirty years in the can for dealing smack. Ouch, baby! Hope someone writes a book about him.

Fun Facts!

According to the trivia on *Goodfellas* I purchased through Amazon Prime, "Martin Scorsese first got wind of Nicholas Pileggi's book *Wiseguy* when he was handed the galley proofs. Although Scorsese had sworn off making another gangster movie, he immediately cold-called the writer and told him, 'I've been waiting for this book my entire life.' To which Pileggi replied, 'I've been waiting for this call my entire life.'"

Oh, and guess who actually *did* knowingly meet their maker as a result of Joe Pistone? That's right – Dominick Napolitano. On August 17, 1981 (three weeks after Pistone was pulled out of the mob by the feds), Sonny Black was called for by then new acting boss Joe Massino.

Sonny handed his gold watch, jewelry, wallet, and apartment and car keys to his favorite bartender at the Motion Lounge in Williamsburg with instructions to give them to Sonny's girlfriend. He was driven to the Flatlands home of Bonanno associate Ron Filocomo, where he was shoved down the stairs. Capo Frank Lino put the barrel of his .38 to Napolitano's head and squeezed the trigger. CLICK. *Misfire.*

Sonny Black then said, "Hit me one more time and make it good." Lino did as instructed. As co-conspirator Frank Coppa later testified, Sonny Black "died like a man."

One year later on August 12, 1982, a badly decomposed corpse was found in a shallow grave on Staten Island with a telltale sign of Mafia disrespect – the hands had been chopped off. It would take months for forensic dental testing to verify what everyone in the New York underworld and law enforcement already knew – it was Sonny Black.

CHAPTER NINETEEN – ROBBERIES

"Better to be nouveau riche than no riche." – Imelda Marcos

Ahem. If I, uh, somehow gave you the impression that hijacking was the most exciting crime you can pull off in the mob, then I apologize. For the record, *Generalissimo* Martín hereby dictates that pulling robberies is the single most adrenaline-inducing activity of all non-lethal crimes you can commit as a wiseguy. Who better to agree with me than thrill junkie JR.

Roberts' favorite activity was robbing suckers, even though there was far more money in taking over nightclubs. Pulling rip-offs was better than sex, but far more addicting and dangerous. He knew the robberies could get him into serious trouble, but he couldn't resist the thrill of sticking a gun into someone's face whom he had just befriended. "I loved turning their world upside down. The look of shock on their faces was better than any orgasm I ever had."

What's that? You say you're not totally convinced about the psychoactive euphoric effect of jacking some fool at gunpoint? Well, if you've read *The Sinatra Club*, then you would have to agree with me that Crazy Sal Polisi was the most fun-loving Big Apple gangster during the '60s and '70s.

Having said that, then, would your sweet Uncle Sally lie to you? Heck no! He says that the best thing about living the Life was the action, the excitement in pulling down heists, hijackings, scores, and robberies. Sure, the money was nice, but it was the pure rush of these dangerous capers that made the Life worth living. "It's better than sex, and I could never get enough."

For God's Sake, Would it Kill You to Wear a Disguise?

With the advent and proliferation of smartphones, as well as the overall increase in surveillance cameras, it's easy these days for someone to snap and upload your face to YouTube. And then you're properly fucked.

Remember when Tommy Two Guns foolishly removed his mask during the Lufthansa Heist? One of his accomplices even yelled at him to put his mask back on. But the damage was done – several employees got a good look at his face. Didn't take long for the cargo workers to identify him from a photo lineup.

Jimmy Burke, for your information, wasn't present during the heist itself. He was in a halfway house after being released from prison following his extortion stretch with Henry Hill. But The Gent did manage to sneak out in the middle of the night to transfer the loot from the work van to one of his secure warehouses.

You know, I've always wondered – and have never been able to ascertain – why Henry Hill was not directly involved in the Lufthansa Heist. As accurately depicted in *Goodfellas*, he originally got the tip from Marty Krugman (who actually did have a wig store with cheesy late-night TV commercials). But Henry only heard about the heist after the fact.

In fact, Hill had such little involvement that even when he flipped, he didn't have enough information to pin Lufthansa on Burke. He did, however, testify against Burke for helping him fix Boston College basketball games, which got Burke twenty years. Hill also ratted him out for the murder of drug dealer Richie Eaton, who ripped off Burke for a quarter of a million bucks. That landed Jimmy a life sentence. He died in prison on April 13, 1996, from lung cancer at age sixty-four after serving fourteen years. Is it just me or do an inordinate number of mobsters seem to die of cancer, and typically in prison? Karma's a bitch.

One of the other participants, fellow mobster Angelo Sepe, despised Hill and convinced Burke not to bring him on board.

But according to Henry himself in *The Lufthansa Heist*, he didn't want to risk the heat that everyone knew would come from the score because he had only been paroled five months earlier. Besides, as he explained to author Daniel Simone, strong-arm work wasn't his forté (which was true).

Finally, Hill was hardly hurting for money at the time, as he was heavily involved in large-scale drug trafficking, as well as fixing the Boston College basketball games. Therefore, he didn't need to participate in the heist.

But something about Hill's excuses just don't add up – namely because the Robert's Lounge gang (as Burke's crew was known) were all aware the Lufthansa haul would be at least two million. Who the hell turns down that kind of fruit? Plus, for these guys, there was always a need for *more*. Have no fear, gentle readers, Big Dawg Martín shall get to the bottom of this sooner or later.

Don't Rob People You Shouldn't Be Robbing

I realize I'm beating a dead horse, what with our comprehensive discussion about John Mendell burglarizing The Big Tuna's mansion, but will it kill you to have this drummed into you once more? On the contrary, brainiac – it might just kill you if I *don't*. Besides, where you gotta go you can't spend sixty more seconds max reading this section?

So I'll provide a poignant anecdote on the kind of people you shouldn't stick up. According to Joseph Bonanno, a.k.a. Joe Bananas (a nickname the press gave him, which he despised), if someone outside the Mafia fucked with a *Mafioso*, that individual became an enemy to the *entire* Family. And if the dude was particularly vile, he might land on *the entire LCN's* Most Wanted List.

Bonanno recalls one incident involving thieves who burgled the house of Mafia boss Joe Profaci's nephew and stole a safe stuffed with cash and jewelry. The *Mafiosi* first tried negotiating with the burglars for the return of the loot. The thieves just laughed. So the *Mafiosi* resorted to Plan B – they put the thieves on a hit list that went out to all Five Families. (New

York is the only city that has ever had more than one *borgata*.) Bonanno explains that it was the duty of every made man in the city to ensure that justice was meted out. Shortly thereafter, the robbers were executed.

Do Your Homework

If you're gonna take off a big-money target, it's critical that you conduct thorough surveillance on that individual so you can determine the best time to jump him. This is when he will have the most amount of loot on his person, coupled with the best time to ensure your escape. This obviously requires a small, trustworthy team, like Tony Spilotro had with Frank Cullotta and other righteous Chicagoans going back to the early '60s.

Spilotro and Cullotta were barely eighteen when they began robbing bank messengers. They stationed one of their crew outside the bank and one inside. The inside man would wait in a teller line until he spotted the messenger withdrawing large amounts of cash, which he placed into a leather satchel. The messenger would then exit to return to his business with the cash. As soon as he did, the inside man would signal the outside man through the bank's windows. The outside man would then follow the messenger and clock his routine, and, when the time was right, Tony and Frank would pounce. This racket was so lucrative, he and Spilotro were pulling down $25,000 a month *each*.

As Cullotta explains in Pileggi's *Casino*, in Las Vegas, sometimes if they were short on dough, they'd pull armed robberies. That's how they took down the Rose Bowl sports book. As Spilotro had predicted, one night at six o'clock on the dot, the elderly female owner and her hulking bodyguard exited the joint and entered its parking lot. As she walked towards her car with a bag of cash, Cullotta's boyish-looking accomplice from Chicago cut them off, gun in hand. With his free hand, he grabbed the money bag.

The bodyguard lunged at the accomplice, who simply backhanded him, knocking him on his ass. The robber then sprinted away, running parallel to the Strip. Following right behind was Crazy Larry Neumann, who had been waiting in the parking lot as backup. Together they jumped in the getaway car, driven by Ernie Davino with Cullotta riding shotgun. By the time they heard the sirens, they were four blocks away.

Take Off Only Promising Targets

Only rob people worth robbing, right? Then why are so many of you bad guys out there pissing into the wind by pulling short-change, no-upside robberies?

I was recently on the Greek island of Mykonos doing research for this book. Perched at the poolside bar, I was reading Selwyn Raab's *Five Families*. A guy who turned out to be a former Organized Crime Strike Force prosecutor in Chicago noticed my book and struck up a conversation. He regaled me with stories about how stupid so many of the mobsters he prosecuted were.

"It's amazing the lengths these guys would go to just to avoid working," he said. He told me about one crew who had spent months planning to rob the grave of a famous movie actress they believed had been buried with a fortune in jewels. When they finally pulled off the caper, they discovered ... *nothing*. The only objects in the coffin were her bones.

The grave robbers got popped as they were leaving the cemetery. Reminds me of that scene in *Donnie Brasco* where Lefty Guns is trying to bust open a parking meter for the spare change. Pa-*thetic*. The former Assistant US Attorney was a true gentleman for speaking with me. He even gave me his card so I could do a formal interview with him under less intoxicated circumstances. Unfortunately, I lost it. Suckin'. Fuck it, I never claimed to be Bob Woodward.

Gambling Stick-Ups

When all else fails, rob high-stakes card games. Surprisingly, many of these games are not connected. For decades, there has been a weekly floating big-money poker game in Hollywood packed only with whales (A-list actors, directors, producers, etc.). Ben Affleck, Matt Damon, Leonardo DiCaprio, and Tobey Maguire were reportedly only four of the big fish who attended these games for *years*. These guys play for $10,000 a hand, and always bring hundreds of thousands of dollars in cash with them. So rob *those* people!

Molly Bloom, a former real estate assistant, somehow managed to single-handedly build up an illicit poker empire. She hosted floating high-stakes-only games in mansions and five-star hotel suites all over LA. She became infamous not only for the size of the stakes, which often reached pots of $2 million, but for the A-list actors who played. Machine-gun-wielding security guards kept watch over the pots, as well as the piles of cocaine and roving high-class sex workers.

Unfortunately, "the Poker Princess" finally got popped in 2011, although the floating game still continues. The film *Molly's Game*, based on her 2015 eponymous tell-all, opened in January 2018, with Jessica Chastain playing her.

In *The Last* Mafioso, Ovid Demaris writes about the easy pickings of non-mobbed-up card-game robberies. This was a favorite caper of Jimmy the Weasel in his younger days when he was a member of The Combination (again, the Cleveland *Cosa Nostra* family).

In the summer of 1936, Fratianno and his *amici* realized they could make more money sticking up gambling rooms than running their own crooked card games. On their first outing, they took down a poker game. He and his best friend Tony Dope Delsanter stormed in, whipped out their revolvers, and screamed at the nine men in the room to take off their clothes and kiss the wall. The total haul: $5,800 in cash and jewelry (over $105,000 now). Not bad for five minutes' work.

For their second score, they raised the stakes considerably: a swank gambling hall. They knew there would be many more people, so he and Delsanter brought along sawed-off shotguns, which are ideal tools for crowd control. They were also concerned someone in the crowd might recognize them so they pulled silk stockings over their faces.

They charged in with the shotguns and were momentarily startled by the size of the crowd – 200 patrons. Quickly regaining their composure, they jumped on top of two tables and yelled at everyone to put their hands against the walls. All 200 people did as instructed. This time the haul was a whopping $70,000. That was some serious fruit back then, *mijos* – near $1.3 million today!

Be Careful About Whom You Work With

I'm not just talking about *not* working with goofs – that ship has sailed, son. I'm talking about you being careful when you work with *killers*. It's not the little scores you need to worry about, but the big kahunas – especially those once-in-a-lifetime scores. Because when there's millions of dollars at stake, even when there's more than enough to go around, your fellow heisters will start thinking about how to increase their own share by bumping off crewmates. The Lufthansa Heist should immediately jump to mind – Jimmy Burke wasn't exactly a gent when he murdered thirteen people (including three women) over several years to cover his tracks and keep the lion's share for himself.

According to Gaspipe, Big Paulie Vario gave Jimmy Burke the green light to whack everyone involved in the heist. Jimmy was a sociopath with no honor. I wonder how much he gave Tommy D and his own son, Frankie. He loved both men and so presumably would not have cheated *them*. However, he probably gave Tommy very little since DeSimone was murdered by Gotti's crew shortly after the heist. Jimmy admitted to Henry Hill that the Lufthansa money was cursed and had driven him insane with greed, bloodlust, and paranoia.

My devoted fans, please help me answer a few related questions: why did Paulie give the go-ahead to Jimmy to murder all these people? Why didn't Pileggi or Hill discuss Paulie doing so in *Wiseguy*?

A final note: none of the men Jimmy the Gent clipped in connection with Lufthansa were made men – that would've caused too many obvious problems, particularly since Burke himself was merely an associate.

Plan Meticulously

There's a strange dichotomy inherent in Dominick Montiglio – he was capo Nino Gaggi's nephew, a Gambino associate who eventually flipped and became one of the primary subjects of *Murder Machine*. On one hand, Dominick (whom I like, so don't get me wrong) saw intensive, prolonged combat as a highly-decorated Special Forces black-ops warrior in Vietnam. This means he was intelligent. For you peaceniks out there (and I am certainly no warmonger), put aside your anti-military prejudices and stereotypical views of commandos and get one thing straight – being a shadow warrior requires a high IQ. You have to be exceptionally proficient at numerous complicated sciences and skills. I've known a few of these guys and they all struck me as being inordinately sharp.

But on the other hand, virtually everything Dominick did when he got out of the military and went to work for his uncle were the actions of an imbecile. (No offense, Dom – I think you'd have to agree with me, right?) This particularly applies to his planning of robberies after he left the protective (if smothering and tight-fisted) wing of Nino. He pulled off several robberies where he barely escaped by the skin of his pearly whites – all because of piss-poor planning caused in no small part by his alcoholism and cocaine addiction. This too resulted in his final bust, which, in turn, caused him to flip.

On January 6, 1983, Montiglio and two accomplices were arrested by sheriff's deputies after botching the robbery of a jewelry broker in the town of Westlake in Ventura County, north of LA. It was a stupid plan to begin with, not least because it went down in broad daylight in a suburban neighborhood.

First, as the lookout, Montiglio hung around outside the jeweler's house, which makes no sense because a second gang member sat nearby in the getaway car. In other words, Dominick's role was not only redundant, but greatly increased the gang's chances of being spotted by neighbors.

Second, a third accomplice, armed with a pistol, home-invaded the house by himself. You always want at least two or even three people when you do a home invasion. Here, the idiot lost control because there were four occupants inside. As he was trying to herd them all into one room, one of them managed to slip away and climb out a bathroom window. Sure enough, a nosy neighbor saw the man escape and run down the street, then immediately called the heat.

When the inside robber realized he had lost one of his flock, he panicked, ran out the door, passed Dominick, and screamed, "Let's get the fuck out of here!" Dominick followed him into the getaway car, which roared off. But not before the nosy neighbor noted their license-plate digits.

Fifteen minutes later, a sheriff's roller lit them up with a siren and pulled them over. All three were taken into custody and chauffeured back to the sheriff's station.

As usual, Dominick was his own worst enemy. Instead of keeping his mouth zipped (which you should *always* do in this situation), he cockily waived his right to shut the fuck up. He gave a bullshit alibi that he thought would provide an innocent reason for his presence in the getaway car. However, because he was a moron and likely coming down off *yeyo* at the time, he put himself in the car at the time of the home invasion.

If it wasn't for his long-suffering, quick-thinking wife Denise, who provided Dominick with a sound alibi, well... as the detective who interviewed her put it best, "Your husband will talk his way into prison without your help." It took her a while thereafter, but she *finally* divorced his useless, philandering, coke-sniffing ass.

Lessons to Be Learned

Whenever the cops question you, always keep your fucking mouth shut! *Never* try to talk your way out of trouble. All you are required to do as a matter of law is provide your name, address, and nothing else. The cops will keep pressing you for information, so simply tell them, "On the advice of counsel, I respectfully decline to answer any more questions. I hereby invoke my Fourth, Fifth, and Sixth Amendment rights under the Constitution of the United States of America, for which it stands, under God, and liberty and justice for all. Amen."

Once you request an attorney, the cops are legally bound to stop questioning you. Never be a dick about it, but as politely as you can manage, tell them to lick each other's balls and give you your one phone call.

With maximum respect and empathy for Dominick, he was clearly a ding-a-ling who never should have gotten involved in crime in the first place. Deep inside he was a good, decent human being. He even blew the opportunity to marry Paul Castellano's daughter, Constance. This would have ensured him a life of untold riches. As Dominick explained to Nino Gaggi, "I'm not in love with her."

As a result, on the rebound from Montiglio, Connie ended up marrying Frank Amato, a stick-up man and hijacking partner of Edward "Danny" Grillo. Amato despised Connie, and thrashed and cheated on her every chance he could. Imagine what happened when Big Paul found out about this fucknut beating his precious daughter – particularly when five years earlier, Don Castellano had Vito Borelli iced just for making fun of his appearance. I'll give you a hint – he called Roy DeMeo.

On September 20, 1980, DeMeo summoned Amato to the Gemini Lounge on the pretense of conducting criminal business. Roy and his crew employed the tried-and-true Gemini method on him: they shot, stabbed, and dismembered him, then dumped his body parts at sea over the side of a cabin cruiser at midnight.

Cue Christopher Cross' "Sailing."

Fun Facts!

By the way, Jon Roberts became so famous after the hit documentary *Cocaine Cowboys* was released in 2006, celebrities like Snoop Dogg and 50 Cent counted him as a friend. So cool. Unfortunately, he passed away several years ago from cancer. I can't believe no one's made a movie about his life yet.

We're walking, people, we're walking...

You may also wish to know that in an incredible stroke of bad luck for Jimmy Burke, Edward MacDonald, the AUSA who turned Hill, had actually played basketball for Boston College, his alma mater. Hill first mentioned fixing games as an afterthought – he didn't think it was a big deal in light of all his other crimes. MacDonald was so incensed that he literally lunged across his table and tried to strangle Hill! The other feds in the room had never seen him so furious.

Also, years later when he retired and went into private practice, MacDonald shocked his colleagues when *he* flipped against *them* and joined Team *Cosa Nostra* by defending mobsters. He even represented Big Joey Massino when he joined Team America in 2004, helping him negotiate a cooperation deal that ultimately resulted in Massino serving only ten years of a life sentence.

What else, what else? Oh yeah...

Many of The Combination's members were related to Kenny Gallo's good friend Johnny Fratto, who sadly passed away in November 2015 from lung cancer. I had the pleasure of spending time with him on several occasions. You can catch more of Johnny as the star of a 2011 documentary you can find on Netflix about the 1929 St. Valentine's Day Massacre in Chicago called *Inside the Mob's Bloody Valentine*. Johnny, you are sorely missed. I'm looking forward to reading his autobiography with Matthew Randazzo V, *Now That I'm Dead, Here's the Real Dirt*.

Next, did you know that Ben Affleck once won the California state poker championship? He was such a good player that in 2001, he won $800,000 playing Texas Hold 'Em at the Hard Rock Casino in Vegas on a three-day bender, tipped a hundred grand to the staff, then had himself limo'd straight to Promises in Malibu for rehab! Now that's what I call drying out in style, baby.

To quote the late, great Rick James, "Cocaine is a *helluva* drug."

By the way, Ben has been banned for life from playing blackjack at that same casino after security guards allegedly busted him that night counting cards!

And did you know that "Player X" in the movie is Tobey Maguire? Don't know 'bout you but I, for one, was heartbroken when I found out that he's a toxic buttdart who, as he admits in the film, loves "to destroy people's lives." Hard to imagine that the hero in some of my favorite flicks (*Ride with the Devil, The Cider House Rules, Seabiscuit,* and the Raimi's *Spiderman* flicks) is a vile, poison-spitting wood nymph. Don't believe me? Don't blame ya, but check it out on the Google machine – he's apparently so reviled in Hollywood (Charlize Theron, for example, hated working with him), he can't get a job now!

Let this be a lesson, kids: with great power comes great responsibility, and clearly tiny Tobey abused his mojo. What made you so mean, Maguire? Mommy didn't breastfeed you when you were a baby? Doesn't matter, but just know this: I haven't been in a fight since kindergarten, but try to pull that Jedi-mind-fuck shit on me and I'll shove my fist up your ass and work you like a hand-puppet.

Having said that, I loved you in *Wonder Boys*.

Chapter Twenty – Bookmaking and Gambling

"There's a sucker born every minute." – P.T. Barnum

Aside from prostitution, the oldest pay-to-play vice in the world is gambling. As part of my four-week research jaunt through Italy, I had the privilege of taking a private tour of Pompeii, just outside of Naples. (Pompeii is the ancient city that was completely decimated by a volcanic eruption in 79 A.D. At its peak, twenty thousand people lived there.) My guide was twenty-five-year-veteran historian Nello DiMaio. His father had been an archeologist who excavated the city. Nello showed me no less than thirty-four fast food stalls (bread, pizza, wine, etc.) where evidence of gambling had been found. This is two thousand years ago!

This fascinating tour led me to one simple realization: since the beginning of mankind, people have been filthy degenerates, engaging in whatever vice available. Goddamn, people love to roll them dice, spin that wheel, and throw down those cards! In the American LCN world, gambling as a tightly-controlled racket goes back to at least the 1870s. That's when the first Sicilian gangsters made their new home in New Orleans, the true American birthplace of *La Cosa Nostra*. (Prior to that, gambling in general had become fairly widespread in Wild West saloons and gambling halls following the Civil War, as well as in Irish-dominated areas in New York decades earlier.)

Making book has been considered a stable, dependable, and almost genteel criminal racket for over a century and a half.

Indeed, the bookmaker was once considered to be a gentleman in comparison to other crooks – a man who rarely, if ever, engaged in acts of violence. Nevertheless, the bookmaker was virtually always connected to a criminal organization that could and would employ brutal methods to make collections when necessary.

Advantages for Customers of Illegal Gambling

Why bother becoming a bookmaker when online gambling is so readily available? When Vegas or Atlantic City are only a few hours away by plane? There is a veritable cornucopia of advantages for a gambler to go with a mob bookmaker as opposed to legitimate venues.

First, if you bet with a Mafia bookie and win, you don't have to pay taxes on your winnings. Conversely, declaring winnings from a legal casino is a tried-and-true method of laundering ill-gotten gains, so long as you don't do it too often.

Second, you don't need a high FICO score to obtain credit from your bookie as long as he knows you're good for the markers, or if someone sufficiently connected can vouch for you.

Third, if you're a high roller, a bookie or mobbed-up gambling joint can often prove more flexible by raising the maximums on your preferred game of chance.

Fourth, there is always the illicit thrill of being bad and rubbing shoulders with unsavory characters, which makes for scintillating cocktail-party conversation.

Fifth, the mob's payouts are typically superior to those of the legit outlets since they don't have high overhead.

Sold yet?

Andrew DiDonato is an expert on the Mafia's historical gambling rackets in New York City. This is hardly surprising as he ran all of Nicholas "Little Nicky" Corozzo's gambling rooms. He was so successful that Nicky himself gave him the nickname "Good News" because every time DiDonato gave him his weekly envelope, he'd deliver happy tidings about their gambling enterprises. Andrew's book *Surviving the Mob* provides an in-depth and comprehensive description of the Mafia's gambling rackets in the Big Apple.

Nicky was so powerful that for a brief period following the commencement of Gotti Senior's life sentence, and before he himself was sent away to prison for various racketeering crimes, Little Nicky was part of the triumvirate that ruled the Gambino Family. In fact, but for his constant legal problems, Nicky would have eventually taken the throne. He was that strong.

Anyways, Andrew explains why many people prefer the mob to, say, Vegas:

> Betting with bookies is the same as betting in a sports book in Las Vegas, only easier. When working with our bookies, the customer didn't have to show up in person to make a bet. Instead, he was assigned a number and we handled the transactions over the phone. The customer called into a central office, would identify his bookie, give his number, and place the bet.
>
> When the office received a call, we first checked the player's 'sheet' to see how much credit he had. If his bet didn't put him over his credit limit, we took his action.
>
> As a rule of thumb, when a guy owed, we allowed him to play for cash. If he won, we took a piece toward what he owed when he cashed out. We worked with these guys because getting heavy over a debt usually meant losing a customer that you knew would have money again and would find somewhere else to bet. Then you'd have to chase that money. If a customer ran away with a big tab, we definitely tracked him down.

"There's a Lot of Money in that Shit, Pop"

And, of course, there are distinct advantages to *you* in making book and operating a gambling ring – namely, raking in the *beaucoup* bucks. Few players in OC enjoyed these proceeds as much as Mickey Cohen. By 1947, his gambling empire was raking in $80,000 a week (over $903,000 present day).

During the 1940s in LA, Cohen was living large. He had a fleet of luxury cars, each containing secret compartments for his cash and guns. He owned a fabulous custom-built home in Brentwood worth $2.6 million now, which doesn't get you jack in LA these days. The crowning glory of Mickey's sweet pad was his closet, which ran the entire length of the master bedroom and contained more than two hundred suits shimmering under fluorescent lights. He also owned hundreds of monogrammed silk shirts and man-panties carefully displayed in custom-built chests. Another dandy after my own black heart!

Too bad Jack Dragna, Jimmy the Weasel, and friends-whose-names-all-end-in-vowels ruined that house when they blew it up during one of their many unsuccessful attempts to kill Cohen. (Big surprise: they wanted to take over his gambling rackets.)

Hell, Mickey was rolling big enough to pay the LA County Sheriff himself tens of thousands of dollars a month in graft to protect his rackets. That price included the occasional round-the-clock sheriff's-deputy bodyguard. LA has always rivaled New York, Chicago, Miami, and even New Orleans as the most corrupt law enforcement city in America.

By the mid 1970s, the Winter Hill Gang was earning $75,000 a week from gambling alone. All the shotcallers bought deluxe houses. Stevie Flemmi bought one in the affluent Boston suburb of Milton for his girlfriend Marion Hussey, their three kids, and her daughter from a prior relationship. The latter was Deborah Hussey, whom he would later molest as a teenager and eventually murder with Whitey's help. Flemmi then had a swimming pool installed in the backyard, and even sent his three kids by Marion to private school.

Before you start nominating The Rifleman for Father of the Year, know this: Stevie Baby insisted that their three kids' birth certificates all identify her ex-husband as the father. Flemmi was concerned that one day Marion might drag him into court for failure to pay child support.

He also purchased the house next door to Marion's family for his parents. Never one to waste a good opportunity, he secretly installed a large hidden compartment in the house where he could stash his weapons. His elderly parents had no idea they were sitting on The Hill's arsenal. Many years later, after the shit hit the fan with Whitey, Steve's brother Michael Flemmi, a retired Boston police officer, would be sentenced to ten years in prison for moving this same arsenal to another hiding spot.

Speaking of Bulger, he finally moved out of his mother's apartment in Southie after she died and bought his own home in the same neighborhood. Howie Winter purchased a big place in nearby Somerville. Johnny Martorano, always generous to a fault, bought two houses, including one for his ex-wife.

Now this wasn't Mickey Cohen money, considering the numerous splits of the take and adjusting for net present value, but even old Mick himself would have been proud of these earners.

Bookmaking Leads to Loansharking

The best part of bookmaking is the immediate and never-ending supply of shylocking customers it feeds you. These games-of-chance addicts are constantly in need of a grand or two to keep the night's festivities going. And that's really the entire point of bookmaking, isn't it? Aside from creating tipsters and corrupting cops, your primary motivation for running card and dice games is to generate loanshark vig. Hence, gambling is at the very root of organized crime.

Breaking In

Big money bookmaking and gambling in most major cities is usually rigidly stratified and tightly controlled by organized crime syndicates. Gambling constitutes a major percentage of all Five Families' rackets. Indeed, by 1987, when Andrew first became deeply immersed in Nicky's gambling rings, certain crews in each Family were annually pulling down tens of millions of dollars *each*.

Thus, you can't just waltz into town as a lone wolf, plant your flag, and set up shop. Apart from being suicidal, it's simply not a practical way to become an operator. To do so, as a wiseguy, you first need to get the okay from your superior officer, with a typical 70-30 split. Guess who gets the 70?

On the upside, however, your percentage will improve the more successful your game becomes. There are even periodic performance-based bonuses. Finally, for the lion's share you will pay the higher ups, they will provide you with the bank to run your game, and the connections to lay off for sports betting. The latter provides you insurance against your book taking too large of a position on any particular game. This keeps your operating risks nicely balanced and ensures you get your profit regardless of who wins or loses.

Fortunately, your entry-level position in the Mafia will likely be in these rackets. This is how Nicky Scarfo gained his entrée into LCN. From the late 1940s to the early 1950s, his uncle, made man Nicholas "Nicky Buck" Piccolo, and his two gangster-brothers began schooling him on bookmaking, gambling, and loansharking. During this period, Scarfo was forced to tend bar to make ends meet. At the same time, he apprenticed under Felix "Skinny Razor" DiTullio, who was also mentor to future hitter Frank Sheeran.

This is also how The Grim Reaper's protégé first jumped into the Life. As I said, after giving eighteen-year-old Larry Mazza permission to keep *schtupping* his common-law wife, Greg Scarpa Sr. folded him into the Wimpy Boys crew. Mazza began running numbers for Scarpa, and even started shylocking with the Reaper's financial backing. Mazza was also able to take over a major sports-betting operation that serviced professional gamblers. By the late 1980s, Mazza's ring was generating $2.5 million a year in pure profit.

Talk about having your cake and eating it, too! Hell, this almost made up for all the murders Scarpa eventually forced

Larry to participate in. But before establishing himself as a capable shooter, Mazza was first placed by The Grim Reaper on brain detail, cleaning up after homicides in blood- and gore-splattered rooms. *Yuck!!!* Or as Agent Pistone likes to say, "nothing for nothing."

Laying Off

Without the local *Cosa Nostra* family backing you, you'll make more money in the short term but your chances of surviving long term will decrease with time. Every once in a blue moon, one of your customers is going to win big against you, the house, because that's simply how the gambling cookie crumbles.

Most of you older cats recall when Mike Tyson suffered his first defeat as the undisputed heavyweight champion of the world against Buster Douglas in 1991. No one thought Douglas had a snowball's chance in Hell of winning, and so the gambling odds were, say, 50-to-1 in favor of Tyson. So if you were an independent bookie giving those odds, all it took was a handful of guys who bet a grand each on Douglas to wipe you out. You either paid up, or if you couldn't or wouldn't, you skipped town; either way, it was curtains for you. Same goes if you refused to accept these Hail Mary bets in the first place 'cause refusing to take a wager is a surefire way to ruin your rep as a stand-up bookie.

However, with the Mafia backing your book, you'll be able to lay off these lopsided wagers, thereby significantly reducing your exposure. We have LCN founding father Frank Costello to thank for this betting insurance. Towards the end of the 1920s, Costello saw the writing on the wall and understood that Prohibition would be repealed in the coming years. As a forward-looking godfather, he focused on shoring up his bookmaking operations.

And then one day he had an epiphany: by creating lay-off pools, he could not only ensure the financial integrity of his own Family's gambling rings, but he could charge outside bookies a fee to spread out their own bets to his organization. It worked like a charm and millions rolled in overnight.

"Don't Get High On Your Own Supply"

Sage advice from Cubano Frank Lopez, which Señor Montana should have taken to heart, and which hopefully you neophyte bookies *will*.

Phil Leonetti's father Pasquale strayed off this path of righteousness with devastating results. Papa's sterling reputation as a top-flight gambling operator was known throughout Philly, New Jersey, even in the Big Apple. He was so well known that famous reporter Walter Winchell once wrote about him.

Unfortunately, Pasquale did the one thing pro bookmakers should never do: gamble. He ended up personally owing the mob big bucks. When he couldn't pay up, he abandoned his wife and baby Phil and fled South Philadelphia. That didn't quite satisfy Family boss Angelo Bruno, who seized Pasquale's pest extermination business. Philip and his mother were left destitute.

This bitter memory scarred Leonetti as a youngster, so whatever you do, don't be a human shit stripe like his dad. If you're stupid enough to have a family while you're a gangster, the least you can do is financially care for them.

Aside from Danny Grillo and John Gotti Sr., who take first and second place, respectively, for the worst degenerate gamblers in Mafia history, the number three spot must go to Gaspipe's longtime crime partner, Burton Kaplan.

The downhill ball started rolling when he placed large wagers with Christopher "Christie Tick" Furnari Sr., who would one day become the Lucchese Family *consigliere* and Anthony "Gaspipe" Casso's mentor. Even the millions Kaplan was earning as a major player in New York's garment trade were not enough to keep him afloat. And so he turned to crime.

He started out easy, illegally selling passports from Peru, counterfeit designer duds, and stolen appliances. Then things heated up considerably when he began hawking pilfered

US Treasury bonds with a crook named Israel Greenwald. Kaplan caught wind of a federal investigation, most likely from his human crystal ball, FBI agent Lindley DeVecchio. Kaplan prudently surmised that Greenwald would fold under questioning and rat him out. And that's when Burtie crossed the line and became a *real* gangster.

On February 10, 1986, Mafia Cops Lou Eppolito and Steven Caracappa followed Greenwald's car in their unmarked roller. Blasting their siren, they pulled him over and arrested him as a hit-and-run suspect. They explained that they were taking him to an auto body shop for witness identification. Israel wasn't concerned as he hadn't been involved in any such incident. He was unaware cops would never take you anywhere except the station house for a witness lineup. Not that he could have done anything about if even if he had.

But as soon as the trio entered the garage and emerged from their car, Eppolito's cousin, Lucchese associate Frank "Junior" Santora, shot Greenwald twice in the head. Kaplan paid the Mafia Cops thirty grand for their efforts.

In total, Kaplan gambled away three million dollars. He once paid off a big marker by helping a murderous loanshark – a former detective – dispose of a corpse in a Connecticut river. Sex workers and blow, Burt, baby – you shoulda stuck to that.

Look, I don't mean to be a party pooper – it's perfectly fine if once in a great while you need to blow off some steam, especially after a big score. In 1991, Gallo and Marco flew to Sin City after conning an extremely violent street gang in Santa Ana called The Avenue Boys out of $60,000 in cash on a bogus dope deal.

Back then, The Avenue Boys were a small-time clique of *vato locos* with whom Marco had hooked up through his uncle, who was an OG (original gangster/*veterano* gangbanger) from one of Santa Ana's oldest street gangs, *Los* Delhi Aces. The Avenue Boys were an offshoot from that gang. Gallo and Marco supplied them with multi-kilo loads of coke and hundreds of weapons over half a decade – almost all of which *they* had purchased through the local paper or at gun shows with fake

IDs. With the coke and guns, The Avenue Boys became one of the biggest and most powerful gangs in Orange County. They have a heavily respected presence in West Coast penitentiaries, boasting of deep ties to *La Eme* and to the Mexican Cartels themselves.

I started down this tangent to talk about how after Gallo and Marco ripped off The Avenue Boys, The Crew flew to Vegas after paying attorney Roger to cover Gallo's extortion defense. During the flight, the boys dropped acid and X (as it was called then), then rented the Presidential Suite at the Hilton for a week. They stashed the loot from the score in the hotel's safe deposit box.

For seven straight days, Gallo gambled like a blackjack fiend while Marco and the rest of The Crew had the time of their lives. Gallo also had a blast, and even bought a small but real working *cannon* that he had driven back to Irvine. When the fuzz finally raided their house, imagine the coppers' surprise when they discovered *that* little home-protection device.

But now that I'm thinking about the monsters they unleashed, and the lives and families they must have destroyed through The Avenue Boys, I'm kinda feeling bad about the whole dealio. I guess you could say that of all the evil shit Gallo and Marco ever did, propping up these psychos must rank near the very top. *Gulp. Walk it off, baby – walk it off.*

Lessons to Be Learned

So, as far as gambling – and, hell, as well as with everything illegal that feels good – everything in moderation, my friends. Including moderation.

Piss on Your Fire Hydrant

Now, by and large, the bookmaking/gambling rackets are benign and peaceful. However, they are also highly lucrative and, therefore, competitive. Indeed, aside from drug trafficking, these rackets invite the most conflict from other criminal groups.

In the late 1960s, up and comer Anthony "Tumac" Accetturo made his bones several times over in Newark, New Jersey. At that time, a group of Black Panthers began violently taking over numbers territories from white bookies. (They were probably infiltrators sent by J. Edgar Hoover as part of the FBI's evil COINTELPRO program, as opposed to true civil rights militants.) Tumac chose the toughest Mafia headbreakers he could find and went after the African American criminals. After murdering several of the top guys, the New Jersey faction of the Lucchese Family retained its profitable numbers rackets.

So even if you have soft hands as a Mafia bookmaker or gambling operator, you'll still have an army of killers at your disposal to enforce your zero-tolerance policy. (That is, unless you're with LA's feeble Mickey Mouse Mafia.)

Gambling Ain't All Fun and Games

As with virtually all of the crimes discussed in this book, gambling is a predicate act for a RICO charge. In 1961, thanks to efforts by US Attorney General Robert F. Kennedy, the federal government enacted the Interstate Travel in Aid of Racketeering Act. ITAR, as the feds called it, made many of the Mafia's activities federal crimes. Thus, crimes that were previously considered state law violations, such as extortion, bribery, and gambling, now carried far more severe penalties.

So for Pete's sake, chipmunks, take all necessary precautions. Johnny Martorano almost took a major pinch as a result of his involvement with bookmaker Dick O'Brien. He was a major player for the Winter Hill Gang. The Massachusetts State Police tapped one of O'Brien's phones, which caught many of his associates having incriminating conversations about gambling. One of them was Martorano, who was using phones in one of his offices. The Staties soon had enough evidence to arrest everyone in O'Brien's organization on gaming charges. They even recorded Johnny taking bets from one of O'Brien's clients.

Naturally, the Staties intended on using those recordings as evidence against Johnny in court to prove he and O'Brien were equal partners in the gambling ring. Martorano knew he was screwed if that happened. He was then subpoenaed to appear at the state police headquarters to provide a voice print so the cops could confirm it was indeed his voice on the tape.

So thank the Lord for corrupt Massachusetts State Police Trooper Richard Schneiderhan. He recommended Martorano have his dentist insert a bridge into his mouth to throw off the test. And so he did just that. Sure enough, the bridge changed the oscillation of his voice to such a degree that the DA's office tossed the case. That's a new one.

Craps

Thanks to Andrew DiDonato (and Dennis N. Griffin), we can now get into the nitty gritty of specific types of gambling operations. By the '80s, craps had become one of the most highly lucrative games run by the Gambino crime family. But to play, you either had to be known by the operator, or vouched for by someone who was known. The games themselves were typically held at two or three secret locations in the city each night. Once you were vetted and approved, you would be provided an address where a shuttle would transport you to one of the games. The bank (the house's cash drawer from which winners were paid) was always kept off-site, for obvious reasons. And every hour, the *house's* winnings would be shipped off to that ultra-secret location.

Typically, betting limits were set between $300 and $500 per roll to reduce the house's potential exposure from hot players. When the house adhered to a $300-maximum limit, it would keep $30,000 on hand (at the off-site location). With a $500 limit, it would have as much as $100,000 off-site.

Because of the historical, nostalgic reverence mobsters and gamblers felt towards craps, the games were virtually always honest (so no loaded dice). With a low but guaranteed cut of all winnings for the house, profits were steady.

The expertise of the dealers is what set the Gambino Family games apart from their competitors – they were either former pros from Vegas or A.C., or otherwise had grown up around craps games their entire lives.

Surprisingly, the Gambino's games were always dry, meaning no alcohol was served. Waitresses would serve lunch or dinner, but only with espresso, coffee, soft drinks, or water.

I wonder why they didn't serve booze like they do in most other Mafia-run games or even in the legit casinos? This makes no sense – don't you *want* your players to get wasted and gamble away their kids' college tuition?

Personally, I think you *should* ply your players with mass quantities of free, top-shelf booze, as well as good food and complimentary limo rides. But if you really want to distinguish your craps game from all your competitors' games, follow the lead of Texas crime lord and gambling czar Benny Binion. Again, shortly after World War II, Binion moved from Dallas to Vegas and opened Binion's Horseshoe Hotel and Casino.

While other casinos set strict limits on craps bets to minimize the damage from the occasional player's winning streak, The Cowboy had no such ceiling. On the contrary, his casino displayed his Texas Longhorn-sized testes by allowing the player to set his own limit. This depended entirely on the gambler's first bet – if he was willing to lay down a million, then that was the limit. And never once did Binion ever refuse a bet, regardless of the amount. This fueled the Wild West fantasies of professional gamblers and ordinary players alike. As a result, the Horseshoe became the number-one craps casino in the world.

Go big or go home!

Just so you know, Benny Binion was the first casino operator in Vegas to offer free drinks, limos, and rooms to players. So light a candle for his eternally damned soul.

Cards

Another lucrative gambling racket for the Gambino crime family were card games. These operations differed from craps because they specifically targeted squares or other Family outsiders. The take was always a guaranteed five percent off the top of any pot. Even a single round of a high-stakes poker game could generate thousands of dollars in commission for the Family.

If you feel the need to occasionally gamble (which I highly frown upon), at least stay the eff away from blackjack games. They are virtually all swindles that target high-net-worth outsiders. Indeed, in the Volcano, no *amico nostra* or Family associates are ever allowed to play these strictly larcenous games.

Race Betting

The ponies are also a major source of revenue for the mob, though never as lucrative as other professional sports. The Gambino Family's race-betting business is operated out of the same bookmaking venue, known as a sports office. Horses draw far less action than sports, but they're still a good moneymaker. The Mafia attracts its customers by offering superior payouts than its primary competitor, the New York Off-Track Betting parlors. The mob can afford to undercut the OTBs, which have expensive overhead covered by deducting from the players' winnings.

Online Gambling

Even though the feds have cracked down in a big way, there's still plenty of money and opportunity in hosting Internet casinos. You want to have your server physically located in a Third World non-extradition-treaty country where you can bribe the local *junta* to set up shop.

Marco made a valiant if somewhat misguided attempt to do this when he was living in Miami after he fled Newport in 1992 to escape the clutches of the FBI and the local bulls. Marco did extensive research and decided he would set up his operation in Belize. He even flew out an ambassador from Belize first-class and put him up for the weekend in an oceanfront suite at the famous Fontainebleau Miami Beach hotel.

Over several days, which included dining and imbibing at only the finest restaurants and watering holes, they worked out all the details. The ambassador confirmed to Marco what he already knew: Belize had no extradition treaty with the United States; had no money laundering or tax-evasion laws; did not require foreigners to pay income taxes on money generated in Belize; had never had a civil war, or problems with those revolting guerrillas or annoying *narcos*; and only suffered the occasional Category Five hurricane.

The debonair, impeccably-dressed gentleman also told Marco something he *didn't* know: the Belizean government had recently passed a law allowing Internet gambling! As a well-connected attorney, the ambassador said he would personally handle all the details and be Marco's liaison with the government, which just happened to be run by his own uncle.

Marco couldn't believe his luck! He took the dapper little bastard to the fanciest strip club in town, the Dollhouse IV in Broward County, just outside the Ft. Lauderdale city limits. You long-tooths know the place – it's commonly known as Thee Dollhouse and was immortalized in Mötley Crüe's *Girls, Girls, Girls* song and video. The Champagne Room, of course.

After recovering from the weekend, Marco set his Machiavellian scheme in motion. He went to the University of Miami, and through some drug connections was introduced to several brilliant (if slightly crazed) computer programmers who jumped on board. The World Wide Web, as it was called back then, was only a couple years old and the possibilities were limitless.

So Marco got his dream team together, and things appeared to be going swimmingly after only a few meetings. Then the other shoe dropped; these idiots showed up to a meeting with his investors, their brains frying out on LSD. True, Marco was a little gacked out on booger sugar himself at the time, but no big whoop. All his dreams of world domination suddenly came crashing down around his perfectly tapered ears. Again.

And guess what happened shortly thereafter? The Gambino Family set up a massive Internet gambling business in Belize, making hundreds of millions of dollars until the operators in NYC got busted, and off they went to federal prison.

Sigh.

Fun Facts!

I've changed the true name of "the Avenue Boys" gang to avoid my being turned into a pincushion by one of their esteemed colleagues. To wit, after *American Me* came out in movie theatres in 1992, three consultants on the film were murdered by *La Eme*. The Mexican Mafia prison gang was deeply offended by the depiction of one of their founding fathers, Rodolfo Cadena – director/star Edward James Olmos' "Montoya Santana" character – getting raped in a juvenile prison. There were even widely-accepted rumors that the Mexican Mafia had put a green light on Olmos, and that he was forced to pay them $50,000 to get it rescinded. See, I'm not afraid of mobsters coming after for me for this book, but gangbangers have nothing to lose so they'll shoot first and ask for autographs later.

And before I forget, did you know that aside from The Westies, the Winter Hill Gang was the last Irish-American organized crime group whose origins went all the way back to Prohibition?

Travel Tidbits

The Gambino Family's dice games may have been strictly on the up and up, but the same certainly cannot be said about the games in ancient Pompeii. According to my illustrious guide Nello DiMaio, archaeologists had discovered loaded dice in the gambling stalls. These were dice which had a little hole cut into a side, into which a pebble had been inserted to load the dice. This greatly increased the chances of the roller crapping out.

I offered Nello my theory that where there is gambling, there is loansharking, and where there is loansharking, there is organized crime. "Nello, based on that irrefutable causal link, is it your professional opinion that it is more likely than not that organized crime existed in ancient Pompeii?"

Nello's brow furrowed in deep concentration for several moments before finally answering, "No."

Chapter Twenty-One – Burglaries and Home Invasions

"If you wanna earn in this Life, you gotta be a fuckin' self-starter." – Dominick "Little Dom" Cataldo

There's a simple yet critical distinction between burglaries and home invasions: in the former, nobody's home when you do a B&E (breaking and entering) on the target residence. In the latter, someone's home *and you know they'll be home* when you do the B&E. In more Biblical terms, the former crime is relatively benign, while the latter is pure unadulterated evil. I'm not making judgments or casting implied aspersions here – as a great man once said, "It makes no difference to me what a man does for a living, you understand."

Don't Defecate Where You Masticate

You fine old folks breathing through oxygen tanks remember the infamous May 1962 M&M murders in Chicago, right? Where Jimmy Miraglia and Billy McCarthy were burglarizing homes in the affluent Chicago suburb of Elmwood Park, where all The Outfit bosses lived? They were the psychos who shot up an Outfit bar, killing three people. Seriously, you don't?! C'mon, fogies – Tony Spilotro popped one of the robbers' eyes out with a friggin' vice!

Oh good, we're all on the same page again. Well, the obvious lesson to be gleaned from that rigmarole is that you shouldn't commit burglaries (or *any* crime, for that matter) in mobbed up locales *or* in your own. *Keep it clean, killas!*

Back in the day, South Brooklyn was an ideal neighborhood in which to raise the *bambinos*. There, women were able to walk around late at night by themselves without having to fear getting mugged or worse. There were few burglaries and minimal street crime for one simple reason: the prevalence of *Mafiosi* residents. The combined presence and vigilance of the boys, as they were called by the locals, ensured that the locale was virtually crime-free. They kept the neighborhood safe. Again, mobsters do not shit where they eat.

Lesson to Be Learned

The last thing you want to do as an up and coming mobster is rock the Ozzie-and-Harriet boat in these microcosms.

In all fairness, mobsters don't always make the best neighbors – just ask those of Philly crime boss Joseph "Skinny Joe" Merlino. In 2011, he moved to an upper-middle class enclave in Boca Raton, Florida, after a ten-year RICO stretch. His affluent neighbors were repeatedly forced to call police because of the constant screaming, yelling, and fighting going on inside. But what the stressed out neighbors found most disturbing were strange banging noises in the wee hours of the night, as if either furniture (*or bodies*) were being moved around. Another source of friction was the never-ending parade of visitors coming in and out of Merlino's manse.

But Skinny Joe ain't got diddly squat on Benny the Cowboy in the neighbor-from-Hell department. On October 23, 1934, Binion's daughter Barbara was born. Unfortunately, she contracted whooping cough and spent most nights coughing and sobbing. The neighbors who lived in the upstairs apartment complained to the landlord that baby Barbara was keeping them up at night. When the landlord brought this to Binion's attention, he told him not to worry, and that he would take care of the problem right away. And take care of it he did.

That night, The Cowboy waited patiently until his neighbor returned home. He then calmly loaded six bullets into his .45

sidearm and fired every single one of them into his ceiling. And when he heard his troublemaking neighbor run into another room, Benny followed, reloaded, and fired away again. The neighbor and his wife immediately moved out, wisely foregoing the option of calling the authorities.

Burglary Pays

Burglary had always been a favorite pastime of Tony Spilotro, going all the way back to his Chicago days in the early '60s, not least because it paid healthy dividends. Tony wasted little time hooking up with the Windy City's high-line jewel thieves, safecrackers, and burglars. After spending years learning the trade from the best (and without ever taking a pinch), including *wunderkind* jewel thief John Cook, Spilotro took his B&E show on the road.

During the summer of 1964, Tony and his new wife Nancy went on a double-date vacation to Europe with their friends, John Cook and *his* frolicsome wife Marianne. They flew into Amsterdam, rented a Mercedes, and drove straight to Antwerp, Belgium, the diamond capital of the world. The foursome then cruised all over Europe. Interpol and local heat lock-stepped the quartet all along their journey until Tony and John slipped away in the French Riviera.

After the fun-loving quad returned to the States, the French authorities and their Monaco counterparts learned Tony and John had broken into the hotel room of a wealthy American woman in Monte Carlo and stolen $533,220 in jewels. The burglars caught a break because she had been shacking up with her young boytoy without her husband's knowledge and so delayed reporting the loss. Spilotro and Cook were tried and convicted *in absentia* – not that they ever planned on returning to that part of the world.

This grand adventure happened during Tony's honeymoon! Wow, talk about combining business and pleasure. Since this was essentially a business trip, I wonder if Tony deducted the whole thing from his taxes. Lame joke, you chortle – not so fast, Pilgrim. Tony did something far more ridiculous when he sued the IRS in 1970 after agents seized $12,000 in gambling proceeds from one of his spots. Tony not only lost the suit, but it gave the feds evidence that he had filed a false mortgage application for his house. No wonder he left Chicago the next year.

Beware of Freak Accidents

Always expect the unexpected when pulling B&Es. And always wear appropriate footwear. Writer Selwyn Raab explains that by age fourteen, John Gotti Sr. was stealing cars, rolling drunks, and pulling off minor league burglaries. Things were going splendidly until one fateful day when he and his accomplices attempted to heist some equipment from a construction site. A portable cement mixer toppled onto his left foot, crushing a toe, which then had to be amputated. This resulted in Gotti striding with an unusual spring in his step, making him bounce jauntily.

Cue Katrina and the Waves' "Walking On Sunshine."

Get Paid Coming and Going

The nice thing about being a well-known burglar is that with a little networking and elbow grease, you can also become a fence. In addition to supplementing your income by middling swag between your clients (burglars and retail buyers), you'll also be able to get top dollar for your own hot merch (the stuff you *personally* burgled). As with most rackets, the earlier you get started on burgling and fencing, the better.

By the time he was thirteen, Henry Hill was running numbers and selling illegal fireworks. He paid cabdrivers from Paul Vario's cabstand to buy six packs of beer for him, which he then sold at a significant markup to his fellow classmates in the schoolyard. He paid off the local heat with free smokes so they'd look the other way. He also made money middling hot goods for the neighborhood's juvenile burglars. Hill even fronted them money to finance their crimes, for which he received some of the stolen merchandise. He then sold radios, sweaters, or whatever was glommed to the men at the cabstand.

Thirteen is a splendid age to start engaging in petty larceny. You're just entering puberty, whacking off like a fiend, and desperate to pop your cherry – all those hormones exploding in your body, screaming for release. *Voilà!* The next best thing to coitus for a strapping young lad is crime. Put all your adolescent energy and pent up frustrations into *that*.

Hell, even Marco took his first pinch at age thirteen while breaking into apartment carports in Costa Mesa (about the same time Gallo got popped for vandalizing cars in reaction to his parents' unfortunate domestic situation). Marco called his aunt from the police station, and bless her heart, she came down to pick him up, pretending to be his mother. The cops were so forgiving because of his age, ingratiating politeness, and cherubic Anglo appearance, they didn't even charge him for carrying a concealed weapon – a butterfly knife, which is a felony in Cali.

Cue Oingo Boingo's "Only A Lad."

Take Your Time Setting Up Your Scores

Sometimes Gallo would take several months to set up a big score. Although he describes Marco as a "passable burglar" who "was down for anything, anytime," Marco admits he was otherwise "half-a-'tard," utterly incapable of coming up with his own scores. It wasn't his fault, Marco claims – back then, his penis led him around like a guided cruise missile. Anyways, Gallo described how they pulled off one particularly notable burglary; specifically, the safe-cracking of "Blinky," whose real name has been lost to the sands of time.

Anyways, step one was befriending Thor, a 175-pound Rottweiler who guarded Blinky's house in Mission Viejo. Anytime they spotted Blinky at a club or bar, they would sneak over to his crib and feed Thor raw steaks. After several visits, Thor was literally salivating when they showed up.

Thus, when they finally made their move and broke into his house, the guard dog was practically dry humping their legs when they showed up with several pounds of ground beef. Gallo explained that the majority of people keep their safe dial only several notches away from the last digit of their combination because they are too lazy to enter the whole sequence every time they open the safe. Sure enough, the pointer on Blinky's dial had been left only two or three notches from a clearly worn spot. Gallo simply spun the dial over to that worn number and the door popped open. The total haul: $36,000 in cash and $100,000 in diamonds. He, Marco and Babar each made over $60,000 in one hour.

They celebrated by renting a big suite at the Newport Beach Marriott for the weekend and raging with The Crew. But the planning of the burglary wasn't quite as simple as Gallo implies. He left out the fact that in order to gain Blinky's trust, Marco had to party with him for weeks on end. Now God knows he never turned down a bit of *ye ole schniffy schniffy*, but Blinky was such a degenerate cocaine addict, Marco would get sick from clubbing with him. Since Gallo never touched the devil's dandruff himself, the task of being Blinky's *yeyo* co-pilot fell to Marco. Ahhh, but it was more than worth it in the end.

In any event, as they were emptying his safe, Blinky was doing the limbo at a big bash they were throwing at their house in Irvine just to keep him out of his own crib. Before Gallo and Marco had left the party, they told Blinky they had to go to neighboring Santa Ana to give Marco's gangbanger uncle some money he owed him for dope.

After stashing the loot somewhere safe, they drove back to their house where the shindig was in full swing. To make it look good, Gallo slapped Marco hard across the face, leaving a healthy bruise. They explained to Blinky that Marco's uncle had punched him for being late on his money. Blinky was so sincerely concerned, Marco almost felt guilty. Almost. In one night, they had covered their extravagant nut for the entire summer.

When All Else Fails, Burglarize Your Own Home

If you ever find yourself hitting rock bottom (and take it from it from me, you will at some point), and you're hard up for scratch, commit insurance fraud and burgle your *own* crib. That's what Gallo and Marco did right after Kenny bailed out of jail on that extortion charge. They had retired from the dope game so things were tight. (Sweet Lord, where did it all go!) This was before they embarked on an epic three-month $250,000 summer crime spree. Their most pressing concern was paying Roger – an attorney of his caliber ain't free, and he sure as hell ain't cheap.

Although they were running low on funds, Marco was impressed by Gallo's equanimity and *sangfroid*. Gallo knew, in a matter of mere weeks, the tanks would be topped off again. Roger shared his confidence – he knew a hustling gangster like Gallo would be flush soon enough, so he expressed no qualms about representing him *pro bono* in the interim.

So they plundered their comfy three-bedroom, single-story, ranch-style home in Irvine. Although that's not one hundred percent accurate. See, Blinky was a *putz* but he wasn't entirely dull-witted. It took him about an hour to figure out they had burgled *his* house. So he returned the favor and broke into *their* home when they were chilling at their Palm Springs condo, and stole most of their gun collection, among many other sundry items.

Realizing they could turn lemons into limoncello, Gallo and Marco immediately proceeded to empty their home of all other valuables (including non-existent goodies), and then reported the burglary to the IPD and Farmers Insurance. Ironically, they had taken out a renter's insurance policy only several weeks earlier. How's that for fortuitous timing?

Gallo kept the lion's share of the check. Marco didn't mind 'cause Gallo was still pissed at him for using his one week jail stay on the extortion beef as an over-the-top, hedonistic vacation. Like when Whitey Bulger and Steve Flemmi would take off to Europe, Kevin Weeks would relax and have fun since he otherwise worked 24-7. So Marco went on a one week party train, from Tijuana to Newport to LA to Vegas and back. Cue Miami Sound Machine's "Conga."

Gallo was understandably irked because he was unable to get a hold of Marco, since back then you couldn't make collect calls to cell phones from jail.

One last thought on this subject: don't do this renter's insurance scam more than once, lunkheads.

By the way, as you can imagine, Gallo was hopping mad about Blinky's payback. So he did what came naturally – he blew up Blinky's Mercedes with a car bomb. *Booya!* Blinky backed down after that, but it was too late – like that, he disappeared, never to be seen or heard from again.

Lesson to Be Learned

Don't do gangster shit if you're not a gangster. Nuff said.

If You're Gonna Be a Bear, Be a Grizzly

You've heard me utter this phrase before, and I like to think that I came up with it on my own. As it relates to burglaries, it simply means this: once you've gained sufficient experience, form your own tightly-knit crew.

The most successful B&E ring in the mob's history was Tony Spilotro's Hole in the Wall Gang. It was based in Vegas but fanned out all over the West Coast and Southwest, committing hundreds of burglaries – all without kicking up to the Mustache Petes in Chi-raq. The gang got its name for its signature method of entering luxury homes in Sin City. It worked like this:

To bypass alarm systems on doors and windows, they used a five-pound sledgehammer to break a big hole in the stucco walls. Then, once the stucco was cleared away, they would clip the remaining chicken wire with metal shears and simply climb into the home. They'd be in and out in five minutes, tops. Meanwhile, they had a gang member in a spotter car outside, monitoring local police and FBI radio chatter on a descrambler.

Ali Baba and his Forty Thieves never had it so good. They knocked over scores of local places in this manner. After the first dozen or so, local newspaper reporters anointed them with the *tres apropos* nickname.

These smash 'n' grab jobs were highly profitable because the homes were often stuffed with jewelry and cash – often as much as $50,000 crammed into dresser drawers. For example, one time the gang hit the house of a *maître d* from one of the ritziest restaurants on the Strip. They found over sixty grand in tip money, as well as a wafer-thin $30,000 Patek Philippe watch.

And how did they know which places to hit? Tipsters! Their best sources were the brokers who sold the homeowners' and renters' insurance policies to the victims – policies which identified the valuable insured items. Thus, the gang could pre-sell the items to be stolen since they knew exactly what was there and how much it was worth. The brokers even laid out where in the homes the items were located, as well as the alarm systems.

The crew only got busted because of a rat in their midst (crewmember Sal Romano), although Bill Roemer conspicuously omits this fact in his book *The Enforcer: Spilotro – The Chicago Mob's Man Over Las Vegas*.

This crew was as professional as they come, filled with only real-deal villains that Tony had imported from Chicago for that specific purpose. Dennis N. Griffin wrote a book with Cullotta called *The Hole in the Wall Gang*, which I've ordered on Amazon. Read it and we'll talk about it.

Holla!

Tipsters

Tipsters are your best source for burglary targets. Anthony Fiato provides an illuminating vignette involving the wife of a Beverly Hills jeweler. After losing big at backgammon at the Cavendish Club on Sunset Boulevard, she came to the Fiatos with a scheme. Since her husband knew every big jeweler in town, she could tip the Gangster Brothers off to big scores.

She also drove a hard bargain, demanding half the take. Although Tony the Animal was skeptical, within a few weeks, she began paying off in spades. Her dead-on information enabled them to pull off burglaries all over the West Side. She gleaned the valuable intel by eavesdropping on her hubby while he made deals with other jewelers. For example, she would find out a visiting jeweler was in town and keeping his diamonds in a particular safe. Sometimes she was even able to provide the combination to the safe.

After taking down a score, the Fiatos would then sell the diamonds to one of their fences for twenty-five percent of their face value (which seems awful low to me). With her fifty percent cut, the woman not only paid off all her gambling debts, but began accumulating quite a tidy little nest egg. This made her even hungrier.

One night, her husband was entertaining a group of visiting jewelers at his own palatial home in The Flats – it's the priciest area of Beverly Hills, for you yokels. While the men were enjoying Louis XIII cognac and fresh Cohibas, the wife snuck into the coat room, opened up one of their briefcases, and saw it contained *thousands* of diamonds! She immediately called the Fiatos, who drove right over, snuck in through a window, grabbed the briefcase, and scrammed.

Cue Donna Summer's "She Works Hard For The Money."

Don't Burgle People Who Shouldn't Be Burgled

Admit it, people – you can't get enough of these cautionary tales about stupid robbers doing stupid things to extremely dangerous people. But for those of you who are rolling your eyes and sighing about my flogging this dead pony, I say this: fuck you, you ungrateful whelps. If it wasn't for me, you'd be serving phosphorescent ICEEs and synthetic-cheese nachos at your local multiplex.

During the early '90s, an asinine pair of burglars – husband and wife Thomas and Rosemary Uva – began burglarizing Mafia social clubs. This became such a problem that Big Joe Massino and his underboss, Good Lookin' Sal Vitale, met with

Junior Gotti about who was going to kill them first. It was agreed an open contract would be issued, meaning anyone from the Five Families could whack 'em (although it's unclear what the reward entailed).

On December 24, 1992 (*ho ho ho!*), the couple was found shot to death on a street in Queens. To this day, the murders remain unsolved, although the homicide dicks suspect it was Baby Gotti's doing. And, of course, Gotti Junior has always denied any involvement, although he supposedly bragged to Massino, "We took care of it."

Mafia social clubs?! Of all the places to rob, *this* is what these cohabitating thinktanks came up with? Some people are simply too dumb to live.

Home Invasions

If I were a gangster, I would have no problem shoving my way into someone's home, herding the occupants into a single room at gunpoint, gagging and binding them with duct tape and zipties, and ransacking the place for valuables – as long as they're *bad* guys.

Doing this to civilians, especially women and children, exemplifies atrocious manners. Unless you're a psycho, doing this kinda shit will haunt you down the road in more ways than you can imagine. Understand that home-invasion crews are comprised of two-to-three armed thugs who dress up in various uniforms to trick the homeowner into opening the door, while another accomplice waits in the getaway ride.

Once that happens, even if the security chain is still in place, the invaders will force their way in and pistol whip the occupants. Sounds exciting, right? The problem is that these desperados often terrorize women, the elderly... even children. Thus, it takes a certain lack of moral fiber to pull off these jobs.

Joe Pistone provides an example of this method of entry. At one point in the mid '70s, two killers from Colombo soldier Jilly Greca's crew, Frankie and Patsy, had emerged fresh from a penological sabbatical following armed robbery convictions. Their coffers depleted, they commenced home invading stately mansions during the daytime in search of cash, jewels, and guns.

First, they would park their car around the corner and case the properties, including big homes on Long Island, by posing as morning joggers. This enabled them to pass by the same place several times while they studied the doors, windows, alarm systems, and even the occupants.

Second, they gained entry by pulling up in an unmarked, government-looking sedan, wearing cheap suits, flashing gold shields, and claiming to be NYPD detectives.

Once inside, they would force everyone to face the wall at gunpoint, then handcuff them. One of them would ransack the home while the other stood guard. A third crewmember would sit behind the wheel of the work car outside.

Similarly, Marco's preferred method of casing houses in expensive neighborhoods was to borrow a cute dog to walk in the particular 'hood, dress casually-upscale to fit in, wear designer sunglasses so no one would notice him scrutinizing the houses, and pretend to read a book (and later, an iPhone) while strolling. In fact, he'd use the reflection from the iPhone to check his six to ensure no one was watching or following him as he was casing these houses.

Okay, let's get back to the frequent unpleasantness inherent in doing home invasions. I can't think of a single Mafia home-invasion robbery that went as terribly awry as the one committed by the so-called King of Miami, Chris "the Binger" Paciello. He was nicknamed for his propensity to binge on violence, but his real surname is Ludwigsen. Paciello is his Italian-American mother's maiden name, which he adopted to fit in with the full-blooded Italian-Americans with whom he grew up.

He committed this particularly heinous crime with his fellow Bath Avenue Boys, a dangerous Mafia farm team associated with the Bonanno Family through acting boss Anthony "Old Man" Spero. The Bath Avenue Boys were largely comprised of younger relatives of mobsters, and they terrorized Bensonhurst during the '80s and early '90s.

Paciello had heard that Mr. Sami Shemtov, an Israeli émigré and owner of half a dozen adult bookstores and related porno businesses, kept upwards of a million dollars in cash in a basement safe in his home. Paciello, who was about to be evicted from his apartment, was desperate for cheddar.

On February 18, 1993, at 9:45 P.M., pretty boy Paciello and three fellow Bath Avenue Boys – James "Jimmy Gap" Calandra, Tommy Reynolds, and Michael Yammine – headed in a Mercury sedan to a cul-de-sac on Staten Island ringed with million-dollar mansions.

While The Binger remained behind the wheel (as he always did on these occasions), Yammine, Reynolds, and Calandra pulled down facemasks, checked their pistols, and headed for the target's front door. Jimmy Gap rang the doorbell.

Sami, who should have known better, had never bothered to install a peephole in his front door. He was expecting company, so had temporarily turned off the alarm system. His attractive and vivacious wife, Judy Shemtov, approached the door and asked who it was. Jimmy Gap answered, "The police!" Judy, who had only been married to Sami for one year (so may not have known he was a smut peddler, since he also owned legit businesses), foolishly began to open the door...

BAM! Reynolds and Calandra slammed their shoulders into the door, knocking Judy backwards into the foyer. They shoved a gun in her face and demanded to know the location of the safe.

Meanwhile, Sami, who had been in the kitchen, heard the commotion and entered the foyer. His appearance startled Reynolds, who accidentally squeezed the trigger of his .45, shooting Judy in the face, killing her. The three would-be robbers fled.

"I'm going to Hell for this one," Reynolds said after entering the getaway car. It was a prescient statement. The Binger raced off to his own nearby home in Staten Island, after which the four men vowed never to speak of the incident to anyone. On the way back to Brooklyn later that night, Reynolds tossed the murder weapon off the Verrazano-Narrows Bridge into the water below.

Eventually Mike Yammine got busted for something major (not sure what) and flipped on two of his three accomplices, but not Chris, whose last name he didn't know. Not a problem for the feds 'cause Jimmy Gap, in turn, flipped on Paciello, bringing his entrepreneurial rise (temporarily) to a halt in December 1999. What a bummer 'cause he was just about to open another Liquid nightclub in West Palm Beach. At least Sofia Vergara helped him raise his *$15 million* bail. Now that's loyalty for ya.

In October 2000, Paciello flipped against both the Bonanno and Colombo Families, taking a plea deal for his monumental home-invasion fuckup. He was sentenced to a ten year federal prison term and eventually served six years, plus the two he did while awaiting sentencing.

Having rejected WITSEC, Paciello returned to South Beach in 2012, after his LA restaurant chain failed, and after he allegedly stabbed someone in a street fight there. He opened a swanky Italian restaurant called Bianca and a nightclub named FDR. The good times finally returned, as did all the celebs, including Casares and baseball superstars A-Rod (Alex Rodriguez) and Sammy Sosa. Oh, *and* he sold the movie rights to his life story to New Line Cinema.

If J.D. Salinger had known Paciello (or Michelle "Nici" Braun), he might never have coined the phrase, "There are no second acts in American lives." Ironically, Sami Shemtov reportedly now lives only a few miles away in Miami.

As for the triggerman himself, almost exactly eight years after the botched robbery, on February 27, 2001, Tommy Reynolds' prediction of going to Hell came true. After admitting to six murders, including Judy's, he was sentenced to life in prison.

Jimmy Gap also did some time, but I believe he thereafter entered WITSEC.

Damn, now that I think of it, Gallo went around Hollywood with his agent and producer pitching a reality TV show called

Mob Stars, starring himself, Andrew DiDonato, Jimmy Gap, Billy Cutolo Jr., Colombo capo Joseph "Joe Campy" Campanella, and some other ex-mobsters. It didn't fly because the network wanted all the guys to live in one city during filming, which was logistically impossible. The real reason, of which he heard credible rumors, was the network suits didn't believe Gallo, who would've been the top cast member, was a real mobster because he was half-Asian! Hollywood's racist? Say it ain't so!

Lessons to Be Learned

When doing a home invasion, keep your safety on and don't shit where you eat. And instead of the home invasion, the gangsters should have grabbed Sami as he left one of his spank banks when his family was gone from the house. Then they could have forced him back there to open the safe. (Sami wasn't a civilian, he was a pornographer, and his family should have been off limits. FYI, he was so cheap, he reportedly only offered a $15,000 reward for info leading to his wife's killers.)

Oh, and if bad shit like this does go down, please don't hesitate to kill every one of your criminal accomplices so if you do get busted for it, you can always point the finger at them. It's not like they're gonna be around to dispute your version of events.

Fun Facts!

Anthony Spero personally inducted Tommy Karate into the Bonanno clan, and was himself badged with Joey Massino on June 14, 1977, in a Queens bar. That ceremony was presided over by then street boss Carmine Galante two years before he was famously rubbed out on July 12, 1979, at Joe and Mary's Italian-American Restaurant in Bushwick, Brooklyn.

More than twenty years later, after the disastrous home invasion, Chris Paciello took the proceeds of a reported one million dollar bank robbery in Bensonhurst, Paciello headed down to South Florida, where he reinvented himself as a nightclub and restaurant impresario. He opened a club called Risk, and after it failed to catch on, he allegedly burned it down for $250,000 in insurance money. He then used that cash to open another nightclub, Liquid.

Overnight, the new joint became the hottest spot in town. It was frequented by all the cool celebs who made South Beach sizzle, which it did until spree killer Andrew Cunanan gunned down Gianni Versace on July 15, 1997. Marco's Love Tribe got the call one hour after the shooting, before it made international news, from friends who lived near Versace's *palazzo*, the Villa Casa Casuarina on Ocean Drive. Thanks to his new partnership with Madonna's former lover, socialite Ingrid Casares, Paciello himself became a hit, reveling in the sexy Mafia rumors swirling around him.

Did I say that Gallo enjoyed more sexual perks than anyone else in the history of the mob? Sorry, but I do believe I was talking out of my ass. Paciello easily takes that crown, having dated Madonna, supermodels Niki Taylor and Naomi Campbell, actresses Daisy Fuentes and Sofia Vergara, and then crappy dance music diva Jennifer Lopez.

Coincidentally, both Paciello and Marco co-existed in the South Beach shark tank at the same time. But when I asked Marco about this, he started screaming and cursing at me in Portuguese, then suddenly hung up. Not sure what to make of that.

Travel Tidbits

While doing intensive empirical research in Mykonos, I splurged on a pair of titanium LPLR sunglasses (which stands for *la petite lunette rouge* – French for "the small red line"). What drew me to the high-end eyewear was the fact the lenses are perfectly flat. I was amazed to discover that when I put them on and slowly panned my head from one side to another, I could see everything and everyone *behind* me in the side reflections of the inner lenses.

The lenses worked even better outdoors. All day long as I lounged on my daybed by the infinity pool, I could see everyone coming and going on my six. Thus, I highly recommend all you discerning thugs-in-training (and classy pervs) out there snap up a pair so no one can ever sneak up on you.

CHAPTER TWENTY-TWO – BANK JOBS

"Because that's where the money is." – Willie Sutton
(responding to a reporter who asked why he robbed banks)

Bank jobs are an entirely different animal than other heists; hence, they merit their own chapter. But just like heists, these capers require huge *pelotas*. Thus, bank robbers occupy the highest echelon of respect in the Mafia. This kind of crime is particularly dangerous because people will actually shoot at you during its commission. It also typically results in a relatively low payout.

But there's another reason you may want to pass on this one – bank robbery is extremely habit-forming. Few crimes provide the intoxicating rush this type of cowboy job mainlines into your central nervous system.

Now while I may not proselytize acting like Bonnie and Clyde, I can certainly understand and appreciate the incredible jolt of adrenaline. Sal Polisi compares robbing banks to getting high as a motherfucking kite. Indeed, following a successful heist in 1971, he felt like Sinatra coming off the stage at Madison Square Garden. Even after divvying up the loot and driving away from criminal associate Joe Vitale's pad, he was still shaking from the rush. Sally had to go straight to a high-class brothel just to calm down.

Notwithstanding this glorification, even Crazy Sal himself urges you young'uns to find something better to do in your leisure time. He believes anyone who tries robbing banks today has to be crazier than he ever was. Even one job can plaster you all over the Internet, with your stats cross-referenced across the desk of every interested local, state, and federal agent.

And God forbid you end up on some local crime show. Your neighbors will love ratting you out and collecting the reward. According to Polisi, bank jobs are so dangerous nowadays, bosses rarely give their consent. After all, a wiseguy facing a twenty-five year federal rap is one bad meal away from turning canary.

Finally, say what you will about the follies and foibles of the FBI, but even its most ardent detractors agree that the feds excel at investigating and capturing bank robbers. And, of course, busting bank robbers always ensures headlines, which, again, the FBI craves more than anything.

Papi Needs a New Pair of Ferragamos

So why then do wiseguys rob banks? Da money, sucka! But just be careful about exactly *whose* money you're robbing at a particular bank. If you're entertaining any doubts about this cautionary proviso, look no further than the infamous Medford Depositors Trust Bank break-in.

On Saturday night during the 1980 Memorial Day weekend, a gang of highly organized thieves, including three current local police officers (Capt. Gerald Clemente, Lt. Thomas Doherty, and Sgt. Joseph Bangs), broke into the Depositors Trust Bank in Medford, Massachusetts. They cut a big hole through the shared wall of the adjacent watch repair shop, and then cut through the roof of the vault. Meanwhile, Lt. Doherty kept watch outside in his police cruiser, monitoring police and FBI radio frequencies.

They spent through Monday, with the gang returning twice on successive nights, popping open and cleaning out seven hundred safe deposit boxes. Some belonged to LCN members, including Jerry Angiulo, who then ruled the Boston LCN. The thieves absconded with $1.5 million in cash, plus $3.5 million in luxury watches and jewelry, including pearls, diamonds, and gold coins.

The mastermind behind the heist was thief Arthur "Bucky" Barrett, who was simpatico with Boston *Mafioso* and proficient whackman Cadillac Frank Salemme. After Cadillac Frank informed Bucky he had inadvertently heisted shotcallers from In Town, Bucky did the right thing and returned their loot.

Unfortunately, Bucky forgot there was another organized crime group in town who wanted tribute. He failed to kick up a share of the haul to Whitey and Stevie, who exacted their 160 pounds of flesh (or whatever Bucky weighed) in August 1983. Bucky was lured to "the Haunty" (Whitey and Stevie's charnel house) on the false pretense of buying cheap, stolen diamonds.

Kevin Weeks testified that Whitey and Flemmi tied Bucky to a chair and interrogated him for hours. He eventually coughed up $47,000 in cash from his home after he called his wife and told her to leave the house so the money could be retrieved from a potted plant. They also grabbed $10,000 in additional cash which was being held for him at a local bar.

Afterwards, Whitey told Weeks that Bucky was "going to lie down for a while." Weeks knew all too well what that meant. Whitey had Bucky walk ahead of him down the stairs to the basement, where crook John McIntyre's body was already buried, to be joined in January 1985 by Deborah Hussey's. Whitey pulled his gun out and squeezed the trigger. *CLICK.* Nothing. Whitey then released the safety and blew Bucky's brains out.

Stevie then used a set of dental pliers that Bulger's flame, former dental assistant Cathy Greig, had allegedly provided Whitey (though it's unclear if she knew what he was going to do with them) and extracted Bucky's teeth. Then Weeks and (allegedly) Pat Nee dug a grave. Meanwhile, Whitey – for whom murder was apparently like great sex – did what he always did post-mortem: he immediately took a nap, thoroughly spent and at peace with the world. The gang members then threw quicklime on Bucky's corpse to expedite decomposition.

Lesson to Be Learned

Give a taste to *everyone* who should be getting one – or at least to those who will kill you if you don't.

In *Deal with the Devil*, investigative reporter Peter Lance claims that The Grim Reaper's own Bypass Gang pulled off a bank break-in over the July 4th weekend in 1974. After popping open the safe deposit boxes, this single score supposedly resulted in a mammoth haul of $15 million in cash and jewels.

But that would make this the single greatest heist in American history, adjusting for inflation. This sounds farfetched to me; hence why I didn't mention this caper in my chapter on heists and scores. (But I'm not infallible.)

Still, even Whitey Bulger would agree with me: the risk is not worth the reward in pulling down bank scores. Whitey got his start in crime in Southie at a young age by tailgating (stealing goods off the back of delivery trucks). By 1955, he had become one of the top tailgaters in Boston, though he was eager to move up to more lucrative crimes.

And, of course, it's bank robbery that landed Whitey in federal prison for nine hellacious years – a stretch that would have been considerably longer had he not volunteered to participate in the G's insidious MK-ULTRA, the LSD, mind control testing program.

I know what you're thinking – dropping acid every single day for months on end sounds like a *pretty, prettttty* good way to do time, right? Wrong! These CIA-sponsored experiments gave Whitey lifelong nightmares and insomnia.

Oh, in case you're wondering how Whitey got busted after a bank robbery spree covering the Eastern seaboard, the answer is simple: he did something incredibly stupid. He went back home and started hanging around his favorite nightclubs, being (as Marco says) the big man, buying drinks.

But wait, perhaps I'm being a bit unfair. After all, he dyed his hair black, donned nerdy eyeglasses, and – this is my favorite part – clamped a giant cigar in his discolored teeth to hide his *visage*. This brilliant disguise lasted about as long as Whitey took to buy the first round of drinks at a nightclub in Revere, just north of Boston. Someone recognized him and dimed him out to the bulls. I hope he ordered a fine, oaky smooth, eighteen-year-old single-malt Scotch, 'cause it was the last drink he would enjoy for the next nine years (excluding pruno).

"Ah, Shaddupa Your Face!"

Keep your trap shut after you pop your bank-robbery cherry. Sal Polisi knew better than to start boasting to his buddies after he pulled off his first heist. He knew the walls had ears and even those in his inner circle might rat him out someday. But most importantly, he wanted his Mafia rabbi, Colombo soldier Dominick "Little Dom" Cataldo, to respect him as a serious heister. A man who knows how to keep his mouth shut after a big score is a man whom other professional robbers will want to work with in the future.

Use a Proven, Reliable, Fearless, and *Intelligent* Guy as Your Lookout

Contrary to popular opinion, the lookout is *not* the least significant role a bank robber can have in your gang. In fact, the opposite is true – the lookout is the most important guy in your bank-robbery crew. If he fucks up, you all go down. That's why the lookout is typically the must trustworthy man on the job.

Robert DiLeonardi was such a lookout man, and likely would have had an admirable criminal career had he not succumbed to his own ego. During the early 1980s, Greg Scarpa's Bypass Crew pulled off a major score at a bank in Queens by jackhammering into the vault. The safe deposit boxes alone netted a cool million in cash, gold bars, diamonds, and jewelry. Scarpa later had DiLeonardi whacked because he had been overheard bragging about the gang's bank heists.

Ergo, it should therefore be patently obvious: if you serve as the lookout, any screw up on your part will be visited upon your head tenfold.

In late August 1980, Scarpa's Bypass Gang tried to break into the Dime Savings Bank in Queens. Donald "Big Donny" Somma and The Reaper's son, Greg Junior, acted as the lookouts. Their sole task was to radio the inside burglars if any trouble came their way. But Junior dropped the ball and allowed a security guard to enter the bank and startle the inside men.

Thank God for Joseph DeDomenico, a.k.a. Joe Brewster – thinking fast, he told the security guard they were the nighttime cleaning crew! While the guard made a call to confirm this claim, the gang got the fuck out of there.

Big Donny bitched to Colombo capo Anthony "Scappi" Scarpati (a former Garfield Boy with Carmine Persico) about Junior's fuckup. Big Daddy was pissed Somma dared criticize his son, regardless of whether it was merited. So he summoned Big Donny to the Wimpy Boys Social Club. The moment Donald entered Scarpa's office, Greg Senior opened his desk drawer, withdrew a revolver, and put one in his hat. So long, Somma.

Cue Til Tuesday's "Voices Carry."

Lessons to Be Learned

If you're gonna foul up as the lookout, make sure you're the boss's son. Equally important, if the boss's son *is* a lookout who drops the ball on a bank job, don't beef on the kid to *anyone*. Oh, and if he *does* drop the ball, think fast on your feet like Joe Brewster.

By all accounts, Scarpa Junior was a capable young gangster. So I'm gonna reach out to him – since he's doing forty years in federal prison, I'm hoping he'll have nothing better to do than talk to me. (I'd better hurry, though, 'cause apparently he's dying of cancer. Suckin'.) Greg Scarpa Jr. was definitely the real Mafia McCoy. Read Peter Lance's book *Deal with the Devil*, which covers the incredible lives of both father *and* son, including the latter's exploits in thwarting several major terrorist plots, including one involving Timothy McVeigh! And read about how the G completely shafted him even after he derailed these plots.

You'll Need a Solid Upfront Man

A thousand pardons, I once again misspoke – the *upfront man* is the most important crewmember in your bank squad. I would normally explain in painstaking detail the responsibilities of the upfront man, but his title is fairly self-explanatory.

Among numerous tales of derring-do recounted by Good News DiDonato, the following is the most exciting – an account of how to pull off a near-flawless bank robbery, thanks largely to his proficiency at being said upfronter:

> One day I met up with [Bonanno associate/bank robber] Paul Mazzarese. Paul lived in New Jersey. He cashed his checks at a Sovereign Bank branch. He noticed that the Brinks money truck came every Thursday and dropped off bags of money. But the procedure was lax: the bags were left on the floor next to the vault until an employee got around to putting them inside. And there was no partition in that facility between the customers and tellers.
>
> Our plan was for Paul, Tommy Scuderi, Joe Miraglia, and me to do the robbery on the Thursday before a holiday weekend. They usually brought in more than usual then to fill the ATM machines for the long weekend.

Andrew and his three crewmembers began clocking the Brinks armored car before Labor Day. They sat at a roadside diner, then as soon the armored car passed by, they would follow in their car. They did this every day for almost a week until they clocked the armored car's timing.

The night before the big day, the crew practiced dry runs of their escape route. The next morning, Andrew used same color tape to change the numbers on their work car's license plate. Then the foursome headed off. Sure enough, like clockwork, the armored car pulled up right on time. Also as expected, one of the guards was carrying two extra money bags for the big holiday. He loaded a total of four money bags onto a handcart and rolled it into the bank. He emerged a few minutes later with the now empty handcart, got back into the armored car, and drove off.

Andrew continues:

> I exited Paul's car, followed by Tommy, and we headed for the bank. I had on doctor's exam gloves and a sweatshirt that covered a bulletproof vest, sunglasses, and a New York Yankees ball cap. I went directly to the counter and jumped over it. I heard a couple of screams but kept my focus on the money bags. I grabbed the first two and threw them over the counter to Tommy. Then I took the other two bags and jumped back over the counter. Some hero moved at me. Tommy threw him on the floor.
>
> A female customer came in and saw what was happening. She started screaming and ran outside. Tommy and I followed her out and went behind the bank. We threw the bags into Paul's car, got in, and laid down on the back seat. We were safely inside Paul's house a minute after the robbery.
>
> Everybody changed clothes. We bagged up our robbery clothes and gear and disposed of everything. The take was just under a half million dollars. We split it four ways. We stayed at Paul's for several hours, listening to the police scanner and watching the news.

Booya!

My favorite photo of Andrew is the one he emailed me of him sitting in the dealer-fresh big-dog black Benzo he had just purchased with proceeds from this very same bank job – a cool 60 G in cash. And, yes, he looks radiantly happy. Admittedly, he was somewhat less thrilled when he had to serve more than four years for his jug run. Ain't nothin' free in life, baby ducks.

If You're Good Enough, You Can Be a Busy Little Bee

Again, not only did the Grim Reaper and Gaspipe both have bank crews called the Bypass Gang, but often shared members. Joe Brewster was one of them. Assuming you somehow avoid a twenty year federal stretch while you're coming up in the bank job world, you too can aspire to be as talented as Joe B. One of his buddies worked for the alarm company ADT. He was kind enough to teach Joe B. and the rest of the crew how to bypass intricate alarm systems so they could break into banks on weekends.

Gosh darn it, did I forget to encourage you wannabe Dillingers to seek employment with an alarm company so you can learn the trade from the inside out? That obviously requires a clean record and at least a modicum of self-discipline. You babes in the woods know by now I have a physical aversion to working a nine-to-five, or even a ten-to-four, or any diminishing contraction thereof. However, in this instance, I think becoming a working stiff works to your advantage. But as William Forsythe says to Nicholas Cage in 1987's *Raising Arizona*, "You're young and ya got yer health – what fer ya want with a job?"

'Member When I Said Bank Robbery is Hazardous to Your Health?

In the jug knockin' game, lackadaisical preparation can mean *your ass*. Case in point: as described by big-ballin' grifter Nicky Crow in George Anastasia's *Blood And Honor: Inside the Scarfo Mob*, one failed heist made the local primetime TV news. Three of Nicky's pals had driven into the bank's parking lot and parked. With pistols and ski masks in place, the trio exited the car and entered the bank.

"This is a stickup!" screamed mobster Tony Perpiglia, forcing the dozen patrons to hit the floor.

In a stroke of terrible luck, it just so happened an FBI stakeout team had been hiding in a back office, waiting for these very same robbers to show up. The feds spotted the heisters as soon as they pulled up in their car through a tinted window, and so had their shotguns racked and ready.

"FBI!" the four agents bellowed as they burst out of the back office. Without waiting for a response, the feds blasted away, critically wounding a second robber named Bakey and killing Perpiglia. The third gang member, Tony Esposito, managed to get off a few errant shots before catching a fusillade of buckshot flush in the chest.

One of the FBI agents knelt down next to Esposito and pulled up his ski mask. As soon as he saw his face, the agent burst into tears. Turns out they had grown up together in the same South Philly neighborhood, and had been close friends as kids. Esposito perished after arriving at the local hospital.

The three crooks should have listed to Nicky Crow, who passed on the bank job after spotting that suspicious back office with tinted windows. Crow had recently gotten wind the FBI had started staking out local banks, and was concerned agents could be hiding therein.

Add a Fed to Your Bank Crew

This is exactly what Machiavellian mastermind Greg Scarpa Sr. did – a gangster so utterly cunning, ruthless, and downright evil that he made John Gotti look like... well, John Gotti *Junior*.

Greg Scarpa Jr. served as his dad's bookkeeper and so was intimately familiar with The Grim Reaper's expenditures. These allegedly included bribes to his handler, FBI Special Agent Lin DeVecchio, in exchange for inside info that would keep the Scarpas out of the pokie. Junior testified that his father had paid DeVecchio more than $100,000 in cash over the years, as well as five-star ski vacations to Aspen and top-drawer sex workers.

As part of this *quid pro quo*, Junior testified that DeVecchio provided him and his pop FBI surveillance videos of their HQ, the Wimpy Boys Social Club. Even more disturbing is the allegation DeVecchio acted as a lookout during bank robberies for The Grim Reaper's Bypass Gang. In fact, the younger Scarpa testified DeVecchio had watched over several bank robberies, in which he participated as a *favor* to his dad. This included the botched 1980 job at the Dime Savings Bank. Speaking of genetic predispositions to organized crime...

Lessons to Be Learned

Taking a page from Whitey Bulger's painful flub...

After a successful run at knocking over jugs (bank robbing virtuoso Sal Polisi's term) across multiple states, maybe *don't* go back to your hometown where the coppers are onto you? And if you're gonna wear a disguise, how about one that actually covers your effin' face?! Wear one of those anti-pollution masks that you always see those germ-phobic tourists wearing.

Whitey, I mean seriously – a *cigar*? Why didn't you simply chew gum and blow a giant cartoon balloon whenever a flatfoot came by? At least add some Groucho Marx glasses, nose, and mustache to perfect the subterfuge.

Oh, and how about this – if you're lammin' it, maybe stay out of motherflippin' nightclubs near your own 'hood? To Whitey's credit, he smartened up considerably during his time in stir and rarely did anything stupid again (with several notable – and, for Whitey, catastrophic exceptions).

And as far as firepower, why fuck around with a puny .38 peashooter? Use a .45 man-stopper next time! And enough with the pre-shooting epithets – remember The Chinster and Frank Costello? Once again, never telegraph your punches!

Fun Facts!

Did you know that John "the Teflon Don" Gotti's grandson, John Gotti III (son of Johnny Boy's other son, Peter, and nephew of Baby Huey), is also a gangster? Far from being a mobster *savant*, this young Turk got popped in August 2016 for dealing Oxy in Howard Beach and Ozone Park. In February 2017, he took an eight year plea deal. He also had to forfeit $260,000 in drug money. His downfall came from – brace yourself – a *bug* planted in his Infiniti. Wow. The acorn didn't fall far from the family tree in this case, huh?

In September 2016, IRS agents raided the six-thousand-square-foot Long Island mansion of the Dapper Don's daughter, Victoria Gotti (the same house where A&E's hit reality show *Growing Up Gotti* was filmed). The IRS also raided an auto parts store in Queens operated by her three sons John, Carmine, and Frank. The feds apparently suspected the three men (who all reportedly *still* live with Mommy!) of tax fraud. One of the boys, John Gotti Agnello, apparently blew through the $2.5 million in cash(!) he had received from five hundred guests at his September 2015 wedding.

Next, in the summer of 1985, John Gotti Sr.'s youngest brother, Gambino associate Vincent "Vinny" Gotti, allegedly strangled twenty-five-year-old Robin Lynn Vitulli in a Queens motel room after doing drugs with her. According to Vitulli's daughter Stacy Swearingen, who was six years old when her mother was murdered, it was common knowledge that on the night in question, Vitulli had been at a local nightclub. Vitulli had supposedly gotten into an argument with the Dapper Don's other brother, Peter Gotti (whose mob nickname is literally Retard), and slapped him in the face. According to Swearingen, it was Peter who ordered her death. No one was ever charged with her murder. In any event, Vinny was such a degenerate druggie that he was banned from the Gambinos' social clubs by his brothers John and Peter.

Finally, in December 2008, Vinny was sentenced to eight years in prison for ordering a botched hit on bagel store owner Angelo Mugnolo, whom Gotti suspected was having an affair with his wife. Can you blame her?

Will someone puh-*lease* tell these Neapolitan Neanderthals to stop dropping baby batter?! I'm gonna set up a crowdfunding campaign to raise enough money to get all of these *Jersey Shore* rejects snipped. Who's with me? Let's end this line of demon seed once and for all!

I should probably shut my mouth right about now in light of the fact that Baby Huey *allegedly* had Mikey Yannotti shoot Guardian Angels founder Curtis Sliwa for slagging off the Gottis on his NYC radio show.

In 1992, Sliwa began railing against the Gottis on his popular radio show on WABC-AM. Alite testified that Baby Huey told him he wanted to whack Sliwa, but Alite talked him out of it. Alite explained to Junior that it's against the Rules to kill a reporter. (How ironic that a non-Italian associate has to explain one of the most basic Mafia tenets to an Italian-American capo who's the son of the godfather.) Instead, Baby Huey decided to throw Sliwa a beating to teach him a lesson not to fuck with "the Chief" (Junior's obsequious nickname for Papa Bear).

One month after Gotti Senior's April 2, 1992, RICO conviction, three thugs attacked Sliwa on the street with baseball bats. Amazingly, he managed to fight them off and escaped without serious injury. Sliwa is a Brooklyn native who grew up streetfighting and studying martial arts. Undaunted, Sliwa continued his harangue, gloating over Dad's conviction and all-but-certain life sentence.

As Gambino soldier Michael "Mikey Scars" DiLeonardo later testified, several months after the assault, Junior ordered a "hospital beating" (Junior's term) of Sliwa to shut his mouth once and for all. As with Alite, DiLeonardo also cautioned Baby Huey against attacking a member of the media.

For some inexplicable reason, Sliwa didn't bother changing his routine after the baseball bat attack. He continued taking a taxi at the same time each day from his home in the East Village to work, including on the morning of June 19, 1992. But the (stolen) Yellow Cab that picked him up that day was driven by Gambino mobster Joseph "Little Joey" D'Angelo, with none other than Michael Yannotti allegedly curled up on the floor of the front passenger seat.

The unsuspecting Curtis plopped into the back, and the doors automatically locked on him. Mikey Y. – BLAM! BLAM! – allegedly shot him twice with a .38 in the thigh and groin after shouting, "Take this, you sonofabitch!" As Sliwa would subsequently testify (at no less than three trials) against Junior Gotti, he savagely fought for his life. Incredibly, as the taxi barreled through traffic, he somehow managed to climb over the front seat, past Mikey Y., and out Mikey Y.'s window!

I've gotta admit, I'm impressed. Even Andrew DiDonato said Mikey Y. was the most dangerous man he'd ever known, and Sliwa bested him. D'Angelo eventually pled guilty to the assault. Although Mikey Y. was not acquitted, he did get a hung jury which voted seven-to-five in favor of guilty. Even Manhattan federal judge Shira Scheindlin said the evidence indicated Yannotti was indeed the shooter. (Mikey Y. wisely wore a bandana around his face when he supposedly did the deed. Remember what I said about disguises?) Mikey Y., however, went down hard on racketeering charges in a subsequent trial and received twenty years in November 2006. *Ouchie!*

For your own edification, five days after the shooting, Gotti Senior was sentenced to life. No doubt Sliwa, who was recovering in a hospital at the time, had a shit-eating grin on his face.

Finally, according to testimony at Baby Gotti's three trials (none of which resulted in a conviction!), Nick Corozzo and Junior both had approved Sliwa's shooting. In addition, in his May 25, 2011, online *Gang Land* column, writer Jerry Capeci states that he had confirmed with the FBI that Andrew DiDonato had, in fact, told the feds of Little Nicky's plan to whack Baby Huey.

Travel Tidbits

Can someone please explain to me why most mob guys are named after the Twelve Apostles? A tour guide in Florence, Italy told me that previous generations of Italians named their sons in this manner to ensure they had a special day on the birth or death day of the respective apostle. Fuck, I don't know... I wasn't really listening. Not my fault 'cause I was super hungover and it was very early in the morning. Suckin'.

CHAPTER TWENTY-THREE – ARSON

"Burn, baby, burn – burn that mother down!" – The Trammps

And I *am* talkin' 'bout burnin' down a building. Seriously, I can't think of a more horrific way to die than being immolated, or a more hideous wound to suffer than a third-degree burn. For the former, please recall what Paul Vario did to his eager-to-please but inexperienced, arsonist son Lenny when he went up like a Roman candle on a torch job. *Ho-kamo po-kamo, talk about a hot foot!*

Nevertheless, I would be sorely remiss if I didn't discuss this most basic yet enduring of all Mafia crimes – lightin' shit up for money or revenge. Still, I wouldn't want to inflict thermodynamic injuries on my worst enemies, and those are individuals whom I would happily feed to a great white shark. But fuck it…

Arson as Vengeance

If you're willing to accept the relatively high risk of spontaneous combustion, arson can be a superb method of extracting your pound of flesh. I've previously regaled you with tales of Gallo and Marco using car bombs as payback. Good News had similar experiences. In January 1984, an ongoing feud with Gaspipe's neighboring crew and Corozzo's literally exploded. The beef started the previous year when the nephew of future boss Vittorio "Vic" Amuso engaged in an altercation with Corozzo crewmember Salvatore "Sally the Lip" Bracchi.

Andrew explains:

Vic's nephew and his friends from Gaspipe's crew tuned Sally the Lip up pretty good. We wanted to retaliate and send a message that you didn't fuck around with our guys. The kid knew we were after him and kept a low profile. It took a long time, but in early 1984, we found out that he was gonna be spending the night at a home right around the corner from the Sixty-Ninth police precinct in Canarsie.

That night me, Anthony Gerbino, and Albert Lattanzi went to that house and broke into the garage, opening the overhead door just enough to crawl under. There were two cars inside. We'd brought gasoline and doused both cars. As we left, we let the gas run down the driveway and make a stream leading to the vehicles. Once we were safely outside, we lit a rag, threw it into the little river of gasoline, and got out of there. There was a tremendous explosion. The garage door was blown all the way across the street. The heat was so intense that every one of the tires blew out. Nobody in the house got hurt, but we'd sent a message.

FYI, Andrew was such a badass, he actually backed down Lucchese powerhouses Gaspipe, Vic Amuso, *and* skipper Danny Cutaia, and even stood up to his best friend Billy Cutolo Jr.'s legendary father, powerhouse Colombo crew chief (capo) William "Wild Bill" Cutolo. Read Andrew's book if you want to hear the juicy details about his long-running, extremely violent feud with Gaspipe's crew, as well as his other crazy beefs. It's *so* choice.

Marco's number-one crime partner from his Dade County days, a Filipino-American doper known as Jimbo X, also used this most painful of all four ethereal elements to get even against some assholes who fucked him big time. While they were out of town, which Jimbo ascertained from their social media postings, he drove over to their house in the middle of the night, doused their basement with a five-gallon can of gasoline, and dropped a lit match. WHOOOSH!!!

Jimbo was shocked by how instantly the conflagration erupted. He ran down the street to his waiting muscle car and roared off, tossing the can in a dumpster several blocks away. The resulting fire burned the entire building down, bringing out scores of firefighters, as well as all the local media outlets.

Incredibly, after an extensive investigation, the fire department blamed the blaze on an electrical malfunction they believed had sprung from the neighboring building! Man, talk about lucky.

When Jimbo called Marco to tell him he had torched the building, Marco said, "You realize you're crazy, right?" But the way Jimbo saw it, those idiots had gotten off easy 'cause he was otherwise planning to shoot them both dead. It was all Jimbo could think about night and day.

The next day, Jimbo drove by the scene of the fire and saw one of the two idiots standing in front of the house, sobbing. Jimbo shouted at him, "Karma!" and took off. The look on the dude's face said it all.

Oh snap, motherfucker – SNAP!!!

Those Gomers should have known better than to mess with a cray-cray like Jimbo. Years earlier, a couple of thugsters from the neighborhood (a father-son team, no less) home-invaded Jimbo. They held him at gunpoint with a MAC-11 submachine pistol while they tried to steal the bountiful marijuana plants he was cultivating in his back room.

When the younger one dropped his guard, Jimbo sprang from the couch like a king cobra and attacked him. They struggled over the submachine gun, which – BRAAAAAAPPPP!!! – sprayed bullets throughout the house. Unfortunately, the rounds barely missed Jimbo's wet-weeping-wussy-of-a-bodybuilder boyfriend, who was hiding in a closet the whole time. *He* died of a heroin overdose a year later. Suckin'.

Anyone who thinks gay guys are wimps has clearly never been to prison or at least watched *Oz* on HBO. In his book, Andrew DiDonato talks about how some of the homosexuals he did time with were among the most dangerous people he'd ever met, and not to be fucked with under any circumstances.

If in doubt, one need look no further than Ronnie Kray, one of the most infamous and violent gangsters in British history. (You Anglophiles will recall that he was the twin brother of fellow homicidal villain Reginald "Reggie" Kray.) Ronnie was a proud poof, and if you were suicidal enough to make a homophobic remark to his face during the '60s when the twins and their firm ruled the London underworld, he'd open you up with a *sword*. Then again, Ronnie was a diagnosed psychotic schizophrenic. Alas, par for the course, life ended badly for the Krays. Anyways, after hearing the MAC-11 discharge, Papa Bear-home invader rushed back into the living room and split poor Jimbo's scalp with the butt of his 9mm. Then he and his prodigal son got the hell out of there. For his trouble, Jimbo received a lovely row of staples in his head and a great story to tell. But he kept his weed. And his dignity.

****

If there's one thing I've learned as a humble grain of sand on the oil-slicked beach of humanity, it's this: you're never too old to fall in love or to burn some fuckwad's car after he cuts you off in traffic. Guess which scenario applies to our favorite Bonanno brokester, Vincent Asaro?

On April 4, 2012, some joker sideswiped Asaro in Howard Beach. Asaro then chased the poor schmuck at an excessive rate of speed until he finally got close enough to get his license plate digits. Using his mob connections, Asaro found out where the man lived, then sent three leg-breakers to his house in the middle of the night to torch his car with gasoline. One of the terrible trio was the Teflon Don's own grandson!

Which one, pray tell? Well, none other than cross-my-heart-and-born-to-lose John Gotti III, who was arrested on this latest faux pas nary two weeks after taking his eight-year plea on his Oxy case. But wait! Only two weeks after *that*, this same criminal mastermind allegedly committed a bank robbery (also in Queens) with two other Bonanno associates on April 18, 2012, netting a whopping $5,491. That's just over $1,800 each.

After torching the car, according to a cop who witnessed the arson from an unmarked police cruiser, which happened to be parked nearby at the time, the three mobsterteers then jumped into the young Gotti's Jaguar. But the kid lost the police after an action packed, tailormade-for-Hollywood, high-speed chase. Nice driving, Gotti the Third!

In late June 2017, both Asaro, then 82, and Gotti-cubed pled guilty to the arson, and now each face up to twenty years in federal prison. I say, "Good trip, babe." And good riddance.

Lessons to Be Learned

You see what road rage gets you, ducklings? I strongly encourage all of you wannabe wiseguys with anger management problems to take up yoga.

Insurance Fraud

Arson is obviously a favorite method of the Mafia to collect on insurance policies, typically following a business bust out. Like we gabbed about earlier, Chris Paciello made a cool score when he allegedly burned down Risk nightclub in South Beach. Gallo tried to do the same for his nightclub, Genesis, in Lake Forest (south OC). Unfortunately, he imported Johnny, an Italian-American New York gangster and cousin of one Gallo's crewmates, Keith. Equally unfortunate, Johnny failed miserably, barely managing to burn up a couch and causing only minor smoke damage to the spot.

Anyways, in addition to robbing banks and getting copious hummers, Sal Polisi was also a gifted firebug. So let's hear what Mr. *Upazzo* has to say. He cautions budding firebugs to avoid using gasoline if you want the fire department or insurance company to blame the blaze on faulty wiring or spontaneous combustion from paint rags. That's 'cause petroleum products leave a distinctive residue.

Instead, he suggests using pure grain alcohol, the kind used in racing fuel. Polisi, who I didn't realize was an amateur botanist, explains the alcohol isn't a petroleum product, and is derived from plants. Therefore, it leaves zero residue when it ignites.

And so his *modus operandi* went something like this: he would load a five-gallon jug of racing fuel into the trunk of his car, along with a flat-nosed funnel made of sheet metal. Once at the jobsite, he would insert the funnel under the door and pour in the alcohol. He'd allow forty-five minutes for the liquid and fumes to spread, then toss in a lit match and KA-BLOOEY! The flames would instantly shoot up two full stories.

Damn, just like with Jimbo!

What's that? You say you can't get enough of Chris Paciello? Well, neither could Sofia Vergara, so you're in good company. Look, I ain't throwin' shade here – she's currently the highest paid actress on TV and is *smoking* hot. Well, your wish is my command, loyal readers, so here's the dirty lowdown.

Arson for Hire

Aside from revenge and insurance money, this is the most prevalent form of incendiary fun in which the mob partakes. This doesn't take much smarts, but certainly enough to T.C.O.B., as attested by Lucchese street boss Alphonse "Little Al" D'Arco. When he was a lowly soldato, Little Al proved to be quite the accomplished firebug. His first torch job was a local trucking company whose owner was beefing with Lucchese mobster Ralph Masucci's brother-in-law. No one was supposed to get hurt.

Late that night, after the business had closed, D'Arco and Masucci used lockpicks to break into the warehouse. After checking to ensure no one else was still inside, they hauled in several gallons of gas, which they started pouring on the second floor, retracing their way back downstairs. Finally, they stuffed some rags into an empty bottle, lit the fuse, and got the hell out of there.

After walking one block, they paused to look back, befuddled as to why they hadn't heard any explosion. Perhaps the fuse had gone out? As they were pondering this mystery... BOOM!!! The fireball blew out all the windows on the second floor, along with a large object which landed on the street below –a security guard who had been copping a nap.

Cue The Commodores' "Flying High."

He only broke his shoulder. Hope Little Al sent flowers. Similarly, as you no doubt gathered from *Goodfellas*, Henry Hill also stacked some Benjies after shouting, "Fire in the hole!" As Henry himself explains in *Wiseguy*, Paul Vario's brother Tuddy paid him two grand a pop to torch restaurants, bars, and other businesses. His favorite method was to mold Sterno and toilet paper along the ceiling beams, then douse the place with gasoline or kerosene. He would then insert a lit cigarette into a book of matches and flee. By the time the cigarette burned down, the petrol fumes would have wafted to the ceiling. The flash would instantly ignite the structure.

Arson for Profit

I know, I know – I told you at jump street I would explain why I traveled to Greece. As the cradle of Western civilization, I wanted to know if Greece was also the birthplace of organized crime. And if so, I wanted to actually meet some Greek gangsters, hopefully even "Godfathers of the Night" (as their dons are called).

For all you stooges, please note that every country on Earth has at least one major organized crime syndicate – particularly in countries like Greece, where the government is rife with corruption. For example, in France, the indigenous mob is known as *le Milieu*, and in the Netherlands, it's called the Penose. But all of the foreign tourists I met in Greece seemed surprised at what I was doing. As one Texan exclaimed, "Boy, y'all mean ta tell me there's a

May-fia in Greece?" Hell, there are even Greek mobsters in *America*.

Indeed, Greek-American gangsters have played a not-insignificant role in the history of *La Cosa Nostra*, particularly in cities that have large Greek communities like Chicago and Philly. During the '60s, '70s, and '80s, The Outfit's number-three man was Gus Alex, a Greek-American political fixer and former Capone torpedo. Gussie's skills and connections were so highly prized that he maintained his lofty position throughout the various upheavals in the Chicago LCN's administration over the decades. Alex was so beloved by the bosses, he was personally entrusted with depositing untold millions of dollars in secret numbered Swiss bank accounts during his reign.

Anyway, it stood to reason that if there were Greek gangsters in the good ol' US of A, there were probably Greek gangsters in *Greece*. But truth be told, my search for Greek mobsters there failed miserably. It wasn't for lack of trying, however – I asked every concierge and bartender I met if they knew any. They all gave me a strange look and shook their heads "όχι" (Greek for "no").

However, they did all agree that at least my *theory* was sound: you know, that Greece was likely where the very first "mafia" (in the generic sense) originated. These individuals were less convinced about my second theory, i.e. that my best chance of finding Greek mobsters would be at five-star resorts on the country's poshest islands of Hydra, Santorini, and Mykonos, and in the exclusive seaside resort of Nafplio.

Although I did not find the Greek mafia, the Greek mafia found *moi* – sort of. On July 23, 2018, coordinated forest fires were strategically set by unknown persons in two towns near the Greek capital of Athens, where I was then staying. The first fire alarm sounded at 12:30 P.M. in Kineta, an hour west of Athens. The second went off at 4:57 P.M. in Rafina, just east thereof.

Whoever set the fires knew exactly what they were doing. The blazes were timed to coincide with the maximum temperature and wind velocity that day. The fires swept down towards the ocean, devouring everything in their path, and destroying the seaside resort of Mati (twenty miles east of

Athens). The wildfires, powered by gale force winds and one hundred-degree temperatures, consumed more than 2,500 homes, displaced over a thousand families, and killed ninety-six people. It was Greece's worst disaster in modern history.

The national and international newspapers (including *The New York Times*) featured articles rampant with speculation and innuendo, but the consensus in Greece was arsonists had worked in tandem to set the blazes. The wildfires had decimated federally protected forest land, but no one seemed to know why that specific area had been targeted.

But I found out the real reason while staying at Hotel Leto, an exquisite five-star boutique on the island of Hydra, where Pink Floyd co-founder David Gilmour had just purchased a villa. There, I met Niko, an extremely wealthy Greek businessman, who had been raised and educated in London. Niko and I hit it off famously, and over fine Scotch and *habanos* (Cuban cigars), he told me with a mischievous smile that even if I were sitting next to a Godfather of the Night, I would never know it.

"They're not like Italian gangsters," he said. "They are not flashy or ostentatious. The bosses are all highly respected members of the business community, very influential in politics."

After ordering our third round of drinks, I asked Niko about who would have profited the most from the Athens fires. "Land developers," he responded. He explained that major construction was strictly prohibited by the Greek government in the protected forest lands. "But with the forests gone, there is nothing left to protect. The developers will bribe the appropriate officials, who will allow them to build commercial and residential properties. This is how things are done in Greece."

I asked him if these land developers were connected to the Greek mafia. He smiled and replied, "They are one and the same."

Bottom Line: If you play with fire, *someone's* gonna get burned. And that ain't cool. Leave the arson gigs for the psychos in your crime family (unless you're one of them).

Arson to Cover Your Ass

In other words, arson to cover up evidence of a particularly gruesome crime. Now, we've already jawed about Jimmy the Bear Flemmi burning down a bar to cover up a murder, which I think you would agree was a case of overkill.

But not so in the so-called "Three Captains' Murders" on May 5, 1981. Good Lookin' Sal Vitale testified that following the triple hit, the death room resembled a scene from 1974's *The Texas Chainsaw Massacre* (which, by the way, was financed by the Mafia). Blood, brain matter, and carnage splattered the walls and drenched the floor. The mess was so overwhelming, it was impossible to clean. As a result, then crew chieftain Joseph Massino gave the order to burn the entire building down.

Fun Facts!

Sometime in April 1994, Chris Paciello fled the Big Apple for warmer climes and was introduced to mobfucker Mickey Rourke. At the time, the Mickster had a failing nightclub called – what else? – Mickey's, that he was desperate to unload. Like Rourke himself, Mickey's had long ago seen far better days. Paciello, allegedly flush with recent bank robbery proceeds, bought it from him and renamed it Risk, which may or may not have been a front for the Gambino Family (reports differ). Unfortunately, the club didn't take off. Not to worry – in April 1995, as previously discussed, just six months after he opened the club, Paciello allegedly burned it down for the insurance money.

According to the Miami Beach Fire Department, which suspected arson, someone had wedged a cigarette between two seat cushions to start the blaze. This is exactly how Gallo's guy Johnny tried to burn down Genesis, albeit with less impressive results.

However, according to Paciello's superstar mob attorney Benjamin Brafman (who also defended Vincent "Chin" Gigante and "Gemini Twin" Anthony Senter, among other Mafia luminaries, and is currently representing "alleged" serial rapist and all-around hideous fuckpig Harvey Swinestein), "The fire at Risk was determined by the insurance company to be accidental." Again, à *la* Jimbo!

And for you *Donnie Brasco* fans, the triple-murder of Anthony "Sonny Red" Indelicato, Dominick "Big Trin" Trinchera, and Philip "Phil Lucky" Giaccone was the *official* reason the FBI pulled Joe Pistone out of his six-year undercover role – the Feebs were afraid he'd be next. Everyone knew Pistone was with Sonny Black, and Sonny and Big Joe were responsible for the massacre. Thus, the feds were concerned that the three skippers' crews, as well as psychopathic killer Anthony "Bruno" Indelicato, would seek vengeance against (among others) Sonny Black's men.

The unofficial reason, however, was that Sonny Black had given Pistone a contract to waste Bruno – no way was the FBI gonna allow an agent to commit murder. Pistone was enraged he was yanked because he wanted to become the first UC to be formally inducted into the Mafia. Pistone knew that getting badged would open up an entirely new world for him, giving him access to top mobsters, including bosses. He also would have been the first copper ever to record an initiation ceremony, which then could have been used in all future Mafia prosecutions as irrefutable evidence of the LCN's existence.

Presumably, the FBI could have simply snatched Bruno off the street and held him in protective custody long enough for Pistone to get made. They could have easily enough faked the hit. Thus, the feds' fear that Pistone would actually go through with the murder seems unfounded.

My gut feeling is that the FBI was secretly concerned Pistone would go native – forget he was an agent and become a *real* wiseguy. Pistone certainly had no shortage of enemies in the FBI – numerous agents and supervisors hated, feared, and envied him for his unprecedented UC role. I think these enemies were worried that by getting made, Pistone would somehow scandalize the FBI. Again, the FBI hates bad press more than anything. And so, in the parlance of the mob, they clipped his wings. And so he resigned.

Personally, I seriously doubt Pistone would have gone rogue – he is and always has been a true believer. So fuck those *putos*, Joe – players gotta play and haters gotta hate.

In the end, Pistone's undercover exploits and the phenomenal success of his autobiography brought nothing but glory to the FBI. They made their peace with each other, allowing him to return and finish out his twenty-year bid. Pistone retired with a full pension and honors up the wazoo. He also got a shitload of money for the movie rights to his book, plus consulting fees, and a major boost in his book sales as a result of the film's success.

Nicely played, Joe.

Chapter Twenty-Four – What to Do with Your Ill-Gotten Gains

"You don't fuck the future, Tony – the future fucks you." – Tony Manero's papa

When you're a young buck, a Mafia comer, and your pockets are bulging with a gangster roll thick enough to choke an Iberian pig, most of your money will go to women, clothes, cars, and good times. However, keep in mind that a career as an organized crime member or associate typically has a relatively short lifespan. In the immortal words of Depeche Mode, "The grabbing hands grab all we can – everything counts in large amounts." This means you should make as much money as possible in as little time as possible, and both spend and save in a fiscally responsible manner.

Look, gents, I'm not gonna give you a diatribe on how to prudently invest your money – that would bore the hell out of both of us. Instead, I'll simply beseech you to follow my rule of thumb – spend half, save half.

Buy Real Estate, But Not in Your Own Name (Duh!)

No brainer on both counts – real estate is the best place to invest your criminal proceeds. However, it's also the easiest asset for the feds to seize. So put your property in other people's names – people you trust with your life. But don't do what Gaspipe did with Burton Kaplan, who literally stole Casso's house after he deeded the property into Kaplan's name for safe keeping.

Johnny Martorano, for one, did not put his own name on the deeds of the various houses he owned. For example, he listed his trusted pal Charlie Raso as the strawman buyer on his second home. Thus, the mortgage was in Raso's name, but Martorano paid it each month. Johnny then completely renovated the home to his exact specifications, hiring subcontractors whom he paid in cash under the table. This way he was able to launder illicit proceeds while simultaneously increasing the property's value. No paper trail means no IRS investigation. And if the pencil-pushing Poindexters do come after you, Johnny recommends telling them, "The market is going only one way – *up, up, up!*"

I likes it, Johnny! Indeed, I can't think of a single mobster who ever put their name on a property deed, although, again, Tony Spilotro once applied for a mortgage in his own name – a decision he came to regret.

If you are going to invest in real estate, I highly recommend the Trump Tower on Fifth Avenue in Manhattan. According to an article in the "Holiday 2017/2018" issue of *Vanity Fair* entitled "Fawlty Tower" by reporter Suzanna Andrews, you'll be in fine company with residents who include...

> Gangsters, minor celebrities, and gamblers. Another resident is Vadim Trincher, a Russian who pleaded guilty in 2013 to money laundering and to having run an international gambling ring with a Russian crime lord that laundered some $100 million. Hillel Nahmad, the art dealer, served five months in prison in 2014 for running a gambling ring out of his Trump Tower home. Susetta Mion, an Italian heiress, is alleged to have stolen her dying mother's $15 million fortune in 2007.

Indeed, as Ms. Andrews explains,

> Trump Tower is known for the high proportion of anonymous owners. These are LLCs registered in Panama, Puerto Rico, Dubai, the British Virgin Islands, and other locations. One reason

for the corporate facades is privacy. Wealthy people don't want to be found, some for reasons of personal security. For these residents – who feel safer having their bags checked by police or being stopped by Secret Service agents – the scanners at the entrance, the police, and even the Secret Service hanging around in the stairwells have been a godsend.

Yes, that's right – buy here and you can brag to your friends about the Secret Service amenity. They lease a duplex on the 66th and 67th floors – for a whopping $130,000 a month, or roughly double the fair market rental value (thanks, taxpayers!).

You can actually buy these condos at a steep discount right now. Indeed, since Trump's November 2016 presidential victory, several dozen apartments have been listed for sale, most of which remain unsold to this day despite major price reductions. (FMV has dropped more than thirty percent since the election, while comparable properties in the same neighborhood have only dropped eight percent.) It's a buyer's market at Trump Tower, which also serves as the headquarters of the Trump Organization, so get 'em while they're hot! Better snatch one of these condos fast though, 'cause as the day I write this, The Donald's approval rating is the lowest in recorded history for a sitting president so chances of re-election are doubtful at best.

Caveat emptor: for you filthy degenerates out there, it might be better to lease your condo out to others instead of living there yourself. AIRBNB the shit out of that crib! As an anonymous real estate broker told Ms. Andrews, "Such high-level security makes it hard to get your cocaine and prostitutes up to your apartment discreetly." I'm talkin' to you, Johnny Depp!

Now you don't necessarily need to buy in Trump Tower to hide your loot, as numerous buildings in the Big Apple allow shady investors to launder their money through strawman purchases. But beware, my little droogies – so much blatant money laundering has put the feds on high alert. As a result, buyers paying a certain amount of cash for these so-called black hole properties must now reveal their true identities. For example, the threshold in Manhattan is three million dollars. (Before, buyers would purchase through LLCs or dummy corporations set up in foreign tax havens.)

Buy Toys, But Again, Not in Your Own Name

The same principle applies to cars and boats, for which you should always pay cash through strawman buyers. Sal Polisi, for example, owned several luxury vehicles, yet had no driver's license in his own name, much less the pink slips for these cars. In fact, everything he owned, including his house, was purchased through strawmen, such as his wife and in-laws. He didn't pay taxes or vote, and none of his numerous firearms were legally registered.

A wise policy, *bubeleh*. Again, even to this day, Gallo doesn't know his own Social Security number. He was even jailed for contempt during his divorce proceedings because he wrote down "$0" on his asset disclosure form. Tabitha's lawyer (she got a new one after Gallo threatened to ventilate the other) went apeshit, waving reams of evidence in the air that proved Gallo was living large. But the judge blinked after Gallo calculated how much it was going to cost the county to jail him each day. He was released later that same afternoon. Go figure.

Owning a pleasure craft screams successful gangster, so please follow Paul Vario's lead. Big Paul never put his name on anything, and always instructed Henry Hill to do the same. Vario loved pleasure boats, but his was the only one in Sheepshead Bay without a name. Paulie never even put his name on a mailbox or buzzer. He refused to have a telephone installed in his home, and always gave his mother's address whenever he was arrested.

Too bad Paulie didn't exhibit such laudable judgment when he brought Henry into his crew. He should've put a rocket in his pocket as soon as he discovered he was dealing dope after Henry finished his five-year stint for extortion in 1978.

Besides, then Paulie could have continued shagging Henry's wife, Karen.

Henry Hill, on paper, did not exist. He had no driver's license, marriage certificate, tax returns, insurance policies, bank accounts, checkbooks, credit cards, or even a Social Security number.

Hell, even gruesome sickboy Charles Carneglia, who was the best man at fellow mobster Peter Zuccaro's wedding, refused to sign the marriage license because he didn't want to give the feds an opportunity to obtain his signature.

****

The same concept applies to bling. To celebrate their successful revenge against Lalo for allegedly murdering Clyde on February 20, 1989, Gallo and Marco went to Bailey, Banks & Biddle at South Coast Plaza (a famous jewelry store that went bust after the 2006 mortgage crisis). They bought two Rolies – an 18-karat-gold Day-Date for Gallo, and a two-tone gold and stainless steel Datejust for Marco.

They moonwalked in rockin' their usual daytime attire – neon pink or Day-Glo-yellow Quicksilver shorts, Bad Boys tank tops, Reebok hightops with white jazz socks, gold Turkish rope chains, and a cloud of Drakkar Noir. The young, uptight female sales clerk ignored them in favor of a young couple who could have leapt off the pages of a Ralph Lauren catalogue. The newlyweds were asking about finance terms for a puny lady's steel Rolex. The silver-haired male manager in a Brooks Brothers suit also glided over to help the couple. He too gave Gallo and Marco the frosty shoulder.

THUD.

All four of them froze at the sound of Gallo plunking down a six-inch stack of rubber-banded street cash on the glass counter. Bet your sweet onion that got their attention. The clerk and manager immediately rushed over to the boys, leaving the yuppie lovebirds staring at them in awe.

It was just like that famous scene in *Pretty Woman* – the manager and clerk were practically Velcro'ing their lips to the boys' overly tanned, shredded glutes. The clerk even brought Marco a Heineken! The Rolex President – and it's *not* called a "Presidential Rolex" – was a smidge over eleven Gs back then.

But Gallo told the manager, "I'm not paying a penny over nine thousand, nine hundred, and ninety-nine dollars."

Gallo didn't even wait for a response before he started counting out C-notes. The manager nodded – he understood that Gallo wanted no forms sent to the IRS, which would have been – and still are – mandatory for all cash purchases of ten grand or more.

You can thank Tricky Dick for that one. In 1970, President Richard Nixon helped pass the Bank Secrecy Law (a.k.a. the Currency and Foreign Transactions Reporting Act), which requires banks to report daily cash transactions of at least ten grand.

Marco almost laughed when he heard the yuppie girl whisper to her preppie boyfriend, "Chad, why doesn't he want to pay more than that?" Chadster was no dummy – he shot her a look and whispered, "I'll explain later, Ashley."

Asset Forfeitures

If you're dense enough to get married and sire children as a mobster, the last thing you wanna see is them getting tossed into the street after the IRS seizes your McMansion. The main reason Bonanno Godfather Joe Massino flipped against all his underlings in 2004 – an unprecedented occurrence in LCN history – is because his beloved wife would have otherwise lost the family home. (He even wore a wire against his own underboss, Vincent Basciano, while both were housed in Brooklyn's federal Metropolitan Detention Center.) Thanks to Massino joining Team Fed, his wife not only got to keep the impressive family home, but also more than a million dollars in cash – enough to live comfortably for the rest of her days. Too bad Massino was forced to surrender over eight mil in other assets.

A similar situation arose in July 1997, when Genovese boss Vincent Gigante finally dropped his hilarious crazy-guy act. He had been pulling it off for over thirty years to avoid prosecution by stumbling around Greenwich Village in old pajamas and a ratty bathrobe, muttering incoherently. His act was so unique and successful that he prohibited any other *Mafioso* from imitating it upon pain of death. The Chinster was forced to do so as part of his guilty plea.

In fact, he did so as part of a secret deal with the feds so his son Andrew Gigante could get a sweetheart deal on an extortion plea. Thanks to Daddy, Andrew received a two-year sentence and "only" had to forfeit two million. Pennies on the dollar for what Chin must have stashed away as the most powerful don on the East Coast since Carlo Gambino passed away in 1976 at age seventy-four of natural causes. Not a bad run, Vincenzo. Or you either, Don Carlo. But what happened to The Chin's self-righteous proclamation to Gotti years earlier that Gigante would never bring his own sons into the Family biz?

By the way, one of the reasons I dislike the feds so much is their blatant hypocrisy (and their woefully misplaced self-righteousness). Do you know that even if you're acquitted in, say, a criminal RICO trial, the G can still keep all the assets it seized from you? That's because when they grab your stuff, it's a *civil* action as opposed to a criminal one. This means they only have to prove by "a preponderance of evidence" that the assets are proceeds from illicit activity. In other words, they only have to convince a jury that your stuff is fifty-one percent or more likely to have been derived from ill-gotten gains in order to keep it. So even if you beat the criminal charges, you still have to go to civil court and prove you bought all your assets and possessions with legally-earned income!

****

You also want to hide your assets in case you get sued by the decedents of your alleged murder victims, which is precisely what happened to Kevin Weeks. He was sued for wrongful death by the family of Debra Davis, who, again, was horrifically murdered by Whitey and Stevie. Despite Weeks' vehement denial of any involvement in her killing, or that he had ever even met her, the family still *civilly* prosecuted him. To settle the case, he agreed to fork over all the proceeds from his autobiography, including (I assume) the hefty advance he received.

Indeed, according to Weeks, the only reason he agreed to write his autobiography (a *New York Times* best seller) was to pay off these civil claims with the proceeds.

Legal Fees and Related Expenses

Not to rain on your parade, but you should put aside ten to twenty percent of all your profits for criminal attorneys and related costs. These include investigators and expert witness fees (for trial), bail funds, bribe money for witnesses, payoffs to cops (and if you're really lucky, to FBI agents), and ransom money (in case you get kidnapped). (As of October 2019, California will abolish the payment of bail money as a condition of release. Bail will then be determined on a case-by-case basis, depending on the individual defendant's flight risk.)

Most successful criminals will spend hundreds of thousands of dollars on legal bills during their career. I know that sucks ass but there's nothing you can do about it and no way to avoid it. In America, you're entitled to the best legal defense you can afford.

Fact, now I'm thinking about this, if you love the gangster lifestyle but don't want the gangster headaches, you should just stay in school, study super-hard, and become a big-time criminal defense attorney. Then you can hang out with wiseguys all you want (and even dress, talk, and act like them à la Bruce Cutler). Then you won't have to worry about going to prison. This is assuming, of course, you don't cross the line like mob lawyers Mike Coiro (in New York) and Robert "Bobby" Simone (in Philly). They both got way too chummy with their *Mafiosi* clientele and ended up getting disbarred *and* going to prison.

Then again, if you actually did get your shit together and changed your wicked ways, you wouldn't need to buy this book. ¡*Ay, caramba*!

So don't take my word for it on this topic – take Kevin Weeks'. He dealt with one particularly mercenary *scheister* who told him he needed to cough up $120,000 for the initial retainer. Plus he wanted $20,000 per week thereafter, as well as all costs – in other words, roughly $600,000 all in. (See, kids, *that's* the racket to get into – screw all this crime nonsense. Personally, I wouldn't like having to make my own Merlot, much less in my cell's toilet.)

Dude, this is no effing joke. You can easily pay over $100,000 alone just to have your legal eagle spend the necessary hours to listen to all the wiretaps the feds made on your loquacious ass. One LA white-collar swindler I interviewed spent over *$1.6 million* to defend himself against criminal fraud charges in federal court. Oh, did I forget to mention that *federal* criminal defense attorneys charge way more than state court sharks? Mama-fuckin'-mia!

Benny Binion paid his federal mouthpiece $200,000 in 1951 to defend him against tax-evasion charges. (Unfortunately, the expenditure did him little good. Benny was convicted in 1953, did a couple years in Leavenworth, and was forced to hand over control of his casino to his adult children. Just as with Lefty Rosenthal in *his* Vegas casino, however, Benny still called the shots as the Horseshoe's public relations director.)

Without question, John Gotti Sr. has the best quote ever – caught on tape by Bruce Mouw's Gambino squad – about what a pain it is to pay your lawyers. Gotti was bitching about the fact that he had already paid $300,000 in legal fees for the RICO appeal of former Gambino underboss Joseph "Joe Piney" Armone and consigliere Joe N. Gallo. These were two old timers who had been so loyal for so long that to *not* cover their legal bills would have been *déclass*é. Gotti also whined about the outrageous fees he was paying to Bruce Cutler and Gerald Shargel for defending him in the assault case of Manhattan carpenters' union official John F. O'Connor, whom he ordered to be shot in 1986: "Where does it end? *Gambino* crime family? This is the Shargel, Cutler, and whattya-call-it crime family!"

Listen, you cheap bastards – an excellent lawyer is worth his weight in gold. There's three things in this life you shouldn't look for bargains on: plastic surgeons, sushi restaurants, and criminal defense attorneys. Whenever Marco bitched and moaned to his soft, pin-striped barrister about how much he was charging, the shark just barked, "You pay peanuts, you get monkeys!"

No one knows this better than Sal Polisi, whose favorite legal eagle Michael "Mike" Coiro launched his career as a mob shark by defending Polisi's mentor, fellow heroin trafficker Dominick "Little Dom" Cataldo. In 1965, Cataldo was swooped up by the FeeBees for stock fraud and possession of counterfeit bearer bonds. Coiro successfully negotiated an outstanding plea deal that sprung Cataldo from the slammer after only a year and a half. After that, many Colombo and Gambino friends hired him to work his magic. By all accounts, Coiro was a highly talented defense attorney.

And 'member when I told you about Sal's hilarious fuck up at his bank robbery trial (where he rocked the same sweater he wore during the heist)? Polisi hired the best gun money could buy: Gerald Shargel. Incredibly, against all odds, Shargel convinced the US Court of Appeals for the Second Circuit to overturn his sentence and order him set free. After serving just over a year of his eight-year sentence, Sal Polisi was unleashed upon the world.

Unfortunately, however, after trying to go straight and blowing $600,000 on a go-kart racetrack business in upstate New York, Sally went back to dealing drugs and got popped again. This, of course, led to him switching sides. *Suckin'*.

Demeaning Post-Prison Jobs

Chances are that after you finish a prison sentence, you're going to have to get a low-level job just to keep your P.O. off your ass. This means you won't have much money if you haven't put some fat stacks aside while you were footloose and fancy free on the street.

Jimmy the Weasel was the king of crappy post-prison gigs. In 1960, after being released, he was washing dishes at Sambo's, a chain restaurant with a racist mascot depicting a young African boy, for minimum wage (ten dollars a day!).

Ten years later, after yet another prison stint (Fratianno burned seventeen years inside on the installment plan), he was forced to drive a furniture-delivery truck. As one of his friends lamented, with all the fortunes Jimmy had made, how could he possibly stomach driving a tow truck for shit money?

If *you're* not careful, *you're* gonna end up driving a certified pre-owned Kia when you get out. With cloth seats. And no SiriusXM radio.

Whitey also had to work shitty gigs after getting out of federal prison, including slaving away as a janitor and riding a jackhammer at a construction site in Quincy, just south of Southie. This was a position his baby brother, then Massachusetts state senator Billy Bulger, had secured for him.

Even the legendary Joey "the Clown" Lombardo, future Outfit boss (and most definitely nobody's fool), had to obtain gainful employment to appease his parole officer. After doing a solid ten-year stretch, his intention was to keep his head down (as it's known in The Outfit). As a result, he ended up working in a Chicago tool-and-dye shop upholstering furniture. *Boring!*

Shrinks

No, I'm *not* going to invoke Tony Soprano's name for this section – geez, give me a little credit, will ya? All bullspit aside, witnessing and committing terrible acts of violence over an extended period of time will almost guarantee that you'll suffer from PTSD. Therefore, you may want to put a tidy sum aside for mental health treatment.

John Alite wisely realized he needed some serious head shrinking. On April 27, 2011, he was finally sentenced on his guilty plea to racketeering, four murders, two attempted murders, drug trafficking, numerous assaults, and extortion. He received a ten year bid, but since he had already served six years (not including two in Brazilian joints), he was released in the spring of 2012.

In what appears to be the new trend (which includes Chris Paciello), Alite turned down WITSEC and returned home to New Jersey, where he now sees a therapist on a weekly basis for what he considers to be an addiction to violence. If you think he's full of shit, just ask any British football hooligan – they'll laugh in your face (before smashing it in).

I sincerely believe that if Frank Sheeran had sought psychotherapy, he would not have died by suicide. He was forever plagued with nightmares of all the carnage he had witnessed and inflicted both during the war and afterwards while in the employ of *La Cosa Nostra*.

Okay, now I *am* going to mention "T." As clearly indicated in *The Sopranos*, you should keep your shrink sessions on the D.L. As Michael Franzese once told a newspaper reporter, any indication that a mobster was seeing a shrink would have resulted in an immediate death sentence – both for the mobster *and* the psychiatrist.

Offshore Bank Accounts

Yes, a great place to stash your money, but make sure you do your homework and pick the right tax haven. For example, Switzerland long ago began cooperating with the feds to out Americans stashing their money in its fabled secret numbered accounts. Even the Cayman Islands have gotten too hot. Things have gotten *really* hot ever since those shady lawyers in Panama, the Mossack-Fonseca law firm, got busted in February 2016. Their arrests exposed thousands of shell companies they had set up for individuals stashing wealth overseas in offshore accounts in places like the British Virgin Islands.

Notwithstanding, the world is still a big place (though it seems to be ever contracting). I interviewed a former hedgefund manager who is a Harvard PhD working on Wall Street about the best way to hide and launder criminal proceeds. Quickly warming to the subject, Mr. SS provided the following insight:

> I've actually given this a lot of thought. If you have at least ten million dollars to work with, you should register an LLC or S-Corp in someplace like the British Virgin Islands. You then open a bank account in Hong Kong in the name of that business entity and deposit as much money as you want. Hong Kong banks do not report financial transactions to the United States government – it's the new Switzerland or Caymans.
>
> You can then purchase any easily liquefiable goods in Hong Kong, from diamonds to art to fine wine or real estate, and either keep it in HK or sell it there and deposit the certified check in the US. There is nothing you can't accomplish in Hong Kong.

Start learning Mandarin, gang!

Diamonds

A splendid way to physically shrink your pallets of cash. Diamonds are ridiculously small and light, and therefore easy to conceal and transport around the world. You can sew them into the lining of your clothes or… well, since most soldati are Catholic, I'll leave that up to your imagination. Beware, however, that many airports occasionally put suspicious-looking people through X-rays (such as LAX and JFK) so, again, please do your homework. That's what the Internet is for. And always go to some Internet café if you're gonna Google sensitive info – you don't want that search history saved on your home laptop.

Safe Deposit Boxes

Safe deposit boxes aren't the cure-all they used to be as far as a good place to stash your loot, but I still like them. Right now in Los Angeles, for example, you literally cannot get a safe deposit box at any major bank anywhere on the West Side because they're all taken. You have to get on a waiting list and wait for one of the owners to kick the bucket – just like good seats at the Met in New York. (You Big Apple opera fans know what I'm talking about. And for the rest of you, watch 1987's *Moonstruck* – like Nicholas Cage says, "It's the best thing there is.")

Instead, there are many legit, highly reputable "private vault" companies out there in major metropolitan cities that offer far more privacy, security, and convenience – and significantly less scrutiny – than conventional banks. You'll also have far more access to your box than you would at a bank – sometimes even twenty-four-hour access. Marco had a great deal going with the manager at one of these businesses near Coconut Grove – a guy he tipped heavily at Christmas, during Hanukkah, *and* on his birthday. The dude would give Marco a heads up if the private vault company ever got served with a subpoena.

Also, these are highly secure facilities with armed guards, alarms, surveillance cameras, the whole shebang. As they cater to a predominantly wealthy clientele, they are extremely professional and discreet, so don't cock swagger in there like the Flatbush Chachi you know you are (or at least aspire to be). As always, do your homework and you'll find a place that's right for you.

Unlike banks, I'd be fine with using my real name at these private vaults. But if you do have loved ones you can truly trust, then it's not a bad idea to have numerous stash spots, so long as they're secure and easily accessible. For instance, by the end of 1970, Gaspipe had been making so much money, his biggest problem was trying to figure out what to do with all the cash. He stashed much of it in safe deposit boxes he put in the names of trusted friends and family members who would simply turn over the keys to him.

Finally, if you have millions of dollars in cash you want to stash in safe deposit boxes, I highly recommend that you shrink your bills by exchanging them for 500-euro notes (€500). This is the largest denomination of currency available in Europe, and one of the largest used in the world. According to Wikipedia, twenty-three countries currently use the euro as their sole currency, with another twenty-two nations using it in addition to their own currency.

As I'm writing this, the exchange rate is $1.16 for one euro. For those of you unfamiliar with Euclidean geometry, this means you can shrink your $1,160,000 in American bills into €1,000,000, which translates into a measly two hundred 500-euro (€500) notes!

Being an aficionado of gangsterism (as racketeering is called in Canada), I instantly realized what would happen when the 500-euro note was originally issued in 2002. Apparently I wasn't the only genius who figured out the obvious, as confirmed by Peter Edwards and Antonio Nicaso in their book about the Italian-Canadian Mafia, *Bad Blood* (which was made into a six-part Canadian TV mini-series in 2017, and is now available on Netflix). Their research revealed that criminal syndicates in Canada immediately began stockpiling the new €500 notes since up to €10 million could fit into an eighteen-inch safe deposit box. In general, gangsters around the globe made them their unofficial currency, using them to transact drug deals, as the equivalent of one million dollars could easily be carried in a standard-sized briefcase.

Better hurry up on this opportunity though because on May 4, 2016, the European Central Bank announced that it would phase out the €500 note by next year. (You geezers reading this might recall the same thing happened on July 14, 1969, when the Federal Reserve discontinued issuing thousand-dollar bills due to lack of use. In reality, international drug lords had quickly scooped them up for obvious reasons and kept them out of circulation.)

I suggest going to major cities where there are hundreds of international currency exchanges, but again, keep the transactions under ten grand.

Bottom Line: Always fly above sonar and below radar.

Storage Units

These are handy for storing drugs, guns, and other contraband (on a short-term basis only, mind you). However, I've never recommended storing cash, even temporarily, in storage units because they're relatively easy to break into. And even if you have a safe therein, the burglars can simply break into *that* or otherwise cart it away. Plus, you'll raise eyebrows if you access it more than once a week, assuming you have to be let in by some pimple-faced teenager who consumes way too much beef jerky and Pornhub.

Retire

Let's pretend for a New York minute that you've made a bundle, invested wisely, and have somehow managed to stay alive, free, *and* solvent. When you've made enough to live comfortably for the rest of your days, then you should pack it in and *call* it a day. Ride off into the sunset on your faithful Appaloosa, never to be seen or heard from again – like Johnny Carson. Now that's class, *papi*.

At least that's the way it *should* work. But as Frank Lopez says, "Not everyone follows the rules." And don't expect or even hope to retire with tens of millions of dollars, which is what Marco foolishly thought would happen to him. Keep your expectations reasonable and you won't be disappointed. Marco's pie-in-the-sky crack-pipe dreams worked out okay but not like he had hoped, and now look at how miserable he is. You think he *likes* sleeping in mosquito netting? Or trying to find lunch that doesn't come directly off a fucking tree?

Retirement does happen, you know – plenty of mobsters have done it. Joe Bonanno did it when he was forced out to pasture after he unsuccessfully (and stupidly) set into motion a

Godfather-finale-like clean sweep of all of the New York dons, including Carlo Gambino and Tommy Lucchese, in 1968.

Here's a more benign example of mob retirement. Upon release from a one-year prison sentence in 1935, Prohibition-era kingpin and owner of the legendary Cotton Club, Owney "the Killer" Madden (Bob Hoskins in Francis Ford Coppola's disappointing 1984 film *The Cotton Club*), saw the writing on the wall as *La Cosa Nostra* began encroaching on his territory. A mutually amicable agreement was reached with the Italians, which enabled Madden to peacefully retire in Hot Springs, Arkansas. With his influence with the local corrupt police force, the town became a safe haven for lamming mobsters. He ended up marrying the city postmaster's daughter and lived happily and wealthily ever after in Hot Springs until his death in 1965 at the ripe old age of seventy-four. You should be so lucky.

****

The last thing you want to do is end up like Jimmy Burke, who had more money than he could possibly spend in a lifetime thanks to the Lufthansa score. (I estimate he kept at least seventy percent of the haul as a result of his murderous campaign against his heist cohorts. The rest was kicked up to Paul Vario, with smaller sums going to the other Mafia *padrinos*, and *much* smaller cuts to the actual accomplices as advances.)

He was so addicted to the Life, he couldn't let it go. He had to keep doing criminal stuff, like selling cocaine and heroin with Henry Hill, which in turn resulted in him "having" to murder Richie Eaton, a con man from Florida, to avenge a rip off. Not that Eaton didn't deserve it. Instead of investing Burke's money in cocaine as promised, he blew it all on expensive women, recreational drugs, weekends in Vegas, and flashy sports cars. In the end, as you know, Henry Hill ratted Jimmy out on that killing, and Burke ended up dying in prison.

Speaking of Henry, don't be a wastrel like him either.

Henry Hill was perpetually in awe of Paulie Vario's savings – a cool $1.5 million stashed in a vault in his Florida home. Vario constantly harped on Henry to save his money, but he wouldn't listen. Hill never believed his own juicy gravy train would come to an end.

Saving money was something neither Hill nor any of his friends ever did. Within a few hours, typically as a result of a bad night at the tables, his once-bulging pockets would be filled only with lint. But then he'd pull down a nice score, and he'd be forced to stuff the $10,000 packets of cash into his underwear. And then it was back to the tables; otherwise, Henry couldn't give his money away fast enough. He lavishly over-tipped wherever he went, including bars, restaurants, and supper clubs all over Nassau County and Queens. When he ran low on funds, he simply borrowed from his buddies until he scored again. There was always a big heist or scam just around the corner, and he always had a dozen deals juggling in the air.

Bitcoin

The jury is still out on whether or not you should invest in or otherwise utilize cryptocurrencies such as Ether, Ethereum, Ripple, and Litecoin. Cryptocurrencies are not tied to any bank, government, traditional currency, regulations, or interest rate. Before we dig into this subject, I think I should first explain Bitcoin, the most popular cryptocurrency available.

When Bitcoin launched in 2009, it was touted as a digital currency that was impossible to trace. It was also a global currency in the sense that anyone in any country could buy and sell it on the Internet, again, without any way for those transactions to be traced back to the buyer or seller. And, of course, Bitcoin could be used to buy anything legal or illegal, so long as the seller of the particular product was willing to accept it as payment.

The benefits of utilizing cryptocurrencies to criminals should be obvious – the feds have no way of tracking what you can buy or sell using them online, much less the source of those funds. And the *overall* increasing valuation of Bitcoin, for example, is also tempting from an investor's perspective. Indeed, if you had invested $100 in Bitcoin in 2010, it would be worth *millions* today.

During the week of December 7, 2017, for example, the price soared eighty-two percent – up more than 2,200% from the same time last year. Ten days later, Bitcoin hit a record high of about $19,200 before plummeting twenty-eight percent the following week, then swinging up thereafter.

(As I'm editing this passage, the price has nosedived to a near three month low of $7,599. Three days earlier, the global cryptocurrency market nosedived over fears regarding tighter regulations.)

You can easily buy Bitcoin online through various cryptocurrency exchanges like Coinbase, Kraken, and Bitfinex, or even through traditional exchanges like the Chicago Mercantile Exchange, where Bitcoin is traded under the XBT and BTC symbols. However, before you go all in, you should be aware of the substantial and numerous risks. And make sure you load up on Dramamine.

First, even between the various exchanges, the simultaneous prices can vary by as much as fifteen percent for Bitcoin. For example, on December 7, 2017, prices varied by more than $2,000, from $15,592 to $18,259. The ramifications of this lack of synchronization among the exchanges are obvious. And don't think you can take advantage of this problem by arbitraging from one exchange to the next – another major drawback of Bitcoin is the lack of immediate liquidity. Frenzied buying and selling of Bitcoin (largely by Asian investors, particularly in South Korea) has caused repeated outages as the exchanges' servers get overloaded. This means you can't immediately buy and sell your Bitcoin when you want, which obviously exposes you to potentially greater losses if the price tanks.

Speaking of South Korea, on December 27, 2017, the government announced its intention to shut down all cryptocurrency exchanges. The Israeli government made a similar proclamation at the same time. More countries were expected to follow suit (including India and China), so *caveat emptor*.

Yet another drawback is the fact that a relatively small number of investors – namely, the original founder(s) of Bitcoin and first-tier investors – control almost half of the Bitcoin in existence. Bitcoin was launched by a programmer or group of programmers operating under the name Satoshi Nakamoto through the website www.bitcoin.org. From there, it spread out to a relatively small group of a thousand supergeeks who collectively own forty percent of all Bitcoin, with individual shares amounting to over $100 million for each investor. (There are sixteen million Bitcoins in circulation, with a maximum of only five million more to be distributed, according to the complex Bitcoin algorithm.)

Many if not most of these founding fathers are presumed to know and perhaps even collude with each other. This means they have the power to manipulate the market in their favor. (Nakamoto's account is believed to hold approximately 980,000 Bitcoins, or five percent of all available Bitcoin, with a current value of more than $15 billion.)

The bottom line is obvious – power outages, government shutdowns, server overloads (during heavy trading periods), monopolistic manipulations, and, hell, even cyberhackers (who have thus far stolen more than *$15 billion* in virtual currencies) can prevent you from timely accessing your Bitcoin account. All of this can result in a good old-fashioned bank run, which, in turn, can crumble the entire cryptocurrency cookie. The fact that Bitcoin is not based on any underlying asset but entirely on human psychology makes this doomsday scenario all the more possible, if not likely.

Having said that, if you're willing to accept the volatility and other inherent risks of trading in cryptocurrencies, I can't think of a better way to transfer vast amounts of illicit wealth around the world. You can even avoid many of the foregoing perils by simply downloading your Bitcoin as a string of software code onto a special hard drive. You can then physically deliver it to your buyer, who can then verify that string of code through a peer-to-peer network called Blockchain, which tracks and verifies every Bitcoin in circulation (and ensures that no single Bitcoin can be sold to more than one party at a time). But if your hard drive is lost, damaged or stolen, there goes your nest egg.

If you're seriously interested in Bitcoin but want to minimize your initial exposure, I suggest buying a single Bitcoin or even a piece thereof (which the exchanges now offer) and get comfortable with the process before upping your ante. And if you're intending to invest a large sum, it behooves you to consult with respected experts on cryptocurrencies, such as analyst Mr. Park Nok-Sun at NH Investment and Securities in Seoul. Meanwhile, go on Coindesk, a website that tracks Bitcoin's value, and start educating yourself.

A final note: be careful about running your big mouth about what a Bitcoin baller you are 'cause you never know who's listening.

On January 22, 2018, four balaclava-clad home invaders kicked in the front door of a home in rural England (Moulsford, Oxfordshire). Once inside, the attackers put guns to the heads of cryptocurrency traders Danny Aston and his girlfriend Amy Jay, and forced them to digitally transfer more than one million dollars in Bitcoin. Mr. Aston used his real name when servicing his clients and providing online advice about his trades, thereby enabling the assailants to track him.

According to *The Daily Beast* reporter Kelly Weill in her January 26, 2018, article "FORGET HACKING, THIEVES ARE STEALING BITCOINS AT GUNPOINT":

> Recent robberies have grown more sophisticated as Bitcoin's price rises. In November 2017, Turkish officials announced the arrest of a group of five people who allegedly posed as police and forced a prominent Bitcoin owner into a car, where they forced him to transfer 450 Bitcoins: worth more than $5 million today.

In December 2017, thieves kidnapped the head of a major Ukrainian Bitcoin exchange on the streets of Kiev. Pavel Lerner, CEO of cryptocurrency company Exmo Finance, was reportedly exiting his office when men in ski masks pulled him into a black Mercedes-Benz. They later released him after he paid a $1 million ransom in Bitcoin.

So be careful out there!

And start thinking about the cryptogeeks *you* should be plundering. All you and your cohorts need are some low-hanging fruit, trusty sidearms, and that special thumbdrive onto which you can transfer your pilfered Bitcoin.

Bueno suerte!

Fun Facts!

When Trump broke ground on the Trump Tower in 1980, he paid a company called S&A Concrete eight million bucks to pour the concrete. S&A was wholly owned by Big Paul Castellano and Genovese Godfather Anthony "Fat Tony" Salerno. According to journalist David Cay Johnston in a May 22, 2016, article in *Politico* entitled "Just What Were Donald Trump's Ties to the Mob?":

> Trump has a record of repeated social and business dealings with mobsters. Trump didn't just do business with mobbed-up concrete companies: he also probably met personally with Salerno at the townhouse of notorious New York fixer Roy Cohn, in a meeting recounted by a Cohn staffer who was present. Trump's career has benefited from a decades-long and largely successful effort to limit and deflect law enforcement investigations into his dealings with top mobsters, organized crime associates, labor fixers, and corrupt union leaders.
>
> Salerno and Castellano and other mob families controlled both the concrete business in New

York City and the unions involved in delivering and pouring it. With Cohn as his lawyer, Trump apparently had no reason to personally fear Salerno or Castellano – at least, not once he agreed to pay inflated concrete prices. What Trump appeared to receive in return was union peace. That meant the project would never face costly construction or delivery delays.

The indictment on which Salerno was convicted in 1988 and sent to prison, where he died, listed the nearly $8 million contract for concrete at Trump Plaza as one of the acts establishing that S&A was part of a racketeering enterprise.

FBI agents subpoenaed Trump in 1980 to ask about his dealing with John Cody, a Teamsters official and associate of the Gambino crime family. FBI agents suspected that Cody, who controlled the flow of concrete trucks, might get a free Trump Tower apartment. Trump denied it. But a female friend of Cody's, a woman with no job who attributed her lavish lifestyle to the kindness of friends, bought three Trump Tower apartments. Cody stayed there on occasion and invested $500,000 in the units. Trump helped the woman get a $3 million mortgage without filling out a loan application or showing financials.

In the summer of 1982, Cody, then under indictment, ordered a citywide strike – but the concrete work continued at Trump Tower. After Cody was convicted of racketeering, Trump sued the woman for $250,000 for alteration work. She counter-sued for $20 million, and in court papers accused Trump of taking kickbacks from contractors, asserting this could 'be the basis of a criminal proceeding requiring an Attorney General's investigation' into Trump. Trump then quickly settled, paying the woman a half-million dollars.

In his article, Mr. Johnston also details how in 1979, Trump hired "200 non-union men to work alongside about fifteen members of the House Wreckers Union Local 95. Normally the use of non-union workers at a union job site would have guaranteed a picket line. Not at this site, however. Work proceeded because the Genovese Family principally controlled the union."

Trump, as usual, emerged unscathed from all this hullabaloo. That is, aside from the rejection of his 1987 bid for the first casino license in Sydney, Australia, which was denied because of his past Mafia connections.

I, for one, was certainly not surprised to learn that Trump was mobbed up – rumors of his Mafia connections have dogged him since at least the mid '80s. This is apparently why he used to brag that he could get any building completed in half the time of his competitors.

But I *was* surprised to learn that his own father, penny-pinching slumlord and alleged KKK member Fred Trump (Google it!), was apparently the man who had introduced him to the mob. In Pulitzer Prize winner Maureen Dowd's July 23, 2018, article in *The New York Times*, "THE DON AND HIS BADFELLAS," she quotes Trump biographer Michael D'Antonio: "In his first big apartment project, Trump's father had a partner connected to the Genovese and Gambino crime families. He dealt with mobbed-up suppliers and union guys for decades."

If you won't take my word for it, how about The Donald's? According to a January 7, 2019, article in *The New Yorker* entitled "HOW MARK BURNETT RESURRECTED DONALD TRUMP AS AN ICON OF AMERICAN SUCCESS" (by Patrick Radden Keefe):

> During a 2004 panel at the Museum of Television and Radio, in Los Angeles, Trump claimed that "every network" had tried to get him to do a reality show, but he wasn't interested: "I don't want to have cameras all over my office, dealing with contractors, politicians, *mobsters*, and

everyone else I have to deal with in my business. You know, *mobsters* don't like, as they're talking to *me*, having cameras all over the room. It would play well on television, but it doesn't play well with them."

Nuff said.

Hey, here's another fun fact for ya: Rolex raises the prices each year, even adjusting for inflation, to keep out the riffraff. The same model will run you thirty-five grand plus tax today. Trust me, that's the first thing I'm buying when this book hits *The New York Times* Best Seller list. You really want your favorite author running around with a fucking Seiko? *Just kidding, Moo-Moo!*

Okay, people, please try to keep up. Did you know that President Nixon's favorite restaurant when he retired to Orange County was the Avilas' El Ranchito in Laguna Niguel? It *is* damn fine Mexican cuisine – my favorite location is on Balboa Island in Newport, where Lalo shot Joey's cuckolded assailant in the back. Still, I find sweaty Dick's choice ironic in light of the fact that he was a virulent racist who despised Mexicans.

Also, unless you're a friggin' mook, you should know that Joe Bananas' failed coup was the inspiration for the climactic sequence in *The Godfather* where Michael Corleone has the heads of the Five Families assassinated.

Did you know that Mario Puzo, the author of *The Godfather* novel (first published in 1969), never knew a single gangster growing up in New York? He made everything up, based mostly on newspaper accounts of gangland events.

Did you also know that Frank Sinatra was so furious at Mario Puzo for depicting him as "Johnny Fontaine" that right after the movie came out, he approached Puzo at a restaurant in New York and tossed a drink in his face?

Did you also know that at the time, *The Godfather* sold more copies than any other work of fiction in history (aside from the Bible – JK!)?

Travel Tidbits

Speaking of Vincent Gigante, I interviewed several of his Greenwich Village neighbors while I was having dinner in Hell's Kitchen during my research tour. On my first night in the city, I was strolling blissfully down Ninth Avenue when I came across Mama Mia's West 44 SW, a lovely indoor-outdoor restaurant located at the southwest corner of 44th Street. While gorging on scrumptious, authentic Neapolitan cuisine, I grabbed a menu and read the history of the restaurant and its owners. In 1971, recently arrived Naples emigrés, husband and wife Anna and Guido Schiattarella opened it, much to the delight of the local residents.

Fastforward forty-seven years later. I simply *had* to speak to the owners. Luckily, I was able to jaw at length to Anna herself, as well as her daughter Cristina, who translated. I explained who I was and about the book I was finishing, and their faces lit up with mischievous smiles.

First, I told Anna my theory that *Mafiosi* would happily have driven in from all five boroughs to eat excellent, authentic Neapolitan cuisine, particularly from authentic Neapolitans. Anna confirmed that her restaurant had indeed been extremely popular with mob guys, including the Genovese Family, back in the day. My heart began palpitating!

Next, Anna confirmed that she had been well aware of the neighborhood Irish mob war during the mid '70s between Jimmy Coonan and Mickey Spillane. However, she said that The Westies had given her restaurant a wide berth and never came in as they knew it was favored by their other enemies, the Genoveses. (In the early '80s, the two groups almost went to war over The Westies' penchant for kidnapping mobsters, and over control of the construction of, and employment at, the Jacob K. Javits Convention Center in Hell's Kitchen.)

I asked her if Vincent Gigante – the Godfather himself – had ever frequented her fine establishment. Both ladies confirmed this fact, and even told me that they had lived right next door to him for decades. Yes, The Chin was always shuffling around like a brain-damaged ex-boxer, they said, but everyone in the

Village knew it was just an act. He was always quite lucid and friendly to them, particularly because he too was from Naples. *Buona sera!*

    I promised the lovely ladies I would send them a copy of this book when it was published, but I look forward to delivering it in person next time I'm in the city. For all you foodies out there, don't forget to visit Mama Mia's and tell 'em Roman Motherfuckin' Martín sent you. *Mangia, mangia!*

Chapter Twenty-Five – Flippin' Ain't Easy

"I can do wheelin', I can do dealin', but I can't do no damn squealin'." – James Brown

This particular chapter has terribly vexed me. See, at first I thought, why should I give advice to people who are considering going over to the other side? As you'll see, it's not a simple black-and-white issue, and thus my feelings are both complicated and ambivalent.

Take Marco for example: as a pee-wee gangbanger-wannabe growing up in the *barrios* of Orange County, he was taught that only rapists and child molesters were lower than rats. This ethos continued to be drilled into him when he became a serious professional crook. And this is obviously still the prevailing wisdom in the underworld, as it should and always will be.

But hold up. Something is amiss. If it wasn't for stool pigeons, we wouldn't have all these amazing books about the mob or the wonderful films. And let's face it – if it wasn't for canaries singing, I wouldn't be writing this book.

It gets even more problematic. My favorite mobsters have all been finks. Gallo was one of the biggest rats to flip in the last two decades. And what about his pals Andrew DiDonato and Frank Calabrese Jr.? And what about other guys I respect, including some I even like on a personal level, like Billy Cutolo Jr.?

Bottom Line: Here's what's taken me this long to figure out – you *can* be a snitch and still have honor. As long as you flip for honorable reasons, you can and should be able to hold your head up high. I know what you're gonna say. *"Well, that's just like, your opinion, man."* Fair 'nuff but let's look at a few examples.

But first, always remember two things: one, you cannot push people without them pushing back; and two, people will fight back with whatever means they have at their disposal. With gangsters, sometimes it's guns and sometimes it's words.

In his book, Gallo claims he became disgusted and disillusioned with the Mafia, but I think he somehow grew a conscience and realized the mob is an evil, destructive entity. He sincerely wants to destroy my beloved LCN. And that's okay with me, despite the fact most people will assume I'm trying to do just the opposite with *this* manuscript. And I'm cool with that too.

Frankie Junior came to the same realization as Gallo, but for him it was more personal. He knew his father, Frankie Breeze, had murdered more people than most serial killers, and so Junior simply wanted the carnage to stop. See, deep down, just like Andrew D., Frankie the Second was clearly a decent human being. Like Gallo's former friend John Baudanza, Frankie would never have gotten involved in the Life but for his bloodthirsty, psychotic, gangster father.

Even more personal is the decision of Billy Cutolo Jr., who flipped in order to investigate and eventually convict the men who murdered his father, Colombo capo Wild Bill. Billy Junior finally got his man (or two men, as it were) as a result of his eight-year-long effort, which included him wearing a wire. However, one of the main architects of his father's disappearance and slaying, Greg Scarpa Sr., died of AIDS-related complications on June 4, 1994, after receiving a tainted blood transfusion from one of his underlings after a hernia operation.

Cue Justin Timberlake's "Cry Me A River."

You Might Get Your Head Blown Off

This is the most obvious drawback of flipping. Case in point: the double murders of Mr. and Mrs. John and Frances DuBeck in the pre-dawn of March 19, 1974, in Las Vegas. The couple had just finished their night shift at one of the casinos, where John supervised dealers and his wife served cocktails.

They parked in their carport and shuffled to their apartment, exhausted from the long night. As they entered their complex's courtyard, a man in black stepped out and blew them away with two blasts from a sawed-off 12-gauge. They were scheduled to testify in the upcoming gambling trial of the LA Family for running a floating craps game in the San Fernando Valley. The DuBecks had foolishly declined the G's offer of WITSEC.

This occurred three years after Spilotro had moved to Vegas. Thus, I'm certain The Ant either pulled the trigger himself or had one of his homicidal minions do it. In any event, the murders were payback against John DuBeck for his anticipated testimony against several top mobsters in the Milano Family (including the top gangster I met through Gallo – the same wiseguy authorities believed had ordered the hits). The couple was murdered only one week before the trial was to commence. Remember what I said earlier about LA reaching out to Chicago for help? And what happened to the decree against leaving bodies in Vegas? I'm stumped on that one.

Earlier we talked about how decade-long FBI informant, San Diego skipper Frank "Bomp" Bompensiero, was executed in 1977 with a silenced .22 while talking to the LA boss in a phone booth. Bomp flipped after his family starved during the five years he spent in Soledad state prison.

Bompensiero was deeply embittered by the fact the LA Family had failed to help out his wife and kids during that time. This *infamia* had been particularly cutting as Bomp had always been a loyal, stalwart killer who reported directly to Godfather Jack Dragna himself. Unfortunately, Dragna croaked of natural causes after Bomp went inside.

Lots of guys flip for this reason, i.e., that their *Famiglia* doesn't take care of their wives and kids while they're in the paint. This is what flipped Willie Boy (that, plus John Gotti's racist backstabbing). Just like Bomp, Willie Boy – who also did plenty of heavy work for his *borgata* – met the same fate at the hands of Tommy "the Butcher" Pitera, with help from Bonanno associate Vincent "Kojak" Giattino. The hit duo ambushed and shot Johnson fourteen times outside of his home on August 29, 1988, just after he left for work at a nearby construction site. They used Glaser rounds for maximum damage and dropped jack-spikes on the street to hinder any potentially pursuing vehicles. Tommy Karate was no dummy.

In 1992, Pitera and Giattino were indicted and tried for the murder. Giattino was convicted. Pitera was acquitted, but was subsequently convicted of six other murders and sentenced to life without parole.

Willie Boy was also quite intelligent and had been a two-fisted earner for many years. He was murdered because he foolishly dropped his guard and believed John Gotti when he said he more or less forgave Johnson for singing. While they were in custody during the Giacalone RICO trial, Gotti had promised Johnson that so long as he didn't testify against Gotti, his only punishment would be permanent banishment from the Mafia. Johnson naively accepted the offer.

Lessons to Be Learned

People always believe what they *want* to believe. Never make the same mistake. Never bullshit yourself.

Personally, I don't think that flipping against your boss simply because he broke his promise to financially support your nagging wife and screaming brats is an honorable reason. It's your fault for being so fucking dim that you thought getting hitched and having kids would somehow miraculously work out for you. You're equally idiotic for not having planned for these certainties.

We also gabbed earlier about how William "Billy the Chopper" Dauber and his wife Charlotte were murdered on

July 2, 1980, after The Outfit learned *he* had flipped. Again, they were shotgunned by Frankie Breeze and pals.

And how 'bout John Otto Heidel, who was changing a flat tire in Brooklyn on October 8, 1987, when someone snuck up on him – presumably the same guy who flattened the tire – and domed him. Heidel was a member of Gaspipe's Bypass Gang, as well as a wire-wearing informant. Mafia Cop Lou Eppolito exposed him to Burton Kaplan, who in turn notified Gaspipe.

****

The second-most famous murder ever of a mob turncoat is that of Abraham "Kid Twist" Reles. The Kid was widely considered to be the most prolific killer for Murder Incorporated, the enforcement arm of both the Italian and Jewish mobs in New York during the 1930s & '40s.

In 1940, Reles was arrested for several homicides. To save his own neck, he flipped against his boss Louis "Lepke" Buchalter, the founder of Murder, Inc. As a result, Buchalter became the only major traditional, organized-crime boss to be executed in the United States – a dubious distinction he holds to this day. Reles' cooperation also sent seven other major mob figures to the electric chair. He was also set to testify against Albert "the Mad Hatter" Anastasia (don of the future Gambino crime family), and that's where Reles truly overreached.

At the crack of dawn on November 12, 1941, while Reles was being guarded as a material witness by police at a Coney Island hotel, he decided to get some fresh air – by diving out of the fourth-floor window and splattering onto the sidewalk below. A local newspaper reporter referred to him as "the canary who could sing, but couldn't fly."

Reles, who'd been tossed by his own police guards, was scheduled to testify against Anastasia later that same morning. The five cops guarding him were all demoted. Hopefully the $100,000 fellow Mafia boss Frank Costello supposedly paid them for the hit took the sting out of the reprimand. Split five ways, it came out to roughly $342,000 *each* in today's money.

****

And, of course, the number-one most famous murder of a rat in the entire history of American organized crime has to be that of our very own beloved Jimmy Bulger. On October 30, 2018, eighty-nine-year-old Whitey was horrifically slaughtered in his cell at the max-security US Penitentiary Hazelton in West Virginia. (This was just over seven years after his 2011 arrest in Santa Monica, and five years after his conviction at trial.) And when I say horrifically, I mean right out of a freakin' horror flick.

At 6 A.M. that morning, all the doors on Whitey's cell block automatically opened so the inmates could go to breakfast. Suddenly, two masked prisoners entered his cell and attacked poor Bulger, who was confined to a wheelchair due to numerous health problems. One attacker gouged out Whitey's eyeballs with a shank, while the other sawed off the tongue that had sent so many people to prison or the afterlife. Whitey actually died during this initial phase of the assault from a massive cardiac arrest (read: shock).

Phase two involved the two men smashing Whitey's face into an unrecognizable cherry-pie mess with a lock-in-a-sock (a padlock in a knotted-off sweat sock). The killers then wrapped Whitey up with blankets in his cot to make it appear as if he was asleep. After placing his head on a pillow and singing him a lullaby, they exited. (Video footage captured this ingress and egress.) He was discovered at 8 A.M. when the guards made their morning rounds.

Bulger had been transferred from a federal medical prison facility known as Coleman II in central Florida to Hazelton less than twelve hours before his murder. Incredibly, he had been assigned a gen-pop cell instead of protective custody where federal informants are automatically placed. The transfer was payback against Whitey for threatening a female staff member at Coleman. (Apparently, the eight months he had to serve in solitary confinement were not sufficient retribution.) An anonymous US Bureau of Prisons employee told the *New York Times* that the transfer was "a death sentence" and "a monumental failure" that would have required the approval of *many* different officials.

By all accounts, the primary assassin was fifty-one-year-old Fotios "Freddy" Geas, a Greek-American Mafia hit man from West Springfield, Massachusetts (ninety minutes west of Boston). In 2011, he was sentenced to two life terms for the 2003 contract murders of Adolfo "Big Al" Bruno, the Genovese Family boss who controlled Springfield, MA., and state-police informant Gary Westerman. Bruno was killed in a power play by a rival who was close to Geas, and who enlisted his help in the coup. The plot was set into motion by Anthony "Bingy" Arillotta, a rival made man with the Genoveses who had groomed Geas as he was coming up. Freddy was reportedly heartbroken when Arillotta testified against him at the Bruno murder trial.

As for his former crime-partner Westerman, Freddy killed him by caving his head in with a shovel, then shooting him in the face at point-blank range. After dumping his corpse into a pre-dug pit in Agawam, MA (ninety-five miles west of Boston), he used white vinegar to eliminate the gun residue from his hands. (Shit, did I misunderstand what Nicky Crow was saying about using vinegar after a shooting? My bad.)

Anyways, Freddy was such a prolific gangster, he was even widely believed by authorities to have been involved in at least five separate murder plots in one particularly productive year alone. No surprise, then, that he was the top dog at Hazelton, wielding an extraordinary amount of power and influence over cons *and* bulls. He was housed on Whitey's tier, which begs the question as to whether prison officials intentionally placed Bulger in the lion's den.

Personally, I can't help but like this Freddy guy – he's everything you'd want in a movie-star mobster: looks, muscles, brains, charisma, and an unshakeable Mafia ethos that mandates the immediate extermination of all vermin informants and woman-killers whenever possible. (I smell a book deal!) Seriously, Freddy is known for despising rats and woman-beaters. His own attorney said Freddy was not denying the Bulger hit.

The second killer was allegedly Paul DeCologero Jr., another mobster with enviable bone structure and musculature who was serving a twenty-five-year bid for RICO violations. He was a member of the Patriarca Family's Boston crew that was then run by his uncle (also named Paul DeCologero). I'm decidedly less fond of Junior than Freddy as the former was apparently involved in the 1996 murder and dismemberment of nineteen-year-old Aislin Silva. She was the civilian-girlfriend of a DeCologero crewmember who had, without her knowledge, stashed a cache of guns and drugs in her Boston-suburb apartment. When the cops raided her place, she became a liability to the boss (again, DeCologero's uncle "Big Paul") and the rest of the crew. Fortunately, Big Paul was later sentenced to life for her murder. (Hey, Freddy, might I suggest giving the younger DeCologero his own lock-in-the-sock party? Just sayin'.)

Hazelton itself should be a major character in the movie that will hopefully be made about this tantalizing melodrama. Nicknamed "Misery Mountain," U.S.P. Hazelton was literally the worst place the B.O.P. could have sent a Mafia rat like Bulger. It was chock full of extremely dangerous mobsters from the East Coast, including Boston, and was considered to be one of the most violent and overcrowded prisons in the federal system. In fact, two other inmates had already been murdered earlier the same year, and two more in as many preceding years. The guards are also known to physically assault and abuse the inmates. Christ, this hellhole makes Shawshank Prison look like Romper Room. Way to go, B.O.P.!

To date, the feds have done fuck all to solve the Whitey whacking. As of this writing, no one has been charged for Whitey's murder, and no explanation has been given as to why he was placed in gen pop. On one hand, I understand, since Bulger had brought nothing but grief to the FBI. On the other hand, however, such a brazen assassination has proven to be a major embarrassment for the B.O.P., so you'd think the feds would want to get to the bottom of it. Plus, you'd think the DOJ would do everything in its power to ensure the killers, as well as the long line of B.O.P. employees responsible for Whitey's transfer, were held accountable. I mean, don't the feds *want* their Mafia informants to believe that even if they're in prison, they'll be protected from revenge-seeking hitmen???

As of November 30, 2018, the B.O.P. was "considering" firing the apparently-inbred warden, Joe "Okily-Dokily" Coakley, who essentially fed Whitey to the Hazelton wolves. Further, Geas and DeCologero were placed into segregated housing (but not prosecuted). Otherwise, it appears that absolutely nothing has been done by the G to deal with this debacle, despite the fact that the B.O.P. assigned a whopping twenty officials to investigate it. 'Member when I told you the last thing the Department of Justice cares about is justice?

Postscript: Whitey's five surviving siblings – William "Billy-Goat" Bulger, brother Jackie, and three sisters – are, as this book goes to press, about to file a wrongful death and negligence lawsuit for millions of dollars in damages against the B.O.P. I have no doubt the Bulger brood will obtain a huge settlement; the question is, however, whether they will ever see a dime of it. That's 'cause the family members of some of Whitey's murder victims plan on attaching a lien on any settlement to compensate them for their own losses.

Legally, I think they're screwed since they're only entitled to Whitey's assets, *not* to his siblings' (which would presumably include the settlement proceeds). Nevertheless, I sincerely wish them the best of luck. So far the only money they've seen is their respective shares of the $822,198 in cash the feds seized from a wall in Whitey's Santa Monica apartment. Still no sign of the millions he stashed away in safe deposit boxes around the globe.

In the end, it all comes down to the fact that this couldn't have happened to a nicer psychopath. *Bon voyage*, Whitey! Cue Theme from *The Love Boat*.

****

Fortunately for you would-be flippers out there, *La Cosa Nostra* has been so decimated by RICO prosecutions (virtually all because of other snitches), urban gentrification, and a host of other reasons I don't feel like going into right now, that rats face little threat of retribution. That is, unless they're suicidal enough to go back to their old stomping grounds.

This is what happened to Mafia rat Mario "Sonny" Riccobene, who was kicked out of WITSEC in 1989 after repeatedly contacting old friends. Three years later, he was back in action in South Philly. Less than a year after that, on January 28, 1993, Sonny was sitting in his Ford Taurus outside a New Jersey diner when someone walked up and shot him to death.

No one exemplifies this embarrassing decline in Mafia vengeance standards more than Chris Paciello. Here's a guy who put away seventy mobsters (including Joey Massino), refused WITSEC, and then eventually moved back to Miami to open up shop again. I'm amazed someone hasn't blown him away. The LCN founding fathers must be writhing in Hades right now at this pitiful state of affairs. *La Eme* and the Hells Angels would *never* have let that shit fly. My theory is that Paciello paid off the godfathers in NYC and bought himself a pass – like Michael Franzese presumably did when *he* allegedly flipped.

Similarly, Frank Calabrese Jr. currently makes his dough leading tour buses around Chicago, providing his intimate knowledge about The Outfit's history. See https://www.familysecretstours.com. Holy cow! More power to you, Frankie!

You Can't Protect Your Real Friends When You Wear a Wire

We talked about this earlier, but when you wear a wire, it never stops recording. There's no way to stop and start it, and no pause button. It's like a giant fishing net, catching dolphins and tuna alike. When you agree to flip, you agree to have your entire life wired up – your house, your car, your *ass*.

Kenny Gallo provides a particularly painful example in *Breakshot*. You see, John "Johnny Goggles" Baudanza was the first true friend he ever ratted out. Indeed, from the first time they met, Gallo was wired, so literally every conversation they ever had was on tape.

Such a retroactive betrayal made Gallo nauseated and ashamed every time he was around JB. Gallo even began avoiding him in an admittedly misguided attempt to minimize Johnny Goggles' exposure. Alas, Gallo knew it was all for naught. All Kenny could think about was Baudanza would never see his children grow up. And, sadly, that was JB's greatest fear.

Thus, if you think you can simply dodge your buddies to avoid taping them, guess again. How many excuses can you conjure up before they get wise? And they'll suspect you're either planning on whacking them, are in on a hit plot against them, or are at least aware of such a scheme. Remember earlier when I talked about how if there's a green light on you, people – especially your closest friends – will stay away from you? So if you're avoiding your pals to spare them from getting pinched, your altruism might just blow up in your two-faced face. *You* might be the one getting popped, and not by a fed but by a .22.

You Might Off Yourself

I was surprised to learn about how often this happens to those who flip. They become so tortured by betraying their closest friends, loved ones, and even their own family members, that they take the cowardly way out.

Gerry Scarpelli was a prolific hitman for The Outfit during the '70s and '80s, and even helped Frank Calabrese Sr. shotgun Billy Dauber and his wife. On July 31, 1988, Scarpelli was busted by the feds for a robbery in Indiana. After he was confronted with wiretaps of him discussing various murders, he joined Team USA, admitting to the Dauber homicides, as well as other contract killings.

But the guilt and pressure over his upcoming testimony against his buddies proved to be too much for him. On May 2, 1989, two days before a court ruling on his robbery charges, Scarpelli did the pirate two-step and hung himself in a shower stall at the federal Metropolitan Correctional Center in Chicago.

Gambino soldier Nicholas "Nicky Skins" Stefanelli was another rat who did the honorable thing and offed himself. Beginning in 2009, after getting jammed up on a dope case, Nicky Skins began wearing a wire against his friends. He did so not only to protect his own wrinkled ass, but that of his son Nicky Junior, who otherwise would have caught the same case.

On February 24, 2012, Stefanelli entered a video poker machine distributorship in Bloomfield, New Jersey, approached owner Joseph Rossi and – Pow! Pow! – pumped bullets into his head, killing him. Rossi had reportedly been cooperating in an investigation of the mob's control of the video poker machine industry, and supposedly was the cause of Stefanelli's 2009 drug bust.

Later that day, Stefanelli checked into the Renaissance Meadowlands Hotel and enjoyed a last hurrah. Two days later, his dead body was found – he had overdosed on drugs. Stefanelli paid for his own funeral in advance.

Finally, in January 1999, infamous Gambino capo Greg DePalma and his made-man son Craig pled guilty to racketeering and extortion charges stemming from the Family's shakedown of Scores strip club in Manhattan. On June 13, 1999, Greg was sentenced to almost six years in federal prison, and Craig to just over seven. Craig would have gotten significantly more jail time if he hadn't flipped.

Unfortunately for Craig, however, Big Daddy expressed his displeasure in a handwritten note, apparently encouraging him to take his own life. Being the dutiful son, in 2002, Craig hung himself in prison. He barely survived and remained in a coma for ten years before finally passing away in December 2012 in a private nursing home. His death was a major inconvenience for Greg, who had been using his son's room as a regular meeting place for Gambino business. According to former FBI agent Jack Garcia, Greg would often have as many as eight or nine other hoods in attendance at these coma meetings.

No reason why they both should have suffered, right?

Your Family Might Abandon You

When you flip, your wife and kids might turn their backs on you when you need them the most, when you're at your lowest point. This is what happened to Joey Massino when he turned. Flipping cost him the love of his wife Josephine, as well as his daughters Joanne and Adeline. They were all disgusted and ashamed of him. Joanne effectively disowned Massino, vowing never to see or speak to him again. Adeline confirmed Massino had forever lost his family by becoming a cheese-eater. They saw him as the ultimate hypocrite – a Benedict Arnold who had preached to them their entire lives the importance of loyalty, only to turn against everyone who had been loyal to *him*.

Massino's family felt particularly betrayed because they had supported him throughout his trial, including through the humiliating revelations of his numerous extramarital affairs. Last but not least, of course, they were justly terrified his cooperation with the feds could endanger their own lives.

Ironically, Joey flipped so he could spare his family from homelessness and poverty. Oops, I forgot to add one tiny little detail: he also cooperated to spare himself the death penalty. My bad.

In July 2004, Massino was convicted of eight homicides (and racketeering), including the *Cinco de Mayo* (May 5, 1981) massacre of Anthony "Sonny Red" Indelicato, Dominick "Big Trin" Trinchera, and Philip "Phil Lucky" Giaccone; and also the August 17, 1981, murder of his former rival, Sonny Black. He was sentenced to two life terms. But on July 10, 2013, US District Judge Nicholas Garaufis re-sentenced him based on his cooperation, and released him two months later after a decade in custody.

And this is precisely what both Dominick Montiglio and Andrew DiDonato's wives did when each of their men went into WITSEC. In fact, when Denise Montiglio left, she took their daughter Camarie with her. It would be four agonizing years before he would see them again. Even worse, Andrew's ex-wife Dina took away their eight-year-old son, Andrew Junior, never to be seen or heard from again. And it absolutely broke Andrew's heart. Brutal.

Can you blame your significant others if they refuse to follow you down the WITSEC rabbit hole? Who the hell wants to live in some hick town where the only Italian restaurant in a hundred-mile radius is the Olive Garden? If you're lucky to have even that – otherwise it's Dairy Queens and Piggly Wigglys.

The Montiglios' pre-WITSEC experience in America's Bible Belt underscores this particular downside of flipping. Surrounded by Deputy US Marshals, they were abruptly transplanted to a no-name town in the Midwest. Their nine-year-old daughter Camarie spiraled into a depression as their Con Air plane descended. The cause: the sight of nothing but wheat fields as far as the eye could see. Her parents also felt that they had landed on a distant planet.

When Henry and Karen Hill entered WITSEC in 1980 with their children Gregg and Gina, then ages thirteen and eleven, they were relocated no less than ten times. They lived in less-than-exciting locales like Omaha, Nebraska; Independence, Kentucky; and Redmond, Washington, near Seattle. Each time they moved, they were given new identities and had to start all over again.

After finally landing in Redmond in 1987, Henry got busted in Seattle trying to sell $10,000 worth of cocaine to an undercover narc. Fortunately, he received only five years' probation after his FBI handlers stepped up for him. *Un*fortunately, that was a short-lived victory. Two years later in 1989, Karen finally had had enough and officially separated from him after twenty-five years of domestic misery. Things didn't improve much for hapless Henry thereafter.

The following year in 1990 (after *Goodfellas* came out), he got shitfaced on booze and drugs at a barbecue party he threw for his neighbors and revealed his true identity. Henry's new name was – I'm not making this up – "Martin Lewis." Henry himself had chosen it as an inside joke – get it, Dean *Martin* and Jerry *Lewis*, who collectively went by the professional name Martin and Lewis?

As a result, the US Marshals whisked him off to sunny Sarasota, Florida. Several years later, through the early '90s, Henry repeated his drunken *faux pas*, and so was finally booted from the Program. And that's how he ended up in Malibu, California – after Karen finally divorced him. This strife, including allegations of domestic violence by Henry against Karen, are detailed in a book their embittered kids wrote many years later called *On the Run: A Mafia Childhood*.

After leaving WITSEC, he was arrested three more times for drugs and once more for drunk and disorderly (in December 2009) at an exhibition of his art work at a strip club(!) in St. Louis, Missouri. Some things never change.

Lessons to Be Learned

If the G doesn't fuck you one way, they'll fuck you in another. So when you enter into your cooperation agreement, make damn sure your lawyer obtains a waiver from the IRS *in writing* for any and all unpaid taxes, including those that would otherwise accrue from the money the feds pay you. Now this could be a bit tricky as the IRS falls under the purview of the Treasury Department. However, since both the Justice and Treasury Departments are part of the federal government, you should be able to get your way if you throw a hissy fit.

Even if your wife does join you in WITSEC, the strain of living next to a cornfield, milking cows, shitting in an outhouse, and riding a John Deere tractor could cause *you* to subsequently follow *her* out of the Program. This is what happened with Gambino flipper Michael "Mikey Scars" DiLeonardo, and to Colombo capo Carmine Sessa, The Grim Reaper's right-hand axeman. According to an October 26, 2007, article on www.abcnews.go.com ("START SNITCHING: INSIDE THE WITNESS PROTECTION PROGRAM") by Marcus Baram:

> Upon his release on bail in 1997, Sessa was relocated with his family as part of the Protection Program. Prone to depression and suicidal thoughts, he pleaded guilty two years later to terrorizing his wife and son after his release and admitted that he had punched out his wife several times. In 2006, Sessa signed himself out of the federal witness program and disappeared, according to mob reporter Jerry Capeci.

FUDGE-THE-FEDS SECRET REVELATION #7

Remember that 1990 comedy with Steve Martin and Rick Moranis, *My Blue Heaven*, where all the rats live in the same town? Yeah, that's actually true! For some bizarre reason (probably to save money, the cheap bastards), half of the ex-WITSECers I spoke to in researching this book all lived in or around Phoenix or Tucson! WTF?! That's where they stuck Sammy the Bull, Crazy Phil Leonetti (who hung out with Gravano), as well as Outfit snitches Willie Bioff, Frank Calabrese Jr., and Lou Bombacino. Christ, half the cast members of Gallo's erstwhile reality show *Mob Stars* lived in or around Tucson or Phoenix, so that's where the network wanted to base the show.

You'll Feel Really, Really Bad About Yourself

Ratting on your homies will prove detrimental to your self-esteem and *esprit de corps*. Take Phil Leonetti's word for it. He claims that testifying against Philly mob attorney Bobby Simone was the most difficult thing he had ever done. He found it far easier killing Vincent Falcone, his first hit, and being sentenced to forty-five years in prison. Simone had always been a true-blue friend to him, but Leonetti felt he had no choice but to fully cooperate with the feds. Nevertheless, there were tears in his eyes as he testified against him.

Cue Roy Orbison's "Crying."

Amazingly, the one person Leonetti didn't testify against was his uncle Little Nicky Scarfo. I've read Phil's book *Mafia Prince* twice, but I'm still confused about his reasons for not doing so, considering how much he hated Scarfo's guts. *Everyone* hated Scarfo, including his own wife, who reportedly gambled away three million bucks he had stashed away for legal fees after he got busted on his RICO case. This led to Nicky trying to put a hit out on her, a contract Leonetti declined in secret disgust. I'm curious as to how Phil was able to cut out Scarfo from his rat agreement in light of the fact that Nicky was Public Enemy Number One.

If you don't have a clear conscience about working for the feds, you could die a miserable death, drinking yourself blind every night in depressing dive bars like Henry Hill did in the San Fernando Valley and Venice beach area. And he was one of the luckier ones, having scored nicely with his numerous book and movie deals. Bill Roemer said as much about Jimmy the Weasel. According to Roemer, the US Marshal's Office felt that The Weasel should finally be financially independent as a result of the large advance and subsequent royalties from his best-selling book by Ovid Demaris, *The Last* Mafioso. Jimmy thought the G was gonna carry him for life! LMFAO!!!

For Jimmy, however, far worse than losing the G's monthly WITSEC check was losing its physical protection. Thus, in the final years of his life, he was constantly looking over his shoulder, terrified that Tony "the Enforcer" Spilotro or his ilk would finally track him down. Indeed, the feds had plopped him down smackdab in the middle of The Outfit's territory (Arizona).

Interestingly, Jimmy frequently called Roemer to vent about this shoddy treatment by the feds. And so the great Fratianno died broke and bitter, deserted by the very people who he felt had sworn to protect him the rest of his life. (Oh, and Fratianno died in the greater Phoenix area.)

The same fate surely awaits Nicky Crow. According to writer George Anastasia, Nicky Crow was despondent after sending all of his friends to prison. As Nicky Crow explained to him, none of them had ever harmed him in any way, but he felt he had no choice but to testify against them. Even though it killed him to get on the witness stand, there was no turning back.

Nick the Crow had cycled through five different identities in even more states while in WITSEC. He was forced to toil in a series of menial jobs and was barely scraping by, even with his (meager) government checks. In the end, he felt utterly exploited by the Justice Department, beaten down to a mere nub of the man he once was. The years spent in hiding had taken their toll on him.

According to Caramandi, life in WITSEC was unbearable. Once he finished his song-and-dance routine in open court for the feds, they couldn't have given two shits about his welfare. They stuck him in a tiny, rundown apartment and gave him a measly monthly stipend of two grand. He had no friends in his new home and, at age sixty with no verifiable work experience, found it nearly impossible to find a job that paid above minimum wage. The worst part was living like a ghost, with no past and no real identity, and constantly plagued by inescapable self-loathing. In hindsight, he wished he had never taken the deal.

Gastrointestinal Problems

Flipping on your friends can also result in irritable bowel syndrome, penile hypospadia, and erectile dysfunction. In

1987, after murdering half a dozen men, Colombo mobster Pete Savino flipped against his boss, Chin Gigante. For the next sixteen months, he wore a wire every single day, recording anyone and everyone he did business with. Each day he was terrified his wire or his informant status would be discovered, and he would be butchered. This constant stress caused him to suffer from severe diarrhea. No doubt this hastened his early death from cancer at age fifty-five, only ten years after he flipped.

Gambino squealer Matthew Traynor, a bank robber and jack-of-all-trades gangster who had known John Gotti Sr. since they were teenage thugs in the Fulton-Rockaway Boys, suffered a massive anxiety attack after testifying against him. The doctor who examined him reported he was pacing around frantically, sweating profusely, and flushed with agitation. Traynor told the doc he was terrified he would be murdered. He was worried that somehow the mob would find out where the feds had stashed him in WITSEC, including by something he might have said on the stand.

In other words, Traynor was soiling his britches.

Larry Fiato adds to this conversation. He claims that every time he wore a wire, something inside him died. He was sickened by the fact he was betraying men he had grown up with his entire life, men whom he greatly admired. This horrible feeling felt like an out-of-body experience, and eventually made him physicaly ill, as if his bodily functions had simply shut down. As he explained to writer John L. Smith, he felt as if he had gone into a permanent state of shock, utterly numbed by a sense of dread and paranoia.

Similarly, Larry's big bro, Anthony "the Animal" Fiato, once told Gallo that ratting out a friend causes physical symptoms, including terrible chills and debilitating nausea. As Anthony explained, all of this arises from the overwhelming self-loathing from committing such an unforgiveable *infamia*.

You Might Have to Rat Out Your Own Family Members

Unless you're a star snitch, you'll almost certainly have no choice but to rat out *everyone,* including your own kin. Philadelphia mobster Mario "Sonny" Riccobene had become disgusted and disillusioned with the senseless violence in the Life, which resulted in the deaths of his brother Robert and his son Enrico. As a result, Sonny copped to a third-degree murder charge and flipped against his half-brother, Nicky Scarfo's arch rival, Harry "the Hunchback" Riccobene.

Similarly, on March 14, 1989, during jury selection for his murder trial, Eugene "Gino" Milano made a deal with the US Attorney's Office and the Philadelphia DA's Office. He also attempted to broker a cooperation agreement on behalf of his younger brother, "Nicky Whip." But Nicky Milano refused to flip against his fellow mobsters. Ironically, this resulted in Gino testifying against his own brother, who received a life sentence.

One week later, on April 5, 1989, the jury returned its verdict: guilty on all counts against all eight defendants. Nicky Whip, Crazy Phil Leonetti, Frank Narducci, Faffy Iannarella, Joseph Ligambi, and brothers Salvatore and Lawrence "Crazy Larry" Merlino were all convicted of first-degree murder.

Even Steve Flemmi secretly ratted out his own *hermano*, Jimmy the Bear, sending him to prison for life with a warm hug and a fraternal tear in his eye.

Cue The Hollies' "He Ain't Heavy, He's My Brother."

Can it get any worse than flipping on your own sibling? It can! Just ask oldfella Sonny Franzese, who had not one, but *two* rats for sons. First, his oldest son, Michael "the Yuppie Don" Franzese, a.k.a. The Prince of the Mafia, *allegedly* switched sides in the late '80s and ratted out crooks, but not Big Papa. Then Sonny's youngest boy and namesake, John Franzese, Jr., wore a wire and testified against The Rock himself in the late oughts (from 2008-2010). Indeed, John (who had a history of drug and alcohol abuse), has the unique distinction of being the first New York City *Mafioso* to ever testify against his own father. Apparently, however, they made up, since Junior is still walking upright.

You Might Have to Rat *Forever* (Or at Least It'll Seem Like It)

FUDGE-THE-FEDS SECRET REVELATION #8

If the feds want you bad enough, you *can* place a limit on the amount of time you're required to make yourself available to testify. This is where a good lawyer comes in handy. Sammy Bull had an exceptional one, and thus was able to put a five-year cap on his trial appearances.

Otherwise, you might end up like Alphonse D'Arco. According to Joe Pistone, Little Al was still testifying at trials as late as 2006 – *fifteen years after he had initially flipped*! Pistone seriously doubts that D'Arco would have made his Faustian deal with the feds had he known what lay in store for him.

And while the feds will pay you a crappy monthly stipend for living expenses *for a while*, plus provide you an equally crappy *used* car, they can't and won't pay you for testifying. That would obviously taint your testimony.

Make Damn Sure You Get Transactional Immunity

When the Justice Department grants you transactional immunity, it cannot prosecute you for any crimes you admit to during what's called a proffer session. In the parlance of the FBI, this is when you get to be queen for a day. This means that over the course of one or two initial meetings, you proffer the information you have to the feds so they can decide whether they want you to join Team USA. If your intel is sufficiently valuable and credible, they'll give you an immunity deal and sign you up. If they decide not to take you on, nothing you say during the proffer session can be used against you in court. (But believe me, they'll figure out a way to indirectly fuck you down the road with that intel. So if you're gonna go down the snitch road, don't lie and don't hold back.)

This is what happened to Junior Gotti, who allegedly tried to rat out a number of veteran Gambino loyalists, including associate Joe "the German" Watts, during a proffer session. Unfortunately for Baby Huey, the FBI agents caught him in numerous lies and rejected him. Regardless, in my book, Baby Gotti is a squealer.

Make sure you have an experienced, competent, and knowledgeable attorney with you during the proffer session, preferably one who's gone through the process at least several times. If you can't afford one, the judge will be forced to appoint you one. And unlike many state-court deputy public defenders, federal public defenders are virtually all intelligent, talented, and competent.

And make damn sure you get your plea deal in *writing*. Your lawyer should then go over it with a fine-tooth comb and have that verbiage read into the record *verbatim* during a closed court session. And your lawyer should hire his or her *own* court reporter to transcribe the hearing, regardless of whether the court has its own stenographer. Never trust the feds. *Ever*.

Before you sign the agreement, ensure you also get a separate "memorandum of cooperation" that lays out your rat status in detail. It should include the AUSA's recommendation to the sentencing judge that you get no more than a certain number of years, a certain amount in fines, and only certain assets to be seized. In fact, tell the feds they can swallow the fines or your balls. And when they start talking about assets, grab your johnson and say, "Seize this!"

You should also have a *third* memorandum that contractually prevents the US Attorney's Office from ever filing any charges against your spouse or children (assuming they were somehow involved in your criminal activities).

All of these memoranda should be countersigned not only by your federal prosecutors, but by the United States Attorney General him/herself. That way, if the AUSAs quit or get fired, or get thrown under the bus by their superiors for giving you an amazing deal, you're still protected.

Finally, make damn sure the feds bring the DA's Office in on your cooperation deal so you don't get prosecuted for *state* crimes. Regardless of jurisdiction, prosecutors will motherfuck you every chance they get.

You Might Regret Your Decision (and Then It's Too Late, Sucka!)

Once you cross that snitch line, there's no coming back. When you sign that agreement, the feds own your ass – or at least until you've finished testifying for them, and until you either voluntarily leave WITSEC or get booted from the Program. Either way, you may very well have made the worst decision in your entire life. Just ask Gaspipe. Everyone he encountered in prison, from the bulls to the cons, glared at him with utter contempt. And he knew he had brought the derision all on himself. Every night he had nightmares because of what he had done – dreams of drowning in a pitch black, shark-infested ocean. He had come to dread his own reflection, overwhelmed by poisonous self-loathing.

Over the years, his rage turned to bitterness. As he told Philip Carlo, "Going over to the government's side in 1994 was like a terrible cancer throughout my body and mind. I lost my family; I lost my friends; I lost my dignity. I lost all respect not only from others but from my own self."

You'll Have to Get a Real Job

This might be the worst thing about flipping – joining the rat race, jostling with the other human detritus. I'm talking about mankind's flotsam and jetsam, the proletarian abyss, the teeming sea of humanity. Imagine slogging your way through rush-hour traffic every single day, or having to ask your boss for permission every time you have to take a piss. How could Hell be any worse?

Andrew DiDonato sums up this horrendous fate. "For most of my life, I'd faced dangerous scenarios and stress that might have brought down a two-ton elephant. But thinking about having to get a real job scared the hell out of me. It might not make sense to most people, but I was terrified."

Similarly, after entering the Program, Dominick Montiglio, who had never worked an honest day in his life, was forced to take a menial job loading and unloading Pepsi trucks. "Oh, woe is motherfuckin' me," you cry. "So unfair!"

And those clock-punching WITSECers are the *lucky* ones. After flipping and ratting out his brother-in-law Joey Massino, no-longer-quite-so-Good Lookin' Sal Vitale (one of the shooters in the *Cinco de Mayo* massacre) entered WITSEC after completing his federal sentence. After he flipped in 2003 (only the fourth underboss to do so, after Crazy Phil, Sammy Bull, and Gaspipe), and entering WITSEC in October 2010, Vitale's marriage collapsed and his four sons disowned him. He struggled to find a job, particularly *because* of his new identity. Take it away, Vitale.

> It's impossible for you to get a job. I mean, you could go work for the local hardware store if the guy's not going to ask no questions. But if you work for any kind of UPS, REA or Target, Walgreens... I've been turned down by every company. Who is going to hire a guy at sixty-five years old with a brand-new Social Security card?

The implication was obvious to potential employers: he was an ex-mobster in the federal Witness Protection Program.

And at some point, as it always does with rats, the US Marshals Service stopped sending him WITSEC checks. He felt they had tossed him on his ear without any means to financially support himself.

Ironically, one of the main reasons Vitale flipped against Massino was because Big Joey had put him on the shelf. This means that he broke (demoted) Good Lookin' Sal by stripping him of his mighty underboss powers. He did so because he suspected Vitale was an informant – a premature and unfounded suspicion, as it turned out.

As Vitale testified, "You don't have real friends in organized crime."

Look, it's not my place to tell you whether you should or should not become a turncoat, as this will undoubtedly be the most important decision of your life. But I will caution you that even if you do flip, always remember that regardless of what sunshine the feds blow up your ass, *they don't give a fuck about you*. You are merely a means to an end for them, and once they're done with you, they'll toss you aside like a soiled prophylactic. Trust me, if you give them the opportunity, they will royally bugger you: one semi-famous mobster whom I interviewed under condition of anonymity told me that the FBI had screwed him out of $60,000 they owed him of his past-due WITSEC stipend. So don't give them the satisfaction – lawyer up and hunker down.

Larry Fiato perfectly captures the FeeBee mindset. He insists that the FBI couldn't have cared less that they had placed his brother Anthony in grave peril by forcing him to wear a wire. He was just a means to an end for them. Larry believed the feds were at least as bad as the mobsters they were hunting. In fact, as he explains in *The Animal in Hollywood*, they were worse because they felt they were on some righteous crusade. In the end, the FBI agents didn't give a shit about whose lives they destroyed in the process.

Fun Facts!

Interestingly, at one point in the '70s, Frank Bompensiero's buddy Jimmy the Weasel was doing a bid in Folsom while Bomp was in Soledad, making them the only made guys in the entire California prison system at the time.

And FYI, Bomp committed a number of murders while working as an FBI snitch, just like Willie Boy Johnson, Joseph "the Animal" Barboza, and Satan only knows how many others.

And lest I forget, make sure you check out Frankie Calabrese Jr.'s 2012 autobiography *Operation Family Secrets*, which was a *New Yok Times* Best Seller. Frankie sold the film rights and sent me the excellent script that a big-time screenwriter had written, but it has yet to materialize. Get your shit together, Hollywood!

By the way, Henry received $500,000 for the sale of his cinematic life rights for *Goodfellas*, as well as for working as a consultant thereon, but the IRS seized virtually all of it to pay back taxes he owed.

Writer Nick Pileggi's wife, the late Nora Ephron, reportedly used Henry Hill as inspiration for the Steve Martin character in writing the script for *My Blue Heaven*, which came out one month before *Goodfellas* in 1990. You rom-com fans will remember Nora as the incomparable screenwriter of *When Harry Met Sally* and *Sleepless in Seattle* (which both garnered her Academy Award nominations). She also wrote *You've Got Mail* and *Julie and Julia*, among many other popular works. They don't make 'em like her anymore.

Oh, and I was kidding about the penile hypospadia; however, I wasn't breaking your balls about the erectile dysfunction that results from informing. According to Daniel Simone in *The Lufthansa Heist*, Henry Hill couldn't sport a woody for two whole years after he flipped – until Jimmy Burke was finally sentenced for the murder of Richie Eaton.

Chapter Twenty-Six – Lammin' It (Gettin' the Fuck Outta Dodge)

"I was gonna take off, but then I thought, where the fuck am I gonna go?" – Nicky "the Crow" Caramandi

O.M.F.G. Here it is at long last – the final chapter of this spellbinding *tour de force* in all its resplendent glory. And what better way to make my exit than to talk about how you should make *your* exit. As you no doubt have gathered, I am quite the proponent of fleeing the United States for safer and more welcoming climes. And why shouldn't you, when the only alternative is doing thousands of push-ups, sit-ups, and knee-bends in a tiny concrete room twenty-three hours a day?

So feck the feds and their draconian Bureau of Prisons 'cause even Gaspipe doesn't deserve to see sunlight only an hour a day. I mean, if our goal is to psychologically torture our worst prisoners, then why don't we do the humane thing and simply execute them? As a recovering humanitarian, this offends my delicate sensibilities. To quote Fyodor Dostoyevsky, "The degree of civilization in a society can be judged by entering its prisons."

I say to Hell with that, and choose Door Number One, which is picked by shockingly few *Mafiosi*. On the other hand, when you look at how truly unsophisticated most mobsters are, then it makes perfect sense.

Gallo could never understand why mobsters in Brooklyn, for example, go back to their old stomping grounds to hang out with their old friends the second they're released from the pen.

They do so despite knowing full well that: (a) that's where they got popped in the first place; and (b) by going back and doing the same shit in the same place with the same people, they will almost certainly get busted again. In fact, they'll probably end up doing far more time since they will be considered a repeat offender. Suffice it to say, Gallo recommends *moving*! Crime is ubiquitous, so a sharp, enterprising hustler should be able to do well no matter where he ultimately plants his freak flag.

Expand Your Horizons

A boxer at Fortune's Gym on Sunset Boulevard sums up this predicament: "When wiseguys cross the Verrazano Bridge, they might as well be in Switzerland." *Amen*. Most crooks grow up in a very small part of the planet, like, say, Bay Ridge. When Gallo lived there for eight years, bouncing around with the Colombos, he was amazed at their miniscule microcosm.

To Gallo, it was virtually impossible to over-emphasize how provincial and backwards the Brooklyn wiseguys were. He likened them to medieval peasants who were terrified of any place beyond their miniscule patch of Earth. Indeed, these same mobsters boasted to Gallo that they had never been on the subway, and had only ventured to Manhattan or other alien boroughs under threat of force.

According to Gallo, these small-minded simpletons had no clue how to get to Lincoln Center, the Empire State Building, or Times Square. And you can freakin' fuggetabout them seeing a Broadway show. Fuck *Mamma Mia*! Aside from Manny Garofalo and John Baudanza, Gallo never met a single gangster who had any substantive connection to the outside world. Even Eddie Garofalo Jr. was thought to be radical simply for dining at the hip new Asian restaurants in Brooklyn.

Paulie Vario was no exception, as confirmed by Henry Hill's mistress

Linda, who told Nicholas Pileggi about a vacation she, Henry, and Paul had taken in the Bahamas. This was to be a last hurrah for Vario before he did time for contempt. But instead of enjoying the crystal blue waters and virgin, white-sand beaches of Nassau, Vario instead clung to Henry and Linda like a newborn kitten. He was absolutely petrified to find himself in a strange country where people spoke a foreign tongue (grammatically-correct English). He refused to leave their side even for a moment. Linda couldn't believe such a powerful and wealthy man had never wanted to leave his own neighborhood.

And this microscopic mentality certainly isn't limited to New York. For example, Nicky Scarfo's gunsels loved vacationing at his home in South Florida. (He cheekily named his yacht *The Usual Suspects* after the famous line from the classic 1942 film *Casablanca*.) For most of them, it was the first time they had ever escaped the Philadelphia-New York-New Jersey diaspora.

It's precisely this type of ignorance and small-town mentality that is going to be the death of you. You must broaden your horizons so you not only don't fear moving abroad, but you will actually enjoy it.

John Alite thoroughly loved his first year living in Rio de Janeiro (after nine months of five-star globetrotting) while on the run from the long arm of the law, which began in March 2003. Granted, the last two years in Brazil, when he festered in hideously disgusting prisons, walking around with the Sword of Damocles shoved up his arse, weren't quite as pleasant. But at least he got to stab lots of people, which always helps pass the time.

Don't Impose on Your In-Laws and Relatives

When you get in the wind, don't hightail it directly to your in-laws' house, particularly without a gilded invitation. If you can somehow peek around your own megalomaniacal ego and narcissistic personality disorder, you might just realize that they despise you.

On October 14, 1984, Colombo boss Carmine "the Snake" Persico (a.k.a. Junior, as no one dared call him Snake to his face) and the rest of the Family administration were indicted for RICO violations. Luckily for Persico, he got tipped off about the pending indictment and fled. The FBI commenced a nationwide manhunt for the slippery godfather, and even added him to its Ten Most Wanted list. Every mobster and lawman on the East Coast was wondering the same thing – oh where oh where could our Carmine have gone?

Not far, as it turned out. He beelined to the Long Island home of his cousin, mob associate Fred DeChristopher. Fred never liked Persico, which wasn't surprising since *no one* liked him; he was a treacherous, venal, bloodthirsty psychopath, hence the derogatory nickname. So Fred was not expecting this uninvited and unwanted houseguest. Carmine simply popped up on his doorstep. "Surprise, *paisan*! What's for dinner? I'm fuckin' famished!"

During the four months he spent living in DeChristopher's attic, Carmine was inconsiderate, selfish, and downright rude. He ordered everyone around in the house, including DeChristopher's wife and kids, as if they were his personal servants. Oh, and the cheap bastard never bothered to pitch in for *anything*.

DeChristopher became so disgusted with The Snake's entitled antics that he finally called the FBI and happily collected the $50,000 reward for Persico's capture. Thus, on February 15, 1985, the FBI pinched Carmine and away to the M.C.C. he went. As a bonus, DeChristopher testified against him at the trial, and Carmine got slapped with a thirty-nine-year sentence.

As of this writing, The Snake had been down thirty-four years so he should have been getting out soon, right? Wrong! He still had another *100 years* to go as a result of his conviction in the famous 1986 Mafia Commission Trial (which Lin DeVecchio, the lead FBI agent on the case, helped put together). Carmine had been twiddling his thumbs in the medium-security F.C.I. in Butner, North Carolina, where he was best friends with Bernie Madoff! (I wonder if Junior had cozied up to John Connolly when he was doing time there before Connolly's transfer to a Florida state pen in May 2011.) But in the end, the Snake cheated Uncle Sam by croaking on March 7, 2019, at the age of eighty-five.

"You Be Gone, and You Stay Gone"

The biggest mistake you can make when you're on the lam is to come home when you think the coast is clear. Listen to how Burton Kaplan slipped up.

In 1994, Kaplan's lawyer informed him that Gaspipe had gone bad (flipped). Burton, who had been Gaspipe's crime partner for many years, soiled his undies, packed a bag, and skedaddled to Mexico. Never one to rest on his laurels, he soon launched a major pot operation, smuggling thousands of pounds of Acapulco Gold into the US. He should have stayed where he was.

In 1996, after a two-year absence, it appeared that no ill winds were blowing in *El Norte* (the US) and so dipstick Kaplan thought, "Hmmm, there doesn't *seem* to be any pending indictments awaiting me."

And so bumbling Burtie flew back to New York where he was immediately arrested, prosecuted, and convicted of being a major trafficker and tax evader. He was sentenced to twenty-five years in federal prison. At age sixty-three, instead of doing the conga line from Cancún to Playa del Carmen to Tulum, he was looking to spend the rest of his life in a tiny zero-star hotel room, courtesy of the US government.

D'oh! How stupid can you be? He should have waited another three to five years, and then hired a well-connected lawyer to find out if there actually *were* any pending indictments or active warrants awaiting him.

Oh, and forget about Mexico, which *does* have an extradition treaty with the US. However, Mexico *is* an excellent transfer point. Cross into Mexico on foot through the Tijuana turnstile, then fly to Cuba, where they still won't stamp your passport if you don't want them to. (The DEA is permanently stationed at the Tijuana airport, so please take a bus to some other airport.) From there, take a boat trip to whatever non-extradition-treaty country you need to retire in. (But not Belize, where every three or four months, the US Marshal's Service sends a special team to scoop up any suspected Yankee lamsters.)

When It's Okay to Go Back

Lammin' it as a defense strategy can work wonders for you. The worst that'll happen is you'll face your original charges, and you won't be granted bail since you're now a proven flight risk. By getting into the wind, however, you can monitor the case from a safe distance. You'll get a bird's-eye view of the prosecution's evidence, as well as which defenses will work and which won't.

If you're gone long enough, your lawyer can work out a sweet plea deal, and you'll serve far less time than you likely would have if you had gone to trial and been convicted with the rest of your esteemed colleagues.

On November 23, 1981, as a result of Joe Pistone's operation, six Bonanno mobsters, including Sonny Black Napolitano, were indicted on racketeering and conspiracy charges based on the infamous "three capos hit," a.k.a. the *Cinco de Mayo* massacre. (Napolitano had actually been murdered three months earlier, in August.)

In March 1982, Massino was tipped off that he too was about to be indicted in the same case. So he bolted for rural Pennsylvania, where he took up carpentry, learned to speak Old Dutch, and was adopted by an Amish family.

Okay, that didn't happen. What did happen, however, was that he moved into a cabin at that campground made famous in the 1987 film *Dirty Dancing*, dropped eighty pounds, and became a mambo instructor.

Okay, that didn't happen either. He actually hid out in a cabin in the Pocono Mountains in Pennsylvania. (That part *is* true. Sorry, I couldn't resist.) Massino understood that by lamming it, he'd have a better chance of beating the same charges facing his co-conspirators. He knew it was unwise to be seated at the same defense table as all the other bad guys since it would create the image of a "mob" in the eyes of the jury. And through his trusty lawyer, he was now able to see what cards the prosecution held.

On July 7, 1984, after successfully lamming it for two years and three months, Massino surrendered to the FBI with defense attorney in tow. While he was eventually convicted of labor racketeering and sentenced to ten years, he was able to beat the far more serious murder and RICO charges.

On November 13, 1992, after doing just over seven and a half years, he emerged from jail as the new, undisputed boss of the Bonannos. Seems his on-the-run defense strategy had paid off in spades for the last true Godfather.

Never Be Predictable

Hands down, the number-one way lamsters get pinched is by making themselves easy to find, e.g., by going to places they're known to go, and doing things they're known to do. In the mid '80s, after learning that his pal William "Billy" Beattie had flipped against him and the rest of the gang, Westies enforcer James "Jimmy Mac" McElroy hightailed it out of Hell's Kitchen. Unfortunately, he was intellectually disabled and so went straight to Mesa, Arizona, where he had previously lammed it. The feds were practically waiting there for him.

So, for example, if you're a hardcore bodybuilder from Red Hook and you have a known history of vacationing in Southern California, the feds will likely be staking out Gold's Gym in Venice Beach. Catching my drift here, pink-eye?

Make All Necessary Preparations

Making a successful run for it requires – say it with me, people – *preparation, preparation, preparation*. Let's gab about lamster Johnny "Gimme Extra Gluten" Martorano, who was in the wind for sixteen years. In preparation for his run, he first set about acquiring new ID documents. His hook up in the Massachusetts Registry of Motor Vehicles provided him a new driver's license in the name of "Richard Aucoin." Next on the agenda involved setting up safe houses in and around Boston in case he needed to return. Finally, he set up a communications system with Stephen Flemmi via a series of public pay phones.

Johnny himself weighs in (no pun intended):

> We'd first set up a system of codes when Stevie was on the lam in Montreal. I would write down KING JM LEAR – ten letters. There's ten numbers on a telephone keypad, including zero. So 1 is K, 2 is I, 3 is N, and so forth. If I want Stevie or anyone else to call me, I give 'em the number of a pay phone near wherever I'm staying, only with letters as the code for the phone number. All of South Florida back then was in the 305 area code. So I'd say, I'll be at N-R-J, and then give the rest of the phone number. Only instead of giving the phone number in digits, I use the letters that correspond to the numbers.

Thus, set up a super-secret communications system so you can keep abreast of pertinent events. *Every* sharp runner sets this up before he takes it on the lam. While Massino was holed up in his comfy cabin in the Poconos for over two years, he stayed in close contact with his underboss, Salvatore Vitale, by calling a bunch of different payphones using coded telephone numbers.

Before he jumped, John Alite also bounced from phone booth to phone booth in New York, ensuring they could receive outside calls. He then jotted down the phone numbers for seven working booths and assigned each a coded number. Step three involved meeting with his tiny cadre of trusted confederates and laying out his communications scheme.

From his overseas perch, Alite would call his bro and have a seemingly innocuous conversation during which he would mention a number and a time. For example, he would say, "Last night I partied with three strippers, but I managed to get out of there at seven before they woke up." This translated to "Call me tomorrow at seven A.M. at booth number three." This system worked flawlessly for Alite, who was thereby able to keep tabs on everything going on back home. For added security, however, transpose your numbers and dates; i.e. this very same conversation would mean that you would call your friend at *three* A.M. at booth number *seven*.

Get a (New) Life

You'll need a new set of ID cards and fresh plastic. Boston Johnny reminds us that since 9-11, it's impossible to lam it without authentic or top quality counterfeit IDs. Again, before he went south for his sixteen-year winter, Martorano was able to obtain a real Massachusetts driver's license.

Then, while hoofin' it in the Sunshine State, he used that license to obtain a Florida driver's license in the same name. He then used that to acquire a pay-up-front credit card with a limit set by the amount of cash he paid in advance. He would use that to rent everything from a car to a hotel room, but even then would always pay in cash.

Andrew DiDonato, who lammed it for many months on both coasts following his bank robbery spree, was also well prepared for his flight. A criminal associate in California had previously provided him a blank California birth certificate, a blank Social Security card, and a blank UPS employee photo ID. With those documents, he was able to reinvent himself as "Joseph Conti."

Using those documents, he was then able to obtain a New York driver's license from a Department of Motor Vehicles office on Long Island. (It arrived in the mail one month after he submitted his application.) As a result, he was able to register and insure his new Benzo in said name.

DiDonato sagely suggests you shouldn't even bother going on the run without having all your ID ducks in a row. One little slip up, such as getting pulled over while driving without a license or getting cited for drinking in public, could land you right back in the cooler.

Never drive while you're on the lam for this very reason. Always take ride-sharing services or live in a city that has decent public transportation. If you light out for Stockholm, Sweden which is the greenest metropolitan city in the world, you can easily ride a bike everywhere – half the population there does it. Or simply walk, you lazy fucks.

****

The key to Whitey Bulger's longevity during his sixteen-and-a-half-year run was due as much to his ability to obtain new IDs as it was to his ample financial resources. Fifteen years before he bailed on Boston, Whitey had carefully set up his first full-fledged alternate ID as "Thomas Baxter." The real Baxter had died in 1979 in Seldon, New York. Through various machinations, Whitey was able to obtain a Massachusetts driver's license with his own photo, Baxter's name, birth date, and Social Security number. Whitey was careful to renew it every four years. In 1990, he was able to use that license to obtain another for Thomas Baxter in New York state, which he renewed in 1994, months before *adios*'ing it.

Similarly, when he was in Santa Monica, Whitey met James Lawlor, a mentally ill, homeless Irish-American man who resembled him. He paid him one thousand dollars for his driver's license, Social Security number, and birth certificate. He was thereby able to open a bank account, pick up prescriptions, register his car, and obtain a senior citizen's ID card.

Be Prepared to Pay Through the Nose

When you take flight, budget as if you're going on a five-star vacation. In 1979, Johnny Martorano fled Boston after all his Winter Hill brethren (minus Whitey and Stephen, who were protected by the FBI) were indicted in a federal horse race-fixing case. After several minor detours, he loafed around in Dade County until he was finally arrested in January 1995.

During his flight from justice, Martorano learned that everything costs at least twice as much when you're a lamster. You're forced to pay whatever price is demanded since you're always at the mercy of your service or goods provider. And everything must be paid in cash to avoid leaving a paper trail. This means you can't obtain employment unless you're paid under the table. And you always need a steady stream of cash to continue financing your trip.

As a result, you must be able to obtain money when you're out of town. Just follow John Alite's moves. He had friends back home wire him money to bank accounts he had set up in Canada, which he correctly surmised would prove more difficult for the FBI to track. In addition, he had his ex-wife Claudia bring him money while he was traipsing across Europe.

Personally, I'd take some serious Bitcoin with me on that special thumb-drive if I hit the road, and then cash them out through one of those foreign exchanges in Hong Kong before moving on to greener pastures.

Jumping Bail

Did I actually imply that if you hoof it, you won't face any more jail time? In point of fact, you'll not only lose your bail money and any property that secured your bail, but you'll also get an additional five-year federal prison sentence for bail jumping. And with federal time, unlike in most state correctional facilities, you'll have to do a minimum of eighty-five percent of your sentence. That's *with* good behavior. The feds abolished parole in 1981 – prior to that, you would get at least one-third shaved off your stretch for good behavior.

Also, whatever cash and jewelry you're blingin' when you get popped on the run is automatically forfeited to the G. So don't run around like Charles Grodin in 1988's hilarious *Midnight Run* with 300 large in thousand-dollar bills shrink-wrapped around your family jewels.

Travel Extensively Abroad

You need to shed your low-class, pedestrian ways and become a citizen of the world. The best way to do this is to travel abroad extensively in preparation for your inevitable flight. Don't be like your pea-brained *paisans*, who think traveling to an exotic locale means catching a three-hour flight to Miami. Be like Whitey and Stevie, who traveled to Europe at least once a year. Sometimes they'd go with each other, sometimes they'd double-date with underage teens (*not* cool, creepies!), and sometimes only with their adult girlfriends.

However, these ignoramuses limited their sightseeing activities to visiting famous battlefields. Apparently, the two uncultured Beantown plebeians had a physical aversion to museums, and were both tragically born without a personality. At least they knew their wine, so they weren't entirely lacking in élan. I know John Morris is grateful for their enological acumen.

Hey, John, if only you had said NO even *once* to John Connolly, imagine how many people would still be alive today. Imagine the infinite, never-ending hell you would have spared all those families. And fuck all your former superiors too. Fuck 'em all the way up the ladder to your regional FBI director, who not only knew about the games you and Connolly were playing with Whitey and Stevie, but actually approved and condoned them. Bet your ass I'll be naming names in the not-too-distant future. And in fact, Irish-American true-crime *auteur* T.J. English has already named them in his book *Where the Bodies Were Buried*.

But as always, just like with the LAPD's Rampart Division scandal in the late '90s, the-powers-that-be simply threw out a few sacrificial lambs and then stonewalled any further investigation. Do you truly believe Morris and Connolly did all of this on their own?

(Okay, calm down, Stormin' Roman – take some deep breaths. As Chief Inspector Jacques Clouseau says, "In with the good air, out with the bad…")

****

But for sheer serendipity, Whitey would have found himself in the cell next to Flemmi's. Whitey had been living a domestic double-life for two decades. He'd spend every evening eating dinner with his long-time girlfriend Teresa Stanley at her home in Boston. Afterwards, he'd drive across town and spend the night with the much-younger Greig in her Quincy apartment. Both homes had been purchased by the magnanimous Bulger.

When Stanley started dating Whitey in 1966, she was a twenty-four-year-old divorcée with four young children and a depleted bank account. Whitey was unquestionably a monster, but at least he financially supported Stanley and raised her kids as his own.

At the time, he had a girlfriend named Lindsey Cyr, who gave birth to their boy the following year in May 1967. Although Whitey eventually lost interest in Lindsey, he was crazy about the boy, whom he named Douglas. Thus, Whitey was then financially supporting two women with five kids between them.

Bulger kept his own apartment during his thirty-year relationship with Stanley. That's a sizeable nut when you factor in Cathy – *four* households and *nine* humans total. No wonder he spent every waking moment being Whitey.

In 1974, seven or eight years after playing house with Teresa, Whitey hooked up with the newly-single Greig. Tragically, six-year-old Douglas had died the previous year after a severe reaction to aspirin. Whitey was never the same after that, and forever more lost his joy for life.

For the next twenty years, he bounced from one woman to the other. Stanley knew Whitey saw other women, but she had no idea he had another *pied-à-terre* set up with Greig. That is, until Greig (who knew about *Stanley*) got fed up with the arrangement in 1994 and spilled the beans to Teresa. Not surprisingly, this created major domestic strife for Whitey. He somehow blamed Stanley for the upheaval. But for Kevin Weeks' physical intervention, Whitey would have strangled her to death (his preferred method of disposing of annoying females).

When Whitey got the tip off from Connolly in late December 1994, it was Teresa he chose to initially hit the road with.

And hit the road they did, spending Christmas in New York City, New Year's in New Orleans, and thereafter traveling to Clearwater, Florida. After slurping up some delectable stone crabs, they made their way up to Connecticut and finally back to Manhattan.

Connolly had retired from the FBI four years earlier with honors and a full pension. Fortunately for Whitey, he had retained all his old contacts even though he was now making $250,000 a year as Director of Security/Public Affairs for Boston Edison. Life was so beautiful. *Sigh.*

In February 1995, after several months with no indictments or arrests, and with Teresa's increasing homesickness, Whitey decided to head back to Boston from New York City. In a stroke of extraordinary luck, on the way back, news reports on the radio announced Flemmi's arrest. Whitey whipped a U-turn and headed back to the city.

From there, he paged Weeks with a prearranged code to go to a certain payphone. An hour later, Weeks answered Whitey's call and followed his instructions to the letter. That same night, Whitey, being a classy gentleman, dropped Teresa off at a Chili's restaurant in Hingham, a suburb of Boston. "See ya," they said to each other. No hugs. No tears. No ballyhoo. As carefully instructed beforehand, Weeks then burned rubber in Stanley's face and blasted Lynyrd Skynyrd's "Freebird" as he and Whitey roared off into the night.

Any regrets or melancholy Bulger was experiencing at that moment quickly dissipated as he drove to Dorchester to pick up Cathy. Greig squealed with delight at the site of her eternal soulmate. Weeks watched awkwardly as they rushed into each other's loving arms in extra-slow motion.

Cue Vangelis' theme from *Chariots Of Fire.*

Then, also as previously instructed, Weeks popped the trunk of his car and released four dozen snow-white doves into the sky. Then, to Greig's amazement, Andrea Bocelli also popped out of the trunk, wearing a white tux and singing *"Con Te Partiro."*

And off the lovebirds went together for the next sixteen years. Needless to say, Teresa was more than a little upset when she found out how the switch-a-roozie went down. She even ratted Whitey out to the FBI about the "Thomas Baxter" alias he had been using when they were on the run together. But Weeks tipped Whitey to the dime-drop, no doubt after getting word from ever-faithful Connolly. Bulger immediately reverted to a back-up identity.

****

Both Sal Polisi and Gaspipe warned John Gotti Sr. about his impending December 11, 1990, arrest. (Gaspipe presumably learned this info from Lin DeVecchio, whom he nicknamed his crystal ball, and whom Philip Carlo did not explicitly identify in *Gaspipe* for some reason.) However, Gotti brushed them off through his *goombah* John Gammarano, who claimed that Gotti not only knew the bust was coming down, but had already made plans to jump.

Not that Gotti needed this head's-up, mind you. After all, Gotti's two top guys, Frank "Frankie Loc" Locascio and Sammy Gravano, as well as other Gambinos, had been served with grand jury subpoenas weeks earlier. Plus, all the local newspapers had been publishing stories about the fact that a major federal racketeering investigation was in the works against Gotti and friends. Gotti never did flee, however, which completely boggles me.

Finally, as you may have surmised, nobody traveled more than Albanian-American gangster John Alite. When he took off, he went to France, Spain, Italy, Amsterdam (The Netherlands), Albania, Senegal, Jamaica, Cuba, the Cayman Islands, Colombia, Venezuela, Paraguay, Uruguay, Argentina, and Brazil. It was the last country, of course, in which he put down roots – the same cosmic blunder Whitey made by staying far too long in one place.

Beware of Interpol

If I have to explain what Interpol is, I suggest you ... well, I don't really know what to suggest. Maybe stop stroking off to *Call of Duty* and read a book sometime? Go to a fucking library?

Anyways, aside from lamming it to countries that lack extradition treaties with the US, you should also find ones that have no connection to Interpol. You can find a list of these countries, as well as oodles of other useful information (such as how to obtain a legit passport from some of these countries), at website http://www.internationalman.com.

After Alite was indicted by the US Attorney's Office in Florida, an Interpol warrant was issued for his arrest after he fled the country. He was eventually arrested after globetrotting for almost two years. In hindsight, he realized he should have stayed put in Havana because Interpol has no presence there and Cuba has no extradition treaty with the United States.

Coulda, woulda, shoulda – and if my aunt had balls, she'd be my uncle.

Don't Overstay Your Welcome

As I indicated nary moments ago, this is your second-worst mistake when makin' tracks. Regardless of how safe and comfy you feel, you should never stay in the same place more than six months at a time. This was what brought down Whitey and Cathy Greig, an attractive woman even in her golden years (though not so much in her mugshot, in which she bears an uncanny resemblance to the Night King). Greig can thank Whitey for her prolonged aesthetic appeal – he paid for her monthly teeth cleaning and extensive plastic surgery, including breast implants, a nose job, and a facelift.

There's no doubt that the love Bulger and Greig shared burned like the heat of a thousand supernovas. That worked out none too good for Romeo and Juliet, and it didn't end particularly well for these two star-crossed White Walkers either. Greig was sentenced to eight years in federal prison for absconding with Bulger – the judge told her he was giving her six months for each year she had spent on the run with him. *D'oh!*

She received an additional twenty-one months on April 28, 2016. Being a stand-up gal, she was hit with a federal contempt charge for refusing to testify before a grand jury investigating who had helped Bulger while he lammed it. Even after she heard the sentence, she still maintained *omertà*. My guess is that she was protecting William "Billy" Bulger, who admitted in front of a grand jury in 2011 that he had been in contact with Whitey while he was on the run. This admission cost him his lofty position as president of the University of Massachusetts (after having retired from the state senate as its longest-running senator ever).Overstaying also jammed up John Alite. In January 2004, he rented a high-rise apartment overlooking Rio de Janeiro's famous Copacabana beach and settled in. He easily made hip friends, taught boxing at a local gym, and sparked a passionate romance with a beautiful young school teacher. Unfortunately, he ignored the little voice in his head that told him with increasing frequency that he should keep moving. In the days preceding his arrest, his sixth sense told him he had fucked up – he knew he had stayed too long.

Interestingly, Messrs. Alite and Anastasia left a critical piece of information out of their book *Gotti's Rules* in regard to how the G-men finally tracked him down. He reportedly did something even dumber than doing the samba way too long in the City of God: he had been e-mailing criminal associates in New York, threatening to rat them out unless they wired him hundreds of thousands of dollars. *John, what the hell were you thinking?*

Don't Get Too Comfortable

John Alite mucked up by thinking he could continue his high-rolling gangster lifestyle in Brazil without blowback. Instead of keeping a low profile, he essentially shouted from the rooftops there was a new bad boy in town. He even moved into a swank apartment building inhabited by gangster-loving sex workers.

He quickly befriended all of them, took them out to clubs and restaurants, and even loaned them money now and then. In turn, the women introduced him to all the local dopers, thugs, and gunmen, who were impressed by Alite's $80,000 diamond-encrusted, 18-carat gold Rolex. In no time, he was everyone's new best friend.

In Brazil, John continued the New York wiseguy lifestyle he enjoyed so much. He openly swaggered around, flashing his money, muscles, and gangster tattoos. He avoided crime but not criminals, befriending all the local hoods. In fact, he seemingly had an unlimited supply of disposable income, which made him extremely popular. He went out clubbing and bar-hopping every single night, including with the upscale prostitutes who lived in his building. He'd even go up into the *favelas*, Rio's notorious slums.

Occasionally, Alite would take brief side trips to different cities in Brazil or to neighboring countries such as Argentina, Paraguay, and Uruguay. These were brief excursions taken solely to test the various ways to quickly get in and out of these countries. He was pleasantly surprised at how easy it was to set up multiple escape routes.

In addition to using his NYC payphone system (via his own cell phone), John stayed in touch with old associates by e-mail, which he would access at Internet cafés. This is how he learned that former criminal accomplices were flipping on him, including his younger cousin Pasquale "Patsy" Andriano.

John's plan was to hoof it for five years. By that point, he thought prosecutors, FBI agents, and witnesses in his federal cases in NYC and Tampa, Florida would have moved on, and evidence would have grown stale or even disappeared. He would then hire a top-notch lawyer and work out a ten-year plea deal. (Ironically, that's exactly what he got after he flipped, though his sentence was subsequently reduced to eight years and four months.)

But after ten months of living large in Rio, he realized he had gotten lazy and complacent. He knew he had overstayed, yet nevertheless stayed put. He knew that some of his new friends could drop a dime on him, but he just couldn't bring himself to leave. He even ignored the whispers from friendly locals that Brazilian police were asking around about him! Sure enough, word had slowly filtered out to the local authorities that a *gringo* gangster named "American John" was in town, playing the bigshot. At the same time, a sealed indictment in the Tampa federal court had been handed down against him and his crew (all Gambino associates) for murder, racketeering, drug trafficking, home invasions, extortion, robberies, and money laundering. The US Attorney's Office wanted to keep the RICO case under wraps until they could locate and arrest Alite.

Eleven months after landing in Rio, that's exactly what happened. On November 23, 2004, he was snatched off the street by a SWAT team and soldiers backed up by a police chopper. Incredibly, that was the very day John had made plans to permanently leave Brazil. He had even purchased a bus ticket to Argentina for that same evening. His arrest sparked a major international press conference. Party. *Over.*

Cue sound effect of Pac-Man dying.

Whatever You Do, Don't Go to Florida

What is it with these Sicilians and the Sunshine State? Florida is the first place they go when they book it. Maybe it's the sun, maybe it's Disney World, maybe it's f'ing Epcot Center. As a result, that's the first place the G-men look when they're after an East Coast crook.

In 1979, thanks to John Connolly's heads-up, Johnny Martorano flew south to avoid a federal horse-fixing indictment. Not long after settling into a comfy condo in Miami, Connolly informed Bulger and Flemmi that Martorano had been spotted strolling around South Beach. So they notified The Executioner, who moved a whopping twenty-four miles away (a thirty-minute drive) to Fort Lauderdale. Once again, Connolly told The Hill that Johnny was bumping into vacationing Bostonians. But after Flemmi called him to warn him yet again, Martorano balked, explaining he couldn't relocate because he had just bought all new furniture. He finally caved in and moved seventeen miles away to Boca Raton.

Don't Do Anything Stupid

And just when you thought Johnny "Toss Me Another Ribeye" Martorano might possibly be a criminal savant...

By late 1994, Boston gangster Joey Yerardi (who could be the identical twin brother of Bighead on HBO's *Silicon Valley*) owed him $365,000. He told Martorano he was going to lam it and asked for his help. Johnny: "What can I do? I feel sorry for him." Joey told him he was short on dough, so Martorano, who was a little light himself at the time, simply removed his beloved diamond pinkie ring and handed it over. Joey took it straight to a jeweler who ripped him off, giving him only 10 Gs. "But what are you gonna do?"

Um, I dunno – possibly **not** loan Joey Y $365,000, and, instead, tell him to hang out at Home Depot if he needs money while he lams it?

According to Martorano, a lamster always needs an ace up his sleeve, such as a hidden cache of diamonds, that you can convert into quick cash when you're in a bind. "So what the hell, the ring served its purpose, right?"

Martorano, loyal to a fault, then bought Joey Y a car and an apartment near his own condo in Boca Raton. "And then I make my big mistake – I buy Joey Y a cell phone. He's only supposed to use it to call me." Big surprise, in early January 1995, Joey Y was arrested in Boca. The police found his phone bill which had only a single number repeatedly called: Johnny's condo. The cops ran the number through the reverse directory and *bada bing*!

As a result, on January 10, 1995, Martorano was arrested at his home after the Massachusetts State Police confirmed his identity from his tattoos.

Try to Enjoy Your New Life on the Run

I honestly can't think of anyone who enjoyed their flight from justice more than Martorano. Certainly not his former crime-partner-crusader Whitey, who lived the last decade of his free life cowering behind drawn shades in a crummy, rent-controlled apartment. Bulger spent his days watching cable TV and reading true-crime books about the mob (including many of those cited herein). This mind-numbing monotony was interrupted only when he took nightly walks with a brow-beaten Cathy to feed stray cats.

Ironically, it was that last activity which led to Whitey and Cathy's arrest. Anna Björnsdóttir, a former neighbor who had moved back to Scandinavia, saw a TV show about Whitey. After recovering from her shock, she called in the tip to the FBI, which had *finally* been shamed into actually mounting a sincere effort to find him. Prior to that, the feds did fuck all to find him since they feared the secrets he would reveal once he was captured. Easiest two million dollars the former Miss Iceland ever earned.

Back to what I was saying about Martorano. With so much time to kill, Johnny the Executioner bought himself a sweet Harley Davidson Fatboy, got a tan, grew a mullet, and started riding down to Daytona Beach. He had no idea that being a redneck could be so much fun. He even splurged on a twenty-two-foot cabin cruiser, which he used to navigate the waters of Biscayne Bay while cracking open one Pabst Blue Ribbon after another. He *lived* for these glorious weekends.

Fuck, I think I need a vacation too.

Fun Facts!

Wanna know the *real* reason John Connolly got assigned to his coveted spot in the FBI's Boston office? He managed to apprehend on-the-run Bostonian Cadillac Frank Salemme as Frank was strolling down a Manhattan street in 1972.

At the time, Salemme was on the run for blowing the leg off John Fitzgerald, a lawyer representing rat Joseph "the

Animal" Barboza, four years earlier in 1968. Salemme and his then partner Stephen Flemmi had rigged a car bomb in an unsuccessful attempt to dissuade Barboza from testifying. As if Barboza gave a flying fuck about his lawyer. (This is the only attack ever carried out against an attorney for his or her representation of a *Mafioso* that I know of.)

Connolly convinced his FBI superiors it was only through his own investigative genius that he was able to track down the elusive fugitive. In fact, all it took was Flemmi dropping a dime on his old pal to his new pal and informant handler FBI Special Agent H. Paul Rico. Flemmi was a Top Echelon Informant *ten years before* Whitey. They left *that* out of the movie.

(*Hey, if I'm wrong about this – or anything else in here, for that matter – let me know and I'll correct any error on both my self-aggrandizing blog at www.underworldblog.com and in the next edition of this book. I'll definitely publish your comments – I love hate mail.*)

At the time, Flemmi was lamming it in Montreal, Canada, on the same charge. It was eventually dismissed, clearing the way for his return home. Prior to that, he and Salemme had lit out west together to Vegas, where they reportedly murdered someone in the desert. But after too much togetherness, they got sick of smelling each other's farts and went their separate ways.

As for Salemme, he was convicted of attempted murder and sentenced to sixteen years. It wasn't until June 3, 1997, when Whitey's informant status was finally revealed in open court, that he learned he had been betrayed by his former best friend and crime partner. He throttled Stevie in a holding cell while they were both waiting to testify against Whitey. Unfortunately, Francis didn't finish the job – probably because he knew the US Attorney's Office would give him a big timeout for strangling its star witness. I bet he regrets not doing so.

Anyways, Bulger and Flemmi frequently traveled to Europe, the Caribbean, and Mexico. Along the way, they stashed millions of dollars in safe deposit boxes for that rainy day they knew would someday come.

That's why I'm so amazed that Whitey didn't *stay* in Europe when he fled. He did apparently visit there a number of times (based on confirmed sightings, including one of he and Cathy Greig in London) after he fled Boston on December 23, 1994. Instead, of course, he and Cathy eventually settled in Santa Monica after bouncing around America. Nor can I believe that Flemmi ignored Kevin Weeks' warning to leave town. Both conundrums are equally perplexing.

Switching gears, this is a good place to apologize to you hayseeds (no offense) - I shoulda mentioned the whole *omertà* thing earlier but I just figured you were all familiar with the concept. You know, that's the Mafia oath you take when you're badged, where you promise never to reveal the existence of the brotherhood or any of its secrets. (Now that I think of it, neither *The Godfather* films, *Goodfellas*, *Donnie Brasco*, or even *The Sopranos* ever mentions *omertà*, much less depicts an actual induction ceremony. Does any film?)

The concept of *omertà* goes way back. Almost two centuries ago in 1828, court documents in the Sicilian region of Cattolica Eraclea identified a criminal organization consisting of more than one hundred officially-inducted members who swore an oath to never reveal the existence of their group upon pain of death.

Better yet, the Camorra's origins can be traced back to the seventeenth century, so clearly *omertà* was instituted back then. Indeed, my trusty Pompeii guide and favorite Mafia historian Nello DiMaio made an excellent case that the Camorra actually dates back to the *fifteenth* century. (I wish I could remember exactly what he said but I was suffering from heat stroke at the time and couldn't really concentrate. Suckin'.) Thus, the concept of *omertà* is over five hundred years old.

EPITAPH

"It's how you finish that counts, not how you start out." – Greg Scarpa Jr.

The Mafia is dead. It just doesn't know it yet. And apparently neither do I. And maybe, with this book, I'm trying to fan the flames from the last glowing embers of my cherished *Cosa Nostra*. By the way, the unnecessary article *"La,"* which means "the" in Italian, was added by J. Edgar Hoover himself. Thus, LCN translates into "The Our Thing," which is obviously nonsensical. Hoover loved acronyms almost as much as he loved violating Americans' civil rights.

Or maybe I'm actually trying to finish what Gallo, Andrew, Frankie Junior, and Billy Junior started – firing the *coup de grâce* into the cranium of the "brotherhood of evil" (as Nicky Crow calls it). Maybe this entire book is simply a cleverly disguised Trojan horse (although that's kinda redundant).

You decide.

****

I have always loved bad guys, particularly those gifted, violent or merciless enough to be members or associates of elite organized criminal syndicates. (I couldn't care less about street gangs or serial killers.) I have always felt very comfortable around them and I'm not sure why – maybe because I understand them; or perhaps it's because I want to emulate their lifestyle, attitude, and strength. After all, the reason we love mobsters so much (er, those of us who *do*) is because they get to do and say whatever they want. It is through *Mafiosi* that many of us live vicariously – at least for those precious few hours on the silver screen or TV.

More likely, I've simply watched far more movies than any mentally sound individual should in one lifetime. Whatever the reason, I love all gangsters (including those I revile), regardless of the incalculable damage they have done to society – that is, unless they're assholes who don't adhere to my rigorous code of Mafia *bushido*.

In any event, I predict that at some point in the not-too-distant future, we'll all be looking back at *Mafiosi* with the kind of rose-tinted nostalgia that we do now with colonial-era pirates, Wild West gunfighters, and even Roaring Twenties-era bank robbers. This self-serving prediction is supported by the fact that modern-day crime groups like the Mexican drug cartels, the Russian *Mafiya*, and MS-13 are so savage that they make *La Cosa Nostra* seem almost quaint in comparison. In the end, the American Mafia may be bad guys, but at least they're *our* bad guys.

So see you on the other side, brothers and sisters – either in this life or the next.

FADE TO **BLACK.**

PRINCIPAL SOURCES, QUOTES, AND REFERENCES

Why I Wrote This Book

Anthony Fiato's quote is from John L. Smith's *THE ANIMAL IN HOLLYWOOD: Anthony Fiato's Life in the Mafia* (hardcover, Barricade Books, New York, 1998), p. 13.

Chapter One – The Benefits of a Career in the Mafia

Lefty Guns Ruggiero's quote is from Joseph D. Pistone's autobiography, written with Richard Woodley, *DONNIE BRASCO: My Undercover Life in the Mafia* (Penguin Group, New York, 1987), p. 360.

Anthony Fiato's quote is from John L. Smith's *The Animal In Hollywood: Anthony Fiato's Life in the Mafia*, p. 120.

Frank Sheeran's quote is from Charles Brandt's book *I HEARD YOU PAINT HOUSES: Frank "the Irishman" Sheeran and Closing the Case on Jimmy Hoffa* (Steerforth Press, Hanover, NH, 2004), p. 135.

Marco Falcón's first quote is from the Discovery Channel documentary about Kenji Gallo, *FLIPPED: A Mobster Tells All* (Killer Bunny Entertainment, 2010), beginning at eight minutes, 48 seconds in (8:48-9:16).

The quote from James Caan is from an interview with the author.

Chapter Two – The Downside of Being Mobbed Up

The quotes from Whitey Bulger and Billy O'Sullivan are from Kevin Cullen and Shelley Murphy's book *WHITEY BULGER: America's Most Wanted Gangster and the Manhunt that Brought Him to Justice* (hardcover, W.W. Norton & Co., New York, 2013), p. 85.

Chapter Three – How to Break Into the Mob

Jimbo X's quote is from an interview with the author.

Chapter Four – How to Prepare for Life in the Mafia

Marco Falcón's quote is from an interview with the author.

Chapter Five – How to Dress, Bling, and Preen Like a Mobster

Marco Falcón's quotes are from interviews with the author.

Chapter Six – How to Behave Yourself as a Wiseguy (Part One – "The Dos")

Marco Falcón's quotes are from an interview with the author.

Kenji Gallo's quote is from an interview with the author.

Frank Calabrese Jr.'s quote is from an interview with the author.

Chapter Seven – How Not to Behave as a Wiseguy (Part Deux – "The Don'ts")

Gallo's quote was relayed to Marco Falcón, who, in turn, relayed it to the author. Marco's other quotes are also from an interview with the author.

Greg Scarpa Jr.'s quote is from Peter Lance's *DEAL WITH THE DEVIL: The FBI's Secret Thirty-Year Relationship with a Mafia Killer* (William Morrow, New York, 2013), p. 504.

Chapter Eight – How to Distinguish Yourself as an Up & Coming Mafioso

Marco Falcón's quotes are from interviews with the author.

Anthony Fiato's quote is from John L. Smith's *The Animal in Hollywood: Anthony Fiato's Life in the Mafia*, p. 31.

Chapter Nine – How to Give and Take Tune-Ups

Excerpt(s) from *AMERICAN DESPERADO: MY LIFE – FROM MAFIA SOLDIER TO COCAINE COWBOY TO SECRET GOVERNMENT ASSET* by Jon Roberts with Evan Wright, copyright © 2011 by Jon Roberts (p. 40). Used by permission of Crown Books, an imprint of Random House, a division of Penguin Random House LLC. All rights reserved.

Chapter Ten – Making Your Bones

Marco Falcón's quote is from an interview with the author.

Chapter Eleven – How to Properly Dispose of Dead People

Marco Falcón's quote is from an interview with the author.

Chapter Twelve – How Not to Get Busted

Marco Falcón's quote is from an interview with the author.

Chapter Thirteen – How to Deal with Rats, Undercovers, and Witnesses

The quotes from Andrew "Good News" DiDonato are from his book with Dennis N. Griffin, *SURVIVING THE MOB: A Street Soldier's Life Inside the Gambino Crime Family* (Huntington Press, Las Vegas, 2010), pp. 20-22.

Chapter Fourteen – How Not to Get Whacked

Marco Falcón's quotes are from an interview with the author.

The quote about the murder of Cathy Lawrence is from Nick Schou's article "The Unsolved Murder of Joe Avila is Only One of Many Loose Ends from O.C.'s Coked-Out '80s", *The O.C. Weekly* (September 24, 2009).

Chapter Fifteen – Extortion, Loansharking, and Debt Collection

The quotes from Andrew DiDonato are from his autobiography with Dennis N. Griffin, *Surviving the Mob: A Street Soldier's Life Inside the Gambino Crime Family*, pp. 42-43.

Jack E. Rausch's quote is from his autobiography *FROM THE CARTEL TO CHRIST: How God Restores Stolen Dreams* (self-published, 2014), p. 130.

Marco Falcón's quotes are from an interview with the author.

Kenji's quote was relayed to Marco Falcón, who, in turn, relayed it to the author.

Frank Sheeran's quote is from Charles Brandt's *I Heard You Paint Houses: Frank "the Irishman" Sheeran and Closing the Case on Jimmy Hoffa*, pp. 95-96.

Chapter Sixteen – Shakedowns

Marco Falcón's quotes are from an interview with the author.

The quote about ADX Florence is from Wikipedia at: https://en.wikipedia.org/wiki/ADX_Florence.

Robert Hood's quote is from Mark Binelli's article "Inside America's Toughest Federal Prison", *The New York Times Magazine* (March 26, 2015).

Chapter Seventeen – Heists and Scores

Frank Cullotta's quote is from Ronald Koziol's article "18 Years Later: Hood's Own Story of Brink's Heist", *Chicago Tribune* (December 26, 1982).

Marco Falcón's quote is from an interview with the author.

Chapter Eighteen – Hijacking

Marco Falcón's quote is from an interview with the author.

Chapter Nineteen – Robberies

The quote from the sheriff's deputy who arrested Dominick Montiglio is from Gene Mustain and Jerry Capeci's book *MURDER MACHINE: A True Story of Murder, Madness, and the Mafia* (Onyx, New York, 1992), p. 362.

Chapter Twenty – Bookmaking and Gambling

The quotes from Andrew DiDonato are from *Surviving the Mob*, pp. 60-62.

Nello DiMaio's quote is from an interview with the author.

Chapter Twenty-Two – Bank Jobs

The quotes from Andrew DiDonato are from *Surviving the Mob*, pp. 164-167.

Chapter Twenty-Three – Arson

The quotes from Andrew DiDonato are from *Surviving the Mob*, pp. 24-25.

Benjamin Brafman's quote is from Suzanna Andrews' article "Chris Paciello's Disco Inferno", *Vanity Fair* (July 11, 2000).

Niko's quote is from an interview with the author.

Chapter Twenty-Four – What to Do with Your Ill-Gotten Gains

The quotes about Trump Tower are from Suzanna Andrews' article "Fawlty Tower", *Vanity Fair* (November-December 2017).

Gallo's quote was relayed to Marco Falcón, who, in turn, relayed it to the author.

SS's quote is from an interview with the author.

Weill, Kelly, "Forget Hacking, Thieves Are Stealing Bitcoins at Gunpoint", *The Daily Beast* (January 26, 2018).

The quotes about Trump's Mafia association are from David Cay Johnston's article "Just What Were Donald Trump's Ties to the Mob?", *Politico* (May 22, 2016).

Michael D'Antonio's quote is from Maureen Dowd's article "The Don and His Badfellas", *The New York Times* (July 23, 2018).

The Donald's own quote is from Patrick Radden Keefe's article "How Mark Burnett Resurrected Donald Trump as an Icon of American Success", *The New Yorker* (January 7, 2019).

Chapter Twenty-Five – Flippin' Ain't Easy

The quote about Carmine Sessa is from Baram, Marcus, "Start Snitching: Inside the Witness Protection Program", www.abcnews.go.com (October 26, 2007).

Gaspipe's quote is from Philip Carlo's *GASPIPE: Confessions of a Mafia Boss* (HarperCollins, New York, 2008). , p. 305.

Andrew DiDonato's quote is from *Surviving the Mob*, p. 232.

The quote re Good Lookin' Sal Vitale is from Anthony M. DeStefano's book *THE BIG HEIST: The Real Story of the Lufthansa Heist, the Mafia, and Murder* (hardcover, Kensington Publishing, New York, 2017), pp. 171-172.

Chapter Twenty-Six – Lammin' It (Gettin' the Fuck Outta Dodge)

Quote from Johnny Martorano is from Howie Carr's book *HITMAN: The Untold Story of Johnny Martorano: Whitey Bulger's Enforcer and the Most Feared Gangster in the Underworld* (Tom Doherty Assoc., New York, 2011), p. 300.

BIBLIOGRAPHY

George Anastasia, *BLOOD AND HONOR: Inside the Scarfo Mob – The Mafia's Most Violent Family* (Camino Books, Philadelphia, 1991).

George Anastasia, *GOTTI'S RULES: The Story of John Alite, Junior Gotti, and the Demise of the American Mafia* (HarperCollins, New York, 2015).

Nick Bilton, *AMERICAN KINGPIN: The Epic Hunt for the Criminal Mastermind Behind the Silk Road* (hardcover, Penguin Random House, New York, 2017).

Matt Birkbeck, *THE QUIET DON: The Untold Story of Mafia Kingpin Russell Bufalino* (Berkley Books, New York, 2013).

Joseph Bonanno with Sergio Lalli, *A MAN OF HONOR: The Autobiography of Joseph Bonanno* (St. Martin's Paperbacks, New York, 1983).

Charles Brandt, *I HEARD YOU PAINT HOUSES: Frank "The Irishman" Sheeran and Closing the Case on Jimmy Hoffa* (Steerforth Press, Hanover, NH, 2004).

Frenchy Brouillette and Mathew Randazzo V, *MR. NEW ORLEANS: The Life of a Big Easy Underworld Legend* (MRV Books, New Orleans, 2014).

Jerry Capeci and Tom Robbins, *MOB BOSS: The Life of Little Al D'Arco, the Man Who Brought Down the Mafia* (St. Martin's Paperbacks, New York, 2013).

Philip Carlo, *GASPIPE: Confessions of a Mafia Boss* (HarperCollins, New York, 2008).

Philip Carlo, *THE BUTCHER: Anatomy of a Mafia Psychopath* (William Morrow, New York, 2009).

Philip Carlo, *THE ICE MAN: Confessions of a Mafia Contract Killer* (St. Martin's Paperbacks, New York, 2009).

Howie Carr, *HITMAN: The Untold Story of Johnny Martorano: Whitey Bulger's Enforcer and the Most Feared Gangster in the Underworld* (Tom Doherty Assoc., New York, 2011).

Al Cimino, Jo Durden Smith, and M.A. Frasca, *THE MAFIA: The Complete Story* (Arcturus Publishing, London, 2017).

Kevin Cullen and Shelley Murphy, *WHITEY BULGER: America's Most Wanted Gangster and the Manhunt that Brought Him to Justice* (hardcover, W.W. Norton & Co., New York, 2013).

Bob Deasy with Mark Ebner, *BEING UNCLE CHARLIE: A Life Undercover with Killers, Kingpins, Bikers, and Drug Lords* (hardcover, Random House Canada, Toronto, 2013).

Ovid Demaris, *THE LAST MAFIOSO: The Treacherous World of Jimmy Fratianno* (Ishi Press Int'l, New York, 1981).

Anthony M. DeStefano, *KING OF THE GODFATHERS: "Big Joey" Massino and the Fall of the Bonanno Crime Family* (previously published as *The Last Godfather*) (Pinnacle Books, New York, 2006).

Anthony M. DeStefano, *MOB KILLER: The Bloody Rampage of Charlie Carneglia, Mafia Hit Man* (Pinnacle Books, New York, 2011).

Anthony M. DeStefano, *THE BIG HEIST: The Real Story of the Lufthansa Heist, the Mafia, and Murder* (hardcover, Kensington Publishing, New York, 2017).

Jay Dobyns and Nils Johnson-Shelton, *NO ANGEL: My Harrowing Undercover Journey to the Inner Circle of the Hells Angels* (hardcover, Crown Publishers, New York, 2009).

Peter Edwards & Antonio Nicaso, *BAD BLOOD: The End of Honour* (previously published as *Business or Blood: Mafia*

Boss Vito Rizzuto's Last War) (Penguin Random House, Toronto, Canada, 2015).

T.J. English, *THE WESTIES: Inside the Hell's Kitchen Irish Mob* (hardcover, G.P. Putnam's Sons, New York, 1990).

T.J. English, *WHERE THE BODIES WERE BURIED: Whitey Bulger and the World that Made Him* (HarperCollins, New York, 2015).

Kenny "Kenji" Gallo and Matthew Randazzo V, *BREAKSHOT: A Life in the 21st Century American Mafia* (Simon & Schuster, New York, 2010).

Joaquín "Jack" Garcia with Michael Levin, *MAKING JACK FALCONE: An Undercover FBI Agent Takes Down a Mafia Family* (Pocket Star Books, New York, 2008).

Sam Giancana and Scott M. Burnstein, *FAMILY AFFAIR: Treachery, Greed, and Betrayal in the Chicago Mafia* (Berkley Books, New York, 2010).

Dennis N. Griffin and Andrew DiDonato, *SURVIVING THE MOB: A Street Soldier's Life Inside the Gambino Crime Family* (Huntington Press, Las Vegas, 2010).

Henry Hill and Daniel Simone, *THE LUFTHANSA HEIST: Behind the Six-Million-Dollar Cash Haul that Shook the World* (Rowman & Littlefield, Lanham, MD, 2015).

Peter Lance, *DEAL WITH THE DEVIL: The FBI's Secret Thirty-Year Relationship with a Mafia Killer* (William Morrow, New York, 2013).

Dick Lehr and Gerard O'Neill, *BLACK MASS: Whitey Bulger, the FBI, and a Devil's Deal* (PublicAffairs, New York, 2000).

Philip Leonetti with Scott Burnstein and Christopher Graziano, *MAFIA PRINCE: Inside America's Most Violent Crime Family and the Bloody Fall of* La Cosa Nostra (Running Press, Philadelphia, 2012).

Peter Maas, *UNDERBOSS: Sammy the Bull Gravano's Story of Life in the Mafia* (HarperCollins, New York, 1997).

Larry McShane, *CHIN: The Life and Crimes of Mafia Boss Vincent Gigante* (Pinnacle Books, New York, 2016).

Gene Mustain and Jerry Capeci, *MOB STAR: The Story of John Gotti* (Alpha, Indianapolis, IN, 1999).

Gene Mustain and Jerry Capeci, *MURDER MACHINE: A True Story of Murder, Madness, and the Mafia* (Onyx, New York, 1992).

Nicholas Pileggi, *CASINO: Love and Honor in Las Vegas* (hardcover, Simon & Schuster, New York, 1995).

Nicholas Pileggi, *WISEGUY: Life in a Mafia Family* (Pocket Books, New York, 1987).

Joseph D. Pistone and Richard Woodley, *DONNIE BRASCO: My Undercover Life in the Mafia* (Penguin Group, New York, 1987).

Joseph D. Pistone and Charles Brandt, *DONNIE BRASCO: Unfinished Business* (Running Press, Philadelphia, 2007).

Sal Polisi and Steve Dougherty, *THE SINATRA CLUB: My Life Inside the New York Mafia* (Simon & Schuster, New York, 2012).

Selwyn Raab, *FIVE FAMILIES: The Rise, Decline, and Resurgence of America's Most Powerful Mafia Empires* (St. Martin's Press, New York, 2005).

Jack E. Rausch, *FROM THE CARTEL TO CHRIST: How God Restores Stolen Dreams* (self-published, 2014).

Jon Roberts and Evan Wright, *AMERICAN DESPERADO: My Life – from Mafia Soldier to Cocaine Cowboy to Secret Government Asset* (Random House, New York, 2011).

William F. Roemer, Jr., *ACCARDO: The Genuine Godfather* (Ivy Books, New York, 1995).

William F. Roemer, Jr., *THE ENFORCER: Spilotro – The Chicago Mob's Man Over Las Vegas* (Ballantine Books, New York, 1994).

George Rowe, *GODS OF MISCHIEF: My Undercover Vendetta to Take Down the Vagos Outlaw Motorcycle Gang* (Simon & Schuster, New York, 2013).

John L. Smith, *THE ANIMAL IN HOLLYWOOD: Anthony Fiato's Life in the Mafia* (hardcover, Barricade Books, New York, 1998).

Doug J. Swanson, *BLOOD ACES: The Wild Ride of Benny Binion, the Texas Gangster Who Created Vegas Poker* (hardcover, Viking Penguin, New York, 2014).

Kevin Weeks and Phyllis Karas, *BRUTAL: The Untold Story of My Life Inside Whitey Bulger's Irish Mob* (HarperCollins, New York, 2006).

Rogues' Gallery

Anthony "Tony" Accardo (a.k.a. the Big Tuna; Joe Batters): A member of the Chicago Outfit for seventy years, including fifty as its leader (boss or *consigliere*). Got his start as a torpedo for Al Capone in the 1920s, and arguably became the most powerful godfather in the history of American crime. He died of natural causes at age eighty-six in 1992 without ever having spent a single night in jail.

Joseph "Joey Doves" Aiuppa (a.k.a. Joey O'Brien): Official boss of The Outfit for fifteen years (1971-86) after being personally selected by Tony Accardo. Started his career as a driver and bodyguard for Accardo in the 1920s. In 1986, he was convicted and sentenced to twenty-eight years for skimming profits from Vegas casinos. Released in 1996, he died a year later from natural causes at age eighty-nine. He appears as "Remo" in the 1995 film *Casino*.

John "Johnny" Alite (a.k.a. Johnny Alletto): Albanian-American associate, enforcer, and hitman of/for the Gambinos. He hooked up with John Gotti Jr. in the mid '80s and became one of the *borgata*'s biggest earners. In early 2004, he fled the US to avoid a RICO case and globetrotted for several years before going down hard in Brazil. He flipped, and after doing some time, emerged free of the G. He is now a writer and motivational speaker, and appears to be living well.

Vittorio "Little Vic" Amuso: Imprisoned since 1994, Little Vic is the longest-sitting boss in the LCN, having been upped in 1987. He and his crime partner, titular underboss Anthony

"Gaspipe" Casso, ruled the Lucchese *famiglia* with a bloody fist during the late 1980s and early '90s. They launched a reign of absolute terror, murdering many of their own men. Amuso is eighty-four years old and will almost certainly die at Cumberland FCI (Maryland).

Albert "the Mad Hatter" Anastasia (née Umberto Anastasio) (a.k.a. the Lord High Executioner): Possibly responsible for more murders than any other individual in the history of American organized crime. A founding father of LCN and leader of the Mafia's most notorious workhorse crew (Murder Incorporated). His *cosca* would evolve into the Gambino Family (originally the Mangano Family). But he ran afoul of his underboss Carlo Gambino, who had him whacked on October 25, 1957, in the barber shop of the Park Sheraton Hotel in Midtown Manhattan.

Gennaro "Jerry" Angiulo: The only Mafia godfather who purchased his throne. Angiulo was the most powerful boss in New England except for Raymond Patriarca Sr. in Providence, Rhode Island. He co-ruled the Boston underworld (along with the Winter Hill Gang) until his own wiretapped conversations brought him down in 1983. In early 1986, he was convicted of RICO and sentenced to forty-five years. He was released in 2007 and died two years later at age ninety.

Joseph "Joey" Avila: A major narco based in Newport Beach, California. Joey and his identical twin brother Sal, along with their older brother Sergio, allegedly ran OC's biggest cocaine trafficking ring for over a decade until his death-by-assassination at age forty in May 1987. Kenny Gallo's mentor.

Sal Avila: After Joey's death, Sal reportedly retired from the drug game to focus on his highly successful chain of Mexican restaurants known as Avila's El Ranchito. He was never the same person after his beloved twin's spectacular murder. He is still alive and well, living in South OC.

Vincent "Vinny Gorgeous" Basciano: Once the acting boss of the Bonannos, his fate was sealed when *el padrino* himself, Joey Massino, wore a wire against him in 2004. In May 2011, he was convicted of murder and sentenced to life. He's doing the big bitch at USP Sandy in Kentucky.

John "JB" Baudanza (a.k.a. Johnny Goggles): A capo with the Luccheses, JB is Mafia royalty – his father and uncle were both made guys with the Colombos, and his father-in-law, Domenico "Danny" Cutaia, was a powerful captain with the Lukes until he died in 2018. JB was released from federal prison for his various shenanigans in July 2015. Current whereabouts unknown.

Lester Ben "Benny" Binion: Starting out as a moonshiner in 1920 at age eighteen, by 1947, Benny had become the king of the Dallas rackets. After The Outfit moved in, he beelined it to Vegas where he opened up Binion's Horseshoe Casino and introduced Texas Hold 'Em and the World Series of Poker to the planet. He died on Christmas Day, 1986 of natural causes at age eighty-five.

Frank "Bomp" Bompensiero: A longtime hitman and capo based in San Diego for the Milano crime family in LA. Demoted after his good friend and mentor, godfather Jack Dragna, died in 1956. He was so disillusioned with his fellow LA gangsters that he flipped in the late '60s. His FBI handlers outed him when they had him pass on a tip about what turned out to be an FBI sting operation called Forex. He was shot to death in a San Diego phone booth in February 1977.

Giuseppe "Joe" Bonanno (a.k.a. Joe Bananas): A founding father of LCN in 1931, Joe became one of the largest importers of heroin into the US and would forever mark his *borgata* as a heroin-trafficking enterprise. His hubris matched his fortune, and in 1964, he overreached when he tried to whack three of his fellow Commissioners. Miraculously avoiding a death sentence, The Commission banished him forever to a fate worse than death – Tuscon, Arizona. And that's where he wilted – on his huge and comfy ranch until his death of natural causes at age ninety-seven in 2002. In the end, he outlived all of his fellow founding fathers and died a wealthy man.

Angelo Bruno (née Angelo Annaloro) (a.k.a. the Quiet Don; the Docile Don): Boss of the Philadelphia LCN family for two decades until he was shotgunned by his successor in March 1980. His murder sparked many other killings that would decimate the family.

Rosario "Russell" Bufalino (a.k.a. McGee; The Old Man): The most powerful godfather of whom the public is unaware. (That's all about to change with Netflix's upcoming Scorsese film *The Irishman*.) He ruled Pennsylvania for thirty years (1959-89), and was one of the most respected members of the Commission. He voted on major issues such as the murder of Jimmy Hoffa. Five years after he retired, Russell passed away of natural causes at age ninety in 1994.

James "Whitey" Bulger Jr. (a.k.a. Jimmy): You know who he is so I'll skip this one.

William "Billy" Bulger: Younger brother of Irish mob boss Whitey Bulger. Billy's eighteen-year reign as the President of the Massachusetts Senate is the longest in US history. For many years, Billy was the most powerful politician in the state. He retired in glory for a much higher-paying position as president of the University of Massachusetts, from which he was fired in the fall of 2003 when revelations emerged about his communications with his lamming big bro.

James "Jimmy the Gent" Burke: Robert DeNiro in 1990's *Goodfellas*. Although Irish-American, Jimmy became one of the biggest earners in the Mafia. As Lucchese capo Paul Vario's top moneymaker and hitman, Jimmy enjoyed rarified status in the LCN. For years he was the biggest hijacker in New York, and masterminded the 1978 Lufthansa heist. He also whacked virtually everyone connected to the heist to keep the lion's share of the loot, and to tie up loose ends. In 1980, his good pal Henry Hill ratted him out for fixing college basketball games and murdering a Florida conman. Died in prison of stomach cancer at age sixty-four in 1996. Karma, baby.

Vincent "Jimmy" Caci: A capo in the Milano crime family, he ruled Palm Springs when he wasn't in prison. Originally from Buffalo, New York, he headed west, where he became disgusted by the pansies posing as mobsters in the City of Angels. Jimmy passed away in 2011 at age eighty-six in his beloved desert home. Truly one of the last of the old-time gangsters.

Frank "Frankie Breeze" Calabrese Sr.: A bloodthirsty capo for The Outfit, he ran the family's workhorse (murder) crew, known as the Chinatown Crew. Responsible for dozens of murders, he was convicted in September 2007 following the Operation Family Secrets trial, and sentenced to life. Died in prison at age seventy-five on Christmas Day, 2012.

Frank Calabrese Jr. (a.k.a. Frankie Junior): The impetus for Operation Family Secrets, Frankie Junior is a former Chicago *Mafioso* who worked for many years under his father's abusive wing. He flipped against him in 2003 while both were in the same prison. Junior entered WITSEC, co-wrote a *New York Times* bestseller, and now runs a successful Mafia tour bus in the Windy City. Well done.

Nicholas "Nicky Breeze" Calabrese: Getting a late start in crime at age thirty-six in 1978, Nicky began murdering people for and with his brother, Frankie Breeze, who was then just a soldier. Like his nephew, Nicky Breeze flipped and testified against Frankie Senior. After doing some time he was released into WITSEC. Current whereabouts unknown.

Alphonse "Al" Capone (a.k.a. Scarface; Al Brown): You know all about him too.

Charles Carneglia: A lifelong criminal and member of John Gotti's Bergin crew, batshit-crazy Charles was the younger brother of legendary *Mafioso* John Carneglia. Charles' only true claim to fame was his ability to dispose of the Gambino Family's murder victims in vats of acid. In 2009, he was sentenced to life after John Alite testified against him. Currently at USP Canaan in Pennsylvania.

John Carneglia: One of the hitmen who whacked Gambino boss Paul Castellano on December 16, 1985, in front of

Manhattan's Sparks Steak House. John was one of John Gotti's closest and most trusted friends. He was also a major heroin dealer, and that's what he went down for in 1987. Released from prison in 2019 after doing thirty years. Current whereabouts unknown.

Nicholas "Nicky Crow" Caramandi (a.k.a. The Crow): Soldier in Nicky Scarfo's *borgata* in Philly. He flipped against Scarfo in the mid '80s and entered WITSEC. Current whereabouts unknown.

Paul "Big Paul" Castellano: You got this one, bud.

Stephen Caracappa: The really skinny guy from the Mafia Cops. Arrested with blood brother Big Lou Eppolito in March 2005, he was convicted in April 2006 of eight murders. Died of stomach cancer in prison in April 2017 after doing more than twelve years.

Anthony "Gaspipe" Casso: One of the most psychopathic killers to ever run a Mafia family, Gaspipe had been a Mafia superstar since he started out with the Luccheses in the early '70s. Came up at the same time as John Gotti, Sammy Gravano, Joey Massino, and Nicky Scarfo. Casso was greatly respected for his earning power and feared for his bloodlust. In prison since July 1991, he's currently decomposing at Terre Haute USP in Indiana. He's seventy-seven.

Lee Matthew Clyde (a.k.a. Clyde): Key member of an OC crew in Newport, Clyde was Kenny Gallo's favorite enforcer. Murdered at age twenty in 1989 by an alleged hitman for the Avilas.

John "Zip" Connolly: One of the most corrupt agents to ever serve in the FBI. Grew up in Southie with Billy Bulger and his brother Whitey. Connolly became the FBI handler for Whitey and Stephen Flemmi. In 2002, he was convicted of RICO. Six years later, he was convicted of second-degree murder, and is currently serving a life sentence in a Florida state prison.

James "Jimmy" Coonan: Boss of the Westies in Hell's Kitchen, Coonan was one of the most murderous Irish gangsters ever during his decade-long reign (mid '70s to mid '80s). But the power and status went to his head, especially after he formed a pact with the Gambinos through Roy DeMeo. In 1988, he was convicted of multiple murders and sentenced to seventy-five years. Currently at FCI Schuykill in Pennsylvania. He'll be released in 2030 at age eighty-three.

Nicholas "Nicky" Corozzo (a.k.a. Little Nicky): For more than thirty years, Little Nicky has enjoyed his status as an überpowerful Gambino captain. Over the years he has served as part of a ruling triumvirate and even briefly as acting boss. Will be released from prison in late 2019.

Frank "the Prime Minister" Costello (née Francesco Castiglia): A founding father of LCN and boss of what would evolve from the Luciano Family to the Genovese *borgata*. In the midst of a power struggle between some of the Commissioners, Costello dodged a bullet on May 2, 1957. He retired and lived a long happy life on his posh Long Island estate, not unlike Jay Gatsby. And that's where he expired in February 1973, at age eighty-two.

Frank Cullotta: Career stretches back to the early '60s when he and Tony Spilotro went on record as associates of The Outfit. After a prison term, he rejoined Tony in the late '70s in Vegas. Cullotta was Tony's top enforcer and leader of their burglary crew, the Hole in the Wall Gang. (Frank Vincent played him in *Casino*.) The entire gang (excepting Tony) was busted on Fourth of July, 1981 in the midst of a burglary. Cullotta flipped, testified, and entered WITSEC. He currently enjoys success as one of the most popular talking heads in Mafia documentaries, and offers tours of all the mob-related locations, events, and murders in Vegas.

William "Billy" Cutolo Jr.: Son of Colombo skipper Wild Bill, who disappeared in May 1991 and whose body would not be recovered for seventeen years -- a casualty of the 1991-93 Colombo War. Billy Junior, an associate with the Colombos, wore a wire for eight years until he helped the feds bust several of his father's killers. Billy's story is begging to be made into a flick.

William "Wild Bill" Cutolo Sr. (a.k.a. Billy Fingers): See above.

Alphonse "Little Al" D'Arco (a.k.a. The Professor): As a Lucchese soldier, Little Al never made waves, kept his mouth shut, and was promoted to acting boss by his on-the-lam superiors, Vic Amuso and Gaspipe Casso. After several bungled murders by Al's underlings, the Professor knew he was next so cut a deal with the feds in late 1991. He testified against wiseguys for the next fifteen years while in WITSEC, and died in March 2019, at age eighty from natural causes.

William "Billy the Chopper" Dauber: Hitman for The Outfit who was murdered along with his wife in July 1980 after his status as a rat had been discovered.

Aniello "Neil" Dellacroce: Arguably the most powerful and beloved Gambino underboss ever. Ruled the family's Manhattan faction. His death of natural causes on December 2, 1985, paved the way for his mentee John Gotti to dethrone Paul Castellano two weeks later.

Roy DeMeo: When DeMeo went to Hell following his murder in 1983, Satan himself offered him a job as a tour guide. DeMeo, a Gambino soldier and top earner, and his Murder Machine crew in Brooklyn whacked more than two hundred people over a nine-year period.

Gregory "Greg" DePalma: Hardluck, can't-catch-a-break Gambino skipper who spent half of his adult life in the can. In January 1999, he plead guilty to RICO charges stemming from the Gambinos' extortion of the infamous Scores strip club in Manhattan. In 2005, he went down hard again after getting suckered by undercover FBI agent Jack Garcia. DePalma died in prison in 2009.

Thomas "Tommy D" DeSimone: Psychotic Lucchese hitman, Tommy D enjoyed the cachet and protection that came from being with capo Paul Vario. Best friends with Jimmy Burke, and participated in the infamous 1978 Lufthansa Heist at JFK Airport. Disappeared in January 1979.

Sam "Mad Sam" DeStefano: A notorious torturer-murderer for The Outfit and Tony Spilotro's mentor. And that's exactly who blew him away with a shotgun in April 1973 after Mad Sam became too much of a liability.

Roy Lindley "Lin" DeVecchio: Highly decorated FBI agent who oversaw the Commission Case investigation in the early '80s. Also the long-time handler for Greg Scarpa Sr., whom he allegedly helped murder many enemies, as well as Gaspipe's alleged crystal ball. Murder charges against DeVecchio were dropped in 2007, and he retired to Sarasota, Florida. He's seventy-nine.

Andrew "Good News" DiDonato: An associate and shooter in Gambino captain Nicky Corozzo's workhorse crew in Brooklyn. He flipped against his former homies in the mid '90s, did the WITSEC thing, and is now living a productive crime-free life in a city I'm not at liberty to disclose.

Ignacio "Jack" Dragna: The last true godfather of the LA fam, which went down the toilet after he died of natural causes in 1956. At his peak in the '40s and early '50s, he ruled over sixty made men. It was the last time LaLa Land would have a single dominant crime syndicate and crime boss.

Louis "Big Lou" Eppolito: The morbidly obese Mafia Cop who went down with Stephen Caracappa in 2005. He's currently withering at USP Tuscon, where he'll likely die.

Marco "Babar" Falcón: Kenny Gallo's Newport Beach crime partner and road dog in The Crew. Fled to Miami in the early '90s to foist his illegal exploits and overactive penis on an entirely new, unsuspecting crowd. After flaming out in a blaze of glory, he once again lit out – this time down *way* south – to escape federal prosecution. And that's where he is now, working on his tan and knocking back Coca-Colas in a thatched-hut bar. *Obrigado!*

Carmine "Charlie Wagons" Fatico: One of the most powerful capos in the Gambino Family, he set into motion a series of events that would almost destroy his own *borgata*. To wit, he plucked a teenage John Gotti from a street gang and showed him the way. Got his nickname from his lucrative hijacking operation. Died of natural causes at age eighty-one in 1991.

Craig Anthony "the Animal" Fiato (a.k.a. Tony the Animal; Tony Rome): Originally a Boston *Mafioso*, he made his bones and moved to Tinsel Town to flex his muscles. As the scariest wiseguy in 1970s and early '80s LA, he had the run of the place until his own brother ratted him out in 1984. The Gangster Brothers entered WITSEC, current whereabouts unknown.

Lawrence "Larry" Fiato: Anthony Fiato's younger brother – see above. A genuine tough guy.

Stephen "Stevie" Flemmi (a.k.a. the Rifleman): A hardcore gangster since the late '50s except for a stint in the Korean War (where he got his nickname for killing Chinese soldiers). Hooked up with Whitey Bulger in 1965, and together they terrorized Beantown until December 1994 when their FBI hander John Connolly tipped them to a pending indictment. Flemmi was too stupid to run, so has been incarcerated since January 1995. Since he's still in WITSEC, the BOP's inmate locator website doesn't identify his current whereabouts (though he will die in prison).

John "Sonny" Franzese Sr. (a.k.a. the Rock): Underboss of the Colombos, Sonny holds multiple world records for being the oldest gangster ever tried for RICO violations, the oldest federal inmate, etc. Incredibly, he's alive and free at age one hundred and two!

Michael "the Yuppie Don" Franzese: Adopted son of John Franzese Sr., Michael is a former Colombo capo and arguably the biggest Mafia earner in the 1980s with his gas tax evasion scheme. He bullshitted his way out of a RICO prosecution by ratting out some non-connected crooks, found religion and lifelong true love, paid off the bosses in New York, and has been living happily ever since in LA splendor. He reportedly stashed away hundreds of millions of dollars. In my opinion, he is the one of the most intelligent captains who ever served in the mob.

Aladena "Jimmy the Weasel" Fratianno: Yet another broke-dick *Mafioso* who chased his pie-in-the-sky dream of casino skimming for decades before finally succumbing to the lure of FBI money in 1976. One of the most colorful and fun-loving mob guys of the twentieth century, Jimmy rarely` had much scratch in his pockets but he was comped everywhere he went. He formally flipped in 1977 after he was demoted as acting boss of the Milanos. Passed away in June 1993 at age seventy-nine.

Christopher "Christie Tick" Furnari Sr. (a.k.a. The Tick): Arguably the most powerful, wealthy, and cunning *consigliere* the Luccheses ever had. Gaspipe's mentor since the mid '60s until his own RICO bust. He also lorded over Gaspipe's Bypass Gang, one of the most successful bank-burglary crews in US history. In November 1986, he was convicted in the Mafia Commission Case and served twenty-eight years. He almost single-handedly destroyed his beloved *borgata* by convincing boss Tony Ducks Corallo to make Vic Amuso and Gaspipe the new boss and underboss, respectively. Tick was released in September 2014 and died four years later of natural causes.

Anthony "Nino" Gaggi: Powerhouse Gambino capo who proved hopelessly incompetent at keeping Roy DeMeo and his Murder Machine crew in check. He was also Dominick Montiglio's uncle and bore a startling resemblance to creepy, disgraced actor Jeremy Piven. In April 1988, he died of a heart attack while awaiting a retrial on a major criminal case.

Carmine "Lilo" Galante: The self-appointed boss of the Bonanno Family, Lilo (nicknamed after his ever-present Italian cigar) was also the leader of an extremely violent faction of major Sicilian heroin traffickers (the Pizza Connection). His greed in hording all the profits and his insatiable thirst for power resulted in his spectacular assassination in July 1979.

Kenny "Kenji Snaps" Gallo (a.k.a. Kenji): A half-Japanese, half-Italian associate of both the Milano and Colombo Families. Became a hardcore criminal at age fifteen after he was expelled from military school. He hooked up with the Avilas, and worked his way up from mule to enforcer to major trafficker. He flipped in the mid oughts, entered WITSEC for several years, and now lives happily on a farm in the Midwest where he owns an gym and trains Parkinson's sufferers.

Carlo Gambino: Like Tony Accardo in Chicago, Carlo never spent a single night in jail and lived a long, happy life with his beloved wife until 1976 when he died of natural causes at age seventy-four. A founding father of LCN, he was the most powerful don in New York during his many decades at the top. His *famiglia* was the largest in the country, tied only with the Genoveses for sheer power. But he sowed the seeds for his own Family's near-destruction when he appointed Paul Castellano as his successor instead of Neil Dellacroce.

Joaquín "Jack" Garcia (a.k.a. Big Jack): Cuban-American FBI agent who went undercover in the mob for two and a half years (in the early oughts) as an associate of Gambino skipper Greg DePalma. Benicio del Toro was supposed to play him in a movie but that never panned out.

Edward "Eddie" Garofalo Jr. (a.k.a the Tall Guy): Feared Colombo war capo whose father was murdered by Sammy Gravano, and whose wife was a cast member of the hit TV reality series *Mob Wives*. Kenny Gallo ratted him out in the oughts, putting Garofalo behind bars for seven years. Current whereabouts unknown.

Sam "Momo" Giancana (a.k.a. Mooney): Aside from Al Capone, Giancana was the most publicity-loving Outfit boss ever. A born killer, he lacked the charm, brains, and elegance of his true boss, *consigliere* Tony Accardo. Giancana was suckered by Joseph Kennedy Sr. into rigging the 1960 presidential election in favor of JFK. Accardo banished him to Mexico for eight years, then, upon his return, had him whacked in his own basement in 1975.

Vincent "the Chin" Gigante (a.k.a. Chin): Cunning and ruthless boss of the Genoveses from 1981 until 2005. Famous for fooling the feds with his crazy-guy act, which kept him out of the pokie for more than thirty years. In April 2003, he pled guilty to various charges and died in prison at age seventy-seven in December 2005.

John A. Gotti Jr. (a.k.a. Junior; Junior Gotti; Baby Huey): Halfwit son of halfwit Gambino boss John Gotti Senior. Still, Baby Huey managed to avoid any convictions after four trials in five years. He finally plead out to various charges and served more than six years in prison. He permanently retired from the Life and lives in a lavish home overlooking prestigious Oyster Bay.

John J. Gotti Sr. (a.k.a. Johnny Boy): Everyone knows *this* John Gotti.

Sammy "the Bull" Gravano (a.k.a. Sammy Bull): Ditto.

Edward "Danny" Grillo: The worst gambler in Mafia history, Danny paid the ultimate price for his addiction. A Gambino soldier, killer, and hard-luck bank robber, Danny was close to both Roy DeMeo and Jimmy Coonan, who raced each other to see who could murder him first. Roy won, personally whacking and chopping up Danny in November 1978.

Jerry H.: Allegedly corrupt undercover narcotics detective for the Irvine PD. Detective Jerry retired with a full pension only two weeks after his criminal exploits were exposed in August 2009 following the publication of Kenny Gallo's autobiography *Breakshot*. He quickly left the OC and moved to Dallas. Current whereabouts unknown.

Henry Hill: This guy you know – he was played to perfection by Ray Liotta in *Goodfellas*.

Anthony "Bruno" Indelicato: One of the most feared hitmen in the Bonanno Family, son of murdered captain "Sonny Red" and mentor to Tommy "Karate" Pitera. One of the shooters of Carmine Galante in 1979. Married Jimmy Burke's daughter and lived lavishly on the millions Burke had stashed away from the

1978 Lufthansa Heist. In December 2008, Bruno plead out to charges stemming from the 2001 murder of Bonanno associate Frank Santoro and sentenced to twenty years. He's currently at FCI Danbury in Connecticut and is scheduled to be released in 2023.

Ronald "Foxy" Jerothe: Gambino associate, quasi-adopted son of John Gotti Sr., and best friend of Crazy Sal Polisi. Murdered by Tommy DeSimone on December 18, 1974, in a dispute over the latter's relationship with Foxy's younger sister.

Wilfred "Willie Boy" Johnson: An informant for sixteen years, Willie Boy was a half-Native American mobster and hitman for John Gotti Senior's Bergin crew. He was outed by federal prosecutor Diane Giacalone and murdered by Tommy Karate as a favor to Gotti in August 1988.

Burton Kaplan: Gaspipe's crime partner and Jewish rabbi in the garment trade, Kaplan stole Gaspipe's home while he was on the lam and eventually turned him in to the feds after flipping. He also testified against the Mafia Cops. Died at age seventy-five in July 2009.

Richard "the Iceman" Kuklinski: C'mon, everyone knows about the Iceman! If not, get HBO. Played by Michael Shannon in the 2012 flick – what else? – *The Iceman* (available on streaming, usually Netfilx with no issues).

Philip "Crazy Phil" Leonetti: Underboss for the Philly family and nephew of Little Nicky Scarfo, Crazy Phil was a proficient hitman who was feared and respected throughout the underworld. He flipped after being convicted of murder in 1988. Current whereabouts unknown.

Joseph "Joey the Clown" Lombardo Sr.: Boss of The Outfit after serving as Tony Spilotro's captain. Convicted in the 2007 Operation Family Secrets trial and sentenced to life. He's currently at Florence ADMAX USP in Colorado, where he'll turn ninety-one in January 2020. Stay strong, baby!

Salvatore Lucania (a.k.a. Charles 'Lucky' Luciano): This is a bloke you know.

John "Johnny" Martorano (a.k.a. the Executioner): Fun-loving hitman for Boston's Winter Hill Gang. Admitted to murdering twenty people after he flipped against Whitey Bulger, Stephen Flemmi, and John Connolly in 1999. Current whereabouts unknown. He's sixty-eight.

Joseph "Big Joey" Massino: First sitting boss of a Mafia family to flip. Went to the dark side in 2005 to escape the death penalty and allow his wife to keep the family home and dough. In 2013, he was released from prison after ten years. Current whereabouts unknown.

Anthony "Tony" Mirra: Psychotic soldier and hitman for the Bonannos. Mirra will be forever known as the dunskie who brought undercover FBI agent Joe Pistone into the Bonanno fold. Mirra paid for this mistake with his life in February 1982 when his own cousin Joseph D'Amico shot him.

Dominick Montiglio: Hapless nephew of Nino Gaggi, former Vietnam Special Forces combatant, and otherwise bottom-feeding Gambino associate. He flipped in 1983 and ratted out Nino and their boss Paul Castellano. Since leaving WITSEC in 2004, he has appeared as a frequent talking head in Mafia documentaries. Current whereabouts unknown. He's seventy-two.

John M. Morris: Former Special Agent in Charge of the Boston FBI office and supervisor of John Connolly. This guy was so fucking stupid he actually brought Whitey Bulger and Stephen Flemmi over to his own home for dinner, horrifying his wife. He also let these psychopaths loose on the public, and in my opinion is equally culpable for numerous murders. For example, he leaked Brian Halloran's informant status to Connolly, whom Morris knew would tell Whitey, thereby directly resulting in the murders of Halloran and civilian Michael Donahue. Ironically, in 1988, Morris leaked Whitey's informant status to the *Boston Globe*, which published a series of articles about Bulger's cozy relationship with the FBI. Morris eventually cut a sweet deal for immunity to testify against Connolly and now works as a "wine consultant." Fuck him.

Dominick "Sonny Black" Napolitano: Seemingly destined for greatness – perhaps even boss someday – with the Bonannos, capo Sonny Black made the fatal mistake of going all in on Joe Pistone, and even wanted to propose him for membership. He pulled the plug on Pistone's six-year undercover gig by ordering him to whack Anthony "Bruno" Indelicato. On August 17, 1981 (twenty days after Pistone came out as a fed), Sonny Black got the whack for his *faux pas*.

Christian "Chris the Binger" Paciello (née Christian Ludwigsen): The former and, amazingly, once-again King of Miami, Paciello was the most glamorous mobster to ever stroll down Ocean Drive, opening his first nightspot there in November 1995. After a six-year stint in prison, he returned to South Beach in March 2012 with new restaurants and nightclubs. Well played!

Carmine "the Snake" Persico (a.k.a. Junior): No imprisoned boss has ever worn the crown as long as Persico, who became the Colombo *padrino* in 1973, then entered the big house for good in 1985. For the next thirty-four years, he ruled the arguably most violent family in LCN with an iron fist until his death at age eighty-five in March 2019. His best friend in prison was Bernie Madoff.

Theodore "Teddy" Persico Jr.: Nephew of the Snake, Teddy did sixteen years for dope, only to emerge in 2004 as the Colombo Family's street boss (acting boss). Too bad Kenny Gallo and his hidden wire awaited him outside the gates. Back in the pen the next year, he reemerged in 2008. He went back yet again in 2014 for issuing a murder contract. He's at FCI Fort Dix in New Jersey, where he's scheduled to be released on August 21, 2020. Sure hope Gallo's not part of the welcome party.

Joseph "Joe" D. Pistone (a.k.a. Donnie Brasco): Nuff said.

Thomas "Tommy Karate" Pitera: The most bloodthirsty, homicidal, and downright creepiest hitman ever shat out from the bowels of the Bonanno *borgata*. A capo from Gravesend, Brooklyn, he whacked up to seventy people before getting popped in June 1990 for numerous murders. He's currently sixty-four and locked up at USP McCreary in Tennessee.

Salvatore "Crazy Sal" Polisi (a.k.a. Sally Upazzo; Sallie Ubatz): Fun-loving Colombo associate who specialized in robbing banks, jacking diamond couriers, and trafficking smack in the '60s and '70s. He got pinched for slingin' *yeyo* in '79 and flipped. Oh, and he ran the Sinatra Club, a social club in Queens that served as the first all-Five Families watering hole and gambling palace. He's been a popular Mafia talking head for years. His would also be an amazing story to see on TV or the big screen – *Pulp Fiction* meets *Sexy Beast* set in the '60s and '80s NYC.

Jon Roberts (née John Riccobono): A Gambino associate in NYC from the late '60s until '75, when he was run out of town by his own peeps for causing too much trouble. He drove straight to Miami, just in time for the dawn of the cocaine cowboys era. He rose quickly to become the Medellín Cartel's top distributor and smuggler in the US. The good times came to an end in September 1986, resulting in "only" a fourteen-year stretch thanks to his DEA cooperation deal. He died at age sixty-three from colon cancer in December 2011. Mark Wahlberg bought his life rights.

H. Paul Rico: Possibly the most cunning, corrupt, and ruthless agent in FBI history, Rico was as vicious and murderous as any Mafia boss. In 1968, he framed four innocent men for murder, sending them off to prison for many decades (including two for the rest of their lives) to protect his own informant, Joseph "the Animal" Barboza. He also set up certain targets whom he personally despised for murder during the Irish gang wars of the 1960s, and set up the contract killing of civilian Roger Wheeler in 1981. Died of a heart attack in January 2004 at age seventy-eight while awaiting trial for Wheeler's murder. What is it about these feds in Beantown?

Michael "Big Mike" Rizzitello (a.k.a. Mike Rizzi): Yet another broke-dick Mafia hitman who never had two bits in his pocket. He made his bones in New York with Crazy Joe Callo in the 1950s before going to Disneyland and hooking up with the Mickey Mouse Mafia. By the time he went down for good after botching the May 1987 murder of strip club owner Bill Carroll, Rizzi had already spent much of his adult life inside. In 1990, he was sentenced to thirty-three years for that fuck up, and died in prison fifteen years later of cancer at age seventy-eight. Suckin'.

William F. "Bill" Roemer Jr.: An FBI agent for thirty years and the G's number-one expert on The Outfit. Roemer retired in 1980 and wrote five outstanding books on the Chicago mob. Man, what I wouldn't have given to hang out with this guy, who loved his job but never took himself too seriously. Oh, he is still the most highly decorated agent in FBI history. Sadly, he passed in 1996 from lung cancer just before his seventieth birthday. He is sorely missed.

George Rowe: Seriously bad-ass, ex-con peckerwood who voluntarily went undercover to help the ATF bust his local chapter of the Vagos outlaw motorcycle gang. Current whereabouts unknown.

John "Handsome Johnny" Roselli (née Filippo Sacco): The Outfit's man in Hollywood during the '40s and in Vegas during the mid '50s. Roselli was one of those few chosen soldiers who answered directly to the boss instead of to a capo. But he got in way over his head with the CIA's plot in the early 1960s to whack Fidel Castro in Cuba (Operation Mongoose). In August 1976, less than a year after he testified before a Senate subcommittee investigating the Castro plot, Roselli was murdered, chopped up, and stuffed into a 55-gallon drum that bobbed to the surface in Florida's Biscayne Bay.

Frank "Lefty" Rosenthal: Robert De Niro's character in the 1995 film *Casino*. Total dick – Lefty, not DeNiro.

Angelo "Quack Quack" Ruggiero (a.k.a. Angie, Big Angie, Fat Angie, Ange): Bull-necked and brain-farted sycophant to John Gotti Sr. Ange's big fucking mouth *alone* almost sank the entire Gambino Family. After his drug lord brother Sal died in a plane crash, Ange took over his heroin-trafficking business with help from the Bergin crew. After getting a tip from Willie Boy Johnson, the FBI bugged Ange's home phone in 1982 and gleaned enough evidence to charge the entire crew (sans Gotti). After boss Paul Castellano demanded the transcripts to the recordings, which revealed the crew's unsanctioned trafficking, Gotti realized he had to make a preemptive strike. Ange, who was one of the eleven assassins, avoided trial and conviction by dying of cancer in December 1989.

Benjamin "Lefty Guns" Ruggiero: No relation to Ange. Lefty Guns was yet *another* total loser *Mafioso*, Bonanno hitman, gambling junkie, and incessant whiner. But he really shat the sheets when he officially put Joe Pistone on record as his associate. Like his capo Sonny Black, he would've been whacked for this *faux pas*, but he got busted before he could meet his maker. After serving thirteen years thanks to Pistone, he was released just before he died of cancer in 1994.

Francis "Cadillac Frank" Salemme: Boston *Mafioso*, hitman, and Stephen Flemmi's crime partner in the '60s until Flemmi threw him to the FBI wolves. After doing fifteen years, he emerged from the pen to become the boss of the entire New England Mafia. Alas, in June 2018, he was convicted of murder and sentenced to life. He's currently at MCFP Springfield in Missouri.

Nicodemo "Little Nicky" Scarfo: Tied with Gaspipe Casso for most psychotic and bloodthirsty Mafia boss of all time. Scarfo was personally responsible for dozens of murders and almost single-handedly brought down the entire Philadelphia *cosca*. Following a 1998 RICO conviction, he was sentenced to life in prison, where he died at age eighty-seven in January 2017.

Gregory "Greg" Scarpa Jr.: A Colombo capo and hitman suspected of up to sixteen murders. He was eventually convicted of RICO violations in 1996 and sentenced to forty years. He's currently at RRM Kansas City (a federal prison facility) and is sixty-seven years old as of 2019. He's also the son of...

Gregory "the Grim Reaper" Scarpa Sr. (a.k.a. Greg; the Killing Machine): Arguably the most powerful capo who ever served in the Colombo Family. Greg Senior – with plenty of help from his FBI handlers (including, *allegedly*, Lin DeVecchio) – probably murdered up to seventy-five people. He instigated the Third Colombo War (1991-93) so he could eventually become street boss (under perennially imprisoned godfather Carmine Persico). Felled by a blood transfusion for a hernia operation from an underling who was HIV-positive. He expired in June 1994.

Anthony Senter: A Gambino associate, one of the Gemini Twins (with lifelong best friend Joey Testa), and one of Roy DeMeo's favorite hitmen. Senter was involved in at least seventy-five murders (and as many as two hundred!) as a member of DeMeo's Murder Machine crew. Ironically (or perhaps not), Senter and Testa murdered DeMeo in 1983 upon orders relayed through Gaspipe Casso from boss Paul Castellano. In September 1989, Senter and Testa were sentenced to life for multiple murders. Senter's currently housed at USP Allenwood in Pennsylvania.

Frank "the Irishman" Sheeran: Irish-American hitman and Teamsters executive. Sheeran graduated from slaughtering Nazi SS guards at Dachau to performing favors (hits) for godfather Russell Bufalino, including murdering Jimmy Hoffa in July 1975. According to his biographer Charles Brandt, Sheeran starved himself to death in a nursing home in December 2003 at age eighty-three. Sheeran also murdered Crazy Joe Gallo in a Little Italy, Manhattan, restaurant in 1972. He'll be played by Robert DeNiro in the upcoming Netflix movie *The Irishman*.

Almost forgot -- he also delivered the sniper rifles used to assassinate JFK in November 1963.

Anthony "Tough Tony" Spilotro (a.k.a. The Ant; the Little Guy): The Joe Pesci character in *Casino*. For those of you haven't seen the film, I suggest *you fucking watch it*!

Joseph "Joey" Testa: See above for Anthony Senter. Damn, he's currently sixty-four and doing life at FCI Terminal Island, which is in San Pedro and driving distance from my crib in LA. Interview?

Joseph "Joe" Valachi (a.k.a. Joe Cargo): First made man to publicly rat on the Mafia (in 1963), which included identifying it as *"Cosa* Nostra" ("our thing"). Valachi was a bottom-rung Genovese soldier, hitman, and smack dealer who married well but could never escape his plebian roots. He croaked in 1971 at age sixty-six while serving a life sentence.

Paul "Big Paulie" Vario (a.k.a. Paulie): The Paul Sorvino character in *Goodfellas*. Nuff said!

Kevin Weeks: Whitey Bulger's favorite bone-crusher for a quarter-century. Weeks had a sweet ride by earning many millions of dollars, participating in "only" five murders, and "only" serving five years after flipping in 1999. Current whereabouts unknown, but I'm thinking Boston.

Salvatore "Good Lookin' Sal" Vitale: Brother-in-law to Bonanno godfather Joey Massino, Vitale rode the gooey wave of nepotism all the way up to acting boss. He flipped in 2003 after being charged with multiple murders, testified against Massino, and entered WITSEC. Current whereabouts unknown.

Michael "Mikey Y" Yannotti: Gambino capo Nick Corozzo's favorite shooter. He allegedly tried to kill Guardian Angels founder Curtis Sliwa in June 1992 upon orders from John Gotti Jr. He got busted for lots of Mafia-related shizzle and sentenced to twenty years. He's currently at FMC Lexington in Kentucky and is scheduled to be released in 2022 at age fifty-nine.

Jerry Zimmerman: World-class Jewish conman, Jerry attached himself to Colombo underboss Sonny Franzese and, more importantly, to his *wunderkind* son Michael Franzese, whom he helped pull off a half-billion-dollar gasoline tax scheme. He eventually ended up in the San Fernando Valley, where he mentored Kenny Gallo in the porn and grifting industries. Died many years ago.

*For More News About Roman Martín,
Signup For Our Newsletter:*

http://wbp.bz/newsletter

Word-of-mouth is critical to an author's long-term success. If you appreciated this book please leave a review on the Amazon sales page:

http://wbp.bz/underworlda

**AVAILABLE FROM DENNIS GRIFFIN
AND WILDBLUE PRESS!**

A FAMILY BUSINESS by DENNIS GRIFFIN

http://wbp.bz/afba

Read A Sample Next

INTRODUCTION

My name is Joseph Silvestri. My mother called me Joseph, but to most everybody else I was Joe or Joey. I was born in Astoria, Queens, on May 1, 1932, and had five brothers and two sisters.

When I was six, we moved to Jackson Heights, also in Queens. We were about the only Italian family there at the time. I'd say I had a normal childhood and was an average or above student.

If I had to name my biggest fault as a kid and young adult, I'd say it was my penchant for using my fists. I was quick to fight and was pretty good at it. I wasn't particularly big, but I packed a wallop that broke some jaws and noses over the years. That talent—if that's the right word—came in handy on some occasions and caused problems other times.

After an abbreviated stint in the US Air Force in 1949, I spent several years working as a bartender or bouncer at various clubs in New York City, including three years at the world-famous Copacabana. I also worked some of the biggest illegal blackjack and poker games in the city. In that capacity, I met and became friends with many of the greats in the entertainment industry, as well as famous sports figures. I had contact with a number of people from the other side of the law too—organized crime. In this book I'll refer to them as "very important people" or "VIPs."

The stories I'll share with you are all true, and in most cases, this may very well be the first time you've heard of them. In those you may have heard of before, such as the 1957 brawl at the Copa involving several New York Yankees players, I'll provide inside details from my position as an eyewitness and participant.

You may find some of my accounts to be serious, humorous, or simply informative. My hope is you will find them all entertaining.

1 : Fisticuffs

One of my early memories is when I graduated from grade school to high school. I was excited because I was in the chorus and we were going to sing on stage during the ceremony. I wasn't much of a cut-up, but I had two friends who were. Before we went on stage, the three of us were talking. Our music teacher told us to quiet down or we'd be excluded from singing. I became very quiet, but not my buddies.

The teacher said to me, "You're out of the exercise."

"Why? I didn't do anything."

"Okay, tell me who did."

I wouldn't give up my friends, and when the chorus was called on stage, I had to stay in my seat. *I was crushed.*

My mother and aunt were in the audience. When the diplomas were handed out and my name was called, they saw me walk up from the student section all by myself and join my classmates. On the way home, my mother asked me about it. I said, "Mama, I got a very special award and they wanted me to walk up there by myself, so I'd get full recognition."

She accepted that explanation and was proud of me.

I went on to Newtown High School in Elmhurst, Queens, where I met the girl who would become my wife a few years later. But my first day there started out with a problem. A kid I didn't know came up to me and said, "Are you Joe Silvestri?"

"Yeah, I am."

"When your older brother went to school here, he beat up my brother. Now I'm gonna kick your ass."

We went to an empty lot across the street from the school to duke it out. There was a big crowd of students around and most of them were rooting for me. I gave that kid a real whipping.

Teaching a bully a lesson was one thing, but I had trouble controlling when and on whom I used my fists. It was an issue that stayed with me most of my life.

* * *

When I turned seventeen in 1949, I quit school and joined the air force. It had just separated from the army and become its own branch. That was one of the biggest blunders I ever made in my life. I didn't know what real racial prejudice was until then.

I went for basic training in Texas, and then on to an assignment in Biloxi, Mississippi. My first problem in Biloxi came when I loaned a black kid in my outfit a civilian sweater I had. He told somebody where he got the sweater and about six guys converged on me in the barracks. They kept saying, "Where is that nigger lover?" They beat the hell out of me with their hands and feet. I sustained some injuries and still have stomach issues after all these years. Following that incident, I became rebellious—the air force wasn't for me and I wanted out.

One day when I was assigned to the company headquarters (HQ), the first sergeant gave me a letter to deliver to another HQ. On my way, I stopped by the field where the football team was practicing and didn't get the letter delivered until about an hour later. When I got back, my first sergeant was pissed off. "Where in the fuck have you been?"

"I got lost. I'd never been there before and couldn't find the right building."

"You lying guinea bastard!"

That was it. I hit him in the face so hard that his eyeglasses became embedded in the bridge of his nose. A bunch of guys grabbed me and took me to my barracks, and then to the stockade. I asked to see a priest and explained the situation to him. He was sympathetic and when I went to my court martial, I was given a general discharge under honorable conditions. I was out of the air force!

They gave me a ride into Biloxi in a Jeep. I was in the back with two MPs, and the first sergeant I'd hit was in the front. He turned to me and said, "If you ever come back on this base, I'll kill you!"

I said, "And if you ever come into town, *I'll* kill *you*."

We never saw each other again.

AVAILABLE FROM DENNIS GRIFFIN AND WILDBLUE PRESS!

THE RISE AND FALL OF A CASINO MOBSTER by DENNIS GRIFFIN

http://wbp.bz/mobstera

Read A Sample Next

1

A Rocky Start

I'll never forget the first time I met Tony Spilotro. I was just a kid, twelve or thirteen, and I hated school. I was always in trouble with the teachers, and my mother had her hands full trying to get me into a school that could handle me. I loved to fight, too, which caused her even more grief.

Anyway, to hustle up some pocket money I started shining shoes up and down Grand Avenue. One day I noticed a kid about my age shining shoes on the opposite side of the street. He saw me at the same time, and we glared at each other for several seconds.

The other kid hollered to me, "What the fuck are you lookin' at?"

"I'm looking at you. What about it?"

We started walking toward each other, met in the middle of the street, and put down our shine boxes.

He said, "This is my fuckin' territory, and I don't want you on this street. Understand?"

He was short but looked pretty solid, and I figured he could probably take care of himself. That didn't bother me, though, because, like I said, I was a scrapper myself. "I don't see your name on any street signs, and I'm not leaving."

We shoved each other a little bit, but no punches were thrown. Then he said, "I'm coming back here tomorrow, and if I see you, we'll have to fight."

"Then that's what we'll have to do."

I went to that location the next day, but the other kid wasn't there. In fact, it was about a week later when we met again on the street. This time his attitude was different—he wasn't combative. He said, "I've been asking around about you. What's your last name?"

"Cullotta."

"Was your father Joe Cullotta?"

"Yeah. So what?"

"Your father and my father were friends. Your old man helped my old man out of a bad spot one time." He told me his name was Tony Spilotro and his father ran a well-known Italian restaurant on the east side called Patsy's.

I remembered hearing about the incident Tony was talking about. My father (who had been a gangster) liked Patsy and was a regular customer at the restaurant. Back then there was a gang called the Black Hand. It consisted of Sicilian and Italian gangsters who extorted money from their own kind, and my father hated them with a passion. Their method was to shake down business owners by demanding money in return for letting the business stay open. They were making Patsy pay dues every week. When my father heard about it, he and his crew hid in the back room of the restaurant until the Black Handers came in for their payoff. Then they burst out and killed them. After that Patsy wasn't bothered anymore.

From that day Tony and I became friends and started hanging around together. I found out he was a few months older than me, and we had some other things in common besides age and being short. We both hated school and would fight at the drop of a hat.

On weekends I'd see Tony at Riis Park, where he hung out. The first time I went there this guy, who was probably in his twenties, dressed in a shirt and tie and looking like a wiseguy, walked up to me and said, "I'll give you five dollars if you fight my brother."

"Who's your brother?"

He pointed to Tony. "Tony, he's right there."

I laughed. "No, I already had a beef with him. We're friends now."

"Oh, you must be Cullotta. Tony told me about you. I'm Vic Spilotro."

I went over with Tony. A little later Vic came over and said he'd found a kid for Tony to fight. Tony beat the hell out of the kid, and then Vic paid him the five bucks. Tony said, "Hey, what about me? I did all the work. Don't I get anything?"

Vic laughed. "Not you, you're not getting shit. I'm doing this to toughen you up, not so you can make money."

We messed around for a while longer, and then Tony said, "Come with me, and I'll show you where I live. It's right off Grand Avenue."

On the way to his house Tony told me he had five brothers. Vince was the oldest, followed by Vic and Patrick. And then came Tony and his two younger brothers, Johnny and Michael.

Tony showed me through the house. All the boys slept in one bedroom with three sets of bunk beds. While we were in the bedroom Tony's mother walked in. She was a very tiny lady, and I had the impression she wasn't very happy about me being there. She asked who I was, and I told her. If she knew about my father and the Black Hand thing, it didn't seem to make any difference. I still sensed she didn't like me. She said to Tony, "Hurry up and get out of here, the both of you."

After she left I said to Tony, "I don't think your mother likes me and probably doesn't want me around."

He laughed. "Don't worry about it. She doesn't like any of my friends. If she had her way I'd only hang around with altar boys."

As we walked out of the house Tony's mother and father were in the kitchen. Tony said something to them, but neither of them spoke to me. My name wasn't mentioned, and I don't think the father even looked at me as I passed by. Over time I got to know Tony's parents better. They were hard working, nice people. I never knew either of them to be involved in anything illegal.

After that initial meeting I didn't see much of Tony during the week because of school. But on weekends I'd catch up with him at Riis Park. I saw Vic quite a bit, too, at Riis or on the streets. I became convinced he was a gangster because of the way he dressed and that he always had a big wad of money with him. At the time I didn't really understand what it meant to be a bookie, but I'd see Vic getting slips of paper and money from people. I found out later that he was taking sports bets and his operation was backed by the Outfit. He used to run crap (dice) games, too, in the alleys behind the houses in the neighborhood. Although Tony and I were just kids, sometimes Vic let us in the games. Even then, it was obvious to me that Tony was in his element when he could bet on something.

Another guy I met hanging around with Tony was Joey Hansen. Next to me, he probably came to know Tony as well as anybody. He was jealous of my relationship with Tony, and we had a couple of fights over it. I mention him here because he played a role in some of the incidents I'll tell you about later.

Did I know then what the future held for Tony? No, I didn't. But looking back, it's my opinion that Vic Spilotro was the person most instrumental in Tony taking to the criminal life and becoming an Outfit guy. Tony idolized Vic and his lifestyle. Vic introduced Tony to a lot of his associates as he was growing up—more guys with nice clothes, women, and money. And what may have been even more important: power.

* * *

About a year after first meeting Tony we started spending more time together. The reason for that was we both got placed in the same facility—Montefiore School. It was a place that provided educational services for troublemakers—kids who couldn't get along anywhere else. I was sent there first, and Tony showed up about a week later. I don't think he was into criminal stuff then. But like me, he was a kid that most teachers couldn't control.

The student body of Montefiore was primarily black. (We called them "colored" at that time.) Tony and I were two of the half-dozen or so white kids in the place and were constantly in physical confrontations with the blacks. Another thing we didn't like was having to use public transportation to get to and from the school. We couldn't do much about the blacks, but I figured out how to take care of the other.

I'd already learned how to hotwire my mother's car. I started using that knowledge to steal cars from around my neighborhood. I drove the hot car to school and parked it a couple of blocks away. After school I'd drop Tony off at his father's restaurant, where he worked every day, and then I'd drive it back to my neighborhood. Having our own transportation was nice, but it didn't stop the fighting inside the school.

One day when I came out of wood shop I found Tony in the hallway surrounded by four or five blacks. One of them wanted to fight him alone. "Come on, white boy," he said, "just you and me."

Tony agreed. The black kid picked him up and flung him over his head to the floor. Tony got up and put a beating on the guy. Then one of the other blacks said, "Let's kill that white motherfucker," and they started to attack.

I grabbed one of the long poles with a hook on the end that was used to open and close the upper windows. I swung it at the blacks and caught a couple of them in the head, and then Tony and I ran out of the building.

When Tony told Vic what was going on with the blacks, Vic said it was time we taught them a lesson by going after their leader—a kid named Jackson—and he'd go with us.

A few days later Tony and I didn't go to classes, and Vic drove us to the school in his four-door Mercury. We got there at lunch time when we knew all the students would be in the cafeteria. Vic brought along a .45-caliber pistol.

Vic crashed the car through the gates of the fenced-in playground and parked it near the cafeteria. Tony took the gun, and he and I ran inside and grabbed Jackson out of his seat at the lunch table. As we dragged him outside to the car he was scared to death, crying, and screaming. The other blacks were shocked. They followed us outside but didn't do anything. We drove away, pistol-whipped Jackson, and then drove back to the school and dumped him off.

Tony said he wasn't going to go back to school. His father didn't want him to and said he needed him at the restaurant. I did go in the next day, and the juvenile officers were waiting for me—they wanted to throw me in jail for the Jackson thing. They wrote me up and told me I couldn't come back to Montefiore. And then they contacted my mother and said we had to appear before a juvenile court judge.

Tony got charged, too, but his lawyer told the judge that Tony worked at his father's restaurant and any action against him would cause a hardship on his family. It worked, and Tony was released to work at the restaurant. I wasn't as lucky and got placed in a reformatory for six months.

After I got out, I got into more trouble and drew nine months in another reformatory called St. Charles. So I didn't see much of Tony again until we were seventeen or so. We would run into one another from time to time and catch up on the latest happenings in the neighborhood. By that time he was making quite a name for himself as a tough guy and a thief. People already respected and feared him.

Just before Tony turned eighteen we talked about the Outfit. I'll never forget his words to me at that time: "Frankie, I'm going to become one of them. Someday I'm going to be a boss, and I'll take you with me."

At that time I didn't want anyone to run my life for me. I said, "I'm not interested in becoming a gangster."

After that we kind of went our separate ways. I was content with being a thief and running my own crew. Tony was pursuing his ambitions of becoming a member of the Outfit, and I heard he was hooked up with some big time gangsters out of Cicero.

And then one day, about a year and a half later, Tony stopped in to see me. He said he and some other guys had a big job coming up with a lot of money to be made. They were short a man, and he offered me the spot. I immediately said I was in. It was then I learned we were going to take down a bank.

http://wbp.bz/mobstera

AVAILABLE FROM SALVATORE LUCANIA AND WILDBLUE PRESS!

THE GANGSTER'S COUSIN by SALVATORE LUCANIA

http://wbp.bz/tgca

Read A Sample Next

Prologue

I didn't realize as a child that my life was vastly different from the lives of most people. I spent a lifetime looking for a thread that would help me make sense of it all. Here's what I came up with:

There are four classes that make up all societies. These societies are governed by laws created by the wealthy few who neither intended to, nor have ever had to live under them. Those few are referred to as our leaders, or the *ruling class*, if you will. Politicians are not the leaders; they are the paid help. The real leaders pay the politicians to do their work for them.

The next class is the *law-abiding citizens*. They live under these laws because they are indoctrinated at a very early age to obey them. They mistakenly believe that laws are somehow rooted in moral principles rather than the resolve of the ruling class to protect their power and wealth, and, most importantly, to maintain control of the citizens who actually generate that wealth.

Only a small segment of the population truly understands the intent of these laws and the nature of those who create them. This segment has two sub-classes: the "criminals" and the "outlaws."

The criminal class survives by taking from others, by any means, what does not belong to them (not so different from the ruling class).

Then there are the outlaws. Outlaws see through the game. They see very clearly the life of the lower class to which they and their families are relegated, and they are having none of it.

Outlaws are different from criminals. For a criminal to make money, someone has to lose money. This is immoral. No one loses anything when the outlaw makes money. There is a difference between robbing someone at gunpoint and being a bookie or growing pot. Making book and growing pot may cross legal lines created by the elite ruling class, but neither is inherently immoral.

I was born an outlaw in outlaw culture. I refused to be forced into the powerless class of the ordinary, law-abiding citizen. I always saw things from outside the box because I was born outside the box, so I was free to think for myself. This does not mean I did illegal things my whole life. I did not. Whatever I did through the years to make a living, I kept one rule: *Do no harm.*

I am seventy-five years old now. I've lived through almost eight decades. I turned sixteen in October of 1959. Two months later the sixties arrived, and with it, a new decade of huge cultural change and experimentation.

Self-betterment groups like *est* and Scientology sprang up all over the country, followed by widespread inner exploration through various religions and gurus. I spent years involved in these "spiritual" adventures trying to find the answer to the question, *Who am I?* Only to realize after years of disappointment that I was asking the wrong question. If you want to know who you are, find out what made you who you are now. That will tell you everything you need to know.

I was born Salvatore Charles Lucania, a second-generation Sicilian in East Harlem, on October 19, 1942. I had an older cousin, also named Salvatore Charles Lucania, who became the infamous Lucky Luciano. I'm sure this had something to do with my outlaw view of life.

My early mentor was my father's cousin Carl Lucania. He was Lucky's nephew and my father's closest friend. It is always difficult for a young person to step out into the world on their own for the first time. My own entrance into the world was a little more complicated owing to the fact I was married at sixteen and had three children by the time I was twenty.

My life was a lot of things, but one thing it was not, was *boring*. When I first decided to write this book some twenty years after I left New York, it was in response to a question I was often asked here in California: "What was it like to grow up in East Harlem in the forties, fifties, and sixties?" I didn't originally intend to write an autobiography, but rather a day-in-the life kind of read with all its colorful characters.

Be that as it may, this book is the end result. Come along for the ride. If nothing else, I think you will be entertained.

Chapter 1

The Perfume Business

I started bootlegging Chanel No. 5 perfume in 1959, when I was sixteen. I got into the business through my cousin Carl, who first introduced me to Cue Ball Kelly that same year. Kelly owned the 7-11 pool hall in Midtown Manhattan. He was also the ref for Brunswick's TV Pool Tournaments.

Kelly was short, Friar Tuck bald, stocky, and fiftyish, His complexion, like his hair, was cadaver gray. Besides running the pool hall, Kelly was in the bootleg perfume business, the subject of our meeting that day. Arranged by my cousin Carl, a member of the Gambino Family, this meeting was to kick off my "business career." Kelly had only one line of perfume, Chanel No. 5, which at the time sold for twenty-five dollars an ounce.

I was excited but nervous. It was highly unusual for someone my age to be given this opportunity. This was my way out of the limitations of Harlem. These men were high rollers to a boy like me.

The two-landing walk up was dimly lit by a nineteenth-century alabaster light that hung from a long, dirt-encrusted chain. *It must have been gaslight,* I thought to myself. The wooden stairs creaked, and the stairwell smelled like an abandoned warehouse.

It was strangely quiet as I approached the swinging green doors of my destination, the loft. I stepped through into a fog of cigarette smoke with scant patches of light. When my eyes adjusted, I was surprised how crowded and large the hall was.

About twenty ornately carved walnut pool tables with a Mark Twain-era look about them were placed throughout the area. Six were in action, but action was what this joint was all about. There were at least thirty guys in the hall watching different games. You could tell by the seriousness of the spectators that this was a high-stakes place. *The Hustler* should have been filmed here.

"Hey Butch," Carl called out. "Over here!"

I loved Carl. He was my father's first cousin, thirty years my senior. Out of respect, I always called him Uncle, as I did with all my older relatives. His charm was his self-assured attitude. "Know what to say, who to say it to, and you can get anything you want done," Carl would say. He was right, except for one detail. You also needed access, but Carl always had access.

"Kelly, this is my nephew Butch," he proudly introduced me.

"How are you, Butch?" Kelly smiled warmly as he shook my hand with both of his, his eyes searching mine. I never looked away, maybe because it was natural for me or maybe I was doing the same thing he was doing. He seemed pleased by it.

Kelly got right down to business, which I liked.

"Sit down, Butch." He gestured to the curly, wire-backed chair. "Your uncle has spoken well of you. He's asked me to help set you up in my business. What do you know about perfume?"

"Nothing," I declared candidly. "Why don't you give me a crash course?"

Kelly looked at Carl across the white marble table and smiled, "I like him already."

As Kelly began to give me the rundown on the perfume business, he placed two little white boxes with black print on the table.

"This is Chanel No. 5 perfume, Butch. It is one of the most expensive perfumes on the market. It retails for twenty-five dollars an ounce. I can supply you with as many bottles as you can sell." He said it as if he were awarding me the first MacDonald's franchise.

"How good is it? How much does it come to me for? How much inventory do you have? What can you supply on a monthly basis, and what are the discounts for quantities," I asked, almost in one breath.

Carl and Kelly glanced at one another and started laughing. Kelly looked directly into my eyes, his blue ones lighting up, and said, "Butch, you will never be poor. Poor is a state of mind, a state you will never visit." Carl nodded his agreement.

"The quality is the same as the legit stuff. I import the bottles from France." Proudly, he opened the package and showed me the bottom of the bottle, with *France* molded into the base. "I sell it by the gross, that's 144 bottles to the case. I want five dollars a bottle; you can sell it for ten. If you give me ten days' notice, I can deliver ten to fifteen cases at a clip."

My mind was racing in two directions as he spoke. I was doing calculations in my head, trying to figure out how to sell those quantities.

After that first meeting, I grabbed a cab back to East Harlem, where I was born and raised. I met with Vinnie and Tom-Tom, my two partners, in the back of Joe's bar on the corner of 106th and Third Avenue.

Joe's was the classic Italian restaurant—little white octagon floor tiles, a long, old mahogany bar and checkered tablecloths. It was our main hangout. We could drink there even though we weren't eighteen. The three of us were all connected by blood to various "Mafia families," but were by no means *members* of those families. We were relatives, still in our teens.

I explained the perfume deal to them. I knew Vinnie's cousin ran a fencing operation out of a large printing plant in Jersey. I believe they printed *The New York Daily Mirror*. They would print the paper at night for the morning edition and use the facility during the day to unload hijacked trucks and distribute goods.

As I was showing them the bottles, Vinnie leaned forward, "I think the first thing we ought to do is buy the real stuff and see if it's as good as Kelly says it is. If it is, we can dump it in those quantities to the guys in Jersey."

"Yeah, but not at those prices," Tom-Tom chimed in.

"He's right, Butch, goods that sell out of the trunks of cars go for one third of the stores' retail prices. That would be about eight dollars a bottle. The fences won't pay more than ten to fifteen percent of that. That puts it between $2.50 and $3.50 for each bottle. We would have to get it for half that price to make any money."

"There go our careers in the perfume business," Tom-Tom laughed.

"Butch, let me check with Jersey, I wanna see what they will pay and what kind of quantities they can handle. You check with your cousin and see what you can do with the price."

"Okay, I will."

"Are you going to tell them it's bootleg stuff?" Tom-Tom asked.

"No, not yet. If it's as good as Kelly says it is, they won't know—or care for that matter." Vinnie casually leaned back in his chair as he spoke.

Vinnie was seventeen, a year older than me. He lived in Yonkers, where you could get a driver's license at sixteen, something you couldn't do in New York City. He drove a 1957, metallic-gray Ninety-Eight Oldsmobile Coupe. I loved that car. Standing at about five foot seven, with a round face capped by a sandy brown crew cut, he was always neatly dressed in slacks and a starched shirt.

Tom-Tom, on the other hand, was tall for a Sicilian, about five-eleven, an inch or so taller than me. He had honey-blonde, short-cropped hair and smooth white skin that tanned easily. His eyes, like mine, were more green than brown, and he spoke with a deliberate stutter, which was why we called him Tom-Tom.

I called Carl the next day to set up a meeting. We met at the Roman Gardens restaurant in Whitestone that Carl used as his "office." He and his "friends" would eat there every day, but never received a bill.

Always curious, that day I finally asked, "Uncle Carl, why doesn't Joe ever give you a bill?"

Carl smiled. "Because we're his draw. His customers come to see the gangsters. Joe's business has tripled since we started hanging out here. So tell me, what's up."

"Okay," I jumped straight into it, "so I am fairly sure I can move large quantities of the stuff, but the prices need to come way down."

"How far down is way down?" he asked, clearly enjoying the moment.

"Between $1.50 and $2 a bottle, but we would move quantities quickly and take five gross to start." I felt like I had just asked the impossible.

"Butch, Kelly would have to turn over his sources for you to get it at that price," he looked amused.

"Yeah, that's what I thought." I felt the wind coming out of my sails.

"But, let me see what I can do."

He smiled warmly at me. Carl had an olive complexion, nappy salt and pepper hair, a flat nose, and dark circles under his hazel eyes. He spoke in short, quick sentences, and was heavy for his five feet, ten inches, about 240 pounds, yet still tall for a Sicilian. Except for my father, we were all tall on that side of the family.

I didn't think Carl could do anything about the price, but he had a knack for making things happen. I liked watching him handle things. One day, a young girl from the Whitestone neighborhood came into the restaurant very upset. Carl and I were having lunch when Joe Abbondola, the owner, approached us and said, "Carl, do you have a minute."

"Sure Joe, what's up?"

"The girl I was just talking to, she's pregnant, but wants an abortion. She's a nice kid from a good Sicilian family. Do you know anyone that can do it?" Abortions were illegal in those days. He met with the girl and her parents later that evening and made a deal with them.

Carl, who was childless, set her up in an apartment and covered all her living and medical expenses. The night the child was born, he went to the hospital and gave his name as the father. A week later, he picked up the mother and her baby, a little girl whom he named Sophie, after his mother, and took her home. He and his wife raised that girl into a fine woman. It was classic Carl.

I was always amazed how Carl moved through life. He always made money but lived modestly. Once in a conversation about money he said to me, "Butch, most people don't understand money. It's not about cars, homes, and fancy things. Ultimately, money is about freedom, freedom to do what you want when you want. It's about the freedom of time to enjoy life."

"About time or life, I don't get it," I asked, perplexed.

"Listen, from the time we are born, until the day we die, all we have is time."

"Right."

"So, in that sense, the only real thing we have to spend in life is our time. Money gives us the freedom of time. How we spend that time, where and who we spend it with, determines how good our life will be.

"It's very important that you understand money is about freedom, because when someone takes your money without giving you something in return, they are robbing you of your freedom, your very life."

"You mean like taxes?" I laughed.

"Bingo!" Carl laughed too.

He called the very next day. "Meet me at Angelo's on Mulberry Street at 2:30."

When I walked into Angelo's, I saw Carl, Kelly and two other men I didn't know sitting at a large red leather booth in the back of the restaurant. They had just finished lunch and were having espresso.

I casually walked over to the table, leaned over and kissed Carl as I always did. The two men immediately stood up and shook my hand as Kelly introduced them.

"Butch, this is Fred Clark my chemist, and this is Abe Flick my printer and bottle supplier. They will supply you with all the materials you need. Between the bottles and packaging you've got fifty-one cents in the deal. The perfume comes by the gallon and works out to twenty-five cents an ounce. You will have to supply your own labor. Here is a list of what you will need to assemble the package," he explained, handing me a yellow sheet of paper. "Fred's and Abe's phone numbers are on the list. They will help you set up."

I was stunned. "Kelly, I appreciate what you are doing. I don't know what to say I…"

"Please, there is no need to thank me. This is the first time I've had the opportunity to return one of the many favors your Uncle has done for me over the years." Kelly was beaming. He looked like Saint Patrick. "Besides, you and I are the only ones doing this in the country. There is plenty of room for the both of us," he said graciously.

Kelly, Fred, and Abe got up from the table, shook my hand, wished me luck, said goodbye, and left. I sat there for a moment, reading the yellow sheet of paper: candle wax, syringe, black twine….

I looked up at Carl, "Why is he doing this?"

"He told you why. He is the kind of man who doesn't forget favors. He's the only kind of man worth doing a favor for. I've helped Kelly throughout the years. I never asked for or accepted money for what I did, but that's what makes it a favor. You will find out that being successful in life is a matter of how you handle relationships.

"Helping others is like putting money in the bank. It's rare in life when people do favors like that, but it's precisely because it's rare that it's not forgotten, unless, of course, you are dealing with a five-dollar man."

"What do you mean, a *five-dollar man*?"

"I mean, never give a five-dollar man, ten dollars. Kelly is a ten-dollar man. Had he been a five-dollar man, he'd see me as a chump. Instead, he showed gratitude. A five-dollar man will never show you gratitude or loyalty. He will never acknowledge that you had anything to do with his success. It's his way of getting something for nothing. That's what makes him a five-dollar man. So just remember, never give a five-dollar man, ten dollars."

"But, how will I know if someone is a five-dollar man?"

"You won't. That's a chance you'll have to take. People who want something from you will appear humble at first. They will tell you what you want to hear. It's after they get what they want that you'll begin to see the change in them. The first sign is the humility disappears. Later on they'll start acting arrogant. It's my experience that arrogance and stupidity are two sides of the same coin. Whenever I see one, I always see the other. The moment you notice that change, distance them, cut off any help and never have anything to do with them again," he warned.

"Just like that."

"Yes, just like that." He got louder as he spoke, "You see, arrogant people think they know it all, but no one knows it all. That's how you know they're stupid. Stupid people are dangerous. They're unpredictable. A dummy will break you quicker than a thief. I would rather deal with a smart thief. At least he's predictable; a dummy isn't. They're losers, short-term thinkers. Get them out of your life as fast as possible."

I got up from the table and gave Carl a long hug, then kissed him goodbye. He held my face in both of his thick hands, looked at me with great affection, and said, "Butch, be careful out there. Things are rarely what they seem to be."

I walked out of Angelo's a foot or two off the ground. Mulberry Street was alive with children, music, and the aromas of Italian home cooking. The redbrick buildings were not so different from the ones in Harlem, but there were many more storefront social clubs down this way. The summer brought everyone out. The men from the social clubs played cards and conducted their "business" outside, while the women sat looking out their front windows, keeping an eye on the children, watching for strangers and cops. It's what a neighborhood is about, everyone watching out for one another.

With Carl's advice bouncing around in my head, I grabbed a cab back to my neighborhood, knowing the deal would work. I also knew that what Carl just said to me was worth more than the deal itself.

"You're shittin' me. I don't believe it!" Tom-Tom said when I told him what Carl had done. "What's his cut?" he asked, as we stood on the corner in front of Joe's bar, waiting for Vinnie to pick us up.

"It's a favor," I said. "If Carl wanted a cut, he would have asked for one. We owe him a favor."

"I'll say. Wait 'til Vinnie hears this! I hope he worked out the other end."

"We'll know soon enough. Here he comes now."

Vinnie pulled up to the curb. I opened the door and jumped into the back seat. When I saw Vinnie's eyes, I knew he had scored, but he was silent. He waited for Tom-Tom to get into the front seat, then reached over him, grabbed two bottles of Chanel No. 5 out of the glove compartment, handed them to Tom-Tom and said, "One of the bottles is ours. The other is legit. See if you guys can tell the difference."

Tom-Tom and I tested the bottles. Neither of us could note any difference whatsoever.

"You'd have to be an expert to tell the difference," I said.

"Right, and that's who I gave it to," Vinnie laughed.

"Who d-d-do you know that's an expert, Vinnie?" Tom-Tom stuttered.

"My Mother. She's been using Chanel for years. Not only couldn't she tell the difference, but also, she said it lasted just as long as, if not longer than the real thing." Vinnie's eyes were dancing.

"God…God… bless your Mother, Vinnie." Tom-Tom made the sign of the cross with great authority over Vinnie's head, and then, turning to me, continued his gracious benediction.

Vinnie looked at me, then at Tom-Tom, then back at me, and broke into more laughter, "Has he been drinking that fuckin' Holy Water again?"

"Tell 'em Butch... Tell...Tell..."

I leaned over the front seat and put my hand over Tom-Tom's mouth. "Tom-Tom, if you don't calm down, you're going to have a heart attack."

I told Vinnie what Carl had done for us.

"It's seventy-six cents to us, plus labor, but I don't know what's involved with labor. We need to pick up the materials and assemble thirty or forty bottles to see how long it takes."

"Then what?" Tom-Tom asked.

"Well, I was thinking that my mother makes dresses on an assembly line. That's probably what we are going to need—an assembly line. Anyway, she does piece work and gets a set price for each specific piece of the garment she completes. That way the manufacturing costs are fixed. If we could get the packaging done for twenty-five or thirty cents a bottle, we could make a killing."

We drove to Rao's on 114th Street to have lunch and figure out how to get the packaging done. Rao's had only about six or seven tables, but it was home cooking. On the way, Vinnie broke the news.

"How about $3.50 a bottle for the first ten cases, and $3.25 for the second? That's per week."

There was silence in the car for about twenty seconds.

"That's about three grand a week," I said.

"Thirty-six hundred," Vinnie shot back.

This time Tom-Tom was speechless. He remained that way until after we ordered lunch. "Tom-Tom, what's going on in that head of yours? I can smell the wood burning from here."

"I think I have the solution to our labor problem. My cousin Joanne does piece work, too, but she does it with jewelry. She, her three daughters, and her two sisters put in sixty man-hours a week, and they make less than $50 each. Our project is perfect for them. Just give me a couple days to work it out."

Two days later, Tom-Tom had the deal worked out. Four weeks later, we shipped our first ten cases. We made $3,600. That's more than my mother made in a year. Joanne made $360, almost half her husband's monthly salary. She paid her sisters $200 and stopped working at her other job. Everyone was happy, especially our customers.

I called Carl the day I got my first "paycheck" of $1,200. "Uncle Carl, I just got my first paycheck. I wanna take you to dinner. You name the place."

"Patsy's on 118th. I haven't been there in years."

Patsy's was an old Sicilian restaurant. It looked very much like the restaurant in *The Godfather* where Michael kills the cop. Octagon tiles on the floor and embossed tin ceilings, with a nineteenth-century bar and nineteenth-century waiters. The music was always Italian. This part of Harlem was virtually unknown to outsiders.

Whenever Harlem is mentioned, generally people think of Black Harlem or Spanish Harlem. Black Harlem is West Harlem. East Harlem, later to become Spanish Harlem, was not just Italian, but mostly Sicilian. In those days it was referred to as the *other Little Italy*.

There's a big difference between Italians and Sicilians, both in language and mentality. Italians cannot speak or understand the Sicilian language, which is largely rooted in Greek and Arabic, rather than Latin. Sicily suffered three thousand years of occupation. The citizens survived these occupations by creating and living by their own rules. The so-called Mafia, or Black Hand, as it was called in those days, was a political organization that functioned as liaison between the occupied and the occupiers. A kind of shadow government, if you will. Not much different from our own political parties today. Hence, the Sicilian mentality, which could be summed up as, "There is no authority higher than our own." An attitude that suited me perfectly.

East Harlem was twenty-two blocks long, running north from 103rd Street to 125th, and eight blocks wide, beginning at the East River and running west to Madison Avenue. It was the domain of the Luciano/Genovese family, the destination of the French Connection, and the financial center for the gambling business—both east and west.

"Pasta con sarde," Carl said to the waiter—spaghetti and sardines with fennel, browned breadcrumbs and pine nuts. It's a Sicilian dish, and Patsy's was one of the few places in the city that still made it. I ordered rolled stuffed veal.

"What are you going to do with your money?" Carl asked.

"I really haven't had a chance to think much about it yet."

"You know, Butch, making money and keeping money are not the same thing. If you want to keep it, don't flaunt it. If you do, people will find ways to take it from you. Also, people can be very jealous, and jealous people will do things that you and I wouldn't think of doing.

"Keep a low profile, save enough money to live for a year without an income. That way, you'll always have the time to put another deal together. Do you understand?"

"Yes, I do."

"Good, let's eat."

"By the way, my partners send their regards and gratitude. They wanted you to know, we owe you a favor."

"That's a good sign," he said, smiling.

http://wbp.bz/tgca

Great Gangster and Mafia Reads From WildBlue Press

A FAMILY BUSINESS by Dennis N. Griffin and Joey Silvestri

Award-winning Mob author Dennis Griffin joins forces with Joey "the Fixer" Silvestri to tell a tale of a bygone era when organized crime dominated New York City. Joe Silvestri was a tough kid from the mean streets of New York. He went from street brawler to wearing a tux at the glamorous Copacabana. He eventually provided "muscle" for the Mob, a highly respected and feared fixer- the guy you went to if you had a problem that needed to be resolved.

wbp.bz/afba

THE RISE AND FALL OF A 'CASINO' MOBSTER by Frank Cullotta and Dennis N. Griffin

Tony Spilotro was the Mob's man in Las Vegas. A feared enforcer, the bosses knew Tony would do whatever it took to protect their interests. The "Little Guy" built a criminal empire that was the envy of mobsters across the country. But Tony's quest for power and lack of self-control with women cost the Mob its control of Vegas; and his life. **wbp.bz/mobstera**

THE GANGSTER'S COUSIN by Salvatore "Sal" Lucania

Young Sal navigates the streets of Harlem, defying the ways of people in power-including the bullies in his neighborhood and his own mafia family culture. He experiences the inherent corruption of the US justice system, and discovers the truth about the secret world of outlaw figures like his cousin and namesake, Charles "Lucky" Luciano. **wbp.bz/tgca**

REPEAT OFFENDER by Bradley Nickell

Millions in stolen property, revolting sex crimes and murder-for-hire were all in the mix for a Las Vegas police detective as he toiled to take Sin City's most prolific criminal off the streets. In REPEAT OFFENDER Las Vegas Police Detective Bradley Nickell provides the inside scoop on the most prolific repeat offender Las Vegas has ever known.

wbp.bz/repeatoffendera

www.ingramcontent.com/pod-product-compliance
Lightning Source LLC
Chambersburg PA
CBHW071213040426
42333CB00068B/1734